Cash Transfers in Context

Cash Transfers in Context

An Anthropological Perspective

Edited by
Jean-Pierre Olivier de Sardan and
Emmanuelle Piccoli

berghahn
NEW YORK · OXFORD
www.berghahnbooks.com

First published in 2018 by
Berghahn Books
www.berghahnbooks.com

Library of Congress Cataloging-in-Publication Data
Names: Olivier de Sardan, Jean-Pierre, editor. | Piccoli, Emmanuelle, editor.
Title: Cash transfers in context : an anthropological perspective / edited by
  Jean-Pierre Olivier de Sardan and Emmanuelle Piccoli.
Description: New York : Berghahn Books, 2018. | Includes bibliographical
  references and index.
Identifiers: LCCN 2018008390 (print) | LCCN 2018010084 (ebook) | ISBN
  9781785339585 (ebook) | ISBN 9781785339578 (hardback : alk. paper)
Subjects: LCSH: Income maintenance programs--Developing countries. |
  Poverty--Developing countries. | Poor--Developing countries. | Economic
  development--Social aspects--Developing countries.
Classification: LCC HC59.72.P6 (ebook) | LCC HC59.72.P6 C374 2018 (print) |
  DDC 332/.0424091724--dc23
LC record available at https://lccn.loc.gov/2018008390

British Library Cataloguing in Publication Data
A catalogue record for this book is available from the British Library

ISBN 978-1-78533-957-8 hardback
ISBN 978-1-80073-917-8 paperback
ISBN 978-1-78533-958-5 ebook

https://doi.org/10.3167/9781785339578

Contents

Figures and Tables

Figures

Tables

Cash Transfers and the Revenge of Contexts
An Introduction

Jean-Pierre Olivier de Sardan and Emmanuelle Piccoli

Cash transfer (CT) programs are having something of a field day. In just over a decade they have become the main form of intervention channeled in the direction of the most vulnerable families in low- and middle-income countries (LMICs). Having originated in Brazil and Mexico in the 1990s, they initially spread to Latin America before being adopted throughout the world from around 2005. Their progression is spectacular: from three countries in 1997, they were implemented in twenty-seven countries by 2007 (Fiszbein et al. 2009) and, by 2016, in 130 countries (Bastagli et al. 2016). In 2016, CT's share of total humanitarian aid exceeded 10 percent (CALP 2018).

A Simple Mechanism with Multiple Forms and Functions

The "mechanism" that lies at the heart of CTs is very simple (see Olivier de Sardan, chapter 1): the basic formula involves the occasional or regular distribution of sums of money to vulnerable households in most cases. This mechanism differs from social security payments (which are contributory), "cash for work" (in which payments are conditional on the performance of work), and aid in kind (for example, food). CTs also differ from universal cover in that they are targeted at a particular category of the population. They can be either conditional (in most cases subject to the school enrollment of children or completion of medical checkups) or unconditional in nature.

Notes for this chapter begin on page 22.

Apart from this common basis, numerous variations can be observed in terms of the norms and procedures governing the payments: some are paid in cash, others by bank transfer, and others, again, in the form of "vouchers"; they can be one-off, monthly, bimonthly, or trimestrial; they vary considerably in terms of their duration and can be exceptional (cases of emergency in the context of disastrous events), permanent (hence they become a new form of social benefit), or paid over intermediate periods (a number of years, similar to the "social security nets" that are intended to enable people to emerge from the poverty trap or cope with recurrent food crises); in the majority of cases the recipients are women, but they are sometimes paid to men, and, apart from the main targets of poor or very poor families, the recipients can originate from different social categories—pregnant women, earthquake or famine victims, disabled persons, refugees, demobilized military veterans, etc. Combined with the simplicity of the "game" or "mechanism" itself, this flexibility regarding the rules that govern the game is clearly one of the reasons behind the global success of the CT system.

This plasticity also explains the wide diversity that exists in the institutional embedding of CTs: they are sometimes the product of a proactive social policy adopted by the state (as is the case in Latin America and South Africa); they sometimes involve international aid in the form of "projects" instigated by international institutions (World Bank, ECHO, US-AID, WFP, etc.); and they are often relayed by NGOS (as is the case in Africa, the Middle East, and Asia). In the latter case, the CTs are focused on two main areas: humanitarian aid distributed in the event of food crises or natural disasters, which is usually unconditional, and development aid, which is generally conditional (promotion of resilience to and fight against poverty) and can also assume more atypical forms (disarmament, demobilization, reintegration programs, or DDR [see Chelpi-den Hammer, chapter 11]; displacement of populations in case of dam building; settlement of migrants, etc.).

Hence the explicit or implicit socioeconomic functions of CTs are varied and based on the institutional contexts in which they arise and the political-economic frameworks that guide them. Needless to say, they are located in a global economic context dominated by neoliberalism, the financialization of capitalism, and the growth of inequality, and in which no structural solution can be found to the intertwined issues of poverty, marginalization, and exclusion. However, CTs do not constitute a single answer to these problems—contrary to the belief of Ferguson (2015), who interprets CTs solely on the empirical basis of their implementation in South Africa as a "new politics of distribution of capitalism" and even, more generally, as a sign heralding a new age of capitalism.[1]

On the contrary, CTs are based on multiple agendas. They can represent a provisional response to a cyclical rise in poverty or an attempt to stem its structural growth in the long term; in this case, they can become a new social right. They can have the aim of eradicating extreme poverty or breaking the intergenerational cycle of poverty. They can also set out to integrate marginalized communities into the market and state arena. They can offer a means of increasing school enrollment rates and access to modern healthcare through the mechanism of financial incentives. They can constitute a temporary response to traumatic events and be associated with different forms of reintegration. They can also act as a tool for the empowerment of women. In many cases, they combine several of these objectives.

Perceptions, Reactions, and Contexts

Each CT program is implemented in a specific context that is linked not only to the always varying and specific features of the political, institutional, and social context, but also to the different representations and strategies of the multiple actors involved in their implementation—in other words, the various "strategic groups"[2] of the country or region involved: the enumerators and statisticians, investigators, program officials, extension agents and frontline workers, public servants, local political authorities, and, of course, the populations themselves (direct and indirect beneficiaries, nonbeneficiaries), etc.

In terms of the target populations, the abundant gray literature on CTs (in particular NGO or World Bank reports) insists that a large number of beneficiaries express their satisfaction with this welcome form of financial support. Given that the system involves the distribution of resources to cruelly deprived populations, this positive assessment is unsurprising. This obvious function of providing aid, emergency support, and resilience support forms the basis of the institutions that operate CT systems. These operations demonstrate an increase in "capabilities" (to use the language of Amartya Sen ([2000]) by referring to the distributed sums and vulnerability of the populations involved, and to the comments made at various focus groups held with beneficiaries.[3] The CT institutions frequently engage in the active and emphatic promotion of these successes.[4]

Simultaneously, they show a strong propensity for minimizing or ignoring the problems associated with the CT system. While the advantages of CTs are associated with the mechanism itself and, in a way, have a positive impact a priori and irrespective of the specific contexts involved (receiving money is always "convenient" for people who lack it), the problems are context-dependent. They should be investigated in detail against the background of each new situation—something that necessitates the use of qualitative methods. And this is precisely what this book attempts to do. Each chapter identifies problems associated with the contexts; furthermore, many of them were written by anthropologists who were already familiar with the contexts in question before focusing on the introduction of a CT system there. As a consequence, the methodology used by most of the authors for producing their data was typically a qualitative one (based on long-term familiarity with the settings and the stakeholders, open interviews, repeated observations, and case studies), following the principles of a rigorous policy of fieldwork: triangulation, saturation, management of bias, "emicity," counterexamples, etc. (Olivier de Sardan 2015).

In effect one of the greatest challenges facing a traveling model like CTs is the fact that they are implemented in extremely different contexts with respect to continents, countries, and sectors (see chapter 1). The majority of the problems encountered by CTs arise from this almost inevitable divide between the model and the local realities. The insufficient consideration of contexts lies behind the multiple strategies for "circumventing" the programs uncovered by the authors of this book—irrespective of whether these strategies are adopted by program officials (e.g., extra conditionalities), local authorities (e.g., "elite capture"), program beneficiaries (e.g., failure to comply with instructions), or nonbeneficiaries (e.g., denigration and stigmatization). Countless misunderstandings arise everywhere and sometimes result in the designation of CTs as the "devil's work" or, conversely, as more or less celestial "manna." For this reason, we refer here to the "revenge of contexts." Being underestimated or ignored, the contexts come back and erupt into the game in an unexpected way, widening the implementation gaps and distorting the objectives of the programs.

This revenge of contexts is expressed through a number of "critical nodes" that involve many spaces of ambiguity, division, and confrontation between the CT programs and the strategic groups involved. We provide an initial comparative inventory of these critical nodes here: some are typical of Latin America (or part of it), others relate to the development rent, which is so omnipresent in Africa and the Middle East, others, again, involve the state (real or imaginary, repressive or benevolent) and NGOs, and many concern the CT targeting, gender, and public services. The critical nodes vary according to the contexts and can also extend across several contexts.

Some of the "Critical Nodes"

The State

Despite being relatively ignored in the literature on CTs, paradoxically, the differential position of the state in relation to the implementation of CT programs is probably the most important of the critical nodes. First, many CTs are managed and funded by states, and constitute a central pillar of their social policy. This is the case in Latin America, where all CT programs are derived from the Brazilian and Mexican models, and in some instances also in South Africa. Second, in many—in particular African and conflict-affected—countries, in which the state does not have many resources at its disposal, does not have a social policy, and has disengaged from humanitarian action, the international aid donors and NGOs assume control of the CT programs from beginning to end. Hence there are two extremes here: state CTs and nonstate CTs, and of course, various permutations in between.

Moreover, the role of the state within CT programs can be variable in itself. In Latin America, for example, the objectives of CTs tended to differ on the basis of their successive phases. At the outset, they were intended as a stopgap measure to counteract the effects of the economic crises and political adjustments; they were later conceived as programs aimed at providing a means of accumulating human capital and breaking the intergenerational transmission of poverty; and, finally, in certain cases they acted as a way of redistributing some of the revenues derived from extractive activities[5] (see Dapuez and Gavigan, chapter 7).

State CTs have spread in countries with very different indices of human development (from Nicaragua to Argentina) and have been promoted by governments with extremely wide-ranging political options—with "Chavist" Venezuela constituting a very special case in point (Sugiyama 2011). This broad distribution makes them one of the most widespread and consensual public policies.

The political use of state CTs varies from country to country. Sometimes, as is the case in Brazil and South Africa, they underpin a welfare-state rhetoric, occasionally with populist overtones. As is the case in Peru, they can also be used to promote the establishment of other public policies (in particular programs originating in ministries for development and social inclusion) or form part of broader development policies (in the areas of health, education, and agriculture). In a number of countries, CTs are deployed by the state as an instrument for establishing its presence in remote or marginalized areas, mainly the Andean and Amazonian regions. They arrive in places where the state has previously had little or no presence and facilitate the registration of the population, the development of the administration and public services (schools, health), and the organization of negotiations with companies.

With respect to nonstate CTs, these work on the basis of an external rent, particularly in places where the state is not very present or effective (see Olivier de Sardan and Hamani, chapter 12)

Rent

Some of the LMICs are "under an aid regime" (Lavigne Delville 2010). This means that the resources provided by international aid (in the form of development or humanitarian aid, project aid, sectoral or budgetary aid, public or private aid, and aid provided to associations) are a key element of the conception and implementation of public policies in these countries. What is involved here, in a sense, is a particular type of rentier state,[6] in which the development aid acts as external rent (external revenue) in the same way, but based on different modalities, as mining rent (in some cases the two are combined). The crucial importance of development aid for public budgets and for civil society creates an aid dependency, similar in many ways to oil dependency. It favors many strategies to capture and disseminate the rent flow.

In such contexts, the populations have become accustomed over decades to benefiting from an endless and assorted series of "projects," funding, support, subventions, and aid. Hence the arrival of the CTs is nothing more than the latest formula for the supply of this external "manna." Alain Morice (1995: 50) used this metaphor in relation to development aid some time ago, and we have adopted it again in reference to CTs (Olivier de Sardan 2014).[7] This "manna" can manifest through innumerable mechanisms (the only limits on which are the imaginations of the development experts and the good will of the aid donors). Irrespective of the mechanism involved, in the vast majority of cases it triggers the adoption of a "common sense" strategy among the "beneficiaries," which is found in the most wide-ranging contexts and is very widely perceived as legitimate: that is, the attempt to obtain the maximum while giving the minimum in return. In the context of conditional cash transfers (CCTs), this translates into "take the money, and comply as smoothly as possible with the conditionalities." In the context of unconditional CTs, it translates into a simpler strategy of "take the money," and this obviously accounts for the popularity of this form of CT, particularly compared with the numerous "cash for work" programs, which have been long promoted in the same areas where, in order to obtain the cash, recipients have to work long hours in the sun building dikes or planting trees.[8]

However, these rent capture strategies are not exclusive to the populations; they are also deployed by the staff involved in the implementation of the CT programs. In Africa, CTs come from two main channels. The first of these is the "World Bank channel," which sets out to involve the states by requiring that they contribute to the financing of the CTs and locate each CT program within a state service (while also retaining control through a project management unit) in the (by no means always fulfilled) hope that the state will assume full responsibility for the scheme on completion of the project. It would not be incorrect to speak of semistate or pseudostate CTs in this context. With this type of CT, it is the agents of the state (or various other entities—private operators, consultants, NGOs— with whom they deal) who attempt to benefit as much as possible from the rent.

The second is the "humanitarian channel," which is essentially populated by international and national NGOs that establish CT programs using finance from international institutions and bi- or multilateral cooperation (ECHO, WFP, UNICEF, US-AID, etc.). With this type of CT, the NGOs are the actor primarily concerned by the rent as the CTs account for an increasingly significant if not the main proportion of their turnover.

Targeting

This central device of the CT mechanism, which constitutes the first step in the implementation of a CT program, is particularly complex. It is the topic of countless expert debates and copious gray literature both in relation to the populations being targeted and the targeting techniques to be used (del Ninno and Mills 2015). An initial debate among experts, which is both technical and ideological in nature, pits the supporters of targeted transfers to poor or vulnerable populations (which involve a targeting process)—that is, the majority of CTs—against the advocates of universal cover, the distribution of universal subsidies to predefined and clearly delimited social categories (registration instead of targeting): for example, all persons of a certain age (pensions), all mothers (family allowances), all sick persons who attend a health center (global fee exemptions), all persons with a disability, etc.

Other more technical debates concern methods—geographical targeting, means testing, proxy means testing (by far the most commonly used method),[9] or community-based targeting—and compare their costs, efficiency, and biases (errors of inclusion or exclusion).[10] In this regard, it is astonishing to note in the literature on CTs the knowledge gap between the significant accumulation of technical information about these methods and the lack of information about how the populations involved perceive the targeting. The same knowledge gap exists in the majority of the countless training courses provided on the topic of CTs: most of the attention here is focused on the processes, procedures, and protocols for CTs and very little on the practices and reactions of the populations involved. This book attempts to address some aspects of this knowledge gap.[11]

A common type of local reaction contests the actual principle of targeting. In communities that are characterized as being generally poor, targeting creates an externally imposed threshold effect between beneficiaries and nonbeneficiaries, and, in many cases, this division does not make sense to the populations and appears arbitrary or illegitimate from their perspective. The case of Niger (see Olivier de Sardan and Hamani, chapter 12) is particularly significant in this regard.[12] However, the same type of reaction can be found in very different contexts, for example in Latin America, where the threshold effect generates logics of competition or denunciation (Piccoli 2014) or results in targeting being perceived as a lottery (see Correa Aste, Roopnaraine, and Margolies, chapter 5). The populations involved never have a say in relation to the principle behind the targeting. However—revenge of contexts!—the failure to adhere to this principle justifies the "circumventions," to which the rules governing CTs are often subjected at local level.

Another type of reaction challenges the objectivity of the targeting and generally incriminates the political elites and/or program officials, who are suspected of "favoritism" or "clientelism" (this is a "selection bias" or "inclusion error" in the language of the CT experts). This links up with the well-known body of literature on what was sometimes referred to as "elite capture" in development projects and more specifically in community-driven development projects (Platteau 2004; Wong 2010; Lund and Saito-Jensen 2013; Musgrave and Wong 2016). It also links up with another less familiar body of literature on the low-level staff of the public services and development projects, particularly in Africa and conflict-affected countries, and regarding, among other things, the "fabrication of figures," a practice in which state or NGO agents frequently indulge when carrying out surveys and quantified reports: fanciful, tendentious, or "negotiated" questionnaire administration sometimes lead them a long way away from the formal rules laid down by the statisticians and methodologists, which they are supposed to apply and in which they have received the necessary training.[13]

Conditionalities

One of the major differences between the different cash transfer programs relates to their conditional or nonconditional nature. In the versions found in Latin America, where the CT system originated (and were later adopted across the world), the allocation of the cash is not based exclusively on targeting but also on the compliance of the beneficiaries (in general the mothers of poor families), who must comply with a series of conditionalities. In general, the conditionalities are of three types: possession of identity papers, school attendance by children, and attendance at health checks.[14] These conditionalities are sometimes invested with the language of "co-responsibility" and hence present a quid pro quo or "mutual contract" logic.[15] In practice, they are often perceived as "obligations," however. They may also be incorporated into a logic of a "reciprocal gesture" and gratitude (see Agudo Sanchiz, chapter 2; Correa Aste, Roopnaraine, and Margolies, chapter 5), and less commonly a logic of "responsibility" (see Piccoli and Gillespie, chapter 6). Hence the CCTs combine a logic based on redistribution (through the targeting of poor families) and a logic of the formation of human capital (through conditionalities focused on health and school enrollment of children).

A common indirect conditionality that arises frequently, and is not presented as such but is nonetheless imposed in an institutionalized manner, also warrants a mention here: participation in the banking system. While in some cases the transfers are made in the form of vouchers, cash, and mobile telephones, the distribution systems are very often based on bank transfer (as in Latin America). This means that all beneficiaries must have a bank account. The money is then paid into their accounts, and they must withdraw it themselves, either at an ATM or at a bank counter (a process that mostly involves waiting in long queues: see Balen, chapter 4).

In Peru, the CT program is linked with other financial inclusion programs (Proyecto Capital), savings programs, and programs for the development of microloans. Hence the CTs there are integrated into a system of financial education and are powerful instruments of market inclusion (Lavinas 2013). Moreover, simultaneous to the implementation of the CT programs, there was an explosion in the number of financial institutions in the country's rural areas. This inclusion of the marginalized populations in the financial system obviously involves a large number of risks as it opens the door to debt for precarious rural households, whose most precious possession is land that is regularly coveted by developers.

The significance assigned to the formal conditionalities varies between countries and programs. While the conditionalities are secondary in some countries, as in Brazil and Argentina, in others they are more central and strictly monitored (Mexico, Peru). In countries with nonstate CTs, some CT programs are even based entirely on the conditionalities, and their main objective is to "buy" the frequentation of a public service by a potential user. Hence they go beyond the policies of fee exemption, which merely eliminate the financial barrier to access public services (e.g., health services), and are closer in orientation to a direct financial incentive.[16]

The existence of stringent conditionalities gives rise to a common phenomenon whose existence has been confirmed in various Latin American countries: the emergence of additional "informal conditionalities" or "extra conditionalities" that are imposed by the program or state officials.

As demonstrated by the book's chapters on this topic (see Correa Aste, Roopnaraine, and Margolies, chapter 5; and Piccoli and Gillespie, chapter 6), the nature of these extra conditionalities is particularly well developed in the case of Peru. The state program officials, the health centers, the schools, and the local authorities add their own lists of obligations to the official ones and fill the mothers' timetables with multiple activities and "voluntary participation." These extralegal conditionalities arise on the periphery of public policies and are neither outside the system nor truly official. They sometimes act as "tolerated instruments" for the purpose of satisfying policy indicators (number of medicalized births, vaccinations, etc.) and as stopgap measures aimed at compensating for the underfinancing of public institutions (lack of equipment for school activities, etc.).

These extra conditionalities operate in a largely uncontrollable gray area where debate is not really possible. When faced with the threat of withdrawal of the aid, the beneficiaries have no possibility of publicly challenging the officials who require them to fulfill these extra conditionalities. These extra conditionalities often involve the condemnation of local practices (in relation to hygiene, food, birthing, education, etc.), and various forms of disregard and violence toward the communities (see Piccoli and Gillespie, chapter 6; Nagels, chapter 8).

The Public Services

CT conditionalities always involve the frequentation of certain public services by poor populations. The preliminary diagnosis common to all cases everywhere CCTs have been deployed is the insufficient frequentation of these public services by mothers and children: insufficient numbers of prenatal consultations and medically supervised births, insufficient numbers of medical examinations and vaccinations for children, and weak school enrollment and/or early school leaving. This diagnosis, which is confirmed by all of the available statistics, obviously concurs with the Millennium Development Goals (MDG), which essentially concern the LMICs. It is necessary to combat the maternal and neonatal mortality, illiteracy, lack of education and training, and child labor that are rife in these countries, hence no one can argue with these objectives in principle.

With a view to bringing about a shift in this direction, the strategy behind the conditionalities is to bring about a change in maternal behavior based on the quid pro quo of the cash transfers;[17] this change is seen, of course, as being "in their [i.e., the mothers'] own interest" or "in the interest of their children." To put it in more crass terms, it is the old tactic of the "carrot," which is now repackaged and designated in the form of (financial) "incentives."

The idea is to take action in relation to demand by presenting the implicit hypothesis that the problem lies essentially on the demand side: the low levels of service frequentation are seen as being mainly due to poverty, insufficient awareness among mothers, a lack of "awareness-raising," a lack of information, and even a local ancestral culture that advocates inadequate behavior and represents an obstacle to the promotion of modern healthcare and education (everyone has heard of and encountered numerous examples of this on occasion—for example, women giving birth at home standing or kneeling, rumors about the hidden agenda of vaccinations made by the "whites," the young girls kept for domestic work, etc.).

However, based on our experience in the field and, in some cases, longitudinal research studies on the health services,[18] we believe that the problem originates more often in a lack of faith in the supply side and in the supply side itself. The inadequate quality of the public services provided to the populations is a major cause of the low frequentation rates. The disregard shown to "indigenous"[19] or "bush" women, the prejudice against them, the greed displayed by the public officials, the scheming, "arrangements," and various forms of minor extortion are equally repulsive to the mothers (and fathers). Summary consultations, standardized treatments, drug shortages, the ignoring of children's pain, the failure to respect modesty in the health centers: all of these elements regarding the health system are found in the majority of the locations in which CCTs are operated. In the context of schools, oversized classes and badly trained, poorly motivated, and sometimes absent teachers exist side-by-side with more or less mandatory "contributions" and meetings and "recommended private courses" and exams, in which success is guaranteed if parents are willing to put their hands in their pockets.

Needless to say, the ways in which public services are delivered in the areas of education and health differ from one context to the next; the dysfunctions are not equal in either scale or "variations." Corruption is not the same everywhere and is not even necessarily a relevant factor. Nonetheless, the fact remains that, apart from a few exceptions, the quality of services provided in the health and educations sectors remains a key problem in the majority of countries in which CCTs are used.

It should not be concluded either, however, that there is no problem in relation to demand. Nonetheless, it may be stated, at least, that problems with demand are more or less always combined with problems in relation to supply. Thus there is a certain inconsistency in an approach that involves the promotion of greater frequentation of services through CT conditionalities without attempting to achieve a significant improvement in the quality of the services offered by the public authorities.

A "Maternalist Perspective" between Empowerment and Stigmatization

While the CT principle is not exclusively applied to women, the majority of the programs and the most prominent ones are aimed at women and implemented in the context of combating poverty. With the exception of chapter 11 (Chelpi-den Hammer), which focuses on the army veterans in Côte d'Ivoire, all of the texts contained in this volume involve CTs aimed at women.

The approach to combating poverty using CTs is "maternalist" in its orientation (Molyneux 2000; Jenson and Nagels 2015). As mothers, women are considered a priori the best recipients and users of the aid. The system of reference behind these CTs as a public policy[20] avails of the image of the mother as someone who is naturally inclined to sacrifice herself for the family and make purchasing decisions for the good of the children, in contrast to her male counterpart, who is more likely to be attracted by "temptation goods." Women are perceived exclusively as mothers and efficient channels through which their families can be reached, and not as program beneficiaries in themselves. Of course, some CTs have objectives in terms of women's empowerment, but this empowerment is essentially based on the reinforcement of the maternal figure.[21] It isolates women and assigns them exclusively to the dimension of "care" (Nagels 2011).

The actual relationship between gender and money is far more nuanced in local contexts, however. In northeastern Brazil, for example, women and men both contribute sums of money to the household, but based on different timeframes (see Morton, chapter 3) and, as is the case in many African countries, the men in Niger are responsible for managing the budget for food and healthcare for the children (Olivier de Sardan and Hamani, chapter 12).

Another aspect of the "maternalization" of the aid is the identification of women as "poor mothers." They are included in the CT programs with a view to breaking the intergenerational cycle of poverty, for which they are implicitly recognized as being partly responsible. Hence, based on this co-responsibility (in the case of the conditional CTs), they must act to terminate the reproduction of this poverty. Poverty is not perceived, therefore, as a collective and political problem but as a matter of family and maternal responsibility (see Agudo Sanchiz, chapter 2).

The case of indigenous women in Mexico, Columbia, Peru, and Bolivia (see Agudo Sanchiz, chapter 2; Balen, chapter 4; Piccoli and Gillespie, chapter 6; Nagels, chapter 8) is particularly illuminating in this regard.[22] These women are doubly penalized here: in order to respond to the requirements of the programs, they must comply with exogenous hygiene standards while also being subjected to the violence of the institutions that discriminate against them—sometimes directly, for example through disdainful treatment, insults, and extra conditionalities, and sometimes indirectly, for example through long waits for meetings, checkups, and administrative and banking services. The long queues, which some people perceived as the "gates of hell" in their religious visions (Piccoli 2014), represent the physical staging of the monetary transfer in the public space. Being forced to tolerate heat and humiliation while waiting in a queue is a form of selection (see Balen, chapter 4) as is the public labeling of poor mothers.

The CT Staff

The staff involved in implementing the CT programs—the enumerators, researchers, social workers, NGO workers, public servants, etc.—are more or less completely ignored in the literature. There is no reference to the problems they encounter, their own perceptions, their difficulties, or their strategies. However, they are not simply the transparent executors of a system; they have their own difficulties, constraints, and scope for maneuvering, all of which vary considerably depending on the context in which they operate. These issues are discussed in several chapters of this book.

In Egypt (see Solkamy, chapter 10), the replacement of previous forms of social assistance by CTs resulted in the reclassification and loss of autonomy on the part of social workers. In Niger (see Olivier de Sardan and Hamani, chapter 12), the NGO workers "mess up" the strategic targeting surveys due to a lack of time and motivation.

In Peru, the staff responsible for implementing cash transfers, who are often criticized for their discriminatory attitudes toward the indigenous communities, face an entire series of difficulties. Working in the Andean and Amazonian regions is exhausting (particularly due to the difficulties of getting around), and the staff are under various pressures from the authorities. In effect, in addition to ensuring that the legal conditions of the programs are respected, these CT workers are encouraged to incentivize the women to carry out other activities promoted by them or by other institutions. Their position is precarious due to the risk of denunciation.

When a television program (*Cuarto Poder*) broadcast in 2011 condemned the obligation placed on mothers to paint a flag on their doors, the program reacted by firing an employee despite the fact that the enforcement of this "obligation" was widespread in the Andes. This double bind (enforcing extra conditionalities but not being caught out publicly for it) is combined with having to deal with the potential aggression of the mothers who are excluded from the programs and who perceive the targeting processes as arbitrary. The stress management guidebook compiled by the program seems like a rather weak and inadequate response in the face of these structural problems.

Mutual Adaptations

The "confrontations" between the CTs and strategic groups specific to the different contexts as we have envisaged them through the above-presented critical nodes should not simply be seen from a static and one-dimensional perspective. They evolve over time on the basis of the adaptive strategies adopted by the different parties involved.

Initial phases of refusal or open resistance in the strict sense of the term, as observed in Peru when the CTs were perceived at the local level as the expression of a "diabolical" repressive state, may be followed by phases that combine acceptance and passive resistance, and even actual compliance with the CT procedures when attempts are made to rectify the errors that have been made.

In fact, the three traditional options described by Hirschmann (1970) — "voice," "exit," and "loyalty" — do not cover all of the attitudes adopted by the target populations in response to CTs. To describe the dominant strategy that we referred to earlier — that is, "the attempt to obtain the maximum while giving the minimum in return" — a fourth option should be added to this list: "cunning."

Given that the continuation of the delivery of the resource represented by the CTs is an objective largely shared by the local populations, the "exit" option is very rarely deployed. Some exceptions can be observed here, of course — for example, by staunch evangelicals in Mexico (see Agudo Sanchiz, chapter 2), or people convinced that the money originates from the devil, whether in the form of the monstrous *Pishtaco* in Peru (Piccoli 2014) or freemasons in Congo.[23]

Recourse to the "voice" option is equally rare, at least in the context of humanitarian CT programs (which are operated by NGOs), obviously because in the eyes of the populations it could result in exclusion from CTs and the end of the "manna." This explains why, as demonstrated by various cases in Palestine, Yemen, and Mozambique (see Samuels and

Jones, chapter 9), as well as in Niger (see Olivier de Sardan and Hamani, chapter 12), the complaint mechanisms that are often provided by the CT programs generally remain unactivated. In contrast to this, the voice option is sometimes deployed in the case of state CCTs in Latin America. In Peru, it often takes the form of whispered objections involving the use of diabolical or mythical images to express local fears (Piccoli 2014).

Although "loyalty" can sometimes be demonstrated, this option is far from being the one that triumphs. Our feeling is that "cunning" is the most widely adopted strategy. This is at the root of what the economists refer to as opportunist strategies that "circumvent" the objectives of the CTs discreetly and quietly. Conditional CTs sometimes elicit apparent compliance with the formal conditionalities while the informal condition-alities are sabotaged (see Piccoli and Gillespie, chapter 7). In the case of unconditional CTs involving distribution of "manna" instead, the "cun-ning" option is played out either around the selection of the recipients (what must be done to be included in the list) or around the uses of the manna (the redistribution of the received cash, its use for social spend-ing rather than the recommended food spending, or its investment in the migration of a young family member when the CTs are supposed to prevent migration, etc.).

However, changes may also be induced in the attitudes of the popula-tions toward the CTs through the introduction of changes in the CT pro-cedures themselves. A central element in the implementation of a public policy should be the latter's capacity for self-adjustment and "learning by doing" (Rose 1991). This capacity is often weak, but it can nonethe-less exist in certain circumstances. Sometimes it is the program officials who attempt to modify their own behavior or arguments (as in Peru by clearly specifying the origin of the funds with a view to alleviating fears). Sometimes it is the programs themselves that reform their protocols and mechanisms over the course of time in response to undesirable effects (as is the case in Brazil and Mexico, the two original experiences with the CT system), which in most cases are demonstrated through qualitative studies. The case of Niger (see Olivier de Sardan and Hamani, chapter 12) presents an attempt by certain NGOs active in the area of CTs to modify some elements of their systems (e.g., complaints committees and targeting techniques) in response to the findings of a socioanthropological research study.

For this reason, we believe that this book, which primarily aims to pro-vide information about CT programs' implementation, in particular their interaction with the contexts in which they are deployed, could also enable the CT programs to self-adjust to local realities, should they wish to.

About This Book

Heuristic Value

The four contributions made by this book can be defined as follows:

1. It represents the first comparative study of CTs based on a socioanthropological perspective that prioritizes the study of the contexts in which the CTs are carried out and the representations of the actors involved on the ground. This enables us to demonstrate the significant difference between the countries in which CTs are a national policy implemented by a strong state (Latin America) and countries in which they are associated with the aid sectors (international institutions and NGOS). A second difference exists in Latin America between the countries in which CTs basically constitute a social policy (Brazil, Argentina) and those in which they are also used as an instrument for the "inculturation" of rural and indigenous communities (Mexico, Peru). The absence of case studies from Asia (which appears to range between the African and South-American systems) is, however, one of the limitations of this book.

2. Due to the proliferation of programs, their extension into different fields, and their globalization, CTs have assumed a place among the main "development industries." The CT system is a traveling model that has enjoyed global success: it is not solely a strategy of the World Bank, and it has been adopted by numerous aid donors and states. The "CT business" has become an unavoidable reality in the world of development and humanitarian aid: it is a sector that creates employment (nationally and internationally) and very important markets.

3. Beyond the CTs in the strict sense, the case of CTs in general enables the reconsideration or more detailed examination of a series of classical problems associated with development and, more generally, public policies in the LMICs: the central role played by "traveling models" at the expense of the contexts (Olivier de Sardan, chapter 1); the unintended consequences of development aid rent (chapter 1; Olivier de Sardan and Hamani, chapter 12); the stigmatization of indigenous communities in Latin America (Agudo Sanchiz, chapter 2; Balen, chapter 4; Piccoli and Gillespie, chapter 6; Nagels, chapter 8); the uncertain status of street-level bureaucrats in general and social workers in particular (Solkamy, chapter 10); the illusions of numerous "participative" strategies (Olivier de Sardan and

Hamani, chapter 12); gender representations and their impact on the implementation of programs (Morton, chapter 3; Nagels, chapter 8); the dynamics of resistance, acceptance, and deviation (Agudo Sanchiz, chapter 2; Piccoli and Gillespie, chapter 7), etc.

4. This book shows, once again (however, in view of the quantitavist obsessions, "once again" is never too much in this field), that qualitative methods are in a better position to reveal some important and central issues regarding the implementation of public policies that are not very accessible to quantitative methods (public statistics and questionnaires) and sometimes even evade them. In fact, quantitative methods are not very "context-sensitive." The current fashion for randomized controlled trials (RCTs), which focus on the impact of a single variable (the "mechanism"), is an illustration of this (see Olivier de Sardan, chapter 1). And these extremely costly RCTs consume a large proportion of the funding and attention devoted to the assessment of CTs to the detriment of implementation studies. It should be stressed, however, that some people within the CT world have availed themselves of qualitative methods and have become advocates of their undeniable contribution (Devereux and Getu 2013; Barca et al. 2015; Watson 2016).

Structure and Chapters

Chapter 2 by Jean-Pierre Olivier de Sardan follows up on the introduction and complements it by tracing the transformation in the initial experiences of CTs into a "traveling model" that is now exported to a large part of the planet. The process of production by international experts of a miracle mechanism, at the core of the model, is based on two success stories (Mexico and Brazil). The "mechanism" is accredited with an intrinsic value that guaranteed the specific efficacy of the model and is expressed in three complementary institutional devices. It is distinguished therefore from the contexts in which it is implemented and to which it is supposed to adapt. In this instance, the CTs are a relevant example of a much bigger group of development projects and public policy transfers that follow the same system of standardization and that, like the CTs, encounter the "revenge of contexts": underestimated, insufficiently taken into account, and poorly understood, the local contexts are at the heart of the implementation gaps of CT programs. The strategies of the officials (and their practical norms), and the reactions of the populations (and their social norms), collide with the CT programs (and the formal norms they impose) and produce a panoply of unplanned unintended consequences, circumventions, and informal arrangements.

Following this general chapter, the book presents a series of case studies divided into two parts, which each outline a historical, geographical and political stage in the spread of the CT programs: the first concerns the continent on which CTs originated—that is, Latin America—and the second concerns its subsequent areas of expansion (Africa and the Middle East here). However all chapters highlight the role of the local contexts.

Conditional Cash Transfers in Latin America

As indicated above, in Latin America CTs are conditional, on the one hand, and based on a voluntarist social policy of the state, on the other. These two elements extend across all of the chapters in which the relationships with the state and public services play a central role, both in the reality and representations.

Alejandro Agudo Sanchiz (chapter 2) examines the local reinterpretation of conditionalities in the Chiapas state in Mexico. For women, the informal conditionalities involve the completion of community work or negotiation of compensation for local intermediaries. This chapter confirms the importance of the context in the face of the apparent verticality of public policies.

Gregory Duff Morton (chapter 3) demonstrates how, in the context of the family economy in Brazil, collective needs (e.g., food) are covered financially by the men, while the "women's money" is used to cover everyone's individual needs (clothes, furniture, etc.). Thus masculine and feminine financial resources correspond to different and complementary areas. The author also shows that CTs have the greatest impact on gender relations when they are received by less poor households.

Maria Elisa Balen (chapter 4) addresses a phenomenon that is seemingly anecdotal but nonetheless central to the cash transfer programs in Colombia from the perspective of the beneficiaries: queues (at the bank, administrative services, etc.). Something that might appear to be a simple undesirable side effect functions both as a source of discrimination and instrument of social control. Based on perseverance and the capacity to resist humiliation, the queues select "those whose needs are greatest."

Norma Correa Aste, Terry Roopnaraine, and Amy Margolies (chapter 5) analyze the implementation of CTs in the indigenous context in the Amazon region of Peru. While highlighting the importance of CTs for families, their study reveals a series of problems that arise in the course of their implementation: misunderstandings in relation to targeting, large numbers of conditionalities that considerably exceed the legal framework, and the generation of fears in association with the program.

These observations are shared by Bronwen Gillespie and Emmanuelle Piccoli (chapter 6) who study the implementation of the same program in the Andean region. They return to the legal and extralegal conditionalities, which set out to train "good mothers" in accordance with a modernist and Western vision, and which disapprove of a series of Andean practices that are considered both backward and harmful. The beneficiaries respond with alternating reactions involving a certain degree of resistance, but above all acceptance and reproduction of the alternating hierarchization.

Andres Dapuez and Sabrina Gavigan (chapter 7) present an analysis of the promises and future projections enshrined in the CT programs in Mexico and Argentina. Each stage of their implementation is guided by a specific vision of the future. Thus CTs are alternately understood here as a means of adjusting to the new economic realities of the 1990s, a policy aimed at the accumulation of human capital, and, finally, a redistribution policy, particularly in Argentina.

Finally, Nora Nagels (chapter 8) studies the impact of CTs on ethnic and gender relations in Bolivia. She shows that contrary to the "pro-indigenous" discourses, in practice, the implementation of CT programs contributes to the reinforcement of discrimination and violence toward indigenous women. The practical norms deployed by healthcare staff remain unchanged, in effect, and continue to result in the stigmatization of the women.

Cash Transfers in Africa and the Middle East

The second part of the book contains the case studies carried out in countries in which international institutions and NGOs are largely responsible for the diffusion of CTs in the context of development policies and humanitarian interventions. The contexts, roles of the states, and aims of the programs are extremely varied here. Many of the CTs distributed in these regions are nonconditional.

Fiona Samuels and Nicola Jones (chapter 9) demonstrate how the establishment of unconditional monetary transfer programs in Mozambique, Palestine, and Yemen affects the perception of wellbeing. Their contribution illustrates both the positive impacts and limits of the programs, and highlights the fact that CTs cannot be considered a magic formula. They are dependent in particular on the political contexts in which they are implemented, which also remain the determining elements of social accountability, governance issues, and the wellbeing of populations in conflict-affected contexts (as shown by the extreme cases of war and occupation).

Hania Solkamy (chapter 10) examines the role of officials in the establishment of CT programs in Egypt, where they replace previous social programs. She shows that it is not possible to understand these programs without taking into account the functioning of the administration and strategies of social workers who have relinquished a significant proportion of the scope for maneuvering they previously enjoyed.

Magali Chelpi-den Hammer (chapter 11) analyzes a program for the demobilization and reintegration (DDR) of military veterans of the crisis in Côte d'Ivoire in which cash transfers are used as an instrument for the support of reintegration. Although the cash provides effective aid for the beneficiaries, the impact on the DDR policy is minimal. CTs everywhere have the effect of a breath of fresh air but do not have any miraculous impact on broader and more significant problems.

Jean-Pierre Olivier de Sardan and Oumarou Hamani (chapter 12) focus on a group of CT programs in Niger, developed by international NGOs, from the perspective of the fight against food insecurity in a context of chronic poverty in rural areas. They show how the program norms (targeting procedures, transparency rules, payments to women, etc.) collide with the local social norms and are circumvented as much as possible by the populations. The attempt by some CT operators to take the findings of this research into account should also be noted here.

Conclusion

Although this book highlights numerous problems associated with CTs, which have generally gone unacknowledged within the CT world, and highlights their unexpected effects, it does not set out to take a stand *against* CTs. We do not have a basic ideological position for or against CTs. They are one social policy among others, and are diffused today on a global scale. As social science researchers, we aim to understand how CTs function, how they are perceived, what kind of reactions they trigger in different contexts, and what kind of implementation gaps arise between their objectives and reality.

From the perspective of the beneficiaries, the data on whom were collected using various qualitative surveys, despite all of the reservations and circumvention strategies highlighted in the following chapters, CTs are generally experienced as a largely positive form of aid. They enable people to boost their "dignity" (see Morton, chapter 3; Samuels and Jones, chapter 9); the comments recorded about them frequently focus on "relief" ("positive changes in household well-being," Barca et al. 2015: xii) and the reestablishment of links between the recipients and their communities ("re-entering the social life," Barca et al. 2015: xvi) is also cited in a number of cases. A "reduce[d] reliance on negative coping strategies" (Barca et al.

2015: xii) is confirmed as is the fact that, in rural areas, CTs have "enabled beneficiaries to reduce their engagement in casual labor and use their time to work more on their own farms" (Barca et al. 2015: xiii).

In terms of the institutions that deliver the CTs, the fears regarding certain possible negative effects were not confirmed: the distributed cash is not wasted on "temptation goods" like alcohol and gambling (Evans and Papava 2014), and food markets have not been disrupted (Barca et al. 2015). Finally, even if the methods used and quality of public services provided raise serious questions, the conditionalities of the CTs have led to an increase in the school enrollment and health monitoring of children (Angle 2015).

Nevertheless, the multiple evaluations carried out within the CT business itself reveal certain limits in terms of the expected effects of the programs. "A large gap remains regarding the cost-effectiveness of CT in general and for addressing nutrition outcomes in particular" (REFANI 2015). CTs "did not significantly transform structural gender norms, particularly concerning the gender balance of strategic household decision-making, but instead conformed to existing gender patterns of roles and responsibilities and practices" (Barca et al. 2015: xiv). The "emergence from poverty" is still far from being confirmed.

From the perspective of reforming or improving the CT system, the contribution made by this volume is to demonstrate the importance of the contexts in which they are implemented. This contrasts with a certain glorification (or even "fetishism") of the "mechanism," which can sometimes be observed as thriving within CT organizations and among CT experts. In our view, the main challenge for CT programs is whether the traveling model of the CT is capable of better understanding the contexts in which it is implemented, of taking them in account systematically, and of adapting to the reactions of these contexts to it rather than trying to make the reality adapt to its model. Can the perceptions, limitations, and expectations of the populations—and of the frontline workers and program officials—be taken into account seriously, including when they challenge some of the strategic orientations of the CT programs (e.g., the principle of targeting, the targeting procedures, the conditionalities, and the methods of distributing the cash)? This question remains an open one.

Jean-Pierre Olivier de Sardan is professor of anthropology at the Ecole des Hautes Etudes en Sciences Sociales (France) and emeritus director of research at the Centre National de la Recherche Scientifique (France). He is among the founders of the Laboratory for Study and Research on Social Dynamics and Local Development (LASDEL) in Niamey, Niger (www.

lasdel.net), and is associate professor, in charge of the master's program Anthropology of Health, at Abdou Moumouni University, Niamey. He has authored numerous books in French and in English, and is currently working on an empirical anthropology of public actions and modes of governance in West Africa. Honors and awards include Chevalier des Palmes académiques de la République du Niger, 2004; Docteur honoris causa de l'Université de Liège, 2012; Chevalier de l'Ordre national de la Légion d'honneur de la République française, 2012; and Prize Ester Boserup, University of Copenhagen, 2014.

Emmanuelle Piccoli is an assistant professor in development studies at the Université Catholique de Louvain (Belgium). She previously benefitted from a doctoral and postdoctoral grant from the National Fund for Scientific Research (FNRS) in Belgium. During those mandates, she was an associate researcher at the Instituto Francés de Estudios Andinos, the Pontificia Universidad Católica del Perú, the Université de Laval in Québec, and the University of Michigan. She published a book titled *Les Rondes paysannes: Vigilance, politique et justice dans les Andes péruviennes* (Academia, 2011) as well as numerous papers about the Peruvian Andes.

Notes

The authors would like to thank Susan Cox for the translation.

 1. Anthropology does not lack examples of overinterpretation, alas. On this point, see Olivier de Sardan 2015, chapter 7.
 2. The exploratory concept of "strategic groups," which was originally formulated by Evers and Schiel (1988), and reformulated by Bierschenk (in Bierschenk and Olivier de Sardan 1997), is used in the anthropology of development to designate groups of actors who adopt a similar position in relation to a given issue or "problem"; various strategic groups face each other in a given "arena."
 3. See, for example, Angle 2015: the two major points of satisfaction expressed by the CT beneficiaries surveyed in three countries (Republic of Congo, Nepal, and Philippines) are (1) the capacity for choice (spending of received sums as beneficiary sees fit) and (2) the restoration of dignity (reintegration into local social context). The only source of dissatisfaction concerns the amounts of money paid, which are considered insufficient to enable people to get out of poverty. According to a report from the Food and Agriculture Organization (FAO) of the United Nations (Barca et al. 2015), cash transfers encouraged income-generating activities; cash transfers had positive—if minor—effects on the local markets in all countries; and regular cash transfers improved the access of beneficiaries to economic collaboration with others—the only concerns in this case being the communication and link between worker and beneficiaries).
 4. For example, the Cash Learning Partnership (CaLP) network organized a side event at the World Humanitarian Summit (Istanbul, 23 May 2016) under the self-laudatory heading "Four ways to join the cash revolution."

5. These policies can also function in the opposite way: mining policy is justified by the distribution of CTs, the sum of which merely represents a very small proportion of the taxes received and *a fortiori* of the value generated. This is one of the ways in which the CTs are perceived in Peru (See Correa Aste, Roopnaraine, and Margolies, chapter 6).

6. On the concept of the rentier state, see Beblawi and Luciani 1987; Yates 1996. For comparisons of oil rent and aid rent, see Collier 2006; Olivier de Sardan 2013.

7. We can see how far we are here from the perception of CTs as a new global "social right" in accordance with Ferguson's (2015) interpretation.

8. On the "cash for work" system, see Subbarao 1997.

9. For a critical (but technical) analysis of the use of proxy means testing, see Australian Aid 2011.

10. See Coady, Grosh, and Hoddinott 2004; Fiszbein et al. 2009; Harvey and Bailey 2011; World Food Programme 2014.

11. Nonetheless, a number of studies within or on the periphery of the CT business that have attempted to fill this gap should be acknowledged: Devereux and Gatu 2013; Oxford Policy Management 2013; Watson 2016.

12. It should be noted that, according to the international statistics, around 10 to 20 percent of the African populations benefit from CTs, while the poverty level is around 50 percent. In Niger, the CT officials translate this reality through a form of community-based targeting that is strongly controlled (by them) and requires villagers to classify the local population in four categories: (1) "those who have wealth"; (2) "those who get by"; (3) the poor; and (4) the very poor; the latter category alone will be targeted with CTs (see chapter 12).

13. If the issue of false data in African statistics has already been raised (see "poor numbers," Jarven 2013), including by the World Bank (see "Africa's statistical tragedy," Devarajan 2013), one of its causes remains largely unrevealed, which concerns the practical norms of civil servants (Bierschenk and Olivier de Sardan 2014; Olivier de Sardan 2015): distorting, concealing, or inventing data to fit donors' or governments' objectives and injunctions are not infrequently routinized practices.

14. To this is added the implicit condition of opening a bank account (in cases in which the payments are made through the bank, which happens in the majority of cases).

15. These semantic modifications and the importance of the contractual logic are also reminiscent of the modification of the language and practices associated with social assistance in Europe, particularly in Belgium (obligation to sign a "contract of integration" for all beneficiaries of social assistance from 2016).

16. Thus programs exist in Africa in which mothers receive cash when they take their infants to routine medical consultations. In a completely different context, vouchers are currently being distributed by maternity services in France to pregnant women who stop smoking (*Le Parisien*, 7 May 2016).

17. In effect these are supposed to be the driving force of school enrollment and attendance at health centers by children everywhere. This point, which concerns gender, is discussed later in the chapter.

18. Regarding West Africa, see *Une médecine inhospitalière* (Jaffré and Olivier de Sardan 2003).

19. For an analysis of the "abuses and discrimination" to which the indigenous populations are subjected by health officials (in the case of Guatemala), see Cerón et al. 2016.

20. Müller 2009.

21. As noted by Jenson and Nagels (2015), the Mexican program Progresa, which was at the origin of CTs, highlighted the empowerment dimension. However, in the process of the standardization of CTs and their export to other South American countries, it was abandoned, and the maternal role of women became the real priority.

22. Discrimination against indigenous people is frequently labeled "neocolonialism" in Latin America literature.
23. Ongoing research by LASDEL on CTs in the Democratic Republic of Congo.

References

Angle, Susan. 2015. *Voices and Views of Beneficiaries on Unconditional Cash Transfers: Democratic Republic of Congo, Nepal and Philippines.* Cash Learning Partnership. Accessed 15 March 2018 http://www.cashlearning.org/downloads/calp-beneficiaries-voice.pdf.
Australian Aid. 2011. *Targeting the Poorest: An Assessment of the Proxy Means Test Methodology.* Canberra: Australian Agency for International Development. http://www.unicef.org/socialpolicy/files/targeting-poorest.pdf.
Bastagli, Francesca, Jessica Hagen-Zanker, Luke Harman, Georgina Sturge, Valentina Barca, Tanja Schmidt, and Luca Pellerano. 2016. *Cash Transfers: What Does the Evidence Say? A Rigorous Review of Programme Impact and of the Role of Design and Implementation Features.* London: Overseas Development Institute.
Barca, Valentina, Simon Brook, Jeremy Holland, Mosope Otulana, and Pamela Porzany. 2015. *Qualitative Research and Analyses of the Economic Impacts of Cash Transfer Programmes in Sub-Saharan Africa Synthesis Report.* Rome: Food and Agriculture Organization of the United Nations.
Beblawi, Hazem, and Giacomo Luciani, eds. 1987. *The Rentier State.* Oxford: Routledge.
Bierschenk, Thomas, and Jean-Pierre Olivier de Sardan. 1997a. "ECRIS: Rapid Collective Inquiry for the Identification of Conflicts and Strategic Groups." *Human Organization* 56(2): 238–244.
———. 1997b. "Local Powers and a Distant State in Rural Central African Republic." *The Journal of Modern African Studies* 35(3): 441–468.
———. 2014. "Ethnographies of Public Services in Africa: An Emerging Research Paradigm." In *States at Work: Dynamics of African Bureaucracies,* edited by Thomas Bierschenk and Jean-Pierre Olivier de Sardan, 35–65. Leyden: Brill.
Beblawi, Hazem, and Giacomo Luciani, eds. 1987. *The Rentier State.* Vol. 2: *Nation State and Integration in the Arab World.* London: Croom Helm.
Bouziane, Malika, Cilja Harders, and Anja Hoffmann, eds. 2013. *Local Politics and Contemporary Transformations in the Arab World: Governance beyond the Center.* Basingstoke: Palgrave Macmillan.
Cerón, Alejandro, Ana Lorena Ruano, Silvia Sánchez, Aiken S. Chew, Diego Díaz, Alison Hernández, and Walter Flores. 2016. "Abuse and Discrimination towards Indigenous People in Public Health Care Facilities: Experiences from Rural Guatemala." *International Journal for Equity in Health* 15: 77.
CALP. 2018. "The State of the World's Cash Report: Cash Transfer Programming in Humanitarian Aid." The Cash Learning Partnership.
Coady, David, Margaret Grosh, and John Hoddinott. 2004. "Targeting of Transfers in Developing Countries: Review of Lessons and Experience." Washington, DC: The World Bank-IFPRI.

Collier, Paul. 2006. "Is Aid Oil? An Analysis of Whether Africa Can Absorb More Aid." *World Development* 34: 1482–1497.

del Ninno, Carolo, and Bradford Mills, eds. 2015. *Safety Nets in Africa: Effective Mechanisms to Reach the Poor and Most Vulnerable*. Washington, DC: World Bank, AFD.

Devarajan, Shanta. 2013. "Africa's Statistical Tragedy." *Review of Income and Wealth* 59: S9–S15.

Devereux, Stephen, and Melese Getu. 2013. *Informal and Formal Social Protection Systems in SubSaharan Africa*. Addis Ababa: Organization for Social Science Research in Eastern and Southern Africa.

Evans, David K., and Anna Popova. 2014. "Cash Transfers and Temptation Goods: A Review of Global Evidence." Policy research working paper 6880. Washington, DC: World Bank Group. http://documents.worldbank.org/curated/en/617631468001808739/Cash-transfers-and-temptation-goods-a-review-of-global-evidence.

Evers, Hans-Dieter, and Tilman Schiel. 1988. *Stragegische Gruppen*. Berlin: Reimer.

Ferguson, James. 2015. *Give a Man a Fish: Reflections on the New Politics of Distribution*. Durham, NC: Duke University Press.

Fiszbein, Ariel, Norbert Schady, Francisco H. G. Ferreira, Margaret Grosh, Niall Keleher, Pedro Olinto, and Emmanuel Skoufias. 2009. *Conditional Cash Transfers: Reducing Present and Future Poverty*. World Bank Policy Research Report. Washington, DC: World Bank. https://openknowledge.worldbank.org/handle/10986/2597.

Harvey, Paul, and Sarah Bailey. 2011. *Cash Transfer Programming in Emergencies: Review of Good Practices*. London: Humanitarian Practice Network, ODI.

Hirschman, Albert O. 1970. *Exit, Voice and Loyalty: Responses to Decline in Firms, Organizations and the State*. Cambridge, MA: Harvard UP.

Jaffré, Yannick, and Jean-Pierre Olivier de Sardan, eds. 2003. *Une médecine inhospitalière: Les difficiles relations entre soignants et soignés dans cinq capitales d'Afrique de l'Ouest*. Paris: Karthala.

Jerven, M. 2013. *Poor Numbers: How We Are Misled by African Development Statistics and What to Do about It*. London: Cornell University Press.

Jenson, Jane, and Nora Nagels. 2015. "Social Policy Instruments in Motion: Conditional Cash Transfers from Mexico to Peru." Paper presented at International Conference on Public Policy, Milan, July 2015.

Lavigne Delville, Philippe. 2010. "La réforme foncière rurale au Bénin: Emergence et mise en question d'une politique instituante dans un pays sous régime d'aide." *Revue Française de Science Politique* 60(3): 467–491.

Lavinas, Lena. 2013. "21st Century Welfare." *New Left Review* 84: 5–40.

Lillrank, Paul. 1995. "The Transfer of Management Innovations from Japan." *Organization Studies* 16(6): 971–989.

Lund, Jens F., and Moeko Saito-Jensen. 2013. "Revisiting the Issue of Elite Capture of Participatory Initiatives." *World Development* 46: 104–112.

Nagels, Nora. 2011. "Représentations des rapports sociaux de sexe au sein des politiques de lutte contre la pauvreté au Pérou comme enjeux de citoyenneté." *Recherches féministes* 24(2): 115–134.

Molyneux, Maxine, 2000. "Twentieth-Century State Formation in Latin America." In *The Hidden Histories of Gender and the State in Latin America*, edited by Elizabeth Dore and Maxine Molyneux, 33–81. Durham, NC: Duke University Press.

Morice, Alain. 1995. "Corruption, loi et société: quelques propositions." *Revue Tiers Monde* 141: 41–65.

Musgrave, Michael K., and Sam Wong. 2016. "Towards a More Nuanced Theory of Elite Capture in Development Projects: The Importance of Context and Theories of Power." *Journal of Sustainable Development* 9(3): 87.

O'Brien, Clare, Fidelis Hove, and Gabrielle Smith. 2013. *Factors Affecting the Cost-Efficiency of Electronic Transfers in Humanitarian Programmes*. Oxford Policy Management; Concern; Cash Learning Partnership. http://www.cashlearning. org/downloads/opm-cost-efficiency-of-e-transfers-web.pdf.

Olivier de Sardan, Jean-Pierre. 2013. "The Bureaucratic Mode of Governance and Practical Norms in West Africa and Beyond." In *Local Politics and Contemporary Transformations in the Arab World: Governance beyond the Center*, edited by Malika Bouziane, Cilja Harders, and Anja Hoffmann, 43–64. Basingstoke: Palgrave Macmillan.

———. 2014. "La manne, les normes et les soupçons: Les contradictions de l'aide vue d'en bas." *Revue Tiers Monde* 3: 197–215.

———. 2015. *Epistemology, Fieldwork and Anthropology*. New York: Palgrave Macmillan.

———. 2015b. "Practical Norms: Informal Regulations within Public Bureaucracies (in Africa and Beyond)." In *Governance and Practical Norms in Sub-Saharan Africa: The Game of the Rules*, edited by Tom De Herdt and Olivier de Sardan, 19–62. London: Routledge.

Olivier de Sardan, Jean-Pierre, Oumarou Hamani, Nana Issaley, Younoussi Issa, Hannatou Adamou, and Issaka Oumarou. 2014. "Les transferts monétaires au Niger: le grand malentendu." *Revue Tiers Monde* 218: 107–130.

Oxford Policy Management. 2013. *Qualitative Research of the Economic Impacts of Cash Transfer Programmes in Sub-Saharan Africa: A Research Guide for the From Protection to Production Project*. Rome: Food and Agriculture Organization of the United Nations. http://www.fao.org/3/a-ar422e.pdf.

Piccoli Emmanuelle. 2014. "'Dicen que los cien soles son del Diablo': L'interprétation apocalyptique et mythique du Programa Juntos dans les communautés andines de Cajamarca (Pérou) et la critique populaire des programmes sociaux." *Social Compass* 61: 328–347.

Platteau, Jean-Philippe, and Gaspart, Frédéric. 2003. "The 'Elite Capture' Problem in Participatory Development." Working paper. Centre de recherche en économie du développement, Faculté universitaires Notre-Dame de la Paix, Faculté des Sciences économiques et sociales.

Rose, Richard.1991. "What is Lesson-Drawing?" *Journal of Public Policy* 11(1): 3–30.

Sen, Amartya. 2000. *Repenser l'inégalité*, Paris: Ed. du Seuil.

Subbarao, Kalanidhi. 1997. "Public Works as an Anti-Poverty Program: An Overview of Cross-Country Experience." *American Journal of Agricultural Economics* 79(2): 678–683.

Watson, Carol. 2016. *Shock-Responsive Social Protection in the Sahel: Community Perspectives*. London: OPM.

Wong, Sam. 2010. "Elite Capture or Capture Elites? Lessons from the 'Counter-elite' and 'Co-opt-elite' Approaches in Bangladesh and Ghana." UNU/Wider Working Paper 82. https://www.wider.unu.edu/publication/elite-capture-or-capture-elites-lessons-counter-elite-and-co-opt-elite-approaches.

World Food Program. 2014. *Cash and Vouchers Manual*. Rome: World Food Programme. http://documents.wfp.org/stellent/groups/public/documents/newsroom/wfp274576.pdf?_ga=1.9770421.1052710405.1470867000.

Yates, Douglas A. 1996. *The Rentier State in Africa: Oil Rent Dependency and Neocolonialism in the Republic of Gabon*. Tranton-Asmara: Africa World Press.

Chapter 1

Miracle Mechanisms, Traveling Models, and the Revenge of Contexts
Cash Transfer Programs: A Textbook Case

Jean-Pierre Olivier de Sardan

Preliminary Note

On no account do I wish to adopt in this chapter a position in the debate "for" or "against" cash transfer programs as such. Cash transfer programs have many positive outcomes for very vulnerable households. However, they also have many unintended or adverse effects, mostly due to the perceptions and reactions of stakeholders (pragmatic contexts) in the course of their implementation. All other types of aid (among which traveling models are predominant by far) also have their unintended or adverse effects, and no miraculous form of intervention exists that is spared such effects. But policies are context-sensitive to varying degrees. Analyzing the "critical nodes," bottlenecks, and implementation gaps encountered by any type of standardized intervention, regardless of the form of public action involved, on a solid empirical basis and bringing them out into the open is an indispensable step toward improving development programs, taking better account of the contexts in which they are implemented, and, if possible, adopting some alternative approaches embedded in the "real world." I would like to bring the methodological resources of anthropology (qualitative research) to bear on such analyses.

In the introduction to this book, we attempted to fathom the diversity of cash transfers and to examine the critical nodes indicative of both the variety of the contexts in which CTs are implemented, and the plurality of action logics at work within each context.

In this chapter, I attempt to understand the emergence and global diffusion of CT programs based on the original success stories (Brazil and Mexico). I analyze how, based on this Latin American foundation stone, a fundamental distinction has emerged between a *context* (considered favorable but secondary) and a *mechanism* (considered central and explanatory), how a set of *devices* associated with the mechanism was gradually created and validated, and how this process culminated in a *model* intended for export along with all its specialists, procedures, expertise, training, manuals, evaluations, networks, and conferences (what could be referred to as the "CT business").

I also examine how this model was promoted and has traveled throughout the world, based on different formula and in varying guises with diverging local adaptations in contexts that differ significantly from those in which it originated. I describe how, in the course of this process, local perceptions, practices, and logics were generally ignored (with some exceptions, of course) and how, as a result, the mechanism and its instruments were regularly circumvented by various local actors (the revenge of contexts).

The chapter concludes with the consideration of how CTs are symptomatic of a more general trend in the area of development: the standardization of interventions and the underestimation of the central role played by the contexts in their implementation.

Over the course of this examination, I also undertake three "theoretical digressions" on concepts and analyses used to describe the process of the production and diffusion of CTs, but which are also more general in scope and could form the object of a broader scientific debate.

The Making of a "Traveling Model"

In view of the extremely polysemous nature of the concept of a *model*, its use here should be clearly explained. I will not discuss computer models based on algorithms (simulations or projections as widely used in economy or in meteorology), or the cognitive, descriptive, and interpretive models that are common within the social sciences (Gérard-Varet and Passeron 1995). I am interested in an entirely different category of models: standardized social interventions, mostly development interventions and public policies aimed at inducing changes in behavior. Hence, what is involved here are conscious, proactive, planned, institutionally formalized interventions of a social engineering nature and not simply ideas or technologies that circulate in a spontaneous manner or in accordance with the laws of the market (as generally arises with "cultural patterns" or commercial successes). The *travel of models* (in this sense) is different from the *travel of ideas* (Czarniawska and Joerges 1996; Weisser et al. 2014), although standardized interventions are shaped by paradigms, cognitive frameworks, intellectual fashions, and prevalent ideas.[1] It is also different from the *travel of commodities* (or of business plans), although marketing techniques may be used in both cases. I prefer to focus on a clearly circumscribed category of phenomena that share an indisputable family resemblance on the empirical level, and CTs are emblematic of such a category. I borrow the expression *traveling model* from Rottenburg (2007) and Behrends, Park, and Rottenburg (2014). Bierschenk (2014: 77) proposes the expression "travelling blueprint." For Behrends, Park, and Rottenburg (2014: 1), "a model can be understood as an analytical representation of particular aspects of reality created as an apparatus or protocol for interventions in order to shape this reality for certain purposes." Behrends, Park, and Rottenburg's (2014) theoretical perspective has the merit of involving intervention models; however, it uses the concept of the model in a very general way following the studies by Czarniawska and Joerges (1996) and Czarniawska and Sevon (2005) on "traveling ideas."[2] The concept will be used here in a narrower sense—which is particularly suited to the case of CTs but to other phenomena too—by referring to the "traveling model" as all standardized institutional interventions (a public policy, a program, a reform, a project, a protocol—depending on the scales or areas involved) intended to initiate a given social change and based on a "mechanism" and "devices" (see below) deemed to have intrinsic properties that will make it possible to induce this change in different implementation contexts.

In political science, the "traveling" done by models is referred to as *policy transfer*.[3] This expression focuses on the borrowing (with some adaptations) by decision-makers in context A of a public policy or elements thereof already implemented in context B.[4] However it makes no mention of the process involved in the production of a model of international scope and its standardization, which is typical of development policies. Development policies are nothing more than a specific subset of policies, that are more often than not (especially in African settings) designed, promoted, and funded from the outside. Models are very common in the area of development. Within the *developmentist configuration* (Olivier de Sardan 2005), in which models represent the core business in a sense, they follow on from each other, they travel a lot, and they travel far.

As demonstrated by the case of CTs, the specific production of a traveling model involves three main processes:[5] *narrativization* (a founding success story), *theorization and social engineering* (the construction of a mechanism), and *networking* (global diffusion). These three processes are deeply dependent on international organizations and networks of experts, which come forward as champions of a given traveling model. Needless to say, these processes (which can overlap) arise in an environment that has already been described extensively in policy analyses, either on the basis of a sequential perspective (emergence, formulation, decision, implementation; see Sabatier 1992; Lemieux 2002) or according to the metaphor of the "couplings" between three "streams" (Kingdon 1995): the problems, solutions, and political will. In the case in point, the world economic crisis and the debates and issues surrounding the "eradication of poverty" and humanitarian interventions constitute the sociopolitical environment that presided over the birth and success of the cash transfer model. However, the particular added value of CTs is based on the three processes of narrativization, theorization, and networking. It is these three processes in particular (and not only the actual intrinsic properties of the CT mechanisms as stated in the official discourse[6]) that have underpinned the "career" of CTs as a traveling model and made them into an indispensable point of reference for all social policies and development and humanitarian intervention policies in low- and middle-income countries (LMIC).

CTs are clearly an example of a very successful traveling model. Its multiple peregrinations have taken it to the four corners of the globe. However, it presents all of the characteristics of other traveling models, which include "attempts at the full-scale transposition of organizational models developed somewhere else as solutions to specific problems found elsewhere" (Bierschenk 2014: 82).

A traveling model needs to refer to an inaugural experience somewhere in the world. This is an indispensable stage in its production and subsequent exportation. "In policymaking circles, experience has a unique status as a justification of effectiveness; it shows that a proposal is not just based upon 'head in the clouds' speculation" (Rose 1991: 5; quoted by Debonneville and Diaz 2013: 166). For CTs, there were not one but two inaugural experiences, both located in Latin America.

Brazil and Mexico: The Starting Point

The history of CTs begins in Brazil and Mexico.[7]

Brazil: The Long Evolution to Bolsa Familia

Two parallel, noncontributory benefit systems operated by the federal state and involving payments equivalent to the minimum wage for the elderly and disabled have existed in Brazil since the 1970s.[8] Various experiments involving conditional CT programs were launched at the local level (Federal District, Sao Paulo state, and some municipalities) from 1995. Most of them were aimed at poor families, and focused on education and school attendance with a view to combating child labor and school absenteeism. The federal government contributed significantly to the program from 1997, and many municipalities also joined them. The Bolsa Escola program was taken over by the federal state and implemented at the national level in 2001 under the presidency of Fernando Henrique Cardoso. It was subsequently transformed into the Bolsa Familia program under his successor, Lula de Silva, in 2003, and expanded to cover three other social programs. The new version included new devices, unified the existing programs, and updated the lists of beneficiaries.

The Bolsa Escola and Bolsa Familia benefits were and are paid preferably to mothers with an income below a minimum salary. Bolsa Escola was initially paid to women with children between the ages of seven and fourteen years, and later six to fifteen years, while Bolsa Familia was recently extended to families with children up to seventeen years old, pregnant women, and breastfeeding mothers. The payments are conditional, with the communes responsible for the imposition of the conditionalities: families must fulfill certain educational requirements (minimum school attendance of 85 percent by the children was initially required; however, there was little monitoring of compliance until 2006) and health requirements (one medical check every six months and immunizations) to obtain the benefits.

It must be stressed that this process was not as linear as this summary may suggest and, as highlighted by Fabio Soares (2011) and Sonia Rocha (2014), it involved multiple attempts, continuous adjustments, negotiation between competing views, and extensive institutional pragmatism under both the communal and federal management. The program had numerous failures (many local experiments with the Bolsa Familiar para a Educaçao, Bolsa Escola, or Bolsa Alimentaçao were considered failures), as well as some successes (for example for the city of Campinas and the federal district of Brasilia) generated by favorable conditions that were difficult to reproduce in other locations. Several CT programs were implemented at the same time between 1995 and 2001 and with very variable results. The launch of the Bolsa Escola at the federal level (1998–2001) was a general failure in targeting and coordination with the communes. Lula's rise to power was crucial for the unification of various social programs under the banner of Bolsa Familia.[9] However, just a few months after the launch of Bolsa Familia, Lula created another CT program based on food cards, which was severely criticized and quickly abandoned. In 2012, Bolsa Familia successfully innovated by implementing a new service for families in extreme poverty (around 4.3 percent of the population), which was aimed at guaranteeing a minimum income for these families (Rocha 2014: 208).

In any event, Bolsa Escola and Bolsa Familia were both broadly considered as significant successes on the basis of their scale, and they were progressively more effective: in 2012, benefits were distributed by Bolsa Familia to around 18 percent of Brazilian families (Rocha 2014: 15). According to Galvani (2017: 6), "The Bolsa Familia program is the largest conditional cash transfer program in the world, reaching 14 million families (about 50 million people)."

Mexico: Progresa and Oportunidades

Here too, the first CT program did not emerge in a void. Many food assistance programs had existed previously, and the Pronasol program later encompassed some forms of social assistance (in particular Alimentacion, Nutricion y Salud). All of these programs were sharply criticized for their clientelist use by the dominant political party, the Institutional Revolutionary Party (PRI), which had been in power for a long time and was an expert in the politics of patronage. Procampo, a nonconditional CT program aimed at elderly farmers, was implemented in 1993. Progresa was launched in 1997 in response to the economic crisis of 1995, and was established at the national level from the outset. It targeted three hundred thousand vulnerable rural households on the basis of a statistical selection process (from the perspective of its promoters to avoid the abuses and deviations that would have been possible with community targeting). Basically, the conditionalities were the same as those applied in Brazil (school attendance and medical checkups), but their design was more complex and they played a more central role in this case, as they were more strictly controlled and enshrined in an ideology labeled as "co-responsibility," according to which each of the two "partners" (state and beneficiaries) were obliged to fulfill their side of the contract (providing the CTs for one and complying with the conditions for the other). The program primarily targeted indigenous communities and women (Gil-Garcia 2016). Despite numerous criticisms of the targeting process, Progresa was extended significantly (five million households, including in urban areas) under the presidency of Vincente Fox (following the defeat of the PRI in 2000) and renamed Oportunidades in 2002. It eventually became Prospera in 2014. As is the case in Brazil, CCTs have become a national policy in Mexico that extends across party-political divisions.

The First Stage of the Model: Construction of a Success Story

So how did the Brazilian and Mexican programs become exportable beyond their respective and very specific historical and sociopolitical contexts to the point of becoming a "new paradigm" for eradicating poverty (Sugiyama 2011: 250) and a "development revolution" (Hanlon et al. 2010; Gliszczynski 2015) for some people, or a "mantra" and "a new buzzword in policy circles" (Dreze 2011) for others? How did a "process of standardization" become established as a "process of conversion of local ideas and practices into a 'standard model'" (Ancelovici and Jenson 2012: 3)?

The critical success of the Brazilian and Mexican CT programs in the eyes of international experts in the early 2000s is based on a series of factors.[10] Some of these factors are intrinsic in that they relate to the structure of the model itself (what I refer to as the *mechanism* and its *devices*, see below): for example, the simplicity of the model (distributing money), its capacity to be put at the service of various goals, its natural integration into market mechanisms, and the use of verifiable conditionalities that are widely acknowledged as legitimate. Other success factors are more extrinsic, such as the permanent quest within international organizations for new instruments and devices for eradicating poverty in response to a phenomenon that has increased in scope since the structural adjustment programs began without any effective strategy actually being confirmed—a factor that evokes "humanitarian neophilia" (Scott-Smith 2016). Hence, a void existed that needed to be filled on the supply side. Finally, a factor that is at once intrinsic and extrinsic is the copious documentation on these programs that "emerged" from the two countries involved. A considerable volume of reports accumulated, and the conclusion was drawn from the multiple quantitative data that the CTT programs in Brazil and Mexico were effective in terms of fighting poverty (poverty alleviation) and creating human capital. The United Nations Educational, Scientific and Cultural Organization (UNESCO), United Nations Environment Programme (UNEP), the World Bank, and the International Policy Centre for Inclusive Growth (IPC-IG) carried out positive evaluations of Bolsa Escola. With regard to Progresa, simultaneous to the publication of numerous flattering evaluations (Fizbein and Schady 2009: 6), the "government collected data and made them available: researchers . . . published hundreds of papers" (Sugiyama 2011: 2). "Progresa is also among the most rigorously studied, evaluated, and reformulated CCTs, first by the Mexican government and then by multilateral agencies" (Dapuez and Savigan, chapter 7).

The success story took shape from that point on and was "narrativized" at the international level, which gave it increasing legitimacy. Specialist

journals painted a flattering picture of the Brazilian and Mexican programs (see special issues of *Development Policy Review* 24, no. 5 [2006],
and *Global Social Policy* 9, no. 2 [2009]), and CTs were also dealt with
by newspapers and publications with a much bigger circulation (e.g.,
the *Economist*, the *New York Times*, *Business Week*, *Wall Street Journal*). A
review of the literature by Sugiyama (2011: 263) found that "most of the
articles on CCTs in Mexico and Brazil present them in a favorable light"
(Sugiyama 2011: 263). In other words, from a supply perspective, the
spotlight was focused advantageously on this newly available mechanism: two edifying and converging success stories began to appear on the
radar of institutions, experts, and decision-makers involved in the area of
social policy and poverty eradication. CTs were henceforth trustworthy
candidates for the status of traveling model. Ancelovici and Jenson refer
to this first stage in the "process of standardization" as "certification."
The role of the international organizations was central for the "certification" of CTs and in the subsequent stages: "International organizations
played a significant role in organizing meetings and conferences that
connected policy-makers from various countries. For example the World
Bank has hosted several international CCT conferences" (Sugiyama 2011:
263). Prominent international personalities such as Kofi Annan, Bill
Clinton, and Rolf Wolfensohn (president of the World Bank) extolled the
merits of CTs. The World Bank, in particular, adopted the CT narrative
and disseminated it: this marked the beginning of the model's "travels"
to nearby countries. The crucial role played by IFPRI, the International
Food Policy Research Institute (between 1997 and 2000), in the evaluation
of Progresa, which was based on randomized controlled trials (RCTs),
should also be noted here (Skoufias 2001):[11] indeed, randomized controlled trials have become the mantra of evidence-based policies and the
preferred tool for the certification of traveling models. "The fact that the
IFRI evaluation demonstrated quantitative improvements in the lives of
the children of the poor in the program gave a tremendous international
support" (Teichman 2007: 563).

*The Construction of a "Mechanism" and Its "Devices": Standardization
and Decontextualization*

Nevertheless, despite their originality and specificity, the Brazilian and
Mexican experiences did not become an exportable model under their
own steam, either miraculously or by the sole virtue of their success and
the good things said about them. The common operational elements that
the experts believed to be at the root of their success—in other words, the
mechanism that explained their effectiveness—had first to be extrapolated

from these experiences. "International development institutions [chose] to focus on the similarities between these programs and outcomes related to poverty alleviation and human capital development" (Sugiyama 2011: 255).

Two nested definitions can be provided for the CT "mechanism": first, a broad and more abstract definition that is not widely used (it applies to all types of CTs without targeting a particular audience); and, second, a narrower, more specific, and more common definition that covers the vast majority of CTs (which are based on the objective of eradicating poverty and vulnerability).

The broad definition can be found in the publication *Glossary of Cash Transfer Program Terminology* (Zuodar 2015): cash-based transfers (CBT) "refers to all programs where cash (or vouchers for goods or services) is directly provided to beneficiaries." (see also CALP 2018: 16). The standard and narrower definition may be formulated as follows: "Standard social policy model for the southern hemisphere focused on payments in cash rather than kind [and] aimed at deprived and very poor citizens" (Ancelovici and Jenson 2012: 55).

Whichever definition is chosen, the *mechanism* did not emerge in this form in the minds of the experts but was developed by the latter through an operation involving the simplification and "distillation" of the Brazilian and Mexican experiences. Although multiple factors contributed to the success of these two stories (see below for Brazil), while they were processes of trial and error and "learning by doing," they were progressively stripped of all elements considered secondary. Their complexity and diversity were reduced to an exportable "mechanism" that could explain their success. As Lillrank (1995) describes it in a completely different context (diffusion of Japanese management models), it was a question of "translating local practices into abstractions intended for export" (Ancelovici and Jenson 2012: 39), something that also implies the correlated "omission" of other practices. A particularly complex reality had to be divided into two parts: a "mechanism" on the one hand, and a "context" on the other. This distinction did not arise spontaneously; it was constructed, albeit implicitly, through a focus on the supposed intrinsic effectiveness of the mechanism and was not subject to debate. The CT mechanism could only be produced by extracting it from what was simultaneously produced as the context of its emergence. This is what Ancelovici and Jenson (2012) refer to as the *decontextualization* phase. In the same way, Debonneville and Diaz (2013: 164) associate the production of the CT conceptual model (*theorization*) with a combination of *decontextualization* and *universalization*. In order to theorize the effective intrinsic mechanism at work in the Brazilian and Mexican experiences, it was necessary at the same time to "de-Brazilianize" and "de-Mexicanize" it by reducing all factors external to the mechanism to Brazilian or Mexican contextual elements. The blunders made at the beginning, the multiple trials and errors, the reservations and criticisms, and the sometime harsh debates between the politicians and experts were forgotten. The battles for influence between coalitions and networks that defended different visions of the CTs were erased to make way for a consensus regarding the intrinsic value of the mechanism.[12]

However, on closer inspection, the elements that were reduced to the status of contexts were critical factors in the Brazilian and Mexican experiences. Let us consider the Brazilian case. When Bolsa Familia was launched, with "over 15 years of continuous learning and radical modernization of the methods and content" (Rocha 2014: 16), the CT programs in Brazil were the product of many trials and errors, a protracted and complex process involving many changes (Soares 2011), and very far from an imported standardized system. Moreover, Sonia Rocha testifies to the existence of an "exceptional set of conditions that were favorable to the development of the program" (Rocha 2014: 16). Given that it concerns a key device of the CT mechanism, the most important of these preconditions is the targeting device. In effect, Brazil had an "extremely rich statistical base generated from the national survey involving the sampling of households" (Rocha 2014: 16) and "the open access to the micro data strongly facilitated the simulation exercises for planning the social benefits, and the evaluation studies based on separate information to that provided by the organizations responsible for the programs. The reliable empirical data created a basis for the respectability of the program" (Rocha 2014: 17). In addition, the instrument used to distribute the payments was based on a "modern and highly capillarized banking system" (Rocha 2014: 17), which facilitated, among other things, the reliability and predictability of the payments made to poor families (Rocha 2014: 206).

The effective social infrastructure must also be added to this list of preconditions: "The country is far from presenting a series of shortcomings typical of poor countries . . .; the fact that it has social services which are accessible to the poor constitutes a facilitating element" (Rocha 2014: 17). Moreover, Bolsa Familia coexists with a traditional social assistance system (benefits to poor elderly or disabled people).[13] Finally, the Brazilian state is strong and generally considered legitimate, and average per capita income is high (over $8,000 [US]) and easily accommodates the financing of CT programs. The important role played by municipalities should also be stressed (Soares 2011: 57), as should their collaboration with the federal state through "shared management."

The conclusion is clear: "The Brazilian formula . . . cannot be considered as an exportable product" (Rocha 201418). Nevertheless, it became an exportable product that was applied in countries (particularly in Africa) that do not have a "statistical base," "reliable empirical data," a "modern and capillarized banking system," "effective social infrastructure," and have neither a "strong state" (i.e., a functional state) nor efficient municipalities. A similar remark was made concerning the exportation of CTs to India (Dreze 2011; Dréze and Sen 2012): basic services such as education and healthcare provision are missing or very poor to a large extent in many parts of that country, while they are functional in Brazil and Mexico. In Latin America, poor households are easy to identify, which is not the case in India. "CCT enthusiasm is often based on a superficial reading of Latin American experience" (Dréze 2011).

Within the "developmentist configuration," the reduction of a "success story" to an effective mechanism involves the exclusion of an entire series of other explanatory factors behind the reference success story, which are relegated to the status of contextual elements that no longer need to be taken into account. In other words: "cognitive short-cuts are at work" (Sugiyama 2011: 265). For example, the Mexican program's strong emphasis on conditionalities, which were in a way a kind of inescapable counterpart to the payments, and were presented ideologically as necessary for the empowerment of the families, was significantly weakened and softened during the production of the device of conditionalities suitable for the "exportable" CT mechanism. The conditionalities that were central to the Progresa/Oportunidades programs became peripheral or even optional in the traveling model, and the criticisms of the Mexican program were ignored.[14] The initial female-empowerment orientation of Progresa has gradually decreased in favor of a purely "maternalist" perspective (Jenson and Nagels 2018).

The process involved in producing the "mechanism versus context" dichotomy is, therefore, one of dehistoricization of the initial success story. In order to celebrate the intrinsic efficiency of the mechanism, the story is stripped of all of its (apparently) contingent components, its dead ends, shortcuts, negotiations, failed attempts, misunderstandings, and critics, and of all of the political games that shaped and branded the emergence and the implementation of the policy.

Ancelovici and Jenson justifiably designate this entire process as *decontextualization*.[15] In fact, this decontextualization process is indissociable from what they call the *framing* of the model,[16] which, for them, represents the third step. The two processes are largely simultaneous. The process of reducing the system to a mechanism goes hand in hand with its construction as the core of the new model (like the core a nuclear reactor). A justificatory and legitimizing argument is established that also provides a sales argument for the mechanism. However, the model that is in the process of being created around the mechanism is not merely discursive or rhetorical. The new "expert system" also involves a sizeable institutional architecture, based on the work of experts, promoters, and specialists. "CCT requires bureaucratic systems to determine the scope and size of the program, select eligible families, track conditionality components and distribute cash grants" (Sugiyama 2011: 257).

I consider *devices* here as the fundamental organizational components (or operational extensions) of a mechanism. The CT mechanism involves three major devices (each of which mobilizes various instruments): (1) a geographical and/or economic targeting device; (2) a device for the standardized distribution of payments involving the use of banking systems to a greater or lesser extent; and (3) a device for the application and monitoring of conditionalities imposed on the potential beneficiaries for access to the CTs (Fiszbein et al. 2007). This third device ultimately became optional with the proliferation of nonconditional CTs beyond Latin America, particularly in the area of humanitarian and emergency aid. The presence or absence of this third device eventually came to define the two major CT families—that is, conditional and nonconditional CTs.[17] Additional or auxiliary devices also exist—in other words, complementary components that are grafted on to the three major devices, such as socio-educative activities, income generation activities, microcredit programs, and other "supporting measures."

Each device involves scores of instruments and techniques, described at length in manifold manuals and toolkits. Targeting ("identifying eligible individuals and screening out the ineligible from a population," Devereux et al. 2015) includes, for example, various sophisticated enrollment and screening methods, including means testing, proxy means testing,[18] household economic approaches,[19] and other forms of community-based targeting with participatory or voluntary enrollment components.[20] Similarly, many instruments are linked to the control of conditionalities (by municipalities, education agents, health professionals, social workers, and community agents); for example, Bolsa familia has developed a five-stage process named *repercussao gradativa* ("gradual repercussion") in the event that a family fails to comply with conditionalities (Soares 2011: 58).

Each instrument involves numerous guidelines, procedures, and norms designed by specialized experts. The result is a "hyper-procéduralité" (Courtin 2011) that is typical of the traveling models and development projects earmarked for LMICs. CTs are also part of the top-down management strategies (which paradoxically often include participatory approaches, such as community-based targeting) that are increasingly considered outdated in Northern countries but are still prevalent in the traveling models exported to LMICs (see Lavigne Delville 2012 b).

Theoretical Digression 1: Regarding the "Mechanism" Concept

The production of a *mechanism* corresponds to a certain *theorization* by experts, in other words, the "formulation of patterned relationships such as chains of cause and effects" (Strang and Meyer 1993: 492, quoted by Boneville and Diaz 2013: 164). The "mechanism" concept brings to the fore the presupposed causality chain, an explanatory variable (or a simple configuration of explanatory variables, a system of causalities), on which the experts base the postulated effectiveness of a policy model. The mechanism is then operated using institutional "devices" and operational architectures. My definition of mechanism corresponds in part, and on the one hand, to what is referred to in the cognitive analysis of public policies as the *frame of reference* (*référentiel* in French) and, on the other hand, to what certain program evaluation experts refer to as *program theory* or *logic of intervention* (see "theory based evaluation": Chen 1990; Weiss 1997), in other words a "set of hypotheses that explains how and why the intervention is expected to produce its effects" (Lacouture et al. 2015: 5; see also Ridde et al. 2012). It may also evoke what Akrich (1992) has referred to as a *script*. According to Timmermans and Berg (1997: 27) "[t]he 'script' of a technological artefact refers to the hypotheses, embedded in the artefact, about the entities which make up the world in which the artefact will be inserted". However, the mechanism is not solely composed of hypotheses (or ideas, words or discourses), it is also, and above all, an institutional and organizational arrangement around these hypotheses, in other words a set of "devices."[21]

The "mechanism + devices" set is what defines the core of a traveling model.

Thus my definition of the mechanism differs from the sense recently assumed by mechanism in the social sciences, following Elster (1989) and Hedström and Swedberg (1998), in which it is designated as a "real" but more or less hidden process as deduced/unveiled/constructed by the social sciences (Gerring 2007).[22] What is involved is a generative vision of causality that proposes to go beyond the simple correlation of variables at the center of quantitative approaches and aims to disclose a concealed cause/effect relation. In contrast to this, as I see it, the mechanism of a standardized model is a construct created by experts who deliberately rely on the alleged effectiveness of an explanatory variable.

For their part, the *realist approaches* to evaluation (Pawson and Tilley 1997) also use the vocabulary of "mechanism" and "context." They focus on the fact that the effects (*outcomes*: O) of an intervention (policy, program) depend on the interactions between the context of the intervention (C) and the mechanism of the intervention (M). Accordingly, they are interested in the "CMO" configuration.

I share their concern with considering the context as a crucial element of the implementation of a program or public policy (and hence, also, a traveling model). However, there is an important ambiguity among the authors who claim to support this approach in relation to the exact content of the mechanism and the conceptual and empirical differentiation between the mechanism and the context (Marchal et al. 2012; Ridde et al. 2012; Dalkin et al. 2015; Lacouture et al. 2015; MacDonald et al. 2016).[23] According to the most common definition, following Pawson and Tilley (1997), the mechanism for an intervention is composed of the "ideas and reactions of the actors affected by the intervention" (Lacouture et al. 2015), an enigmatic statement, to say the least. For Pawson and Tilley and many others (see Marchal et al. 2012), "mechanism" refers to Hedström and Swedberg's concept: a "real" but hidden causality, which is based on the reactions of the actors to the intervention and which, beside and through the context, is at the root of the effects of the intervention (outcomes).[24] This interpretation imposes a differentiation between the intervention in the strict sense, on the one hand, and the explanatory mechanism, which produces the "real" outcomes and which it is incumbent on the researcher to reveal (but which remains in fact a "black box"), on the other. It also necessitates the placement of the actors on the side of the mechanism and not that of the context, something that is very difficult to sustain. It appears far simpler to me to not venture into this area and to consider the mechanism as the operational "theory" behind the intervention. At the same time, the perceptions and reactions of the actors involved in the implementation of a traveling model form part of the implementation context, more precisely the pragmatic context, of which they are central elements (see Theoretical Digression 3 below).

Therefore the differentiation between a mechanism and a context is not a scientific operation carried out *a posteriori* by a researcher; it is a social construct created by policy experts at the heart of the production of traveling models, the proceeds of a distinction between (1) elements involving an explanatory variable (the mechanism), which are their concern and around which they construct their interventions; and (2) elements that involve contextual variables, the management of which is always problematic and uncertain. The construction of a mechanism is indissociable from the language of variables (and, within this language, the promotion of an "explanatory variable").

The Spread of Conditional CTs in Latin America

In 2005, the World Bank noted that "Bolsa Familia has already become a highly praised model of effective social policy. Countries around the world are drawing lessons from Brazil's experience and are trying to produce the same results for their own people" (World Bank 2005, quoted by Sugiyama 2011: 263). This global export process started with Latin America, where CTs spread rapidly from the late 1990s, despite the considerable variation in political agendas from one country to the next. One of the reasons for this is that all of these countries had strong bureaucracies, technical services covering their entire territories, relatively reliable statistical tools, and effective targeting methods (Anveloci and Jenson 2012: 54). In other words, the presence of functional states constituted a major common contextual factor, and this explains why throughout Latin America these policies were national policies and mainly financed through the national budgets.

But this does not mean that the design and implementation of CT programs were solely the products of national experts and policies. On the contrary: transnational networks played an important role in the form of "a particular kind of policy network characterized by a highly integrated set of actors, restricted membership, insulations from the public and a clear consensus on basic policy assumptions" (Teichman 2007: 558). Certain institutions were particularly active within these networks: World Bank, Inter-American Development Bank (IDB), and International Food Policy Research Institute (IFPRI) (Teichman 2007: 560–561). Nonetheless, the homogeneity of these institutions should not be overestimated, nor should the conflicts within them be underestimated. Although it may have been the product of some consensus in the world of social policy, humanitarian policy, and poverty eradication experts, the construction of the CT mechanism did not unfold without internal debate, particularly in relation to objectives, devices, and instruments. Some experts were inclined to confine CT programs to giving the money to vulnerable households and sending them on their way to face the market, while others wanted to involve "civil society." Tomazini (2013) makes a distinction between three "coalitions," each with a specific perspective on how to fight poverty: the "human capital" champions, the "unconditional basic income for all" champions, and the "food security" champions. The supporters of purely statistical targeting, particularly with a view to avoiding corrupt or clientelist practices, clashed with the supporters of "participatory" targeting involving the communities themselves in the selection process (Teichman 2007: 560–564). The principle of targeting itself has been called into question by the proponents of universal cover (Kidd 2009), and the "political economy of targeting" (Sen 1995) is highly debatable. "Targeting is one of the most challenging and controversial aspects of the design and implementation of social transfer programs throughout the world" (Devereux et al. 2015: 9). Varying interpretations and objections also arose in relation to CT conditionalities.

However, overall, the same standard conditional model was adopted in the majority of Latin American and Caribbean countries.[25] Sugiyama (2011: 264) highlights the presence of "similar features of CCT policy design among the Latin American programs." The corresponding list of programs includes, among others, Honduras (Asignacion familiar), Argentina (Asignación Universal por Hijo and Progresar), Colombia (Familias en Acción), Paraguay (Tekopora), Ecuador (Bono de Desarrollo Humano), Peru (Juntos), and the Dominican Republic (Solidaridad). It should be stressed that this expansion of CCT arose in a continental context where the political regimes differ and the ruling political elites have varying agendas. In effect, the CT programs combine the simplicity of their mechanism and the considerable plasticity of the objectives they may serve. Different political situations, different power relations, different ideologies, and different institutional architectures can all be accommodated by CT programs. In other words, the various national political considerations, which differ from one country to the next and are necessary for the adoption of CTs, are added to the pressures exerted by the international organizations that promote the CTs. The support of national political actors with their own objectives is needed for the implementation of a standardized policy model (Weyland 2004, quoted by Leite, Peres, and Bellix 2012). As a result, seventeen out of the twenty Latin American countries had CT programs in 2009 (Fiszbein et al. 2009).

Nonetheless, two countries, Chile and Bolivia, implemented programs that represented significant variants of the standardized model, for domestic political reasons. The Chilean program (Chile solidario) highlighted the aspect of providing individualized support for the very poor by having each household monitored by a social worker (Chile had for a long time a very active social assistance network), and also increased the number of conditionalities of access to the program while adapting them to each case (Teichman 2007). The two programs implemented in Bolivia, Bono Juancito Pinto and Bono Juana Azurduy, are conditional (in relation to school attendance by the children and health checks for pregnant women and mothers of young children) but "universal" (i.e., nontargeted); in other words, they have no income-related conditions and are financed by oil revenues (see Nagels, chapter 8).

The Export of Conditional and Unconditional CTs to Africa and Asia

Due to the intrinsic quality of the innovation and direct policy transfers from one country to the other, the export of the CT model beyond the confines of Latin America was not a simple case of snowball or wildfire diffusion. In fact, the intrinsic quality of a social engineering model matters less (although it is not irrelevant) than the role played by its "social bearers" (see Olivier de Sardan 2005) who ensure its "replication" (Darbon 2009: 266). There is nothing spontaneous about this duplication "far away from the original base" and, therefore, far away from the original success story. It is an "indirect transfer" through "model promoters" (Weyland 2004). It is based on the networking of experts and decision-makers, through whom what could be called the "idea" of the traveling model (its core mechanism), its narrative and promotion, are circulated to the extent that the importation of the model is included in the agendas of various distant countries, generally as a result of the convergence of funding and/or international technical aid.

In the case of CTs, once again, the World Bank played a central role through a "narrativization," which was developed over the course of numerous reports and evaluations and which hailed the merits of CTs (see among others Fiszbein et al. 2009; Monchuk 2014) and relayed by even more numerous seminars, workshops, and training courses aimed at development experts and policy decision-makers. This "narrativization" also drew on relayed success stories that validated the capacity of the model to travel a considerable distance—in other words, to adapt to new "macro contexts" (on a continental scale). More often than not the difficulties and shortcomings of the implementation process are concealed or downplayed; papers written by CT experts focus exclusively on positive impacts.[26] CT are henceforth a cluster of "good practices," ready to be reproduced elsewhere. The rhetoric of "good practices," particularly developed by the World Bank (Diaz 2017), is a touchstone of the diffusion of traveling models.

Hence the Philippines acted as a "relayed success story" for Southeast Asia (Debonneville and Diaz 2013; Diaz 2017). The World Bank organized the Third International Conference on Conditional Cash Transfers in Istanbul in June 2006 with a view to extending CCRs toward the Middle East and Asia. At this event, Filipino delegates were able to establish special contact with a Colombian expert, a World Bank consultant, who would subsequently play a key role in advising on the establishment of a CCT program in the Philippines (Pantawid Pamilyang Pilipino Program). This program, in turn, would act as a flagship program for the diffusion of CCTs in the entire region. In Africa, the intergovernmental conference held in Livingstone in Zambia in 2006 also played a catalytic role with its "call for action."

The influence of international institutions in the adoption of CT programs by numerous countries of the South is frequently a determining factor. It is expressed in two ways: through financing ("funding for projects, either in the form of grants or loans, can provide powerful incentives for countries with few resources to reconfigure their social spending programs," Sugiyama 2011: 263) and through advice, expertise, and technical aid in the development of the programs, and norms and "good practice" governing the distribution of the cash (Harvey and Bailey 2011). "In practice, funding and norm-creation work together" (Sugiyama 2011: 264).[27] However, the acceptance of CT programs (proposed by international institutions) by national decision-makers and experts also reflects certain internal strategies of these national decision-makers and experts, which can be either economic (desire to benefit from aid "rent" one way or another) or political (desire to obtain electoral benefits).

It should be noted that the process of importing CTs into a country can follow different routes. I differentiate between two of these: (1) access via international institutions (frequently the World Bank) and the state; and (2) access via NGOs (self-funded by international donors). The diffusion of CTs by the World Bank is directly targeted at the national state (president, prime minister, relevant ministers) through the integration of a "project" (and a management unit) into the official state organization chart. It is usually carried out under the heading of "safety nets" (see Monchuk 2014), prioritizes the CCTs as far as possible in the name of the promotion of human capital (Fiszbein et al. 2009), and is based on "proxy means testing" for the implementation of the social targeting (Del Ninno and Mills 2015). For instance, "the World Bank organized a high-level meeting in 2007 in Luxor in Upper Egypt, in which the whole economic team of ministers in the then cabinet participated, where they introduced these senior policy makers to cash transfers as an alternative to untargeted and expensive subsidies" (Sholkamy, chapter 10). Each country in the Sahel currently has a CT program funded by the World Bank (O'Brien et al. 2017: 18). Safety nets promoted by the World Bank are accepted by the governments of LMICs on the basis of their own agendas (which differ from those of international institutions), with each party interpreting ("translating") the program in a way that meets its own interests and objectives (on translation, see Theoretical Digression 2, below).

Entry via the NGOs is a preferred option in the far more decentralized area of humanitarian aid, in which the NGOs are major players. In effect, the traveling done by CTs is not solely geographical; it is also thematic: they have extended their area of competence from their original field—the eradication of chronic severe poverty (in Latin America)—to other fields and have gradually become the preferential tools of food security policy and humanitarian policy (particularly in Africa), which more or less coincides with the world of "urgentism" and "shock responses" (see Oxford Policy Management 2015). Famines, earthquakes, floods, and refugees have become signals par excellence for the launch of short-term CT programs, far from the Brazilian and Mexican founding stories.

Needless to say, the distinction between the development world and that of humanitarian aid is permeable and often debatable (Atlani-Duaut 2009; Olivier de Sardan 2011a). In Africa, the victims of food crises (and targets of humanitarian CTs) are also the poorest of the rural classes (targets of CTs aimed at eradicating chronic poverty). However, CTs underwent major mutations over the course of their travels in Africa: the NGOs rather than the state took responsibility for the implementation of the humanitarian CT instruments; and because the humanitarian CTs are transitional measures, they also became unconditional in most cases.

In the context of this diffusion of CTs by the NGOs, it is important to note not only the central role played by the international institutions that provide the finances (ECHO, WFP, US-AID), but also to the specialization of certain NGOs in particular niche aspects of the CT business. For example, the household economic approach (HEA) method, which is widely used for targeting, is promoted by the NGO Save the Children, whose expertise in this area is acknowledged (see Seaman et al. 2000). In contrast, Action Against Hunger is the driving force behind the Cash and Learning Partnership (CaLP) network, which is entirely dedicated to the topic of cash transfers, the exchange of information about them, and methodological debates and training courses based on the "communities of practice" models.

In some cases, for example in Niger (see chapter 12), the two access routes—via the state and via NGOs—were adopted simultaneously. On the one hand, the World Bank promoted a multiannual "safety net" type CT program, which, however, was unconditional (but nonetheless with a strong incentive for the women to invest the distributed cash in income-generating activities; see Hamani 2013)[28] and implemented under the banner of eradicating chronic poverty. In a way, this program was billeted within the state of Niger in the form of a project theoretically coproduced by the state; however, the latter was merely supposed to take it over when the period of funding by the World Bank lapsed. On the other hand, following the food crisis of 2005, numerous NGOs working in the humanitarian sector simultaneously established "emergency" CTs, mainly to deal with the recurrent food crises which arise during the lean months in the lead-up to the harvest every year. These programs were funded by international donors specialized in this area (WFP, ECHO).

The issue of sustainability is critical in the context of these two main access routes (World Bank with the state on the one hand, and the NGOs on the other). The majority of African states have very little capacity to take over a project funded by the World Bank or to replace the humanitarian NGOs, and the majority of these programs would appear to be destined to extinction once their external "transfusion" is over.

In a way, it is a kind of testimony to the flexibility of CTs that the model has traveled across the entire range of LMICs, from one extreme to the other: having been supported initially by functional states in emerging countries, they have ended up in the hands of NGOs in the poorest countries with weak states. The question arises here as to whether this property of the mechanism and its devices means that CTs can adapt to any situation, subject to major or minor adjustments. The professional CT world firmly believes this.

Distant Travels: Translations, Vernacularizations, Customizations, and Summary Adaptations?

In the process of the universalization of CTs, undeniable efforts were made to adapt the model to its new implementation contexts (as is the case for all travel undertaken by standardized models). Having been decontextualized in Latin America, the mechanism underwent various adjustments to enable its recontextualization. While respecting the mechanism's basic instruments (targeting, distribution, and eventual conditions), the experts try to find formulas that are suited to the objectives and publics targeted by the process. "It rarely involves a carbon copy but a highly creative act" (Debonneville and Diaz 2013:164). The multiple variants can concern the institutional bearers (states, international organizations, NGOs), the targeted recipients (the categories continue to expand beyond the original poor families and now include disaster victims, the elderly, disabled, etc.), the targeting procedures (based on statistics, surveys, or including "community" and participatory elements), the distribution procedures (cash, vouchers, bank cards, mobile telephones, etc.), the sums paid and the frequency of their distribution, the conditionalities, etc.

Hence, multiple attempts at "customization," "vernacularization" (Levitt and Merry 2009), and "translation" (Campbell 2004) can be observed.[29] However, in the case of traveling models like CTs, these attempts essentially involve work by national or international experts.

Various debates on the balancing of "fidelity" and "adaptation" in the implementation of interventions (Caroll et al. 2007; Pérez et al. 2016) reflect this technocratic perspective on the place that should be assigned to the local particularities and structural contexts, from the perspective of those responsible for interventions. However, these debates do not question the "core components" of the intervention, and ultimately prioritize the quest for fidelity with regard to these core components; in other words, compliance with the mechanism and its devices.[30] The recontextualization process is also based on an extremely reductive vision of what the traveling model experts refer to as "context," reduced to a set of contextual variables (see Theoretical Digression 3 below).

The concept of "translation" (from one model to a context, from one context to another, from one strategic group to another) is an attempt to evade this technocratic reduction. It is essentially used by the social sciences. Nevertheless, it is ambiguous. Who is translating what? From an empirical perspective, "translation" can have two different meanings in relation to traveling models.

On the one hand, there is a *deliberate* process of translation carried out by (national and international) CT experts and decision-makers with a view to rendering the standardized model compatible with what they consider a new national (macro) context. In a way, this process involves "top-down" adaptations for the creation of a "national" variant of a CT program in a given country. This is the final stage in the formulation of a public policy once it is based on a traveling model. The model's devices are amended, streamlined, reorganized, and "nationalized" with a view to its integration into its new (structural) context. It said to be an "institutionalization" or "appropriation" process. An entire literature on policy transfer within political science highlights the work involved in this reformulation process at the national level when an external model is adopted so that lessons can be learned from it (Rose 1991; 1993).

On the other hand, the concept of "translation" can refer to the multiple reinterpretations of the model (once reconfigured in its national variant) and the unexpected transformation it undergoes in the course of its implementation due to the multiple social logics and varying interests of the different "strategic groups" (or "stakeholders") with which it is confronted. This second possible meaning of "translation," which differs clearly from the first, is closer to what I refer to here as "the revenge of contexts." The complex game of the actor strategies directly and indirectly involved in the implementation of CT programs generates an inevitable implementation gap (discrepancy between an intervention as it is planned and an intervention as it unfolds in reality or between the expected and unexpected effects).

In fact, the entire problem consists in appreciating the reality and reach of "top-down" adaptations. Of course, they enable the implementation of CT programs that are less "out of sync" with the local contexts than the original Brazilian or Mexican model would be. However, the fact remains that they involve the development and imposition of a set of expert norms (associated with the model's instruments) developed in a process involving international consultants and senior national officials, validated by national authorities, and on which the field workers, beneficiaries, and local populations are never really consulted. However creative and competent the experts in charge of this adaptation process may be, the rule of the game for CTs remains: "Policy-makers are adopting models wholesale and then, only later, making adjustments to reflect local realities" (Sugiyama 2011: 265). The national variants of the traveling model impose on the local contexts norms concerning access to the resource (the cash) that always differ from local norms—that is, the social norms of the local populations and the practical norms of the field workers, which are always underestimated and frequently ignored in the adaptation process (see Theoretical Digression 3). All of the case studies presented in this book demonstrate this clearly in relation to CTs. Hence, this observation would appear to be valid for other traveling models.

The adaptation of a traveling model to a local context by experts and decision-makers is often carried out by a pilot phase followed by the scaling up of the model if the evaluations are conclusive. This is demonstrated by the CT programs introduced by the World Bank in Africa ("safety nets"). However, these evaluations, which are supposed to provide the "evidence" necessary for an "evidence-based policy," are fundamentally based on a quantitative (and standardized approach, e.g., Gottfredson et al. 2015), focused on the putative intrinsic effectiveness of the mechanism's devices (which have been modified to varying extents by the experts with a view to their adaptation at the national level). They do not enable the in-depth documentation—something that would require qualitative surveys—of the implementation of the pilot intervention in the local contexts. Hence, the scaling up rests on "device-based" rather than "context-based" studies.[31]

Theoretical Digression 2: Regarding Translation

The concept of translation has had multiple meanings in the social sciences for a long time (for anthropology, see, e.g., Geertz 1973; for hermeneutics, see, e.g., Eco 1990). The concept was recently systematized in science studies by Callon (1986) and Callon and Latour (1981; 1986) on the basis of empirical studies on scientific and technological innovations, which led to the emergence of a new school called the "sociology of translation" and also referred to as "actor-network theory." One of the merits of this school was to combine, on an empirical level, the study of networks, which are essential to the success of any program for the dissemination of an innovation, with the study of the technical components of the innovation (Akrich 2006). Various authors have attempted to apply this sociology of translation to the field of development policies and projects—for example, Czarniawska and Sevon (1996), Mosse (2005), Mosse and Lewis (2006), Rottenburg (2007), Le Meur (2011), and Behrends, Park, and Rottenburg (2014). This kind of perspective resonates with a triple ascertainment already made by numerous researchers in the field of the anthropology of development (see Olivier de Sardan 1988; 1995; 2005; Long 1989; Elwert and Bierschenk 1998; Bierschenk, Chauveau, and Olivier de Sardan 2000): (1) the different strategic groups involved in a development project have different interests; (2) within each group, certain actors set themselves up as representatives, entrepreneurs, leaders, or spokespersons; and (3) various interactions arise between these representatives and groups, in particular adversarial and negotiation relationships. This perspective, described as an "entangled social logics approach" (Olivier de Sardan 2005), has widened into an anthropology of public action (Lavigne Delville 2016), public policies (Olivier de Sardan 2017), and public services (Bierschenk and Olivier de Sardan 2014). For its part, the translation perspective has developed a rather similar line of argument, using its specific vocabulary, and concludes from this that the different groups can only coexist to the extent that they each "translate" the objectives and implementation of the project in their own way: "There is always need for translating one set of interests into another. Donor advisors, consultants, and project managers are able to exert influence only because the ideas or instructions they purvey can be translated into other people's own intentions, goals, and ambitions" (Mosse 2005: 8).[32] The vision of translation presented by Callon and Latour was also adopted by public policy analysis (Lascoumes 2004) and policy transfer studies (Stone 2012), including the case of CT programs disseminated in Latin America (Balen and Leyton 2015).

However, the concept of translation is affected by various limitations and ambiguities. The first and most important one is that its content as promoted in science studies by Callon and Latour, and by those who imported it into the anthropology of development and public policy analysis, is very general and enigmatic and somewhat "catch all."[33] Its modalities (various) or perimeter (variable) are not clearly defined; while this undoubtedly ensured its success (and the associated risks of theoretical inflation or rhetorical use[34]), it also makes it difficult to operate.[35]

Accordingly, it does not differentiate different types of translation based on the processes or actors involved. For example, it does not accommodate the—in my view indispensable—distinction between the two above-mentioned processes (i.e., the process of the adaptation of a mechanism by experts to a new context of implementation, and the multiple reinterpretations and reactions by various strategic groups in the course of its implementation). A second limitation relates to the actual nature of the translation metaphor, which mainly connotes operations of a semiological nature (on the level of representation, interpretation, narrativization, staging, and the establishment of a discourse), which are, therefore, maximized with the corresponding risk of minimizing the organizational and institutional processes. "The process of 'translation' . . . permits the negotiation of common meanings and definitions" (Mosse and Lewis 2006: 14). In a translation-based approach, the perspective is focused on "interpretative communities" (Mosse 2005). While remaining loyal to this approach, Behrends, Park, and Rottenburg (2014: 20) are aware of this "hermeneutic" risk and suggest as a result "paying particular attention to practices, materiality and technology."[36] But why then remain locked in the metaphor of translation?

Notwithstanding this, various convergences exist between the corresponding projects in the sociology of science and technology, or of translation, or the actor network theory, on the one hand, and the anthropology of development or public action and even, more broadly, the "anthropology of gaps, discrepancies and contradictions" (Olivier de Sardan 2016), on the other. The case of CTs analyzed here clearly illustrates the statement noted by Mosse (2005: 8): "As Bruno Latour reminds us, the success of policy ideas or project designs is not inherent (nor given at the outset) but arises from their 'ability to continue *recruiting* support and so impose [their] growing coherence on those who argue about them or oppose them' ([Latour] 1996: 78)." More generally, Callon and Latour's concern with a "symmetrical anthropology" is indisputable from a methodological point of view and also aligns with ours in relation to the study of interventions and development (Olivier de Sardan 1995; 2005): each type of actor must be granted "epistemological equality" (see Lavigne Delville 2011), or, in other words, the principle of "emicity" (emic perspective) typical of the anthropological process (Olivier de Sardan 2015b) must be applied to all of the actors concerned, and greater attention must be paid to all of their points of view, irrespective of their status (i.e., international experts, local service users, national decision-makers, or local officials).[37] With reference to Nader (1974), it could also be said that it is a question of studying "up," "down," and "sideways" simultaneously. Another fundamental point of convergence is the rejection of "the great divide" (Latour 1983; 2006) and all dichotomies of a "traditional/modern" and "them/us" nature. Finally, like Callon and Latour, I assign central importance to the networks and disputes, alliances and negotiation processes—whether formal or informal in nature.

It is important to note one important divergence, however. By focusing on the constitution and expansion of networks with a view to promoting an innovation (search for allies, enrollment, mobilization of support; Callon 1986), actor-network theory takes little account of the routines and procedures already in place and the need to come to terms with them. This criticism was already made within the field of science studies itself by Timmermans and Berg (1997): the quest for standardization inherent in the diffusion of a new technology (Latour 1989) involves not only the emergence of new practices but also the incorporation of old ones. Actor-network theory has little interest in preexisting contexts, path dependencies, and the informal norms that regulate daily activities, and in the context of which the innovation must assume a place. These elements are, however, central for the analyses of the processes at the heart of the implementation gap (see Theoretical Digression 3 below)

Poor Awareness of Pragmatic Contexts

Of course, contexts are not ignored by CT programs. "It is now generally accepted that the impact of social transfers on beneficiaries and households depends crucially on the socio-cultural context, especially gender relations and intra-household decision-making power" (Devereux 2006: 14). For instance, a study carried out by the FAO on CT programs in six African countries and based on qualitative methods reaches the following conclusion: "Key overarching finding is that a wide range of contextual factors have effects on the types and scales of CT impacts" (Barca et al. 2015). But the consequences have not really been drawn: "Instead, program designers tend to ignore culture or to impose socio-cultural assumptions on beneficiary communities and families" (Devereux 2006: 14). The pragmatic contexts (the frame of routine interactions of local actors) in which programs are implemented remains a largely unexamined and unresolved problem with CTs and traveling models. Program designers are interested in contexts (although they are primarily concerned with compliance); however, they reduce contexts to structural features and statistical abstractions (see Timmermans and Berg 1997). Therefore, the adjustments made to pragmatic contexts are far from sufficient (for a discussion of the concept of "context," see Theoretical Digression 3 below).

Let us consider three cross-cutting examples of this (and each chapter of this book provides other concrete illustrations): ignorance of preexisting welfare benefits, the ambiguities around the concept of poverty, and the questionable relevance of the "household" as a unit. These three topics are at the very core of the CT mechanism: the distribution of cash (a welfare benefit) to vulnerable (poor) families (households).

Preexisting Welfare Benefits

A characteristic of the projection of the CT model throughout the world in highly diverse contexts is the failure to take preexisting welfare benefits at either national or local levels into account in the operation of the CT system. CTs erupt in the form of an entirely new mechanism with no connection or reference to preexisting forms of solidarity aimed at vulnerable families, which are considered inadequate and inefficient. These preexisting forms of (formal or informal) benefits are ignored by the CT mechanism and devices.

However, the CTs do not land in a social void. Numerous forms of local solidarity exist everywhere, and assume multiple manifestations depending on the context: mutual family or neighborhood support, clientelism and patronage, sponsorship, charity, "remittances" from migrants, and, in the case of Islamic countries, the Zakat, the tithe donated to the poor by Muslims. Of course, some experts acknowledge the existence of these informal "safety nets" along with their advantages and limitations (Devereux and Gettu 2013; Watson 2016)—up to the ranks of the World Bank (World Bank 2012; Tamiru 2013). Nevertheless, once the merits of the local forms of mutual support are acknowledged, they are put aside: the CT mechanism is self-sufficient and self-fulfilling and contains no provision for establishing links between formal and informal "safety nets."

Similarly, at the national level, prior to the arrival of CTs, various public systems, allocations, pensions, exemptions, and measures for the "poor" are present, and emergency instruments can be found which are supposed to be activated in the event of famine or other national disasters. Needless to say, these are sometimes ineffective or dysfunctional; however, they are part of the social landscape. Yet these preexisting formal benefits are just as ignored by the important new model as the preexisting informal benefits. There has been a clear failure to learn lessons from past experiences at local and national levels in this regard. The case of Egypt, analyzed here by H. Sholkamy (chapter 10) is telling: "Neither the international community recommending 'cash' nor the decision makers adopting the recommendations was fully engaged with the history of social welfare in Egypt, with the current capacity of the state to deliver welfare, or with the perceptions and experiences of social service providers."

Poverty

Poverty is at the core of all CT targeting. It should be noted that the experts' poverty criteria (statistical poverty)[38] always differ from those of the local populations (poverty as an emic category).[39] For the targeting to reach the "truly poor", in a laudable endeavor to approach local criteria, various institutional technologies are based on "community-based targeting," or, more generally, so-called participatory approaches are adopted, which appear to take the contexts into account. Of course, comprehensive community-based targeting is very rare; however, various "participatory" elements are regularly combined with classical surveying methods—for example, household economic approach (HEA) and proxy means testing (PMT)" in the customary "technocratic" CT targeting process implemented by the generally humanitarian NGOs. Hence, the populations or persons chosen by them are asked to divide the villagers into four categories: only the fourth of these categories, the "very poor," is eligible for CTs, according to CT programs' norms. There is nothing spontaneous about this classification process; it is imposed on the populations by the program officials, as is the actual framework comprising the four categories (neither the process nor framework reflect local cognitive behaviors; see Olivier de Sardan and Hamani, chapter 12). Furthermore, these so-called participatory "brackets" are contained within a set of other rules imported by the NGOs: preliminary geographical targeting on the basis of statistics or consultations with government experts; surveys of the HEA or PMT type to verify whether those designated as "very poor" are actually very poor; and, frequently, a final selection of beneficiaries from the list of the very poor to comply with the NGO quotas, which exclude certain members of the "very poor" from the benefits (see chapter 12).[40]

Furthermore, the evaluation of a household's resources or expenses is a far from satisfactory proxy for "poverty." Given the numerous biases of both the surveyors and the surveyed, irrespective of the surveying methods used, HEA and PMT surveys are often less reliable than they claim—in certain African contexts at least. Moreover, while many studies have highlighted the fluctuating and labile nature of poverty in Africa, which, apart from the chronic poverty affecting a relatively small proportion of the population, is affected by major economic variations (Watson 2016), the surveys arbitrarily evaluate income at a particular point in time. Moreover, the lack of a support network (social isolation) is often more

constitutive of radical poverty than the lack of income. Finally, access
to minimum resources in one basic area (like food) does not necessarily
mean that access is available to minimum resources in another basic area
(like health) (see Kadio, Ridde, and Mallé 2014).

Hence the identification of "the poor" is a far more complex process
than it appears, both in terms of methods and in definitions of "poverty"
used (Morestin, Grant, and Ridde 2009; Ridde and Jacob 2013). Dréze and
Sen (2012: 38) offer a case in point for the "below poverty line" (BPL) designation in India, where they say the pitfalls of this indicator have become
"increasingly clear in recent years." Causing enormous exclusions errors,
resentment of nonbeneficiaries, suspicion, mistrust, and divisions among
communities, an indicator such as the BPL illustrates the "social cost of
targeting" (Devereux et al. 2015: 34–36).

Household

Although the beneficiaries are individuals (generally women) in most
cases, the "household" category is the social unit targeted by CTs and
taken into account in the evaluations. Women are targeted as "mothers"
and are supposed to manage the cash solely on the basis of the household's interests. However, when it comes to resource seeking and the
consumption of goods, the household does not constitute the basic economic unit in all locations (Watson 2016). This is particularly evident in
the case of pastoralists, specifically those who practice nomadic livestock
raising in large areas of Africa. Pastoralism illustrates the difficulties faced
by CTs, which are based on a standardized "sedentary" model, in adapting to the local contexts, specifically those particularly far removed from
the international standard (Devereux and Tibbo 2013; Sabates-Wheeler,
Linde, and Hoddinott 2013; Watson 2016). A heuristic advantage of this
"collision" between the CT traveling model and the pastoralist contexts
is that it demonstrates particularly clearly how the model is founded on
certain basic categories that are taken for granted both in the (agrarian
and urban) contexts in which it emerged (Brazil, Mexico) and by the international experts, but which are in fact ambivalent, ambiguous, or even
inoperative in many other contexts.

Even in a sedentary context, the widespread theory among CT operators
that the household is the fundamental economic unit organized on the basis
of the pooling of resources for the overall benefit of the family, with the
wife managing the resources in the interest of the children, is far from uni-
versally corroborated.[41] The division of activities and resources is strictly
gender-based in the majority of Sahelian households (Olivier de Sardan
and Hamani, chapter 12): for example, the purchasing of basic foodstuffs,

school expenses, clothing, and medical supplies is the responsibility of the men, who produce both cash and subsistence crops on their land, and the women use their income (sale of poultry and small ruminants, condiments, and cooked food) as they see fit, and regularly send cash to their own parents. In northeastern Brazil, men are in charge of food, while women pay for clothes and school equipment (see Morton, chapter 3).

With regard to the children, the requirement that a child must be biological (as confirmed by a birth certificate) to qualify for entitlements under most CCTs, and sometimes in the nonconditional CTs, is not always relevant: in Africa, for example, a household may include fostered children (*enfants "confiés"*), children being hosted on a temporary basis, and children who officially belong to another household, all situations for which legal proof will not exist. The head of the household considers these children as "his children" and would be shocked if they were not taken into account by a CT program.

Finally, the CT beneficiaries are subject to obligations in relation to the distribution and sharing of the money that extend beyond their immediate households. These social constraints are not taken into account by the CTs. For example, demobilized soldiers in Côte d'Ivoire (see Chelpi-den Hammer, chapter 11) would very much like to receive their entire benefit in a single payment, as this would enable them to minimize the sums they must provide to a large circle of parents and relatives, who approach them for handouts each time they receive a CT payment. This need is not taken into account by the CT distribution instrument, which adheres to its "expert" programming involving several staged payments.

The Revenge of Contexts

Hence, despite the incontestable advantages offered by the income from CT payments, local populations are not unanimously enthusiastic (in private conversation at any rate[42]) in their reception of the system. The populations' reservations and objections differ vastly, depending on the implementation contexts and CT instruments in question and depending on the policies that frame the CT programs: rejection of the state, claiming a right, quest for rent, distrust of public services, feelings of humiliation, imposition of an additional burden on the women, criticism of the formal and informal conditions, inadequacy or irregularity of the distributed sums, circumvention of payments by the elites, etc.

Both full compliance and radical rejection are extreme and minority positions in response to the rules enforced by CT programs, which the actors affected by CTs do not truly adhere to and which they consider arbitrary or illegitimate. As mentioned in the introduction, rather than *exit, voice,* or *loyalty* strategies, it is *cunning strategies* that prevail here. They express a tension (or "double bind") between the desire to continue to benefit from the CT manna (which requires "good" behavior) and the condemnation of the norms governing the access to CTs (which involves the expression of disagreement). However, these circumvention strategies are themselves as varied as the local contexts and the types of actors and strategic groups involved: men and women, beneficiaries and nonbeneficiaries, (formal and informal) local authorities, state and NGO workers, staff from the ministries and NGOs, banks and microcredit institutions, statisticians and surveyors, etc. This complexity of the local contexts in the face of the standardized and imported instruments is at the root of what I refer to as the *revenge of contexts*. This metaphor does not presuppose of course a deliberate rejection of CTs or a generalized hostility against CT programs. It points to the fact that contexts, ignored or underestimated by CT programs, come back into the play and produce a series of unexpected effects.

The term *revenge of contexts* calls attention to the potential mismatch between unique, complex local contexts and standardized, imported instruments. It (surely) does not presuppose a deliberate or generalized hostility against CT programs. However, it underlines that ignoring or underestimating the specificity of each context can backfire and generate unintended consequences. Implementation contexts are a formidable challenge for traveling models.

Numerous examples of this are provided in the chapters of this book, each one associated with a specific context. I will present three of them here: the circumvention of participatory injunctions, the use made of the distributed cash, and the intervention of religious factors.

The Circumvention of Participatory Injunctions

The participatory injunction is a sub-instrument of targeting used by many CT programs. The desire to involve the populations in the selection process is at the root of a kind of "participatory social engineering" that aims to enable the deployment of certain forms of popular control over the selection of CT beneficiaries: village general assemblies, elected representatives, committees of elders, complaints committees, etc. However, this engineering is itself imposed by the national (and sometimes international) experts and has its own "democratic" rules (according to the experts), which do not generally correspond to the forms of power and decision-making that prevail in the local communities and which are also subverted as a result. The case of the general village assemblies organized by the NGOs for CT programs in Niger is significant in this regard: "Contrary to the 'democratic' expectations of the NGOs, for which a general assembly should be an arena for public debate and transparency, a village general assembly is more often than not a space for social control, where taking the floor to contradict a speaker, denounce a cheating neighbor, or, to go even further, publicly criticize the chief in front of strangers is seen as unseemly behavior and is widely stigmatized"[43] (Olivier de Sardan and Hamani, chapter 12).

Of course, the limits of participatory policies, the multiple misunderstandings that seep into them, and the subversions to which they are subjected have already been highlighted by an entire body of scientific literature on development (Nelson and Wright 1995; Mosse 1996; 2011; Crooke and Kothari 2001; Ribot 2002; Olivier de Sardan 2005; Li 2007; Gardner and Lewis 2015). However, the accumulation of knowledge in this area does not lead to an actual modification of policies, which appear to be condemned to a perpetual cycle of repetition.

The Use Made of the Distributed Cash

Another example involves the uses to which the distributed cash is put by the beneficiaries. Two objectives are regularly pronounced by humanitarian CT programs implemented in response to food crises or aimed at fostering the resilience of vulnerable households in the Sahel: to reduce the indebtedness of these households and halt migration among the young. These practices are considered negative risk-coping behaviors (see Dercon 2005) by the international development institutions. However, when beneficiaries repay their debts to traders, very often they do it so that they will be able to run up new ones. Similarly, the cash received through the CT programs is sometimes used for the very purpose of enabling a young person to migrate (departure involves capital outlay, which is considered an investment in view of subsequent remittance payments from the migrant).

The Intervention of Religion

I would now like to present a completely different example of the revenge of contexts, which is found in numerous indigenous communities in Latin America: the intrusion of religious divisions in the CCT programs.[44] Apart from the sometimes attested equation of the distribution of the money and accompanying requirement of school attendance by children with the "buying" of children for the benefit of the monstrous *Pishtaco* bogeyman figure (Piccoli 2014), it has been confirmed that opposition to CTs is often concentrated within the new Protestant evangelist churches, while the legitimist Catholic churches are more willing to support them. However, this pattern is sometimes reversed at the local level: According to Sanchiz (chapter 2 of this volume), "Protestants were more likely to reject the program, although this is also a variable between contexts: in northern Chiapas, the PRI-leaning members of Paz y Justicia who embraced Progresa became close to evangelical churches, as their opponents opted for Catholicism. In ongoing conflicts over land and other resources, identifying oneself with a particular political or religious label may depend on what other available positions have already been appropriated by rivals."

Theoretical Digression 3: Pragmatic Context and Structural Context, Normative Gap and Implementation Gap

Of course, the concept of context itself can appear ambiguous, polysemous, and vague.[45] First and foremost, from the perspective of science studies, every action, whatever its level, unfolds in a context. The construction of a mechanism and global diffusion of a model also take place in contexts, and the offices of the World Bank or those of a given Ministry of Social Affairs are just as much contexts as a village assembly or queue of cash transfer recipients. They all merit the attention of researchers. Admittedly, very different contexts are involved here: those of the think tanks and so-called high-level expert meetings (contexts of the narrativization, theorization, and networking of a public policy) are not those of the poor neighborhoods of Mexico or Nigerien villages (implementation contexts). In this chapter, I have limited the use of the term context to the (national, regional, local) implementation contexts of a traveling model.

However, for traveling model experts, the implementation context is very often reduced to a set of sociodemographic variables (rates, indices, and other indicators relating to incomes, the poverty threshold, schooling, frequentation of public services, GDP, Human Development Index, etc.). These contextual variables are structural in nature; they may be aggregated, weighted, and enumerated in innumerable permutations.

For example, in a review of the literature dedicated to the role of contexts in programs for improving the quality of healthcare (Kaplan et al. 2010), having identified some families of contextual variables, such as the "outer setting" (economic, social, and political environment), "organizational setting," "individuals and their roles," and "networks," the authors differentiate between sixty-six variables that have been the target of measures (Kaplan et al. 2010: 506). This logic of variables, its inflationary drift, litanies of components, factors, key elements or frameworks, and quantitativist obsession (no qualitative study was considered by this review) renders the concept of the context meaningless.

As noted by Abbott (1992; quoted in Hedström and Swedberg 1996: 291): "In the causal modeling tradition, variables and not actors do the acting." Contexts that are seen through variables are structural contexts. I advocate for an alternative approach to contexts, one that puts actors' actions and interactions at the center. Indeed, local reformers (or "reformers from the inside") play a crucial role in changing and reworking pragmatic contexts.[46]

Accordingly, I propose to distinguish between *structural contexts* (in the background and described using statistical variables) and *pragmatic contexts* (in the foreground and described using qualitative methods). The latter prioritize the role of the actors and are associated with the concept of agency, which is widely used in the social sciences today. Developed by Giddens (1984) and imported into the field of development by Long (1992), it designates the cognitive and strategic "margin of maneuver" of actors (that is, their capacity to know and act with relative autonomy). The structural contexts (generally characterized as related to the economic, political, social, or cultural environment) operate on the importation of a traveling model through the intermediary of pragmatic contexts — in other words, based on the actors' game and their interactions. The structural contexts involve a number of constraints and resources that influence the representations and practices of the strategic groups involved in the CTs (experts and national policy decision-makers, program workers, public service and NGO workers, local authorities, beneficiaries, nonbeneficiaries), but it is the representations and practices of the strategic groups that constitute the pragmatic contexts. They are at the heart of what I refer to as the revenge of contexts.[47]

In other words, the implementation contexts are first and foremost the local actors: their networks and interactions, their social norms and practical norms, their organizational and professional cultures, their routines and motivations, their local history, their conflicts and power relations. This perspective clearly diverges from the language of variables.

This central role of the actors — their perceptions and strategies, which are always considerably removed from the expectations and presuppositions of the experts — gives rise to two types of gaps: an *implementation gap* and a *normative gap*.

The *implementation gap* is an inevitable process: however "well prepared" public policies may be, gaps between the intended impacts and what actually happens on the ground inevitably arise in the course of their implementation; in the words of Mosse and Lewis (2006: 9), there are "differences between their formal objectives and goals and those that emerge through the practices and strategies pursued by the actors at different organizational levels. . . . The relation of policy and practice is not an instrumental or scripted translation of ideas into reality but a messy free-for-all in which processes are often uncontrollable and results uncertain." However, the more standardized and ignorant of its implementation contexts a public policy is, the more likely it is that a significant implementation gap will arise.

With regard to the *normative gap* (which is one of the factors at play in the implementation gap), it too is inescapable, but it varies in its scope and modalities. Every public policy delivers not only public or collective goods but also public norms governing the access to these goods (as illustrated by the case of CTs). Traveling models encounter a particularly vast "normative gap" between the norms produced by the experts and the local norms that exist in the implementation contexts.

In fact, it is possible to identify at least two major types of normative registers within the implementation contexts. On the one hand, there are the social norms of the beneficiary populations which relate, among other things, to mutual support, collective action, the definition of poverty, the gender relationships, the education of children, migration, the relationship with the state and, more generally, the populations' "coping strategies." A considerable time ago, Oscar Lewis (1969) referred in a rather similar sense to a "culture of poverty" in Mexican and Caribbean urban environments. Coping strategies, embedded in social norms, were core components of this culture of poverty, and they still are. The social norms of beneficiary populations and their local cultures, which are highly variable from one location to the next, are largely unacknowledged by the CT programs.

Another type of contextual norm exists that is even more ignored by CTs: the practical norms that regulate the real practices and routines (different from what is officially prescribed) of the CT program workers and state officials involved (social workers, communal officials, teachers, healthcare personnel). In reality, the latter do not strictly follow the rules in which they have been trained. In Latin America, for example, they add informal or extralegal conditionalities to the official conditions. These "noncompliant" behaviors[48] are not random; they are relatively predictable and routinized and are governed by latent and implicit norms, which I refer to as "practical norms" (De Herdt and Olivier de Sardan 2015; Olivier de Sardan 2015d). The practical norms of civil servants and NGO's frontline agents, and their professional cultures, are also largely unacknowledged by the CT programs.

The behaviors relating to CT programs involving development or humanitarian aid in Africa are a clear illustration of this dual normative register. From the perspective of the local populations, all aid is very welcome, and the strategies adopted with a view to benefiting from this external manna are integrated into a set of habitual coping strategies (among which remittance payments from migrants assume an important role). With regard to the project workers, they are frequently the victims of double binds (or even triple binds) in that they have to implement (or at least appear to implement) their employers' requirements without having the necessary resources in most cases. Furthermore, they must also manage the revenge of contexts while pursuing their own interests.

Traveling Models beyond CTs

The problems encountered by the CT programs in the course of their implementation also affect the other traveling models, their instruments, their devices, and their mechanisms. In accordance with the dominant strategy shared by the development institutions (including many NGOs) and the promoters of new public management (NPM), all of the traveling models prioritize the mechanisms — and compliance with their rules — and as a result come up against the preeminence of the implementation contexts over the mechanisms.

Numerous examples of traveling models have been described by different scholars, who have highlighted how much contexts have been underestimated and the unexpected effects that have arisen in very different areas as a result: transitional justice (Ancelovici and Jenson 2012), "conflict resolution and management" procedures, and the "equitable" management of oil revenues and gender-based approaches (Behrends, Park, and Rottenburg 2014). Numerous examples can also be cited in the area of healthcare — for example, the training of community-based birth attendants for home deliveries (Mumtaz et al. 2015),[49] the use of community health workers in the efforts to fight malaria (Druetz, Zongo, and Ridde 2015), user fee exemption policies (Olivier de Sardan and Ridde 2014; 2015) and traveling models in maternal health (Olivier de Sardan, Diarra, and Moha 2017). In the battle against corruption, the "most frequent approach has until today been to use the 'tool kits' of ideas provided by the international community in line with the 'one size fits all' approach" (Persson, Rothstein, and Teorell 2013: 431) despite the comprehensive evaluation of repeated failures and the persistence of corrupt phenomena. Of course, each traveling model is specific in nature and based on a mechanism (or set of mechanisms) and devices with specific characteristics that make the model unique. However, all of the models share the experts' belief in the intrinsic effectiveness of the mechanism in multiple contexts.

Nevertheless, all models are subject to local forms of reinterpretation, diversion, circumvention, or fragmentation, and are exposed to unexpected effects caused by the interaction of different rationales that frequently diverge and sometimes come into conflict, and underlie the behavior of the various "strategic groups" brought face to face during the implementation process.

Similar to some more or less community-based targeting methods within CT programs, an entire series of participatory approaches, which are widely practiced today in the development world, aim to accord greater space to implementation contexts by developing procedures and cycles that involve the local communities in the implementation of the project devices that concern them (recruitment of "volunteers," architecture of accountability, "participatory" surveys, etc.). However, as demonstrated by Mosse (2005) for India and Li (2007) for Indonesia in relation to major "participatory" programs promoted by leading international organizations (the UK-based Department for International Development and the World Bank), these "communitarian touches," which, as we have seen for the CTs, involve "participatory injunctions," remain marginal or cosmetic in most cases in comparison to the implementation of the devices of a mechanism and the logic of a project, its promoters, and workers. The marginality of participatory processes within development interventions was expressed as follows in the theoretical language of neoinstitutionalism: "When analyzed in terms of Ostrom's differentiation between constitutional, collective and operational choice (Dolsak and Ostrom 2003; Ostrom 2005), local people have largely been restricted to 'participatory' roles in collective and operational choices" (Haller, Accialoli, and Rist 2015: 3). The "constitutional" choices (in other words, matters relating to institution building and the definition of fundamental rules) remain the privilege of the experts in traveling models, and the participation of local actors remains strongly regulated and supervised by the programs—even with regard to the collective and operational choices. The quest for compliance (with the imposed norms) remains at the core of the traveling models and new public management policies. And it is precisely the "noncompliance" and circumventions of compliance that characterize the "revenge of the context" (the pragmatic context, or whatever we choose to call it). The latter presents as "a heap of 'unintended consequences' and 'unexpected results'" (Czarniawska and Joerges 1996: 14). Various studies, often undertaken from the same perspective of this book, provide an empirical account of this in a very wide range of areas, mainly in relation to development policies and programs like human rights (Englund 2006, for Malawi), focused antenatal consultations (Olivier de Sardan, Diarra, and Moha 2017, for Niger), natural resource management

(Ribot 2002, for Senegal) and the battle against HIV-AIDS (Swidler and Watkins 2009, for Malawi). The conclusion reached in the latter can be applied in other areas, including CTs: "The unpredictable resources donors sometimes provide tend to get incorporated into the same ways of coping with life that villagers usually depend on" (Swidler and Watkins 2009: 7).

Traveling Models at the Heart of Development Aid

The production of a traveling model around a miraculous mechanism like that analyzed here for the CTs is a habitual process in development policies and public policies that present themselves as indispensable reforms in most cases. "For large development agencies . . . organizational imperatives overwhelmingly favor tackling problems, or those aspects of problems, that lend themselves to a technical, universal answer" (Pritchett, Woolcock, and Andrews 2012: 4)

CTs are clearly nothing more than a recent addition to a long series of such universal mechanisms. Based on its inaugural success in Bangladesh (Grameen Bank), the microcredit was one of the most widespread traveling models over the two decades preceding the arrival of CTs. The World Bank referred to a "revolution" in this regard (Robinson 2001). However, the gaps between microcredit programs and their implementation contexts were constantly confirmed (Bedecarrats 2013).[50]

Today another traveling model is promoted at great cost by the World Bank in all of the LMICs, particularly in the area of healthcare (Turcotte-Tremblay et al. 2016): performance-based financing (PBF), also called payment for performance (P4P). It has generated a considerable body of seminars, workshops, training courses, study trips, reports, and manuals, and has mobilized a sizeable workforce. It is also based on a highly acclaimed inaugural success story[51] (in Great Britain) and was imported into Africa on the basis of a "success story relay" (Rwanda: see Soeters, Habineza, and Peerenboom 2006; Basinga et al. 2011). But the fact that PBF has been a success in Rwanda does not mean that it will work in other African settings. Quite the opposite. Many contextual factors were decisive in the "success" of the implementation of PBF in Rwanda, such as "the very specific political situation, the very strong social control that prevails, the regime's capacity to ensure relatively satisfactory functioning of public services, less widespread and less visible corruption than elsewhere, the effective use of sanctions within the administration and the fear they arouse" (Olivier de Sardan, Diarra, and Moha 2017). These elements contrast strongly with the situation of most health systems across Africa, characterized by "every-man-for-himself-ism," weakness of the state, poor functioning of public services, open and widespread corruption, impunity, etc. (Olivier de Sardan 2009).[52]

When implemented in different African countries, PBF programs largely ignore preexisting contexts. For example, all over Sahelian Africa, the national vaccination days financed by the Gavi Vaccine Alliance, which have been operating for years on the basis of a PBF mechanism (a fee is paid per vaccination administered), have had multiple adverse effects (disorganization of health services, systematic multivaccinations, falsification of data, etc.),[53] of which PBF programs take no account.

Of course, the PBF programs are considerably more sophisticated and attempt to take the quality of services into account; however, they are based on the same mechanism. Hence, the PBF in the healthcare sector provides an interesting case involving the combination of (1) a particularly simple mechanism, as old as the world itself (at least as the market economy)—a financial incentive: pay more those who work more and better—and (2) implementation devices and instruments of a rare complexity (and unsustainable cost for African countries). No fewer than twenty-three quantitative indicators and eleven qualitative indicators were developed by the experts for the primary health centers in Burkina Faso alone. In addition to the sixty-one basic evaluation indicators financed by the World Bank (Ministère de la Santé 2015), the program coordination must record and monitor a total of 102 indicators. Various studies have already demonstrated how these programs clash with the local realities (for the case of the Democratic Republic of the Congo, see Fox et al. 2013), and serious doubts arise in relation to their efficiency and sustainability (Paul et al. 2014; Turcotte-Tremblay et al. 2016;[54] Ridde et al. 2017; Seppey et al. 2017; Turcotte-Tremblay et al. 2017).

Examples of Instruments That Are Particularly Suited to Traveling Models: Logical Framework and RCTs

Whatever their nature, the traveling models in the development sector are based on common planning and evaluation instruments with the precise characteristic of being interested in the mechanism alone (and its devices) while focusing on the expected results from the implementation of this mechanism. Hence these instruments are very similar to the traveling models. They are based on the same assumption (appreciating or evaluating the intrinsic effectiveness of the mechanism) and aim to neutralize the role of the contexts in their implementation. Far from being independent and neutral instruments,[55] they actively participate in the promotion of the traveling models. The instrument in question in the case of planning is the logical framework, and in the case of impact evaluation it is randomized controlled trials (RCT).

The Logical Framework

The logical framework is one of the rare procedures to have been adopted by all of the development agencies and to have survived for several decades. It is a quasi-mandatory crossing point for the designers of any program—irrespective of its location or the institution that supports it. It is entirely focused on the compliance with a mechanism and its instruments,[56] which it declines on the basis of operational objectives, the activities to be carried out for this purpose, and the results to be attained, which are measured on the basis of quantitative indicators. Everything to do with the contexts is externalized in a separate column, which is labeled "risks" or "critical hypotheses" and contains political, social, and cultural data that cannot be acted on and which it is hoped will not interfere with the running of the program. This instrument provides no place for studies and "feedback" on the implementation processes, implementation gaps, and the unexpected outcomes arising from the contexts. Originally conceived in the context of technical engineering, the logical framework was extended to the context of the social engineering of development as though the same kind of planning were involved.[57]

Randomized Controlled Trials (RCT)

RCTs, which have been promoted by the Abdul Latif Jameel Poverty Action Lab (J-Pal) throughout the world for around twenty years, are based on the same assumptions as the traveling models, and this largely accounts for their success: they are intended to test the intrinsic effectiveness of a mechanism while neutralizing the effects of the implementation context by comparing a group that benefits from an intervention like CTs and a nonbeneficiary control group. The context, which hinders the evaluation of the specific impact of a mechanism, is seen as the methodological enemy. By constructing two groups that are considered equivalent in all points because they fit the same sociodemographic criteria (i.e., structural contexts), the experiment is intended to eliminate all contextual effects, which are reduced to mere structural contexts .[58] The actors in the field (i.e., the pragmatic contexts) are considered as being outside the context and, in a manner of speaking, are seen as mere guinea pigs reacting to the introduction of a given mechanism. All differences observed and measured between the two groups (in terms of output and program impact) will accordingly be attributed to the intrinsic virtues of the studied mechanism.

This experimentalist vision of the impact of an intervention was, of course, inspired by a methodology that originated in biomedical science (double-blind studies). Traveling models offer fertile ground for the application of RCTs and they have been used extensively for the evaluation of CTs, microcredits, and PBF.[59] However, their results are the subject of intense debate as they do not appear to be as convincing as claimed by their promoters: in particular, their "external validity" (the generalization capacity of their findings—in other words, their validity when they are extended to other contexts than the specific context that has been put under experimental study) is their weak point (see among others Rodrick 2008; Ravallion 2009; Bernard, Delarue, and Naudet 2011; Jatteau 2013). In other words, an RCT on a CT program in Northern Niger provides no reliable indication of what may happen with another CT program in Southern Niger, not to speak of a CT program in Mali or Chad.[60]

Nonetheless, having become established as the mandatory "crossing point" of all "evidence-based policies," and to an even greater extent in the name of "evidence-based medicine" in the healthcare sector, RCTs have assumed a disproportionate place in the market for development policy impact studies today. They are an ideal tool for the standardization of models and contribute significantly to the supremacy of mechanisms and their devices at the cost of sensitivity to pragmatic contexts. At the same time, they cause the devaluation (or delegitimization) of qualitative research on the singularity of concrete cases and the specificities of the "real world."

Context Matters in Words: Traveling Models Prevail in Practice

The standardization of development policies has, of course, long been the object of various critical assessments emanating from the social sciences: in the field of political economy, for example, from the pioneering work of Hirschman (1967) to Naudet (1999) and Easterly (2006); and in the work of numerous authors in the field of anthropology of development (including Mosse 2005; Olivier de Sardan 2005; Li 2007; Gardner and Lewis 2015). Even within large international organizations, the major producers of traveling models, various warnings are expressed about the application of standardized regulations and underestimation of contexts, as can be seen, for example, in this World Health Organization publication: "Considerable caution is needed in scrutinizing formal management structures, rules and regulations, as they may bear no resemblance with actual management practice" (Pavignani and Colombo 2009: 223). In the same way, many World Bank experts and development experts are more and more aware of the inadequacy of "one size fits all" models, and there is a growing consensus among development economists in relation to the validity of more pragmatic and context-specific solutions (Rodrik 2008). The vice president of the World Bank wrote, "There is no unique universal set of rules. . . . We need to get away from formulae and the search of elusive 'best practices.'" (World Bank 2005: xiii, quoted by Rodrik 2008: 25)

However, far from declining in number and volume, traveling models continue to prosper under various labels (for example, the recent "high impact factor interventions"). Although modernization theory is dismissed in principle and although any development agency will proclaim that there is no magic bullet and that context matters, the predominant strategy remains by far, as pointed out by Pritchett, Woolcock, and Andrews (2012: 6), "intensifying a process of reform via the importing of methods and designs deemed effective elsewhere." The underlying theory of change remains "accelerated modernization via transplanted best practices" (Pritchett, Woolcock, and Andrews 2012: 6). Traveling models meet these requirements perfectly.

Hence, the social sciences have had little influence in this area. Indeed, one sometimes gets the feeling that the criticism of a traveling model merely creates the conditions for its replacement with another model. "Better theory, new paradigms and alternative frameworks are constantly needed" (Mosse 2005: 640) but "strangely little attention is given to the relationship between these models and the practices and events that they are expected to generate or legitimize in particular contexts" (Mosse 2005: 1–2).

Why This Surprising Recurrence of Traveling Models?

The question arises, therefore, as to what lies behind this perseverance with the incessant production of traveling models. Five reasons are presented below.

An Employment Market

"Notwithstanding the failure of these systematic transfers of models from the North to the Africas since independence, they continue because experts and consultants from the North and South, professionals from the South and leaders from the North and South derive benefits from them" (Darbon 2009: 275). The production and circulation of traveling models is, in a way, the "core business" of the "developmentist configuration" (the development industry) and provides work for various cohorts of personnel from those involved in program design (international officials) to those who implement the programs in the field (NGO workers). Each new model has its own market of experts, specialists, and practitioners at both national and international levels.

The Institutional Routines

The importance of "path dependency" cannot be underestimated. Over the course of several decades, social engineering consultancies, programming, evaluation and design offices, development agencies, international organizations, and major foundations have developed expertise and technical and accounting methods that mainly involve the creation and diffusion of traveling models (staging of success stories, presentation of mechanisms and design of devices and instruments, seminars and good practice guides, community of practices networks, logistical framework, RCT). Sticking to this path is the simplest strategy for institutions in which the creation and diffusion of traveling models have become routine practices. What we observe here is what DiMaggio and Powell (1983) referred to as "institutional isomorphism" whereby organizations in a given sector tend to behave in an identical way.

Development as Supply-Based Policies and Aid Rent

The public policies in the field of development generally correspond to the ideal type of the "garbage can", i.e, rummaging around an indiscriminate and shifting mix of problems, solutions, influences and choices (Cohen, March, and Olsen 1972). As noted by Naudet (1999), development policies and programs are "finding problems for the solutions." This supply-based policy, which "imposes its products on the basis of its ideological choices and specific managers and not on the basis of the demands and needs of the beneficiaries" (Darbon 2009: 268) is based on models constructed by the development agencies, large NGOs, and international foundations. One reason among others for donors to promote and fund such models is that donors distrust national elites (not without reasons, in some cases at least) and have absolutely no confidence in the capacity of most LMIC governments to promote reforms or to improve the quality of public services delivery. Financing standardized interventions appears more efficient, allows more control, and should enable more people to benefit from foreign aid in principle. These models are almost always accepted by the authorities in the South, which are sheep-like followers and conformists in the majority of cases. They are interested above all in the resources (rent) these policies will provide, and have little regard for prioritizing the contextual concerns that they should focus on. This is clearly illustrated by the rhetoric of "good practice": this basically involves the allocation of "star pupil" status for practices that comply with the norms promoted by the traveling models. This is one of the perverse effects of the dependence on aid (or "development rent"; see introduction and Olivier de Sardan 2013). No pressure (or almost none) from the demand side can counteract or alter the incessant and compelling supply of traveling models.[61] In this regard, the experts and international aid donors cannot be held solely responsible for the hegemony of traveling models. The governments and experts of the countries of the South share the responsibility to a great extent.

Financing Rationales

All development professionals say that it is far more difficult to obtain modest funding for innovative projects initiated in the local context than major funding for traveling models. The compilation and format of the project applications, the funding mechanisms, the disbursement procedures, the management methods, and the auditing practices: everything contributes to the prioritization of exportable mechanisms and instruments that accommodate economies of scale and can be evaluated on the basis of quantitative criteria.

A Mental Framework

The belief—after all, it is one—in the intrinsic effectiveness of a mechanism positioned at the center of a public policy rests on an experimentalist and technologist basis that has proven its worth in certain particular areas: in effect, a vaccination or new drug are the bearers of such intrinsic effectiveness and are scarcely or not at all "context-dependent"—from a purely therapeutic perspective. Hence it is tempting to believe that the same applies to social and institutional technologies and to credit the latter with the same potential effectiveness as biomedical (or industrial) technologies. As we have seen, instruments as the logical framework and RCTs are based on this kind of extrapolation. The belief that what is true for technical and biological engineering is also true of social engineering is a widespread one.[62] Nothing could be further from the truth. The shift from technical or biological engineering to social engineering involves a radical change of "reference world." The traditional experimentalist statement "all other things being equal" makes no sense in the social world: it is impossible to implement (Passeron 2002; 2006). The multiplicity, complexity, and intertwining of the variables involved in all social interventions (pragmatic contexts), however minor they may be, makes all attempts at reduction to a single explanatory variable illusory. Nevertheless, this illusion persists in a few sectors of the social sciences that are still governed by a positivist vision of the world. And it prevails above all in the instances responsible for the development and implementation of public policies and development programs. Traveling models flourish against the backdrop of an inflation of norms, indicators, and procedures, which goes along with the "bureaucratization of the world" (Hibou 2012), fueled by this illusion that the social world can be ruled by benchmarking, scorecards, and codifications in the same way that the biological world is mastered by techniques, experiments, and protocols.

And Neoliberalism?

I did not include the global dominance of neoliberalism as one of the contributory factors behind the permanence of traveling models. Given that a large number of researchers working in the social sciences, including anthropology (Escobar 1995; Comaroff 2006; Hilgers 2012; Crewe and Axelby 2014), identify neoliberalism as the main, omnipresent, and recurrent cause of all the ills of development, this warrants an explanation.

Neoliberalism is, of course, the global backdrop of the world economy. Neoliberalism is the bearer of a certain moral vision of the world that opens the door to the frantic quest for profits, opportunist economic behaviors, corruption, and rentier practices, but also to charitable foundations, humanitarian aid, and poverty eradication policies (Whyte and Wiegratz 2016). Neoliberalism is at the root of the preeminence of the techniques of new public management (which are more heterogeneous than was ever admitted) (McCourt and Minogue 2001). And, of course, the World Bank develops its strategies in a political-economic context dominated by neoliberalism and tends to impose its solutions on the entire world (Hibou 1998).

Nonetheless, traveling models are not an inescapable consequence of neoliberalism. And neoliberalism is not the direct cause of all interaction between public policies and implementation contexts. It cannot be blamed for all the unexpected and adverse effects of development.[63] The World Bank is not a great devil that wants to dominate the world. It, too, is pervaded by differences, uncertainties, and contradictions. The complex game played by the actors cannot be reduced to this single "explanation."

If neoliberalism has a major responsibility for the situation of the world in general, and development policies in particular, it is only through the medium of numerous mediations, translations, contradictions, inconsistencies, and other complexities, which should prevent any reduction to a catch-all explanation. To put it in the Marxist language of my youth, by using the expression of "determination in the last instance" to characterize the effects of the economy on the social world (Althusser 1965; Poulantzas 1973), we were at times more prudent than is the case with certain simplistic contemporary denunciations of neoliberal globalization.

Conclusion: Are There Any Alternatives?

The answer to this question is clearly "yes," and it can be considered either within the process of production and diffusion of traveling models or outside it.

Within the development institutions, including within the CT business itself, multiple attempts have been made, and are still being made at different levels in the chain to be more "context sensitive" and take greater consideration of the constraints, resources, aspirations, norms, and strategies of the local and regional actors (see end of chapter 12 by Olivier de Sardan and Hamani). Numerous development professionals at different levels in the public policy and development production chain have reservations and criticisms or are skeptical about traveling models despite the fact that they implement them. It is our hope that this book will be of use to these internal reformers irrespective of their location and the nature of the traveling models with which they work. Even if it means not always respecting "good practice" in terms of the behavior and the compliance being promoted, the provision of windows of opportunity by the development institutions themselves to local actors for "positive subversions" and innovative adaptations is, after all, one of the best strategies that can be adopted by development professionals who are anxious to go beyond their institutions' "off-the-peg" approach.

There is another pathway. Outside the world of traveling models, attempts are being made, at different levels and just about everywhere in the world, to invent solutions that start from the contexts and the problems on the ground and not from standardized solutions, attempts at designing innovative reforms rooted in local realities, attempts at supporting innovators "from the inside" rather than reformers "from the outside." Some (in reality, very few) of these attempts have attained a degree of renown or even assumed a place within the major organizations and schools of management (for example, the *jugaad* movement; see Radjou, Prabhu, and Ahuja 2013) and within intellectual circles, such as the opening up of the debate on technical innovations to citizens and fieldworkers instead of confining it to experts and decision-makers (Callon, Lascoumes, and Barthe 2001). Others, the majority and the most interesting ones, are more discreet, scattered, heterogeneous, almost invisible, and worthy of being identified and documented. Most local innovators are isolated individuals, entirely invisible to the world of experts and decision-makers. Making them visible, with their success and their failures, is a task that could be assigned to the social anthropology of public action.

It is not the job of the authors of this book to allocate good grades or make a selection. We simply hope that it will encourage both the reformers within the institutions responsible for the production of traveling models and the discreet innovators within local societies to highlight and take into account the preeminence of the pragmatic contexts in all projects that involve social change.

Jean-Pierre Olivier de Sardan is professor of anthropology at the Ecole des Hautes Etudes en Sciences Sociales (France) and emeritus director of research at the Centre National de la Recherche Scientifique (France). He is among the founders of the Laboratory for Study and Research on Social Dynamics and Local Development (LASDEL), in Niamey, Niger (www.lasdel.net), and is associate professor, in charge of the master's program Anthropology of Health, at Abdou Moumouni University, Niamey. He has authored numerous books in French and in English, and is currently working on an empirical anthropology of public actions and modes of governance in West Africa. Honors and awards include Chevalier des Palmes académiques de la République du Niger, 2004; Docteur honoris causa de l'Université de Liège, 2012; Chevalier de l'Ordre national de la Légion d'honneur de la République française, 2012; and Prize Ester Boserup, University of Copenhagen, 2014.

Notes

I would like to thank Jean-François Caremel, Philippe Lavigne Delville, Frédéric Le Marcis, Nora Nagels, Sonia Rocha, Valéry Ridde, and Ilka Vari-Lavoisier for their comments and inputs on an initial version of this text. I want also to express my thanks to our late translator Susan Cox.

1. In the field of public policy analysis, the French school has focused on the link between public policies and cognitive frameworks (Muller 2000; Hassenteufel and Smith 2002).
2. He refers to the particularly abstract concept of the "token," which is borrowed from Bruno Latour but does not have very clear empirical borders and generates more confusion than clarity.
3. For a critique of the reference works on "policy transfers" by Dolowitz and Marsh (1996; 2000) and on "lesson drawing" by Rose (1991; 1993), see James and Lodge 2003.
4. Policy transfer is usually understood as a "process in which knowledge about policies, administrative arrangements and institutions in one time and/or place is used in the development of policies, administrative arrangements and institutions in another time and/or place" (James and Lodge 2003: 181).
5. These stages do not correspond exactly to the classical stages of policy-making (agenda-setting, formulation, decision-making, implementation). The sequential approach has often been criticized (Kingdon 1995); however, once it is acknowledged that the

approach is not explanatory, that the stages can overlap, and that their order is not set in stone, it would appear difficult to dispense with it entirely in that the configuration of actors involved changes at each stage.

6. Nevertheless, it goes without saying that these intrinsic properties also played a role in the success of CTs. For example, the logistic simplicity of CTs compared with the logistic complexity of food aid favored their adoption in the context of humanitarian aid.

7. Of course, it is always possible to go back further in history and find more or less forgotten antecedents, such as the Venezuelan *Beca Escuela* program of 1989 (Kundid 2005). Dapuez and Gavigan (chapter 7) quote an IDB economist who told them that "Progresa was derived from the US food stamp system."

8. I draw here in on Fabio Soares's (2011) clear historical review and Sonia Rocha's (2014) widely documented study. See also Morton (chapter 3).

9. "The initial design of Bolsa Familia reflected a compromise among different views of what this unified program had to be" (Soares 2011: 57).

10. On the diffusion of CTs in Latin America, I draw on the analyses of Teichman (2007) and Sugiyama (2011), in particular, and on Ancelovici and Jenson's (2012) more general and very stimulating analysis of the standardization process in transnational policy transfers, which is based on two examples, one relating specifically to CTs and the second to "truth and justice" commissions. Diaz (2017), focusing on the role played by the World Bank, draws also on Ancelovici and Jenson's paper, and then follows the travel of CTs from Latin America up to Philippines.

11. I will return to the link between traveling models and randomized controlled trials later.

12. "Certainly, the Bolsa Familia and Oportunidades are the products of a 'bricolage' of elements from different coalitions" (Tomazini 2013).

13. Beneficio de Prestaçao Continuada.

14. Regarding Progresa, for example, the criticism concerned the "absence of community participation at all stages (program design, the selection of beneficiaries, monitoring); the exclusion of many deserving poor; and the potential divisive impact on poor communities; they also called for parallel support for productive projects" (Teichman 2007: 562).

15. Decontextualization is a "conscious effort aimed at disembedding a group of ideas or an institution from its social context" (Ancelovici and Jenson 2012: 41).

16. Framing is a "discursive strategic task carried out by the actors to define the problems, simplify the situations and experiences, link several separate issues, and propose solutions and all for the purpose of collective action" (Ancelovici and Jenson 2012: 42).

17. Of course, each instrument can take varied forms, and this has resulted in great diversity among CT-type programmes. The Cash Learning Partnership (CaLP) identified twelve types of such programs (Zuodar 2014).

18. "The term 'proxy means test' is used to describe a situation where information about household or individual characteristics correlated with welfare levels is used in a formal algorithm to proxy household income, welfare or need. Given the administrative difficulties associated with sophisticated means tests and the inaccuracy of simple means tests, the idea of using other household characteristics as proxies for income is appealing" (Grosh and Baker 1995). The methodology is described in Kidd and Wylde 2011.

19. The very voluminous guide to the "household economy approach" published by Save the Children (Boudreau et al. 2008) is an indication of the complexity of the techniques and instruments involved in such an "analytical framework."

20. According to a toolkit on safety nets from World Bank (2016), enrollment includes two main approaches: census-style survey approaches (identification of beneficiaries by program staff) or on-demand approaches (potential beneficiaries should apply). A similar distinction has been made by Castaneda (2005) between "outreach" approaches and "application" approaches (Devereux et al. 2015).

21. The French term *dispositif* is particularly difficult to translate, as its polysemous use by Foucault frequently muddied the waters. By *device* (*dispositif*) I intend a set of operational, technical, and institutional measures that enable the implementation of a mechanism within a public policy. This perspective converges in some respects with the literature on policy *instruments* (Lascoumes and Le Galès 2007; Halpern, Lascoumes, and Le Gales 2014). For their part, Jenson and Nagels (2015) analyze CTs as social policy "instruments." However, I prefer to reserve the term "instrument" for the techniques made available to a mechanism and its devices—for example, the targeting methods (household economy approach or proxy means testing), the logical framework, or randomized controlled trials (see below).

22. It also differs from the use of mechanism by Ancelovici and Jenson (2012), for whom the process of standardization itself is a mechanism, just like each of its stages (certification, decontextualization, and framing).

23. "In realist literature there is as yet no consensus on interpretation of mechanism, even though it is a central element in the realist mode of explanation" (Marchal et al. 2013: 4).

24. Following a review of the variety of uses of the concept of the mechanism in the realist approaches to evaluation, Lacouture et al. (2015: 8) propose a definition which does little to eliminate the prevailing confusion: "A mechanism is an element of reasoning and reactions of (an) individual or collective agent(s) in regard of the resources available in a given context to bring about changes through the implementation of an intervention."

25. "Latin America presidents who adopted CCTs represent a wide spectrum of political ideologies" (Sugiyama 2011: 257).

26. For example, a paper published by the World Bank on CT in Niger (Barry, Maïdoka, and Premand 2017) completely ignores LASDEL's research demonstrating many biases and circumventions in relation to community targeting (Hamani 2013; Olivier de Sardan 2014; Olivier de Sardan et al. 2014).

27. Naturally, the international institutions and national decision-makers both deny the existence of such pressures in public: "Program officers generally argue they do not unduly pressure countries to adopt public policies, but rather respond to country requests and make their expertise available. . . . Similarly, country officials rarely, if ever, state that their decisions are based on directives from IFIs [international financial institutions]. For obvious reasons, domestic policy-makers claim agency and autonomy in decision-making" (Sugiyama 2011: 263).

28. A World Bank expert has, significantly and paradoxically, named these strongly suggested practices "*conditions souples*" (flexible conditionalities) (Premand 2016).

29. Rottenburgk (2007) refers to an entire series of terms denoting the same idea: hybridization, creolization, glocalization.

30. "High fidelity practitioner behavior is created and supported by core implementation components (also called 'implementation drivers')" (Fixsen et al. 2005).

31. It is not unusual for the scaling up to begin before the results of the evaluations of the pilot phases are available (for an analysis of the scaling-up process in the area of health policy in Africa, see Ridde 2015 and Olivier de Sardan 2015c).

32. The importance of informal negotiations, latent compromises, and unstable coalitions between stakeholders around the values, norms, and meanings of an intervention has also been demonstrated by some policy analysts (see Mahoney and Thelen 2010) without using the language of translation.

33. It is sufficient to quote some definitions provided by Callon and Latour themselves: "Translation is the mechanism by which the social and natural worlds progressively take form. The result is a situation in which certain entities control others. Understanding what sociologists generally call power relationships means describing the way in which actors are defined, associated and simultaneously obliged to remain faithful to their alliances" (Callon 1986: 223). "By translation we understand all the negotiations, intrigues,

calculations, acts of persuasion and violence, thanks to which an actor or force takes, or causes, to be conferred on itself, authority to speak or act on behalf of another actor or force. . . . Whenever an actor speaks of 'us,' s/he is translating other actors into a single will, of which s/he becomes the spirit and spokesman" (Callon and Latour 1981: 279).

34. On the role of theoretical inflation in the social sciences, see Passeron 2006.

35. Paradoxically, Callon's (1986) famous article on the domestication of scallops, which in various respects marked the founding of this sociology of translation, does not use the metaphor of translation in its demonstration and interpretation of empirical data; the metaphor of translation only emerges at the end of the text in a purely abstract form.

36. It should be acknowledged that the founders of actor-network theory did not restrict themselves to semiological analyses, due to their interest in sociotechnical processes (Latour 1996). However, this contributed to making the metaphor of translation even more vague as a unifying concept.

37. Of course, the fact of associating emicity and symmetry excludes the "non-human actors (or 'actants')," which Callon and Latour include in their principle of symmetry (see Callon 1986).

38. It is important to remember that statistical poverty is itself a historical construct: "Il fut un temps où on ne parlait pas de pauvreté au Sahel" ("There was a time we did not talk about poverty in the Sahel"; Bonnecase 2011: 9).

39. We encountered people's definitions of poverty in Niger that are very far removed from the international standards: "the poor person is someone who puts leftovers on the roof of his house to conserve them and eat them later"; "the poor person is someone whose daughter does not find a suitor even if she is pretty."

40. Watson's (2016) excellent report refers to similar facts in Mauritania and Chad, based on evaluations that show considerable similarities to what we observed in Niger.

41. This explains why an RCT carried out in Burkina Faso, which compared the impact of CTs paid to women and CTs paid to men, found little difference in the end use of the cash at the familial level (Akresh, De Walque, and Kazianga 2013).

42. The comparative advantage of qualitative methods, which make use of comprehensive interviews, is that they are positioned as much as possible on the level of private discourse.

43. We are, of course, describing a general tendency, and exceptions may well exist involving outspoken opponents or unconventional personalities who are willing to express their opinions publicly.

44. This also occurs on other continents, of course. For example, an ongoing research project by LASDEL in the Democratic Republic of the Congo has discovered that many opponents of the Lisungi CT program, promoted by the state and the World Bank, suspect it to be a freemason conspiracy, which in Congo amounts to the work of the devil.

45. "The terms 'context,' 'setting,' and 'environment' are sometimes used interchangeably in the literature" (Pfadenhauer et al. 2015). See McCormack et al. 2002 for a concept analysis concerning the use of "context" in the health domain; and Lacouture and al. (2015) comment on the different meanings of "context" for Pawson and other theory-based evaluation researchers.

46. On "transformational leaders" and contexts, see McCormack et al 2002; on "reformers form the inside" and practical norms, see Olivier de Sardan 2009b.

47. Organizational and professional cultures could be seen as major components of pragmatic contexts, if (and only if) "culture" is not defined in abstract terms (as values or world views) or culturalist terms (i.e., presupposition of homogeneity and/or traditionality) but instead as a "set of practices and representations that investigation has shown to be shared to a significant degree by a given group (or sub-group), in given fields and in given contexts" (Olivier de Sardan 2015a: 84). This meaning of culture includes "practical norms" (see below).

48. Compliance is a concept borrowed from public health (compliance with medical pre-scriptions). Britan and Cohen (1980: 20) use the term "dependability": "the degree to which an official behaves with the rules and regulations governing his office."

49. "It appears that the rollout of programmes to increase skilled birth attendants in rural areas has been largely based on rational logic and historic evidence without due regard to matching programme design to local context" (Mumtaz et al. 2015: 256).

50. For an analysis of their implementation in Madagascar, see Lavigne Delville 2012a.

51. However, several systematic reviews did not demonstrate that PBF had any major posi-tive impact on the effectiveness and quality of the health system (Turcotte-Tremblay et al. 2016). It is even possible that the cautionary statement of an economist in relation to the adverse effects of P4P on healthcare personnel in the case of Great Britain could also be relevant for the LMICs: "The potential for poorly designed P4P incentives to erode motivation is considerable" (Maynard 2012: 8).

52. For an analysis in the field of maternal health of the differences between Rwanda on one side, and Niger, Malawi. and Uganda on the other, interpreted in terms of collec-tive action, see Booth and Cammack 2013.

53. "In 2000, the Global Alliance for Vaccines and Immunization (GAVI) offered eligible African countries a fixed payment per additional child immunized against DTP3.... We show evidence that this policy induced upward bias in the reported level of DTP3 coverage.... In short, pay-for-performance incentives by a donor directly under-mined the integrity of administrative data systems" (Sandefur and Glassman 2014: 2). Nevertheless, "such schemes appear to be spreading in the region, due to ... donor enthusiasm for results-based aid" (Sandefur and Glassman 2014: 24).

54. This review raises an important point: "Six out of seven articles had at least one author that was or had been affiliated with an organization involved in the implementation of PBF, thereby resulting in a potential conflict of interest" (Turcotte-Tremblay et al. 2016: 10). More broadly, this argument is valid for almost any traveling model, including CTs: in most cases, CT evaluations are carried out by experts from the institutions in charge of the CT programs and responsible for promoting them.

55. Lascoumes and Le Gales (2004), who promoted the analysis of public action on the basis of their "instruments," broadly insisted on their nonneutrality.

56. "The program theory (or theory of change) – or how the intervention is expected to have intended impacts – is embedded in the traditional log frame, though the latter may not make explicit the underlying assumptions" (White 2009: 7).

57. For a critical analysis of the logical framework, see Gasper 2000; Giovalucci and Olivier de Sardan 2009.

58. "The implicit premise ... is that interventions that work in one place can be expected to work in another. This presumes ... that the results of such 'micro' interventions are substantially independent of the 'macro' context" (Reddy 2012: 62). As we can see, RCTs' methodology and traveling models are based on exactly the same postulates. For a critical approach to RCTs in general, see Bédécarrats, Guérin and Roubaud 2017, and to RCT in relation to microfinance institutions, see Bauchet et al. 2011.

59. "The CT field is dominated by large-scale quantitative impact evaluations" (Fisher et al. 2017).

60. Our current research on a safety net program in the Republic of the Congo has yielded very different results than our previous research in Niger (Olivier de Sardan et al. 2015).

61. Lavigne Delville (2012b) stresses that those responsible for development interventions (both their conception and implementation) are not accountable to the users (the target populations).

62. Obviously, as the scientific research has shown, all biomedical innovations are simul-taneously sociotechnological in nature. However, technological innovations are quite

different from organizational, institutional, procedural, and managerial innovations, if only in terms of the relationship between their intrinsic effectiveness and their implementation contexts. Of course, the diffusion of a biomedical innovation (e.g., a vaccine) is always accompanied by a social engineering component, which subjects this diffusion to the vagaries of the social world and the burden of the local contexts (e.g., a vaccination campaign); however, the intrinsic effectiveness of the vaccine, whatever the context, is not threatened by it. In other words, evidence-based medicine makes sense at the biological/epidemiological level, but its extrapolation to public health models (with significant social engineering components) is inappropriate, not to mention its further extrapolation to evidence-based policies (Dopson et al. 2003).

63. Brenda Chalfin's (2010) study, which presents an interesting ethnography of the customs system in Ghana, is typical in falling for this easy game of blaming everything on neoliberalism: see critiques by Bierschenk (2015) and Olivier de Sardan (2011).

References

Abbott, A. 1992. "What Do Cases Do? Some Notes on Activity in Sociological Analysis." In *What Is a Case? Exploring the Foundations of Social Enquiry*, edited by C. Ragin and H. Becker, 53–82. Cambridge: Cambridge University Press.

Adams, V., S. R. Craig, and A. Samen. 2016. "Alternative Accounting in Maternal and Infant Global Health." *Global Public Health* 11(3): 276–294.

Akresh, R., D. De Walque, and H. Kazianga. 2013. "Cash Transfers and Child Schooling: Evidence from a Randomized Evaluation of the Role of Conditionality." World Bank Policy Research Working Paper 6340.

Akrich, M. 1992. "The Des-Cription of Technical Objects." In *Shaping Technologies/ Building Societies: Studies in Sociotechnical Change*, edited by W. Bijker and J. Law, 205–224. Cambridge, MA: MIT Press.

———. 2006. "La construction d'un système socio-technique: Esquisse pour une anthropologie des techniques." In *Sociologie de la traduction: Textes fondateurs*, edited by M. Akrich, M. Callon, and B. Latour, 109–134. Paris: Presses des Mines.

Althusser, L. 1965. *Pour Marx*. Paris: Maspéro.

Ancelovici, M., and J. Jenson. 2012. "La standardisation et les mécanismes du transfert transnational." *Gouvernement et Action Publique* 1(1): 37–58

Andrews, C., L. Bassett, T. Castañeda, M. C. S. Gandara, M. Grosh, J. Lourerio, and R. Quintana. 2010. "Safety Nets How To: A Toolkit for Practitioners." Version 1. Washington, DC: World Bank.

Atlani-Duault, L. 2009. "L'anthropologie de l'aide humanitaire et du développement: Histoire, enjeux contemporains et perspectives." In *Anthropologie de l'aide humanitaire et du développement*, edited by L. Atlani-Duault and L. Vidal, 17–40. Paris: Armand Colin.

Kidd, S., and E. Wylde, eds. 2011. *Targeting the Poorest: An Assessment of the Proxy Means Test Methodology*. Canberra: Australian Agency for International Development.

Balen, M. E., and C. Leyton. 2015. "Policy Translation: An Invitation to Revisit the Work of Latour, Star and Marres." *Global Discourse* 6(1–2): 101–115.

Barca, V., S. Brook, J. Holland, M. Otulana, and P. Pozarny. 2015. "Qualitative Research and Analyses of the Economic Impact of Cash Transfer Programs in Sub-Saharan Africa." Synthesis report. Rome: FAO.

Basinga, P., P. J. Gertler, A. Binagwaho, A. L. Soucat, J. Sturdy, and C. M. Vermeersch. 2011. "Effect on Maternal and Child Health Services in Rwanda of Payment to Primary Health-Care Providers for Performance: An Impact Evaluation." *The Lancet* 377(9775): 1421–1428.

Bauchet, J., C. Marshall, L. Starita, J. Thomas, and A. Yalouris. 2011. *Latest Findings from Randomized Evaluations of Microfinance*. Access to Finance Forum: Reports by CGAP and Its Partners, no. 2. Washington, DC: Consultative Group to Assist the Poor; World Bank.

Bédécarrats, F. 2013. *La microfinance: Entre utilité sociale et rentabilité financière*. Paris: L'Harmattan.

Bédécarrats, F., I. Guérin, and F. Roubaud. 2017. "All that Glitters is not Gold. The Political Economy of Randomized Evaluations in Development". *Development and Change*. https://doi.org/10.1111/dech.12378.

Behrends, A., S. J. Park, and R. Rottenburg. 2014. "Travelling Models: Introducing an Analytical Concept to Globalisation Studies." In *Travelling Models in African Conflict Management: Translating Technologies of Social Ordering*, edited by A. Behrends, S. J. Park, and R. Rottenburg, 1–42. Leyden: Brill.

Bernard, T., J. Delarue, and J. D. Naudet. 2011. *On "Nailing" What Works through Impact Evaluations: Lessons from the Experience of AFD*. Paris: AFD.

Bierschenk, T. 2014. "From the Anthropology of Development to the Anthropology of Global Social Engineering." *Zeitschrift für Ethnologie* 139(1): 73–98.

———. 2015. "The Neoliberalism Effect: Review of Brenda Chalfin (2010). Neoliberal Frontiers. An Ethnography of Sovereignty in West Africa, Chicago, University of Chicago Press." *Zeitschrift für Ethnologie* 139 (1): 73–98.

Bierschenk, T., and J.-P. Olivier de Sardan. 1997. "ECRIS: Rapid Collective Inquiry for the Identification of Conflicts and Strategic Groups." *Human Organization* 56(2): 238–244.

———. 2014. "Ethnographies of Public Services in Africa: An Emerging Research Paradigm." In *States at Work: The Dynamics of African Bureaucracies*, edited by T. Bierschenk and J.-P. Olivier de Sardan, 35–65. Leyden: Brill.

Bierschenk, T., J.-P. Chauveau, and J.-P. Olivier de Sardan, eds. 2000. *Courtiers en développement: Les villages africains en quête de projets*. Paris: Karthala.

Bonnecase, V. 2011. *La pauvreté au Sahel: Du savoir colonial à la mesure internationale*. Paris: Karthala.

Booth, D., and D. Cammack. 2013. "Maternal Health: Why Is Rwanda Doing Better Than Malawi, Niger and Uganda?" In *Governance for Development in Africa: Solving Collective Action Problems*, edited by D. Booth and D. Cammack, 41–72. London: Zed Books.

Boudreau, T., M. Lawrence, P. Holzmann, M. O'Donnell, L. Adams, J. Holt, and A. Duffield. 2008. *The Practitioners' Guide to the Household Economy Approach*. London: The Food Economy Group, Regional Hunger and Vulnerability Program, Save the Children.

Callon, M. 1986. "Some Elements of a Sociology of Translation: Domestication of the Scallops and the Fishermen of St Brieuc Bay." In *Power, Action and Belief: A New Sociology of Knowledge?*, edited by J. Law, 196–233. London: Routledge.

Callon, M., Y. Barthe, and P. Lascoumes. 2014. *Agir dans un monde incertain: Essai sur la démocratie technique*. Paris: Seuil.

Callon, M., and B. Latour. 1981. "Unscrewing the Big Leviathan: How Actors Macro-Structure Reality and How Sociologists Help Them to Do So." In *Advances in Social Theory and Methodology: Toward an Integration of Micro- and Macro-Sociologies*, edited by K. Knorr Cetina and A. V. Cicourel, 277–303. London: Routledge and Kegan Paul.

CALP. 2018. "The State of the World's Cash Report: Cash Transfer Programming in Humanitarian Aid." The Cash Learning Partnership.

Caroll, C., M. Patterson, S. Wood, A. Booth, J. Rick and S. Balain. 2007. "A Conceptual Framework for Implementation Fidelity." *Implementation Science* 2: 40.

Castaneda, T. 2005. *Targeting Social Spending to the Poor with Proxy-Means Testing: Columbia SISBEN Systems*. Washington, DC: World Bank.

Chalfin, B. 2010. *Neo-liberal Frontiers: An Ethnography of Sovereignty in West Africa*. Chicago, IL: The University of Chicago Press.

Chen, H. 1990. *Theory-Driven Evaluation*. Newbury Park, CA: Sage Publications.

Coady, D., M. Grosh, and D. Hoddinott. 2004. *Targeting of Transfers in Developing Countries: Review of Lessons and Experiences*. Washington, DC: World Bank.

Cohen, M., J. March, and J. P. Olsen. 1972. "A Garbage Can Model of Organisational Choice." *Administrative Science Quarterly* 17:1–15.

Comaroff, J., and J. Comaroff, eds. 2006. *Law and Order in the Postcolony*. Chicago, IL: University of Chicago Press.

Cooke, B., and U. Kothari, eds. 2001. *Participation: The New Tyranny?* New York: Zed Books.

Courtin, C. 2011. "Les programmes de l'Union européenne vers les sociétés civiles africaines. Idéologie de la transparence et hyperprocéduralité." *Revue Tiers Monde* 205: 117–134.

Crewe, E., and R. Axelby. 2013. *Anthropology and Development: Culture, Morality and Politics in a Globalized World*. Cambridge: Cambridge University Press.

Czarniawska, B., and B. Joerges. 1996. "Travels of Ideas." In *Translating Organisational Change*, edited by B. Czarniawaska and G. Sevón, 13–48. Berlin: Walter de Gruyter.

Dalkin, S., J. Greenhalgh, D. Jones, B. Cunningham and M. Lhussier. 2015. "What's in a Mechanism? Development of a Key Concept in Realist Evaluation." *Implementation Science* 10: 49.

Darbon, D. 2009. "Modèles et transferts institutionnels vus des Afriques: les nouveaux villages Potemkine de la modernité?" In *La politique des modèles en Afrique: Simulation, dépolitisation et appropriation*, edited by D. Darbon, 245–283. Paris: Karthala.

Debonneville, J., and P. Diaz. 2013. "Les processus de transferts de politiques publiques et les nouvelles techniques de gouvernance: Le rôle de la Banque mondiale dans l'adoption des programmes de conditional cash transfers aux Philippines." *Revue Tiers Monde* 216: 161–178.

De Herdt, T., and J.-P. Olivier de Sardan, eds. 2015. *Real Governance and Practical Norms in Sub-Saharan Africa: The Game of the Rules*. London: Routledge.

Del Ninno, C., and B. Mills, eds. 2015. *Safety Nets in Africa: Effective Mechanisms to Reach the Poor and Most Vulnerable*. Washington, DC: World Bank.

Devereux, S. 2006. "Cash Transfers and Social Protection." Paper prepared for the regional workshop on Cash Transfer Activities in Southern Africa. Southern African Regional Poverty Network (SARPN), Regional Hunger and Vulnerability Programme (RHVP), and Oxfam GB, Johannesburg.

Devereux, S., and M. Getu (eds). 2013. *Informal and Formal Social Protection Systems in Sub-Saharan Africa*. Kampala: Fountain Publishers.

Devereux, S., E. Masset, R. Sabates-Wheeler, M. Samson, D. Lintelo and M.A. Rivas. 2015. "Evaluating the Targeting Effectiveness of Social Transfers: A Literature Review." Institute of Development Studies Working Paper 460. Brighton: IDS.

Devereux, S., and K. Tibbo. 2013. "Social Protection for Pastoralists." In *Pastoralism and Development in Africa: Dynamic Changes at the Margins*, edited by A. Catley, J. Scoones, and J. Lind, 215–230. London: Routledge.

Diaz, P. 2017. "Itinéraire d'une 'bonne pratique': La Banque mondiale et les conditional cash transfers en Amérique latine et aux Philippines." *Critique Internationale* 75: 113–132.

Di Blasi, Z., E. Harkness, E. Ernst, A. Georgiou, and J. Kleijnen. 2001. "Influence of Context Effects on Health Outcomes: A Systematic Review." *The Lancet* 357(9258): 757–762.

DiMaggio, P., and W. W. Powell. 1983. "The Iron Cage Revisited: Collective Rationality and Institutional Isomorphism in Organizational Fields." *American Sociological Review* 48(2): 147–160.

Dolowitz, D. P., and D. Marsh. 1996. "Who Learns What from Whom? A Review of the Policy Transfer Literature." *Political Studies* 44: 343–357.

———. 2000. "Learning from Abroad: The Role of Policy Transfer in Contemporary Policy-Making." *Governance: An International Journal of Policy and Administration* 13(1): 5–24.

Dopson, S., L. Locock, J. Gabbay, E. Ferlie, and L. Fitzgerald. 2003. "Evidence-Based Medicine and the Implementation Gap." *Health* 7(3): 311–330.

Dozon, J.-P., and D. Fassin, eds. 2001. *Critique de la santé publique: Une approche anthropologique*. Paris: Balland.

Drèze, J. 2011. "The Cash Mantra." *Indian Express*, 11 May 2011.

Drèze, J., and A. Sen. 2012. "Putting Growth in Its Place." *Yojana* 56: 36

Druetz, T., S. Zongo, and V. Ridde. 2015. "Le retour de la conception biomédicale du paludisme dans les institutions internationals." *Mondes en Développement* 2: 41–58.

Easterly, W. 2006. *The White Man's Burden: Why the West's Efforts to Aid the Rest Have Done So Much Ill and So Little Good*. New York: Penguin.

Eco, U., with R. Rorty, J. Culler, and C. Brook-Rose. 1990. *The Limits of Interpretation*. Bloomington, IN: Indiana University Press.

Elster, J. 1989. *Nuts and Bolts for the Social Sciences*. Cambridge: Cambridge University Press.

Elwert, G., and T. Bierschenk. 1988. "Development Aid as an Intervention in Dynamic Systems: An Introduction." *Sociologia Ruralis* 28(2–3): 99–112.

Englund, H. 2006. *Prisoners of Freedom: Human Rights and the African Poor.* Berkeley, CA: University of California Press.

Escobar, A. 1995. *Encountering Development: The Making and Unmaking of the Third World.* Princeton, NJ: Princeton University Press.

Farrington, J., and R. Slater. 2006. "Introduction. Cash transfers: Panacea for Poverty Reduction or Money down the Drain?" *Development Policy Review* 24(5): 499–511.

Fassin, D., and A. C. Defossez. 1992. "Une liaison dangereuse: sciences sociales et santé publique dans les programmes de réduction de la mortalité maternelle en Equateur." *Cahiers des Sciences Humaines* 28: 23–36.

Ferguson, J. 2015. *Give a Man a Fish: Reflections on the New Politics of Distribution.* Durham, NC: Duke University Press.

Fisette, J., and M. Raffinot, eds. 2010. *Gouvernance et appropriation locale: au-delà des modèles importés.* Ottawa: University of Ottawa Press.

Fisher, E., R. Attah, V. Barca, C. O'Brien, S. Brook, J. Holland., and P. Pozarny. 2017. "The Livelihood Impacts of Cash Transfers in Sub-Saharan Africa: Beneficiary Perspectives from Six Countries." *World Development* 99: 299–319.

Fiszbein, A., N. Schady, F. Ferreira, M. Grosh, N. Keleher, P. Olintro, and E. Skoufias. 2009. *Conditional Cash Transfers: Reducing Present and Future Poverty.* Washington, DC: World Bank.

Fixsen, D. L., S. F. Naoom, K. A. Blase, R. M. Friedman, and F. Wallace. 2005. *Implementation Research: A Synthesis of the Literature.* FMHI Publication #231. Tampa: University of South Florida; The National Implementation Research Network.

Fox, S., S. Witter, E. Wylde, E. Mafuta, and T. Lievens. 2013. "Paying Health Workers for Performance in a Fragmented, Fragile State: Reflections from Katanga Province, Democratic Republic of Congo." *Health Policy and Planning* 29(1): 99–105.

Freeman, R. 2009. "What is Translation?" *Evidence and Policy* 5: 429–447.

Galvani, F. 2017. "Bridging the Implementation Gap in Poor Areas: A Study of How Municipal Socio-economic Characteristics Impact Intergovernmental Policy Implementation." *Social Policy & Administration* 52(1): 408–434.

Gardner, K., and D. Lewis. 2015. *Anthropology, Development and Twenty-First Century Challenges.* London: Pluto Press.

Gasper, D. 2000. "Evaluating the Logical Framework Approach towards Learning Oriented Development Evaluation." *Public Administration and Development* 20(1): 17–28.

Geertz, C. 1973. *The Interpretation of Cultures.* New York: Basic Books.

Gérard-Varet, L. A., and J. C. Passeron, eds. 1995. *Le modèle et l'enquête: Les usages du principe de rationalité dans sciences sociales.* Paris: Editions de l'EHESS.

Gerring, J. 2007. "The Mechanistic World View: Thinking Inside the Box." *British Journal of Political Science* 38(1): 161–179.

Giddens, A. 1984. *The Constitution of Society: An Outline of the Theory of Structuration.* Cambridge: Polity Press.

Gil-Garcia, O. 2016. "Gender Equality, Community Divisions, and Autonomy: The Prospera Conditional Cash Transfer Program in Chiapas, Mexico." *Current Sociology* 64(3): 447–469.

Giovalucci, F., and J.-P. Olivier de Sardan. 2009. "Planification, gestion et politique dans l'aide au développement: le cadre logique, outil et miroir des développeurs." *Revue Tiers Monde* 198: 383–406.

Grosh, M., and J. L. Baker. 1995. "Proxy Means Tests for Targeting Social Programs." World Bank: Living Standards Measurement Study Working Paper 118, 1–49.

Haller, T., G. Acciaioli, and S. Rist. 2015. "Constitutionality: Conditions for Crafting Local Ownership of Institution-Building Processes." *Society & Natural Resources* 29(1): 68–87.

Halpern, C., P. Lascoumes, and P. Le Gales. 2014. *L'Instrumentation de l'action publique: Controverses, résistance, effets.* Paris: Presses de Sciences Po.

Hamani, O. 2013. "Les Pratiques Familiales Essentielles (PFE) au Niger: Socio-anthropologie d'une intervention à base communautaire." *Etudes et Travaux du LASDEL* 104.

Handa, S., C. Huang, N. Hypher, C. Teixeira, F. V. Soares, and B. Davis. 2012. "Targeting Effectiveness of Social Cash Transfer Programmes in Three African Countries." *Journal of Development Effectiveness* 4(1): 78–108.

Hanlon, J., A. Barrientos, and D. Hulme. 2010. *Just Give Money to the Poor: The Development Revolution from the Global South.* Sterling: Kumarian Press.

Harvey, P., and S. Bailey. 2011. *Cash Transfer Programming in Emergencies: Review of Good Practices.* London: Humanitarian Practice Network, ODI.

Hassenteufel, P., and A. Smith. 2002. "Essouflement ou second souffle? L'analyse des politiques publiques 'à la française.'" *Revue Française de Science Politique* 52(1): 53–73.

Hedström, P., and R. Swedberg. 1996. "Social Mechanisms." *Acta Sociologica* 39: 281–308.

———, eds. 1998. *Social Mechanisms: An Analytical Approach to Social Theory.* Cambridge: Cambridge University Press.

Hibou, B. 1998. "Economie politique du discours de la Banque Mondiale en Afrique sub-saharienne: Du catéchisme économique au fait (et méfait) missionnaire." *Les Etudes du CERI* 39.

———. 2012. *La bureaucratisation du monde à l'ère néo-libérale.* Paris: La Découverte.

Hilgers, M. 2012. "The Historicity of the Neoliberal State." *Social Anthropology* 20: 80–94.

Hirschmann, A. 1967. *Development Projects Observed.* Washington, DC: The Brooking Institution.

James, O., and M. Lodge. 2003. "The Limitations of 'Policy Transfer' and 'Lesson Drawing' for Public Policy Research." *Political Studies Review* 1(2): 179–193.

Jatteau, A. 2013. *Les expérimentations aléatoires en économie.* Paris: La Découverte.

Jenson, J., and N. Nagels. 2018. "Social Policy Instruments in Motion: Conditional Cash Transfers from Mexico to Peru." *Social Policy & Administration,* 52(1) ; 323–342.

Kadio, K., V. Ridde, and S. O. Mallé. 2014. "Les difficultés d'accès aux soins de santé des indigents vivant dans des ménages non pauvres." *Santé Publique* 26: 148.

Kaplan, H. C., et al. 2010. "The Influence of Context on Quality Improvement Success in Health Care: A Systematic Review of the Literature." *Milbank Quarterly* 88(4): 500–559 (doi: 10.1111/j).

Kidd, S. 2009. "Equal Pensions, Equal Rights: Achieving Universal Pension Coverage for Older Women and Men in Developing Countries." *Gender & Development* 17(3): 377–388.

Kingdon, J. 1995. *Agendas, Alternatives and Public Policies*. New York: Harper Collins.

Kundid, L. 2005. "Le programme Bolsa Escola à Belo Horizonte." *Socio-Anthropologie* 16. Accessed 23 April 2018. http://socio-anthropologie.revues.org/437.

Lacouture, A., E. Breton, A. Guichard, and V. Ridde. 2015. "The Concept of Mechanism from a Realist Approach: A Scoping Review to Facilitate Its Operationalization in Public Health Program Evaluation." *Implementation Science* 10(1): 153.

Lascoumes, P. 2004. "Traduction." In *Dictionnaire des politiques publiques*, edited by L. Boussaguet, S. Jacquot, P. Jacquot, and P. Ravinet, 437–444. Paris: Presses de Sciences Po.

Lascoumes, P., and P. Le Galès, P. 2007a. "Introduction: Understanding Public Policy through Its Instruments. From the Nature of Instruments to the Sociology of Public Policy Instrumentation." *Governance: An International Journal of Policy, Administration and Institutions* 20: 1–21.

———. 2007b. *Sociologie de l'action publique*. Paris: Armand Colin.

Latour, B. 1983. "Comment redistribuer le grand partage?" *Revue de Synthèse* 110: 203–236.

———. 1986. "The Powers of Association." In *Power, Action and Belief*, edited by J. Law. London: Routledge and Kegan Paul.

———. 1989. *La science en action*. Paris: La Découverte.

———. 1996. "Lettre à mon ami Pierre sur l'anthropologie symétrique." *Ethnologie Française* 26(1): 32–37.

———. 2006. "Les 'vues de l'esprit': Une introduction à l'anthropologie des sciences et des techniques." In *Sociologie de la traduction: Textes fondateurs*, edited by M. Akrich, M. Callon, and B. Latour, 33–70. Paris: Presses des Mines.

Lavigne Delville, P. 2011. "Une anthropologie symétrique entre 'développeurs' et 'développés.'" *Cahiers d'Etudes Africaines* 202–203: 491–509.

———. 2012a. "L'anthropologie a-t-elle été utile à l'institution de microfinance Mahavotse? Mobilisation des sciences sociales et conduite de projet au Sud de Madagascar: un art du possible." *Coopérer Aujourd'hui* 76 (GRET). Accessed 9 May 2018. https://www.microfinancegateway.org/sites/default/files/mfg-fr-etudes-de-cas-anthropologie-imf-mahavotse-madagascar-05-2012-cooperer.pdf.

———. 2012b. "Affronter l'incertitude? Les projets de développement à contre-courant de la révolution du 'management de projets.'" *Revue Tiers Monde* 211: 153–168.

———. 2016. "Pour une socio-anthropologie de l'action publique dans les pays sous régime d'aide." *Anthropologie et Développement* 45: 33–64.

Le Meur, P. Y. 2011. *Anthropologie politique de la gouvernance: Acteurs, ressources, dispositifs*. Sarrebruck: Editions Universitaires Européennes.

Leite, C., U. Peres, and L. Bellix. 2012. "Cash Transfer Programs and the Multilateral Organizations: The Dissemination of Policies in Brazil, Chile, and

Mexico." Paper for the 22nd World Congress of Political Science. Madrid, Spain.

Lemieux, V. 2002. *L'étude des politiques publiques, les acteurs et leur pouvoir.* Québec: Les Presses de l'Université Laval.

Levitt, P., and S. Merry. 2009. "Vernacularization on the Ground: Local Uses of Global Women's Rights in Peru, China, India and the United States." *Global Networks* 9(4): 441–461.

Lewis, O. 1969. *La vida: Une famille porto-ricaine dans une culture de pauvreté.* Paris: Gallimard.

Li, T. M. 2007. *The Will to Improve: Governmentality, Development, and the Practice of Politics.* Durham, NC: Duke University Press.

Lillrank, P. 1995. "The Transfer of Management Innovations from Japan." *Organization Studies* 16(6): 971–989.

Long, N. 1992. "From Paradigm Lost to Paradigm Regained? The Case for an Actor-Oriented Sociology of Development." In *Battlefields of Knowledge: The Interlocking of Theory and Practice in Social Research and Development,* edited by N. Long and A. Long. London: Routledge.

———, ed. 1989. *Encounters at the Interface: A Perspective on Social Discontinuities in Rural Development.* Wageningen: Agricultural University.

MacDonald, M., et al. 2016. "Supporting Successful Implementation of Public Health Interventions: Protocol for a Realist Synthesis." *Systematic Reviews* 5: 54.

Mahoney, J., and K. Thelen. 2010. *Explaining Institutional Change: Ambiguity, Agency and Power.* Cambridge: Cambridge University Press.

Marchal, B., et al. 2012. "Is Realist Evaluation Keeping Its Promise? A Review of Published Empirical Studies in the Field of Health Systems Research." *Evaluation* 1(2): 192–212.

Marchal, B., et al. 2013. "Methodological Reflections on Using Realist Evaluation in a Study of Fee Exemption Policies in West Africa and Morocco." FEM Health, University of Aberdeen.

McCormack, B., A. Kitson, G. Harvey, J. Rycroft-Malone, A. Titchen, and K. Seers. 2002. "Getting Evidence into Practice: The Meaning of 'Context.'" *Journal of Advanced Nursing* 38(1): 94–104.

McCourt, W., and M. Minogue, eds. 2001. *The Internationalization of Public Management: Reinventing the Third World.* Northampton: Edward Elgar.

Michaud, Y., ed. 2002. *L'histoire, la sociologie et l'anthropologie.* Paris: Odile Jacob.

Ministère de la Santé. 2015. "Guide de mise en œuvre du financement basé sur les résultats dans le secteur de la santé." Ouagadougou: Burkina Faso.

Monchuk, V. 2014. *Reducing Poverty and Investing in People: The New Role of Safety Nets in Africa.* Washington, DC: World Bank.

Morestin, F., P. Grant, and V. Ridde. 2009. *Les critères et les processus d'identification des pauvres en tant que bénéficiaires de programmes dans les pays en développement.* Montréal: Université de Montréal.

Mosse D. 1996. "The Ideology and Politics of Community Participation: Tank Irrigation Development in Colonial and Contemporary Tamil Nadu." In *Discourses of Development: Anthropological Perspectives,* edited by R. Grillo and L. Stirrat, 255–291. Oxford: Berg.

———. 2005. *Cultivating Development: An Ethnography of Aid Policy and Practice.* London: Pluto Press.

———, ed. 2011. *Adventures in Aidland: The Anthropology of Professionals in International Development.* Oxford: Berghahn Books.

Mosse, D., and D. Lewis. 2006. "Theoretical Approaches to Brokerage and Translation in Development." In *Development Brokers and Translators: The Ethnography of Aid and Agencies,* edited by D. Mosse and D. Lewis, 1–26. Bloomfield, CT: Kumarian.

Muller, P. 2000. "L'analyse cognitive des politiques publiques: vers une sociologie politique de l'action publique." *Revue Française de Science Politique* 50(2): 189–207.

Mumtaz, Z., A. Levay, A. Bhatti, and S. Salway. 2015. "Good on Paper: The Gap between Programme Theory and Real World Context in Pakistan's Community Midwife Programme." *BJOG: An International Journal of Obstetrics & Gynaecology* 122(2): 249–258.

Nader, L. 1974. "Up the Anthropologist: Perspectives Gained from Studying Up." In *Reinventing Anthropology,* ed. D. H. Hymes, 284–311. New York: Vintage.

Naudet, J. D. 1999. *Trouver des problèmes aux solutions: 20 ans d'aide au Sahel.* Paris: OCDE.

Nelson, N., and S. Wright, eds. 1995. *Power and Participatory Development: Theory and Practice.* London: Intermediate Technology Publications.

O'Brien, C., C. Cherrier, C. Watson, and J. Congrave. 2017. "Shock-Responsive Social Protection Systems Research. Case study: Regional Approaches to Addressing Food Insecurity in the Sahel and the Contribution of Social Protection." Oxford: Oxford Policy Management.

Olivier de Sardan, J.-P. 1988. "Peasant Logics and Development Projects Logics." *Sociologia Ruralis* 28(2–3): 216–226.

———. 1995. *Anthropologie et développement: Essai en socio-anthropologie du changement social.* Paris: Karthala.

———. 2005. *Anthropology and Development: Understanding Contemporary Social Change.* London: Zed Books.

———. 2009a. "State Bureaucracy and Governance in West Francophone Africa: Empirical Diagnosis, Historical Perspective." In *The Governance of Daily Life in Africa: Ethnographic Explorations of Public and Collective Service,* edited by G. Blundo and P.-Y. Le Meur, 39–71. Leiden: Brill.

———. 2009b. "Development, Governance and Reforms: Studying Practical Norms in the Delivery of Public Goods and Service." In *Ethnographic Practice and Public Aid: Methods and Meanings in Development Cooperation,* edited by S. Hagberg and W. Widmark, 101–23. Uppsala Studies in Cultural Anthropology 45. Uppsala: Acta Universitatis Upsaliensis.

———. 2011a. "Aide humanitaire ou aide au développement? La 'famine' de 2005 au Niger." *Ethnologie Française* 41(3): 415–429.

———. 2011b. "'Compte-rendu de l'ouvrage de B. Chalfin': Neoliberal Frontiers. An Ethnography of Sovereignty in West Africa, Chicago, Chicago University Press." *Politique Africaine* 123: 141–146.

———. 2013. "The Bureaucratic Mode of Governance and Practical Norms in West Africa and beyond." In *Local Politics and Contemporary Transformations in the*

Arab World: Governance beyond the Center, edited by M. Bouziane, C. Harders, and A. Hoffmann, 43–64. Basingstoke: Palgrave Macmillan.

——. 2014. "La manne, les normes et les soupçons: Les contradictions de l'aide vue d'en-bas." *Revue Tiers Monde* 219: 197–215.

——. 2015a. "Africanist Traditionalist Culturalism: Analysis of a Scientific Ideology and a Plea for an Empirically Grounded Concept of Culture Encompassing Practical Norms." In *Real Governance and Practical Norms in Sub-Saharan Africa: The Game of the Rules*, edited by T. De Herdt and J.-P. Olivier de Sardan, 63–94. London: Routledge.

——. 2015b. *Epistemology, Fieldwork and Anthropology*. Trans. A. Tidjani Alou. Basingstoke: Palgrave.

——. 2015c. "Health Fee Exemptions: Controversies and Misunderstandings around a Research Programme. Researchers and the Public Debate." *BMC Health Service Research* 15 (Suppl. 3).

——. 2015d. "Practical Norms: Informal Regulations within Public Bureaucracies (in Africa and Beyond)." In *Real Governance and Practical Norms in Sub-Saharan Africa: The Game of the Rules*, edited by T. De Herdt and J.-P. Olivier de Sardan, 19–62. London: Routledge.

——. 2016. "For an Anthropology of Gaps, Discrepancies and Contradictions." *Antropologia* 3(1): 111–131.

——. 2017. "Les enjeux scientifiques et citoyens d'une anthropologie des politiques publiques." *Antropologia Pubblica* 1(1–2): 7–22.

Olivier de Sardan, J.-P., A. Diarra, F. Y. Koné, M. Yaogo, and R. Zerbo. 2015. "Local Sustainability and Scaling up for User Fee Exemptions: Medical NGOs vis-à-vis Health Systems." *BMC Health Service Research* 15 (Suppl. 3).

Olivier de Sardan, J.-P., A. Diarra, and M. Moha. 2017. "Travelling Models and the Challenge of Pragmatic Contexts and Practical Norms: The Case of Maternal Health." *Health Research Policy and Systems* 15 (Suppl. 1): 60 (doi: 10.1186/s12961-017-0213-9).

Olivier de Sardan, J.-P., O. Hamani, N. Issaley, Y. Issa, H. Adamou, and I. Oumarou. 2014. "Les transferts monétaires au Niger: le grand malentendu." *Revue Tiers Monde* 218: 107–130.

Olivier de Sardan, J.-P. and Ridde, V. 2015. "Diagnosis of a Public Policy: An Introduction to User Fee Exemptions for Healthcare in the Sahel." *BMC Health Service Research* 15 (Suppl. 3).

——, eds. 2014. *Une politique publique de santé et ses contradictions: La gratuité des soins au Burkina Faso, au Mali et au Niger*. Paris: Karthala.

Oxford Policy Management. 2015a. "DFID Shock-Responsive Social Protection Systems Research." Literature review. Oxford: Oxford Policy Management.

——. 2015b. "DFID Shock-Responsive Social Protection Systems Research." Inception report. Oxford: Oxford Policy Management.

Passeron, J. C. 2006. *Le raisonnement sociologique: Un espace non-poppérien de l'argumentation*. Paris: Albin Michel.

Paul, E., N. Sossouhounto, and D. Eclou. 2014. "Local Stakeholders' Perceptions about the Introduction of Performance-Based Financing in Benin: A Case Study in Two Health Districts." *International Journal of Health Policy Management* 3(4): 207–214.

Pavignani, E., and S. Colombo. 2009. *Analysing Disrupted Health Sectors: A Modular Manual*. Geneva: WHO.

Pawson, R., and N. Tilley. 1997. *Realistic Evaluation*. London: Sage.

Pérez, D., P. Van de Stuyft, M. Del Carmen Zabala, M. Castro, and P. Lefevre. 2016. "A Modified Theoretical Framework to Assess Implementation Fidelity of Adaptive Public Health Interventions." *Implementation Science* 11: 91.

Persson, A, B. Rothstein, and J. Teorell. 2013. "Why Anticorruption Reforms Fail: Systemic Corruption as a Collective Action Problem." *Governance* 26(3): 449–471.

Pfadenhauer, L. M., K. Mozygemba, A. Gerhardus, B. Hofmann, A. Booth, K. B. Lysdahl, and E. A. Rehfuess. 2015. "Context and Implementation: A Concept Analysis towards Conceptual Maturity." *Zeitschrift für Evidenz, Fortbildung und Qu lität im Gesundheitswesen* 109(2): 103–114.

Piccoli, E. 2014. "'Dicen que los cien soles son del Diablo': L'interprétation apocalyptique et mythique du Programa Juntos dans les communautés andines de Cajamarca (Pérou) et la critique populaire des programmes sociaux." *Social Compass* 61(3): 328–347.

Poulantzas, N. 1973. *Political Power and Social Classes*. London: New Left Books.

Premand, P. 2016. Tranferts monétaires, mesures d'accompagnement du volet comportemenatal et investissements dans le capital humain: Résultats préliminaires de l'évaluation d'impact du projet filets sociaux au Niger. Washington, DC: Banque Mondiale.

Pritchett, L., M. Woolcock, and M. Andrews. 2012? "Looking Like a State: Techniques of Persistent Failures in State Capability for Implementation." Harvard University: Center for International Development, Working Paper 239.

Radjou, N., J. Prabhu, and S. Ahuja. 2013. *L'innovation jugaad: Redevenons ingénieux!* N.p.: Les Editions Diateno.

Ravallion, M. 2009. "Evaluation in the Practice of Development." *The World Bank Research Observer* 24(1): 29–53.

Reddy, S. 2012. "'Randomise this'! On Poor Economics." *Review of Agrarian Studies* 2(2): 60–73.

Ribot, J. 2002. *Democratic Decentralization of Natural Resources: Institutionalizing Popular Participation*. Washington, DC: World Resources Institute.

Ridde, V. 2015 "From Institutionalization of User Fees to Their Abolition in West Africa: A Story of Pilot Projects and Public Policies." *BMC Health Service Research* 15 (Suppl. 3).

———. 2016. "Need for More and Better Implementation Science in Global Health." *BMJ Global Health* 1(2).

Ridde, V., and J.-P. Jacob, eds. 2013. *Les indigents et les politiques de santé en Afrique: expériences et enjeux conceptuels*. Louvaine-la-Neuve: Academia-L'Harmattan.

Ridde, V., and J.-P. Olivier de Sardan. 2015. "A Mixed Methods Contribution to the Study of Health Public Policies: Complementarities and Difficulties." *BMC Health Service Research* 15 (Suppl. 3).

Ridde V., E. Robert, A. Guichard, P. Blaise, and J. Van Olmen. 2012. "L'approche Realist à l'épreuve du réel de l'évaluation des programmes." *Revue Canadienne d'Evaluation des Programmes* 26(3): 14.

Ridde, V., M. Yaogo, S. Zongo, P. A. Somé, and A.-M. Turcotte-Tremblay. 2017. "Twelve Months of Implementation of Health Care Performance-Based Financing in Burkina Faso: A Qualitative Multiple Case Study." *The International Journal for Health Planning and Management* 1: 15.

Robinson, M. S. 2001. *The Microfinance Revolution: Sustainable Finance for the Poor.* Washington, DC: World Bank Publications.

Rocha, S. 2014. *Allocations Sociales et Pauvreté au Brésil: Le bon combat?* Paris: Éditions de la Maison des Sciences de l'Homme.

Rodrik, D. 2008. "The New Development Economics: We Shall Experiment, But How Shall We Learn?" Social Science Research Network Scholarly Paper.

Rose, R. 1991. "What Is Lesson-drawing?" *Journal of Public Policy* 1(1): 3–30.

———. 1993. *Lesson-Drawing in Public Policy: A Guide to Learning across Time and Space.* Chatham: Chatham House.

Rottenburg, R. 2007. *Far-Fetched Facts: A Parable of Development Aid.* Cambridge, MA: MIT Press.

Sabates-Wheeler, R., J. Lind, and J. Hoddinott. 2013. "Implementing Social Protection in Agro-pastoralist and Pastoralist Areas: How Local Distribution Structures Moderate PSNP Outcome in Ethiopia." *World Development* 50: 1–12.

Sabatier, P., ed. 1992. *Theories of the Policy Process: Theoretical Lenses on Public Policy.* Boulder, CO: Westview Press.

Saetren, H. 2005. "Facts and Myths about Research on Public Policy Implementation: Out-of-Fashion, Allegedly Dead, But Still Very Much Alive and Relevant." *The Policy Studies Journal* 33(4): 559–582.

Sandefur, J., and A. Glassman. 2014. "The Political Economy of Bad Data: Evidence from African Survey & Administrative Statistics." Washington. Center for Global Development, Working Paper 373: 1-28.

Sayer, A. 2000. *Realism and Social Science.* London: Sage.

Seaman, J., P. Clarke, T. Boudreau, and J. Holt. 2000. *The Household Economy Approach: A Resource Manual for Practitioners.* Save the Children Development Manual 6. London: Save the Children Fund.

Sen, A. 1995. "The Political Economy of Targeting." In *Public Spending and the Poor: Theory and Evidence*, edited by D. Van de Walle and K. Nead, 11–24. Baltimore, MD: Johns Hopkins University Press.

Seppey M., V. Ridde, L. Touré, and A. Coulibaly. 2017. "Donor-Funded Project's Sustainability Assessment: A Qualitative Case Study of a Results-Based Financing Pilot in Koulikoro Region, Mali." *Globalization and Health* 13: 86.

Skoufias, E. 2001. *PROGRESA and Its Impacts on the Human Capital and Welfare of Households in Rural Mexico: A Synthesis of the Results of an Evaluation by IFPRI.* Washington, DC: International Food Policy Research Institute.

Soares, F. V. 2011. "Brazil's Bolsa Família: A Review." *Economic and Political Weekly* 21: 55–60.

Soeters, R., C. Habineza, and P. B. Peerenboom. 2006. "Performance-Based Financing and Changing the District Health System: Experience from Rwanda." *Bulletin of the World Health Organization* 84(11): 884–889.

Stone, D. 2012. "Transfer and Translation of Policy." *Policy Studies Journal* 33: 1–17.

Sugiyama, N. 2011. "The Diffusion of Conditional Cash Transfer Programs in the Americas." *Global Social Policy* 11(2–3): 250–278.

Swidler, A., and S. Watkins. 2009. "'Teach a Man to Fish': The Sustainability Doctrine and Its Social Consequences." *World Development* 37(7): 1182–1196.

Tamiru, K. 2013. *What Is the Role of Informal Safety Nets in Africa for Social Protection Policy?* Washington, DC: World Bank.

Teichman, J. 2007. "Multilateral Lending Institutions and Transnational Policy Networks in Mexico and Chile." *Global Governance* 13: 557–573.

Timmermans, S., and M. Berg. 1997a. "Standardization in Action: Achieving Local Universality through Medical Protocols." *Social Studies in Science* 27: 273–305.

———. 1997b. *The Gold Standard: The Challenge of Evidence-Based Medicine and Standardization in Health Care.* Philadelphia, PA: Temple University Press.

Tomazini, C. 2013. "Les conflits autour des politiques de transferts monétaires: les coalitions de causes et le renforcement du paradigme 'capital humain' au Brésil et au Mexique." In *L'analyse des politiques publiques au Brésil*, edited by C. Tomazini and M. Rocha Lukic, 123–153. Paris: L'Harmattan.

Turcotte-Tremblay, A.-M., J. Spagnolo, M. De Allegri, and V. Ridde. 2016. "Does Performance-Based Financing Increase Value for Money in Low- and Middle-Income Countries? A Systematic Review." *Health Economics Review* 6(1): 30.

Turcotte-Tremblay, A.-M., I. Ali Gali-Gali, M. De Allegri, and V. Ridde. 2017. "The Unintended Consequences of Community Verifications for Performance-Based Financing in Burkina Faso." *Social Science and Medicine* 191: 226–236.

Von Gliszczynski, M. 2015. *Cash Transfers and Basic Social Protection: Towards a Development Revolution?* Basingstoke: Palgrave Macmillan.

Watson, C. 2016. *Shock-Responsive Social Protection in the Sahel: Community Level Processes and Perspectives.* London: OPM.

Weiss, C. H. 1997. *Theory-Based Evaluation: Past, Present and Future. New Directions for Evaluation.* San Francisco, CA: Jossey-Bass.

———. 1998. *Evaluations: Methods for Studying Programs and Policies.* Englewood Cliffs, NJ: Prentice-Hall.

Weisser, F., M. Bollig, M. Doevenspeck, and D. Müller-Mahn. 2014. "Translating the 'Adaptation to Climate Change' Paradigm: The Politics of a Travelling Idea in Africa." *The Geographical Journal* 180(2): 111–119.

Weyland, K. 2004. *Learning from Foreign Models in Latin American Policy Reforms.* Baltimore, MD: Johns Hopkins University Press.

World Bank. 2015. "Economic Growth in the 1990s: Learning from a Decade of Reforms." Washington, DC: World Bank.

———. 2016. "Safety Nets How To: A Toolkit for Practitioners." Washington: World Bank.

Whyte, D., and J. Wiegratz, eds. 2016. *Neoliberalism and the Moral Economy of Fraud.* London: Routledge.

Zuodar, N. 2015. *Glossary of Cash Transfer Program Terminology.* Oxford: CaLP.

Chapter 2

Realizing Cash Transfer Programs through Collective Obligations
An Ethnography of Co-responsibility in Mexico

Alejandro Agudo Sanchíz

This chapter discusses the problem of how local power relations shape and are shaped by *co-responsibility*, of which antipoverty policy regimes have made use in specific ways. In line with the cost-sharing and efficiency-driven policies of the World Bank, related concepts like "comanagement" and "self-help" gained traction in the 1980s, when community participation became a means to promote self-sufficiency in development projects. Still premised on the idea that overcoming poverty is not only the government's task but "the whole society's" (Sedesol 2007: 4), the principle of co-responsibility has nonetheless been modified as states moved toward targeted assistance schemes. In conditional cash transfer programs (CCTs) like Mexico's Oportunidades, collective responsibility is devolved to individual households, whose members must discharge certain obligations in return for the entitlements offered by the program.

My aim is to focus on the gap between this contractual formalization of co-responsibility and the actual implementation of Oportunidades, but also to describe how that gap is actually bridged by the intervention of diverse actors, interests, and strategies that give social form to the program's rules and effects. Based on participant observation and interviews with service providers, frontline workers, promoters, and recipients in rural Chiapas (southern Mexico), the ethnography presented here locates the processes on which the promotion of "citizens' participation" is contingent. The operations of this abstract order in particular communities — many of them adjacent to the 1994 Zapatista uprising and exposed to

---

Notes for this chapter begin on page 110.

succeeding and contradictory policies—shows how old and new social roles are maintained and transformed. Apparent convergence with the co-responsibility regime depends on an existing logic of donation and indebtedness, which turns contractual entitlements back into collective duties conveying relationships of power and patronage.

In the first part of this chapter, I outline Oportunidades' aims, components, and assumptions through an overview of the policymaking process that culminated in the program's inception. The second part provides the background context for the reception of the program in rural Chiapas. In the third part, I use ethnographic evidence from my research as an anthropologist-consultant in the impact evaluations of Oportunidades to illustrate my argument about the collective reinterpretation of co-responsibility, showing how private improvements are recast in terms of the common good and community service. In order to have access to the resources of aid, formal principles must still be regularly sustained and disciplines exercised; in the fourth and final section, I focus on the role of particular intermediaries in following procedures, discussing how the position in which operational rules place them fosters a discretionary monitoring of responsibilities that may undermine program goals.

The Adoption of Conditional Transfers in Mexico: Some Domestic Determinants

With roots in the co-optation of the critical "participatory" approaches to development of the 1980s (Agudo Sanchíz 2015: 56–57), the ideology of comanagement was central to the Solidarity program (Pronasol) implemented in Mexico under the administration of President Carlos Salinas (1988–1994). Reduction of public spending was then hailed as a key strategy to obtain funds for efficient development schemes. These were based on the participation of local organizations and communities in anything ranging from maintenance of public works to the provision of labor and informally produced resources. Pronasol was part of a series of programs known as *social investment funds*, implemented in thirteen other Latin American countries and bankrolled by international institutions like the World Bank with the aim of offsetting the consequences of the structural adjustment years. However, this first generation of antipoverty programs was beset with partial coverage and coordination problems between central and local governments, leading to the rethinking that occurred in the design of CCTs (Roberts 2012: 348–351). Pronasol itself was discredited, as it served in practice to redirect scarce resources toward selective political co-optation (Gledhill 1995: 50).

Transparency and accountability initiatives were thus among the policy reforms that succeeding president Ernesto Zedillo, facing a credibility crisis, was compelled to take on after the Mexican peso devaluation of December 1994 and the subsequent collapse of the country's banking system. Zedillo's Cabinet for Social Development (CSD) appointed a working group to devise a new income-transfer program that, dispensing with local intermediation to avoid clientelism, would focus federal aid squarely on needy recipients. Unlike the Brazilian Bolsa Família program, in whose administration municipalities play an important part—albeit in terms of clear guidelines and templates provided by the central government—the new Mexican scheme was designed to make less use of community collaboration and to minimize reliance on local governments and NGOs (Roberts 2012: 353).

Despite coalescing around the consensus generated by the economic fallout, the policy experts and technocrats of the motley CSD group diverged over how to tackle the country's worsening problem of poverty. In the arena of the CSD team, the ultimate aim of officials at the Treasury Secretariat was to attract the rural population to the towns, where services were concentrated, in order to make public spending more efficient, as well as to "boost markets through consumer demand fuelled by cash transfers" (Cortés and Rubalcava 2012: 37). These orientations clashed with those of the economists at the Ministry of Social Development (Sedesol), who brought with them their previous experience in Pronasol and, in line with former president Carlos Salinas's "social liberalism," privileged a wider governmental role in social policy—although without reaching the generalized state intervention to which public health and education officials had been accustomed (Cortés and Rubalcava 2012: 43). To avoid controversies over reception of program stipends, the representatives of Sedesol sought to include all communities in the program; yet it was finally determined that eligible localities must have both schools and clinics or be located in their vicinity—thus excluding the smallest and usually most marginalized hamlets. Treasury officials, for whom cash transfers should have focused on individuals, had nonetheless to yield to the evidence provided by social scientists about the influence of domestic groups over their individual members' economic decisions. Targeting and conditionality thus constrained the range of policy options, but Cortés and Rubalcava (2012: 44) see the resulting scheme as a compromise between distinct orientations: rather than being an individual subsidy oriented to the demand for newly privatized goods and services, as it was originally entertained, cash transfers would exclusively compel households to use public education and healthcare facilities.

The Education, Health, and Nutrition Program (Progresa) was thus launched in 1997. Alongside Brazil's Bolsa Família—but unlike many other similar schemes implemented later in the region—Progresa had a wholly national origin and reflected a novel construction of poverty as a generalized, direct, and impersonal relationship between the state and the population (Roberts 2012: 345). Despite its interinstitutional nature, the program was to be run by a national coordination office that kept control over the "objective and impartial" identification, incorporation, and monitoring of recipient households (Sedesol 2007: 3–4). Geographical information systems analysis identified concentrations of poverty using census data. Teams of subcontracted interviewers went to poor localities to administer a basic questionnaire on socioeconomic characteristics to determine a household's level of poverty. The criteria for poverty were established through survey-derived formulas that converted the questionnaire information into an index of poverty.[1] Visits were subsequently made to houses to check on the validity of the questionnaire information.

Thus, bimonthly transfers went straight to mothers in rural households classified as "extreme poor," conditioned on their members' controlled attendance at health centers for regular checks and workshops on self-care, as well as children's schooling from primary to secondary education—and, since 2001, to the end of high school. Although households got a stipend for "food support" (around $15 [US] at the time of fieldwork in 2007–2008), as well as a nutritional supplement for pregnant and breastfeeding mothers and children under two years of age, the transfers they received were primarily in the form of scholarships for their children. Grants rose with the child's educational level and involved an element of gender sensitivity, since they were 10 percent higher for girls than for boys from the onset of secondary education, when the risk of female dropout is highest. Toward the end of 2007, a household with grantees in primary and secondary education could receive up to $100 (US) per month, with that figure increasing to about $170 (US) in households that also had students in high school (Sedesol 2007: 10–11).

Progresa thus had continuity after Zedillo's Institutional Revolutionary Party (PRI) lost the 2000 elections to the opposition National Action Party (PAN). The program was then renamed as Oportunidades and extended to cover urban areas, which increased the number of recipient households from 2.6 million (in 2000), the equivalent of 50 percent of all rural households (González de la Rocha and Escobar 2008: 133), to five million by 2005—all this on an annual budget amounting to 0.3 per cent of the GDP from federal funds (equivalent to 25 billion Mexican pesos in 2004), although with an eventual loan of $1 billion (US) from the Inter-American Development Bank (Molyneux 2006: 433). With an estimated twenty-five million beneficiaries in 2006, the program was said to reach a near universal coverage of the country's poor, whether urban or rural.[2]

Aside from the multiple studies demonstrating poverty effects for Progresa-Oportunidades (e.g., Escobar and González de la Rocha 2005; Fiszbein and Schady 2010), much has been written regarding the assumptions behind its policy model. Viewed as "active agents" capable of making choices to escape poverty, recipients are largely responsible for regulating themselves under the values, language, and resources provided by the program; it then becomes the poor's fault if they fail in their options to help themselves out of poverty (Luccisano 2003). The program's self-proclaimed gender awareness has also been problematized in view of its hardly imaginative "maternalist" approach to the capabilities of participating mothers, who must stay healthy with a view to their children's good health and administer stipends for their benefit (Molyneux 2006). Here the donor-driven concept of co-responsibility is linked not just to long-established constructions of women as means to the development of others (Nussbaum 2000: 5–6), but also to a particular representation of poor households as a policy *problem:* it is in them that "lie the factors tending to perpetuate the conditions of extreme poverty from generation to generation," as the program's own operational rules state (Sedesol 2007: 3). Blaming the poor is the flip side of the reformulation of aid relationships in the language of local co-responsibility in decision-making, which extends to program recipients the shift from "gift" to "contract" (Eyben with León 2005: 121) that, at a global level, characterizes the links between international financial institutions and national governments.

The actual existence of ideological affinities with notions of contract and entitlement is, of course, a different matter. If we find that diverse actors are not (completely) absorbed by the discipline and rationalities of co-responsibility, then we must also ask how Progresa-Oportunidades is realized at different levels. From Pronasol to the negotiating table of Zedillo's CSD group, the trajectory of co-responsibility in Mexico points to the importance of the domestic political and economic determinants of neoliberal reform. Global policy convergence is an after-the-fact conclusion, since the leverage of international financial institutions must be reworked according to the very national contexts that such institutions seek to deny (Mosse 2005b: 27–28, citing Schwegler 2003). Before advancing a similar argument on a smaller canvas, I need to situate my case against the background of Chiapas.

Progresa-Oportunidades in Rural Chiapas

By 2007, Oportunidades was regarded as a flagship program, and its long-term impact assessment in rural areas called for new methods and larger samples than those employed in previous evaluations. I then coordinated an ethnographic research team whose fieldwork stretched out over nine months (2007–2008) in mostly indigenous communities in north, central, and southeast Chiapas—in the municipalities of Tumbalá, San Cristóbal de Las Casas, and Las Margaritas, respectively. Interviews were conducted with corresponding numbers of recipient and nonrecipient households (around twenty in each case), finding, where possible, nonindigenous (Spanish-speaking) families also for the sake of contrast. Comparable studies were simultaneously conducted by other researchers in the states of Oaxaca, Chihuahua, and Sonora.[3]

Moving beyond a narrow focus on "poverty," defined in terms of static surveys conducted according to normative constructions of income lines, our approach to long-term vulnerability in changing contexts of threats and opportunities (González de la Rocha and Escobar 2008: 139–145) pointed to effects not preselected for in the program's model of impact. The propensity of qualitative evaluations to look at how communities view and receive the program, including the relations developing between beneficiaries and frontline workers and officials, also revealed unscripted practices through which diverse actors gave different meanings and contents to co-responsibilities. These findings made more sense after I became aware of several ethnographic studies that examined how global policy models are produced socially in specific contexts (Wood 1998; Mosse 2005a). In fact, development's actor-networks *make* their context by generating interests and *translating* policy goals into diverse people's own intentions and ambitions (Latour 1996: 86, 133, 142–143). Constructionist analyses have thus enriched earlier actor-oriented approaches (e.g., Long 1992) by challenging further the sort of determinism implied in the notion that programs are about direct implementation with real effects.

By the end of the evaluation, I had thus considered studying policy as a field of academic enquiry in itself, realizing that the anthropology *of* development was difficult to separate from the anthropology *for* development, as the results of qualitative assessments questioned policy models (Long 1992: 3). Like most of my colleagues in the evaluation team— medium-term anthropologist-consultants subcontracted by the same outside body in charge of the program's impact assessment—I held a permanent post at a Mexican academic institution and sought to bring my experience in development to bear on ongoing teaching and research interests. Operating at one remove from real responsibility for implementation and funding, I felt free enough to highlight "hidden" areas of development practice that are critical to understanding how interventions actually work in particular settings.

At the very least, I found that Progresa's rules for the identification of potential recipients were hard to apply when it was first implemented in Chiapas in 1997, as the region was riddled with political turmoil following the 1994 uprising of the Zapatista Army of National Liberation (EZLN). Particularly in northern Chiapas, where I conducted my Ph.D. field research between 2001 and 2004, there was widespread violence related to the conflict between Zapatista sympathizers and members of Paz y Justicia, a paramilitary group supported during the second half of the 1990s by the then ruling PRI party. Progresa frontline operators in such regions had to resort to a "special incorporation" to avoid worsening factionalism on the ground. This meant dispensing with the formal procedures for selection of recipients like surveys and door-to-door interviews. On my return to Chiapas in 2007, in charge of the research team for the program's long-term impact evaluation, I found that all households in some communities had been incorporated en masse to Progresa.

It is hard not to notice the irony of this measure, resorted to by a federal program with the aim of making up for the troubles partly created by the very government's illegal tactics. Alongside dirty war and repression — but also concessions to appease growing mobilization in the wake of the EZLN uprising — such procedures marked the uneven transformation of the Mexican state in Chiapas during the institutional crisis of the 1990s (Agudo Sanchíz 2008). Consistent with the dismantlement of the material and ideological foundations of the PRI regime's hegemonic nationalism by both Salinas and Zedillo, the socially exclusionary policies of that period were variously contested: the changes in policymaking and official discourse were thus not simply prompted by international pressures, but by local struggles showing the limits faced by the transformative project of "a complex and changing state [that] was able to negotiate separate paths among partly distinct and partly interrelated regions and arenas" (Rubin 1996: 98).

It was unfeasible for Progresa to achieve universal coverage in all troubled regions and communities across Chiapas — just as it had proven impossible for the government to use generalized force against popular organizations after 1994. Several spatially and temporally differentiated conflicts witnessed the eviction of would-be program recipients from their native communities, often because their religious and political affiliations challenged those of local authorities staunchly loyal to either Catholicism or the PRI party (when not both).

Yet when the political temperature dropped and resettlement was made possible, returnees found grounds for rejecting exposure to Oportunidades. This was the case of Chacalá, a hamlet founded by Protestant converts who had been driven out of the predominantly Catholic community of Saltillo, in the Maya Tojolabal region of southeast Chiapas. At the time of the evaluation in 2008, forty-three out of a total of sixty-nine households in Chacalá had been incorporated into Oportunidades, but only as late as 2005. A mother of eight children who still refused to participate in the program's surveys told researchers that many in the locality had seen the acceptance of government benefits as an act of "estrangement" from their religion, explaining that "one cannot have two patrons at the same time: it's got to be either God or the government, and I already have a commitment to God." Protestants were more likely to reject the program, although this is also a variable between contexts: in northern Chiapas, the PRI-leaning members of Paz y Justicia who embraced Progresa became close to evangelical churches, as their opponents opted for Catholicism. In ongoing conflicts over land and other resources, identifying oneself with a particular political or religious label may depend on what other available positions have already been appropriated by rivals.

In this kind of context, other cases of self-exclusion from the program stemmed from contrasting political identities related to Zapatismo, which had differential impacts in the Tojolabal area. The rural hamlets in the Las Cañadas subregion of the Lacandon jungle, to the east of Las Margaritas municipality, actively participated in the uprising as support base communities, and rejected any contact with the government. From the 1960s on, these settlements had been established by migrants from other places, like the western part of Las Margaritas itself, where the municipal head town is located, close to a group of indigenous communities created by postrevolutionary land redistribution policies in the 1930s. Unlike the Lacandon jungle colonies, these communities had not developed organic ties with the EZLN, adopting instead a strategic sympathy toward Zapatismo from the peasant organizations through which they had pushed their agrarian demands since the 1970s. If the jungle settlements reflected the limits and irregular presence of the national state, the communities in western Las Margaritas were variously located "on the margins of Zapatismo," although undergoing changes partly related to the 1994 rebellion (Escalona 2010: 174–175). Some neighbors got personally involved in the Zapatista movement as active insurgents. A woman interviewed during fieldwork in 2007, for example, said to have belonged to "the organization" (the EZLN) along with her husband for more than a decade. She had refused to participate in the Oportunidades' surveys ever since "coming down from the mountains" and back to her native community in 2003. Her reason: "I'm still in the resistance."

Both religious and political grounds for rejecting Oportunidades reflect particular understandings of the social bonds related to notions of indebtedness. During the late 1990s, claiming the benefits of govern-mental schemes came to be regarded as an act of commitment or acqui-escence toward the political party of the regime. This is hardly surprising if we also consider that in many communities it was PRI adherents who first brought news about Progresa's benefits. In some cases, PRI-leaning authorities strengthened their control over dissidents through surveillance of program co-responsibilities. In northern Chiapas, Paz y Justicia leaders forced pro-Zapatista women to attend local clinics for health checks and induction courses on family planning—which those women opposed as "contrary to the law of God"—under the threat of "ejecting them from Progresa" (Agudo Sanchíz 2006: 595). Such cases of local appropriation of program rules undermined the claim that Progresa was devoid of political party affiliations. They also ironically illustrate how fulfillment of pro-gram duties can be the outcome of contingent communal power relations and political struggles.

In other cases, Progresa-Oportunidades added up to ongoing develop-ments of which Zapatismo was a determinant among others. The EZLN's proposals for female participation consisted mainly in military training and (domestic) work in its base communities in the Lacandon forest. While sympathizing with the Zapatista uprising from "its margins," men in the Tojolabal communities of western Las Margaritas rejected such pro-posals by saying that it was not customary for women to spend too much time outside their homes (Escalona 2010: 207). The Zapatista approach itself reflected a limited view of female roles that ignored the changes taking place in communities like Saltillo before 1994. Those changes had to do, for example, with women's increasingly active intervention in the spaces left by male outmigration in the community assemblies and the collective farming projects set up by peasant organizations in the 1980s. Such experience allowed women to use informal "Oportunidades' meet-ings" to discuss village affairs and even take into their own hands the organization of community matters going beyond the program (Agudo Sanchíz 2015: 197–199).

Translating Co-responsibility into Practice

Pigg (1992: 495) argues that the results of her research on aid policy in Nepal do not permit speaking simply of an appropriation of dominant visions: international development models "become important in and through a society that is Nepalese." Similarly, the processes I describe below cannot be reduced to a simple assimilation of external categories, even if certain images of co-responsibility seem to have been incorporated into conceptions of social difference and authority in some communities in Chiapas. Paraphrasing Pigg's (1992: 495) argument about the historically contextualized intertwining of distinct meanings of development, it might be said that, rather than perceiving the ideology of co-responsibility as culturally foreign, people in those communities have "come to know it through specific social relationships."

Some of such relationships have to do with the long-established institution of the *tequios*, the community teams devoted to public works to which men are traditionally obliged to contribute unremunerated labor. However, *tequios* have increasingly drawn on Oportunidades' recipient women, with men refusing to work on the grounds that they "are not paid by the government." Accordingly, staff at local health and education centers promoted the correlation of program stipends with the participating mothers' "obligation" to contribute a set amount of hours of work to clearing rubbish or cleaning schools, clinics, and other public spaces. At the time of the evaluation, nearly all interviewed women were aware that this community work was *not* part of program co-responsibilities. However, a conflict witnessed during fieldwork shed further light on the answer "they are part of our duties for getting support from the program," through which many explained *tequios*. The doctor at the clinic in Saltillo was confronted by a group of disgruntled women over withheld Oportunidades stipends. The penalized recipients accused the practitioner of informing program administrators of their neglect of health duties, despite the fact that they had always showed up at the *tequios*. The latter had therefore become an essential component in negotiations with local doctors and nurses, who might in exchange promise not to report women's failure to attend health checks and workshops.

Here it is possible to talk about co-optation of "traditional labor" by some state agents—something that was actually in the spirit of Pronasol's efforts to promote self-help in welfare projects. Regulatory responsibilities are sidestepped and risks shifted to groups whose unremunerated work is ruled by gender, kinship, and community norms. In the ill-equipped and ill-staffed health centers of Las Margaritas, Oportunidades recipients were asked for monetary contributions "on behalf of the program." Doctors and nurses justified these payments by saying that they lacked sufficient resources and that their own wages were scanty and irregular—a situation worsened by the work overload of having to monitor program duties. Participating women also contributed fees to buy food and refreshments for the policemen and frontline workers who oversaw monetary transfers on payment days, an illegal arrangement that shifted program operational costs further to the budgets of recipient households.

All this offers another instance of unloading of public services onto co-responsibilized subjects. Nonetheless, local service providers are also part of more complex action networks in which mutual obligations and constraints involve and affect everybody in a community. While there was a great deal of pressure on doctors and schoolteachers to cover up unfulfilled co-responsibilities, participating mothers kept an eye on one another's compliance with program rules and admonished those failing to attend health checks and workshops. Especially under Progresa, it was widely believed that a missed co-responsibility by a household could affect others and that, accordingly, recipients themselves had the capacity to decide who could be struck off the program. This acted as a powerful incentive to undergo health checks and attend workshops at local clinics—something celebrated in turn as "advancements in the culture of healthcare demand" in impact assessment reports.

The transformation of program entitlements into collective benefits and obligations also compelled recipients to contribute to the funding of public works and services completely unrelated to Oportunidades. Some women made payments through gritted teeth, but others felt that the program's stipends were worth it after all: they represented a reliable income that helped cover basic household expenses on a regular basis, making participant mothers worthy of loans and credit at local shops. The persistent view of stipends as a subsidy "for which to be grateful," however, was reflected in obligations guided by an older logic of community hierarchy and subordination along lines of class and gender. Like Saltillo, many localities in Chiapas are *ejidos*, agrarian reform communities established on lands donated by the post-revolutionary PRI regime. "Peasant" men were thus turned into subjects of a state to which they would be perpetually indebted, while women—and an increasing number of landless neighbors, like those who migrated to the Lacandon jungle—were denied the agrarian rights allocated to men (Nugent and Alonso 1994: 228). Those with direct access to land through *ejido* titles were thus vested with a special authority manifest in contributions demanded of non–right holders (Agudo Sanchíz 2006: 591).

To these dues were added those paid by Oportunidades recipients when their children failed to attend school. The amount of such fines varied according to the reasons for absence (nothing was paid if the child was sick). Similarly, bigger penalties applied to those who missed health workshops or medical check-ups because they were working outside rather than within the locality—which followed the older logic of sanctions imposed on those skipping community assemblies not related to Oportunidades.

Contributions and fines were often collected and administered by the *vocales*, themselves recipient women whom the others elected as their representatives before the program. Being also in charge of organizing *tequios* in coordination with *ejido* authorities and clinic staff, *vocales* demanded monetary contributions from the other women to cover *gastos de manejo del cargo* (office-management expenses), seen in terms of "compensation" for the burden that program-related responsibilities added to their chores. According to the principles of local commitment and self-management, however, their work was voluntary and unremunerated. Oportunidades' operational guidelines did not stipulate collection of fines as part of *vocales'* duties to monitor compliance with program rules either. Yet they used payments as a means for negotiating with doctors and head teachers, so that they did not report absences.

Development programs require these "informal networks of support, built personally through relations of trust and maintained through an out-of-sight 'economy of favours and obligations' existing at the margins of legitimacy (or maybe in some cases legality)" (Mosse 2005a: 125). Such local codes and practices are partially acknowledged by program managers, yet these rather talk about exceptions to which a set of ready-made categories apply: "compassion effect" (when nonattendance is not reported by school directors), "bribe-taking," and "informal co-responsibilities"—any unscripted event must immediately be labeled and stabilized with respect to the policy model. In fact, program recipients did talk about fraud and bribery when they suspected that their missed co-responsibilities had been reported despite paying fines or performing alternative community work. As illustrated by Nuijten's (2003: 62–63) study of organization and politics in an *ejido* in west-central Mexico, people employ the corruption label to refer to unbalances in the transactions through which exchanges of services and favors normally take place between neighbors, frontline workers, and agrarian bureaucrats (cf. Olivier de Sardan 2005: 21n41).

It is these norms and organizational practices that incorporate program rules and enable their realization in specific ways while modifying their logic. Paradoxically, conditional transfers often reinforce rather than supplant the notion of the gift as they draw on it. Recipients may feel that stipends are never wholly theirs because they can be withdrawn if certain duties are not complied with—"a gift may never leave its owner," who therefore keeps while giving (Eyben with León 2005: 120). They never actually get to decide if they are owners or partners of equal status, which is reflected in constructions of the government as a "patron" and in the "obligation to work for the program" or "cooperate" with work or money in exchange for its stipends.

Surveilling Co-responsibility

Inasmuch as conditional transfers can be viewed as a disciplinary attempt to manage poverty, their power dimensions will not be fully understandable from official discourses and representations alone. Real outcomes depend largely on the strategies and improvisations developed by a range of actors in implementing and legitimizing policy orders. This research focus draws on the combination of an open-ended "methodological interactionism" (Olivier de Sardan 2005: 12) with an analysis of actors' construction and management of the social contexts of which they are part (Latour 1996; Mosse 2005a; 2005b). Development "brokers" can thus be seen as intermediaries between different realms of policy and practice, but also as situated within the heterogeneous networks that produce the concrete realities of a program.

Not reporting absences was just part of a series of measures taken by rural school directors to help students reconcile education with the labor provided to their households—for example, adjusting the school calendar to seasonal farm work and migration. Outside school hours, teachers might also advise parents on the benefits and co-responsibilities of Oportunidades, thus playing the more active role of the *promotor comunitario* (outreach worker) typical of earlier indigenist policies. In Saltillo, I found friendship and even fictive kinship ties between community residents and the—also Tojolabal—teachers at the local primary school. The principal was regularly invited to talk about the "importance of schooling" and the program's scholarships at community assemblies, where he encouraged parents to ensure their children's school attendance for the sake of their future.

Another example of mutual enrollment is provided by the strategies used by indigenous schoolgirls to confront the gender bias that hinders their expectations, also regarded as an unanticipated positive impact in the 2008 evaluation. In communities like Saltillo, it was possible to observe how girls teamed up to persuade their reluctant parents that they would be "in good company" by going in groups to the high school at the town of Las Margaritas. These initiatives were part of their wider efforts to seek part-time jobs to supplement the program's scholarships and thus support their own higher education. Information about these diverse options was in turn circulated among the girls' younger siblings and friends in other households.

The translation of program rules into diverse interests and activities also provides the conditions of possibility for the monitoring and fulfillment of co-responsibilities. The displacements through which Oportunidades' intermediaries were instructed and called upon, however, produced a series of local constructions and imageries of control and surveillance that, paradoxically, revealed an uneven capacity and presence of techniques necessary to bring the discipline and administration of individuals into practice.

The attempts of interested local leaders and corporative groups to tamper with cash transfers were deterred in principle by the Committees for Community Promotion, which were made up by the *vocales* or voluntary workers to whom I referred above. These women disseminated information and, in indigenous communities, acted as interpreters of program messages on account of their Spanish proficiency—few Oportunidades frontliners conversed in any indigenous language, since most of them were drawn from predominantly Spanish-speaking towns. *Vocales* were thus in charge of coordinating local program operation in its aimed areas and fulfilling duties of "transparency and social auditing" (Sedesol 2007: 6). Accordingly, the Committee for Community Promotion in each locality comprised not just *vocales* specialized in health, nutrition, and education, but also one who bore the title of *vocal de control y vigilancia* (control and surveillance *vocal*), as it appeared on the program's operational guidelines.

Vocales were counseled by the Mesas de Atención a Comités (MACs)— boards of frontline workers attached to Oportunidades' regional centers that functioned as "field information checkpoints" while "bringing program staff closer to beneficiary families" (Sedesol 2007: 48). MAC members tutored *vocales* as partners in community management and as intermediaries between recipient women and the program's regional centers, a policy task whose implications I could witness firsthand in April 2008 at a workshop held in the town of Tumbalá. On the appointed day, and accompanied by one of the researchers in my evaluation team, I was directed by members of the municipal government to a house normally used for local assembly meetings. The place was teeming with more than two hundred women summoned from indigenous localities in the Chol-speaking zone of northern Chiapas around Tumbalá town—the scarcity of time and resources had forced program workers to contravene the directive stipulating a maximum of thirty-six *vocales* per workshop session. Despite our efforts to be as inconspicuous as possible, the MAC's lead instructor immediately noticed our presence and urged us to abandon the periphery of the event to take the stand alongside the other board members. On resuming the session, he introduced us to the assembly by announcing that my colleague and I—dutifully equipped with camera and notebooks—"came from Mexico City to ensure that all this goes well and check if the induction is conducted in the correct way." Given the situation, it was naïve for us to stress that we were just conducting an external impact assessment and had nothing to do with Oportunidades' staff.

The chief purpose of the MAC session was to keep *vocales* posted on issues of "transparency," "true information," and, above all, on a forth-coming recertification of households aimed to ascertain who was eligible for further transfers: "the government doesn't support you indefinitely"— explained the MAC spokesman—"and that's why the program needs to know whether you have made the most of its stipends over the past three years." This disciplined attempt to transmit policy messages while repro-ducing constructions of the government and the program as somewhat autonomous entities, however, stumbled on the instructor's own elabo-ration: rather than sustained improvement through investment in chil-dren's schooling and capabilities for work, he stressed short-term goals like buying better-quality foodstuffs and resorted to moralizing warnings against spending transfers on alcoholic drinks.

Increasing apprehension filled the assembly house as the instructor reminded women of their responsibilities during the imminent eligibility survey. Particularly the control and surveillance *vocales* would have to accompany surveyors on a "tour of inspection" to check households' real conditions. The MAC convener even reprimanded them for their alleged collusion with frauds: if some recipient families comprised salaried work-ers, or had "a good house and a car," it was because complicit *vocales* had helped to cover up those material advantages by taking inspectors to ad hoc homes different from those of the women previously interviewed. Thus putting the onus of the program's procedural inaccuracies on *vocales* themselves, the instructor concluded that they must think twice before misleading surveyors in this way, especially because the aim of the new recertification would be to "clean up the Oportunidades program."

At this point I uncomfortably felt that our presence in the event was reinforcing and sanctioning a particular enactment of surveillance, whose imagery was regularly disseminated by well-intentioned frontliners in an attempt to realize Oportunidades' normative orders. *Vocales* and other recipient women in diverse localities told us how program work-ers reminded them of the panoptic eye–style scrutiny to which they were subjected. They were warned that "the program knows" whether they attended health checks and that pictures were regularly taken of the food-stuffs they bought with stipends. As a *vocal* in neighboring Oaxaca State said, "I don't quite know how, but they are always watching us; I wonder if they take pictures . . . sure they see us through their computers" (in González de la Rocha with Sánchez and Paredes 2008: 107n117).

Nonetheless, this internalized discipline rests on particular translations of control and supervision that entail relatively autonomous relationships of power, acquiescence, and cooperation—local imageries of surveillance were underpinned by the close scrutiny to which recipient women were regularly subjected in their communities. Through those relationships, intermediaries such as the *vocales* became agents as well as objects of policy. This double positionality was met with uneasy ambivalence, however. On the one hand, these women demonstrated that they had acquired a new sense of authority in their daily encounters with villagers, program staff, and local government bureaucrats, which led them to denounce certain irregularities, such as municipal officials' attempts to meddle with the organization of cash transfers. They also kept records of women's turnouts at health centers and, by random door-to-door calls, checked children's attendance at school—as a *vocal* said, "We spread fear so that people comply."

On the other hand, realizing that being practitioners of policy involved monitoring their neighbors' behavior, *vocales* drew the line at reporting unfulfilled co-responsibilities, misuse of program aid, and errors in the selection of recipients. Showing others up might backfire especially if one was both an aid recipient and intermediary, when the accumulation of social and material resources might have implications that face in diverse directions. If *vocales* and other women did not incorporate the achievement of certain norms and procedures into their subjectivities, then no techniques existed to make them into fully co-responsible individuals.

Conclusions

Consistent with the construction of poverty as an exclusive and direct state-society relation, the rules and mechanisms of targeted-aid programs like Oportunidades (which incorporated only households not covered by the major social security institutions) typically exclude membership in other development schemes—Oportunidades' national coordination office could not legally transfer resources to NGOs, which hindered the establishment of institutional linkages for attending to the same populations. Poverty as administered shortage can thus prove functional to certain programs of governance. Once we see that, given the paucity of medical attention in the overburdened rural clinics, households must resort to private health centers in the towns, we are reminded of the general economy of power in which co-responsibilities were included. After all, "boosting markets" by shifting services to the private sector, as well as reducing the dispersion of population, were on the negotiating table of the group of experts who gave shape to Progresa.

Yet such Foucauldian analyses of the "side effects" of policy (Ferguson 1994) need further research on specific social situations. While wary of the consequences of skipping the structures that constrain individual "capabilities" and decision-making, most anthropologists agree that beneficiaries are not passive recipients or victims of policy designs and institutional mechanisms. However, the advocates of cofinancing and comanagement schemes would concur precisely with this point. The construction of recipients as active participants in meeting the costs of development is, after all, matched by the labor and resources provided by households and communities.

But, again, such convergence is not a given. It is made possible when a host of actors intervenes to link program-related activities with other local interests and events. Oportunidades was sustained not only by a diversity of broker roles, but also by extensive networks of support comprising schoolteachers, health staff, frontline workers, beneficiaries, etc. It is true, however, that the program itself created further social divisions and tensions between beneficiaries and those not selected (Agudo Sanchíz 2015: 193–194); it also brought new rules and opened up spaces for the creative application of the necessary knowledge and skills to abide by them, as exemplified by the fines charged for unfulfilled co-responsibilities and the fees collected by *vocales* for their "work expenses." Illustrating the local hierarchies of knowledge that both shape and are shaped by development interventions, *vocales* showed features of the long-established yet flexible framework of leadership that, in many Mexican rural communities, can accommodate new and changing figures of authority (Agudo Sanchíz 2006: 578–583). Especially where literacy, numerical skills, and bilingualism are still far from widespread, those with basic preparation are often regarded as suitable candidates for a number of responsibilities in various areas that involve interactions with outsiders. These cases bear resemblance to those of development intermediaries in other places like Africa, characterized by a "multiplicity" of norms: "Successive forms of power are piled one upon the other without displacement or substitution taking place" (Olivier de Sardan 2005: 16).

Finally, overlapping roles and meanings of development illuminate more general aspects regarding the dilemma faced by current contractual policy regimes. As we have seen, Oportunidades' implicit type of social regulatory program, with its moralizing ideology of monitored co-responsibility, had to build on persisting notions of donation and reward. Local constructions of co-responsibility operate through, and are part of, a collective logic of indebtedness and obligation that apparently functions to instill self-discipline in program recipients and intermediaries. I do not make a big point of the fact that such local understandings are not directed to the creation of organizational cultures fully adapted to global policy agendas; rather, I suggest that local relations and forms of organization can provide the concrete ground for institutional policy agents to establish explicit programs and objectives.

Postscript

I finished my work in the qualitative evaluations of Oportunidades in 2009. The program was granted another loan of $1,250 million (US) from the World Bank, and its coverage was extended to reach 6.5 million households by 2012. Oportunidades continued to be responsive to suggestions for improvements resulting from the regular evaluations by outside bodies. In 2015, a report published by EvalPartners—an alliance of policy evaluation societies from different countries—summarized the main modifications introduced in response to the assessments in which I participated: training for bilingual extension workers recruited from indigenous youth alumni to enhance program operations in indigenous communities (a novelty which, while providing employment for young men and women, may displace some key translation roles played by *vocales* in such communities); the reinstatement of deprived, drop-out households in small and distant locations through an associated transfer program that did not require the fulfillment of co-responsibilities (health checks and school attendance); and the modification of the program's operational rules to allow full coverage in such regions by incorporating families without undertaking a home survey.[4]

If local and regional contexts mattered in modifying some of the program's rules, its overall logic was not free from shifts induced by national political determinants—as illustrated by the PAN party's attempt to establish itself as the originator of the program by modifying and relaunching it as Oportunidades in 2001. After the 2012 general elections saw the PRI party's return to power, the name of the program was yet again changed—this time to Prospera (Prosper)—and a new "Crusade against Hunger" was announced with much fanfare as the main priority of the incoming administration. Prospera's rules were modified to reorient its interventions so as to contribute to the—as yet unclear—aims of this crusade.

Alejandro Agudo Sanchíz is professor of social anthropology at the Iberoamericana University (Mexico City), and a member of Mexico's National System of Researchers. Among his relevant articles is "Opportunities for the Poor, Co-responsibilities for Women: Female Capabilities and Vulnerability in Human Development Policy and Practice" (*Journal of Human Development and Capabilities*, 2010). He is the author of the book *Una Etnografía de la Administración de la Pobreza* (Universidad Iberoamericana, 2015) and coeditor, with Marco Estrada and Marianne Braig, of the volume *Estatalidades y Soberanías Disputadas: La Reorganización Contemporánea de lo Político en América Latina* (Colmex/ Free University of Berlin, 2017).

Notes

From 2005 to 2008, I worked on successive projects for the qualitative assessment of the program's impacts, led by Agustín Escobar (2005) and Mercedes González de la Rocha (2005–2008) at the Center for Higher Research and Studies in Social Anthropology. Incorporated into the program's operational rules, both qualitative and quantitative evaluations were funded by the Inter-American Development Bank. I am indebted to the Research Division of Universidad Iberoamericana for financially supporting my own ethnographic research on the program. Some parts of this chapter draw on material from my earlier doctoral research, which was funded by the Department of Social Anthropology at the University of Manchester (2001–2002) and by a grant from the Wenner-Gren Foundation for Anthropological Research (2002–2003). Unless otherwise noted, all translations into English are mine.

1. Eligible households are those living on incomes below the line of minimum welfare, equal to the value of the food basket per person per month. This line is now revised annually by the National Council for the Evaluation of Social Development Policy, an agency of the Federal Public Administration created in 2004. See "Evolución de las líneas de bienestar y de la canasta alimentaria," Coneval website, accessed 11 October 2017, http://www.coneval.org.mx/Medicion/MP/Paginas/Lineas-de-bienestar-y-canasta-basica.aspx.
2. According to official estimates, in 2006 there were 21.7 million people (20.7 per cent of the total population) living below the "poverty of capabilities" line (i.e., unable to meet their basic nutrition, education, and health needs), then estimated at about $82 (US) per month in urban areas and $59 (US) in rural areas. See "Comunicado de prensa 002/2007 México, D.F., 03 de Agosto de 2007," Coneval website, accessed 13 October 2017, http://www.coneval.org.mx/SalaPrensa/Comunicadosprensa/Paginas/Comunicado-No-0022007.aspx.
3. The reports with the assessment methods and results are available in English as links under "Evaluación Cualitativa Externa del Programa Oportunidades: 2000–2008," LANIC Etext Collection, accessed 11 October 2017, http://lanic.utexas.edu/project/etext/oportunidades/.
4. See M. González de la Rocha and A. Escobar, "#EvalStories 7: If you don't ask, you won't see it! The Evaluation of a Conditional Cash Transfer Programme in Mexico," in *Evaluations that Make a Difference*, EvalPartners, accessed 17 October 2017, https://evaluationstories.wordpress.com/2016/06/13/evalstories-7-if-you-dont-ask-you-wont-see-it-the-evaluation-of-a-conditional-cash-transfer-programme-in-mexico/.

References

Agudo Sanchíz, A. 2006. "Actores, lenguajes y objetos de confrontación y conflicto en la Zona Chol de Chiapas." *Estudios Sociológicos* 24(72): 569–600.

———. 2008. "Land Recuperation and Conflict on the Margins of State Formation in Northern Chiapas." *Identities* 15(5): 574–606.

———. 2015. *Una etnografía de la administración de la pobreza: La producción social de los programas de desarrollo.* Mexico City: Universidad Iberoamericana.

Cortés, F., and R. M. Rubalcava. 2012. "El Progresa como respuesta a la crisis de 1994." In *Pobreza, transferencias condicionadas y sociedad,* edited by M. González de la Rocha and A. Escobar, 27–49. Mexico City: CIESAS.

Escalona, J. L. 2010. "En los márgenes del zapatismo: Veracruz y Saltillo, dos poblados tojolabales (Las Margaritas)." In *Los indígenas de Chiapas y la rebelión zapatista: Microhistorias políticas,* edited by M. Estrada and J. P. Viqueira, 171–215. Mexico City: Colmex.

Escobar, A., and M. González de la Rocha. 2005. "Evaluación cualitativa de mediano plazo del Programa Oportunidades en zonas rurales." In *Evaluación externa de impacto del Programa Oportunidades 2004,* edited by B. Hernández and M. Hernández, 247–316. Cuernavaca: INSP-CIESAS.

Eyben, R., with R. León. 2005. "Whose Aid? The Case of the Bolivian Elections Project." In *The Aid Effect: Giving and Governing in International Development,* edited by D. Mosse and D. Lewis, 106–125. London: Pluto Press.

Ferguson, J. 1994. *The Anti-Politics Machine: "Development," Depoliticization, and Bureaucratic Power in Lesotho.* Minneapolis, MN: University of Minnesota Press.

Fiszbein, A., and N. Schady. 2010. *Conditional Cash Transfers: Reducing Present and Future Poverty.* Washington, DC: The World Bank.

Gledhill, J. 1995. *Neoliberalism, Transnationalization and Rural Poverty: A Case Study of Michoacán, Mexico.* Boulder, CO: Westview Press.

González de la Rocha, M., and A. Escobar. 2008. "Vulnerabilidad y activos de los hogares: el programa Progresa-Oportunidades en ciudades pequeñas." In *Método científico y política social,* edited by F. Cortés, A. Escobar, and M. González de la Rocha, 129–202. Mexico City: Colmex.

González de la Rocha, M., with G. Sánchez and P. Paredes. 2008. "Documento analítico del estudio etnográfico en Oaxaca." Unpublished manuscript. Mexico City: CIESAS.

Latour, B. 1996. *Aramis or the Love of Technology.* Cambridge, MA: Harvard University Press.

Long, N. 1992. "Introduction." In *Battlefields of Knowledge: The Interlocking of Theory and Practice in Social Research and Development,* edited by N. Long and A. Long, 3–15. London: Routledge.

Luccisano, L. 2003. "Mexican Anti-poverty Programs and the Making of 'Responsible' Poor Citizens (1995–2000)." Ph.D. dissertation. York University, Toronto.

Molyneux, M. 2006. "Mothers at the Service of the New Poverty Agenda: Progresa/Oportunidades, Mexico's Conditional Transfer Programme." *Social Policy and Administration* 40(4): 425–449.

Mosse, D. 2005a. *Cultivating Development: An Ethnography of Aid Policy and Practice.* London: Pluto Press.

Mosse D. 2005b. "Global Governance and the Ethnography of International Aid." In *The Aid Effect: Giving and Governing in International Development,* edited by D. Mosse and D. Lewis, 1–36. London: Pluto Press.

Nugent, D., and A. M. Alonso. 1994. "Multiple Selective Traditions in Agrarian Reform and Agrarian Struggle: Popular Culture and State Formation in the *Ejido* of Namiquipa, Chihuahua." In *Everyday Forms of State Formation: Revolution and the Negotiation of Rule in Modern Mexico*, edited by G. M. Joseph and D. Nugent, 209–246. Durham, NC: Duke University Press.

Nuijten, M. 2003. *Power, Community and the State: The Political Anthropology of Organisation in Mexico*. London: Pluto Press.

Nussbaum, M. C. 2000. *Women and Human Development: The Capabilities Approach*. Cambridge: Cambridge University Press.

Olivier de Sardan, J.-P. 2005. *Anthropology and Development: Understanding Contemporary Social Change*. London: Zed Books.

Pigg, S. L. 1992. "Inventing Social Categories through Place: Social Representations and Development in Nepal." *Comparative Studies in Society and History* 34: 491–513.

Roberts, B. 2012. "Del universalismo a la focalización y de regreso: los programas de transferencias condicionadas y el desarrollo de la ciudadanía social." In *Pobreza, transferencias condicionadas y sociedad*, edited by M. González de la Rocha and A. Escobar, 341–360. Mexico City: CIESAS.

Rubin, J. 1996. "Decentering the Regime: Culture and Regional Politics in Mexico." *Latin American Research Review* 31(3): 85–126.

Schwegler, T. 2003. "Narrating Economic Authority: Pension Privatization and the Discourse of Neoliberal Policy Convergence in Mexico." Paper for the Annual Meeting of the American Anthropological Association, Chicago, November 19–23, 2003.

Sedesol (Secretaría de Desarrollo Social). 2007. "Reglas de Operación del Programa de Desarrollo Humano Oportunidades. Ejercicio Fiscal 2008." Retrieved 11 October 2017. https://www.gob.mx/cms/uploads/attachment/file/79550/2008.pdf.

Wood, G. D. 1998. "Projects as Communities: Consultants, Knowledge and Power." *Impact Assessment and Project Appraisal* 16(1): 54–64.

Chapter 3

Types of Permanence
Conditional Cash, Economic Difference, and Gender Practice in Northeastern Brazil

Gregory Duff Morton

Since conditional cash transfers are typically designed to assist people in poverty, analysts often assume that the recipients are similar in terms of income—all similarly poor. But what if this assumption is wrong?

This chapter examines economic diversity and its results among women in two northeastern Brazilian villages. I argue that conditional cash transfers can have an important impact on gender relations inside the household. But this impact, it turns out, gets mediated by the household's income level. Thus, when policymakers set the program's eligibility cutoff line, they are molding gender in ways that they may not anticipate.

Bolsa Família and the Question of Autonomy

A woman, really, she doesn't do anything.[1] Really all she does is take care of the food, of things inside the house. She helps in the harvest. She helps clear the land as well. She helps with everything. Sometimes there's firewood out in the forest and I go cut it.

Mulher mesmo não faz nada. Só faz mesmo cuidar da comida, das coisas dentro de casa. Ajuda na colheita. Ajuda a limpar também. Ajuda em tudo. Às vezes tem lenha na mata e eu pego.

These are the words that Nicola used to describe her daily work as a woman and a homemaker in the drylands of Maracujá.

Notes for this chapter begin on page 135.

Nicola lived at the place where the street ends and the bean and coffee fields begin, in a white house with two bedrooms. She, her husband, and her children barely fit inside. Nicola toiled in the family's field, and her husband sometimes got gigs as a rural day laborer, "one day for one, another day for another" (um dia para um, um dia para outro). "I think that I work too much," she told me (Eu acho que eu trabalho demais).

Like many others in the village, Nicola's household received a monthly payment from Brazil's national conditional cash transfer program, Bolsa Família. Bolsa Família money is available to women in households living below a level that approximates the World Bank poverty line. Their children must fulfill the program's conditions by receiving vaccines and attending school. Nicola's family qualified. With this benefit, she acknowledged, her situation

changed. 'Cause this is what I mean—if it weren't for that money, there wouldn't be anything here. The money we have here, it's just that money.

mudou. Que eu falo assim, se não foi esse dinheiro aí, não era nada aqui. O dinheiro que nós tem aqui é só esse.

Nicola used the pronoun "we" to represent the owners of the money, and thus she avoided claiming the Bolsa Família as hers. She explained:

The person who receives it is my husband. He's the one who signed up for it.

Quem é que recebe é meu marido. Foi ele que fez o cadastro.

A few meters away from Nicola, in a practically identical house, lived Francisca, her husband, and their two sons. Francisca began a conversation about Bolsa Família with the following observation:

I know it was a door that opened up for me.

Eu sei que foi uma porta que abriu para mim.

The pronoun "me" already signaled her view of the benefit, a view that she later made clear. In the conversation related below, she first spoke about her life before Bolsa Família:

Francisca: Never would I buy anything. I never made debts because I knew that I wouldn't be able to pay them. I never— even though José [Francisca's husband] works and gets paid, he never gave me money. He would say, "Go over there, and buy something," and that would be fine, you know? Like that. But for me

Francisca: Nunca eu comprava nada. Nunca fazia dívida porque eu sabia que eu não podia pagar. Eu nunca— independente de que José [o marido dela] trabalha e recebe, mas ele nunca me deu dinheiro não. Ele falava, "Vai lá, e compra," e tudo bem, né? Pronto. Mas eu myself to go up and buy a thing, no. I never bought. I had never bought. It was after Bolsa Família came that I got to buy. I've bought furniture for inside the house, clothes—

Duff: Really!

F: Me? Yep, I have. DVD—I buy everything. Today I buy. . . . The money from Bolsa Família, I'm the one who gets it, and I manage it. I buy things for the kids, and I buy for myself. . . . There are people who say this kind of thing, "Oh, but that's a right we have." But who ever thought about our rights before? Nobody ever thought about our rights!

mesma chegar e comprar, não. Nunca comprei. Nunca tinha comprado. Depois do Bolsa Família que eu passei a comprar. Já comprei móveis para dentro de casa, roupa—

Duff: É mesmo!

F: Eu já. DVD, tudo eu compro. Hoje eu compro. . . . O dinheiro do Bolsa Família, é eu que pego, e eu administro. Eu compro coisas para os meninos, e compro para mim. . . . Tem gente que fala assim, "Ah, mas é um direito da gente." Mas quem é que já pensou no direito da gente antes já? Nunca ninguém pensou no direito da gente!

And, as if she wanted to eliminate any possible doubts as to the identity of the people in the group that she referred to as "we," Francisca added a conclusion about Bolsa Família:

I think that it's a woman's dream, right? To be independent, to have your money. To be there with no one to be ordering you.

Eu acho que é o sonho de uma mulher, viu? De ser independente, de ter o seu dinheiro. Estar com ninguém estar mandando.

How to understand the difference between these two visions from two neighbors? In the first, women appear to be people who do nothing, only help; the money from Bolsa Família belongs to "us;" the husband receives the benefit. In the second, women are presented as the bearers of rights and dreams; Bolsa Família money goes "for the kids, and . . . for myself"; the woman manages the government cash. And this divergence is not merely personal. Inside the village, many women told stories similar to Francisca's, and several women offered the same responses as Nicola.

The difference can perhaps be illuminated through an economic fact. Nicola lived in one of the poorest households in the village, and Francisca's household, although it had a very low income by national standards, was locally recognized as one of the most prosperous. This connection seemed quite common in the communities where I conducted research. In interviews, the women who associated Bolsa Família with a discourse of personal autonomy were normally those who lived in households with relatively higher incomes, while the women who identified the benefit with their families (or spouses) were the poorest. In every household, the federal government makes strenuous efforts to give Bolsa Família money only to women. But even if the woman technically receives the money, there is some difference that distinguishes the way the money is understood in poorer and in more prosperous households. Why this difference?

Since its inception in 2003, Bolsa Família has had effects both mundane and profound[2] on an immense number of beneficiaries—over thirteen million households, or approximately a quarter of the nation's population (Queijo 2018). The beneficiary group is notable for its heterogeneity.

In this chapter, I explore economic diversity. It should be emphasized that even the people I call "prosperous" are small farmers who still confront sporadic hunger, cannot pay for eyeglasses, and have difficulty buying shoes. But the households benefited by Bolsa Família are not all equally poor, and in the divergence between Nicola and Francisca, we can perhaps detect a difference that has significance in the backlands of Bahia.

Women in comparative poverty speak of Bolsa Família in connection with family and husband, while women in comparative prosperity speak of Bolsa Família in connection with personal autonomy. Why?

I start with an economic explanation. In the more prosperous households, couples tend to divide the household's money into (at least) two budgets, money for the man and money for the woman. The poorest households cannot make such a distinction. It is only in the domestic accounting of the more comfortable families, therefore, that Bolsa Família would appear as an increase in specifically female money.

I will strive to demonstrate that this economic explanation is correct, but needs to be augmented. Why do the poorest recipients not separate the household budget? Why do the more prosperous divide their money? In the context of the villages at the field site, what is the meaning of "autonomy"—the state that Francisca describes as "being independent?"

Autonomy has been a major topic in the scholarship on the gendered effects of Bolsa Família (Suárez and Libardoni 2007; Rego 2008; De Brauw et al. 2010; Pires 2011; 2013;[3] Rego and Pinzani 2013), and autonomy is at issue in the criticisms lodged against the gender politics of conditional cash transfers (CCTs) (Lavinas and Nicoll 2006; Mariana and Carloto 2009: 904; Molyneux 2009; Gomes 2011: 94). Here I try to provide a contextual answer to the question of autonomy, an answer grounded in the practices that villagers use to assimilate Bolsa Família money into a local ideology.

The Field Site

Even in the pastures that stretch out dry, even in the small valleys where corn grows next to beans, one can already see the smoke and hear the voices that seep upward from a long line of houses: that is the Assentamento Maracujá, one of the two villages investigated in my research project. Maracujá is a land settlement run by the Movement of Landless Rural Workers (MST). With very little access to water and without an effective means to transport goods to market, Maracujá today is a place of poverty. Nonetheless, the 205 people who live in its sixty-two households strive to sustain themselves by planting manioc, corn, coffee, pineapple, and beans and raising cows and chickens.

The residents also cultivate a strong bond of friendship with the inhabitants of Rio Branco, a village roughly fifteen kilometers away. For 150 years, Rio Branco has been home to small farmers who live isolated from the city. Today, the thirty-five households in Rio Branco, with 103 people in them, live in economic conditions similar to those that characterize Maracujá.

These conditions include cyclical migration to work in the cities. In both Maracujá and Rio Branco, despite the overt trappings of peasant life, the villagers are, in an important sense, rural semiproletarians. The young and energetic toil in the metropolis, while children, retirees, and the unemployed rely on an inexpensive lifestyle in the villages. Thus the urban economy is exonerated from supporting the social reproduction costs of people outside of the labor force.[4] Or, to see the situation through a lens perhaps more similar to the view of the villagers, the villages appear as islands of permanence in the river of uncertain economic growth.

Bolsa Família played a major role in Brazil's economic growth during the first decade of the twenty-first century (Rego and Pinzani 2013). Bolsa Família was created in 2003, shortly after Brazilians elected their first ever Workers' Party president, Luiz Inácio "Lula" da Silva. The nation had seen a number of previous CCT experiments during the 1990s, and the triumphal rollout of Progresa/Oportunidades/Prospera in Mexico gave international validation to the CCT approach. When the model "traveled" back to Brazil upon Lula's election, the nation's new political context resulted in a distinctive set of modifications and adaptations to the CCT cookbook (Peck and Theodore 2015). Still today, the program bears the marks of its left-wing origin. It covers a broad swath of the population. It allows new applicants to self-declare their income rather than requiring them to prove eligibility. It has no time limits. It has only two conditions for beneficiaries: they must insure that their children attend school and receive vaccines. It is available, in some circumstances, to single adults with no children. It offers a relatively generous benefit compared to other Latin American nations (Valencia Lomelí 2008).[5] Through these characteristics, Bolsa Família proclaims its status as a progressive CCT.

I carried out ethnographic fieldwork in the two villages from September 2011 to November 2012, using both participant observation and a quantitative survey to investigate household economies. In this chapter I focus on the results related to couples who live with children, and I leave for later for later the less frequent but very revealing situation faced by single parents.[6]

The results of the survey, presented in figures 3.1 and 3.2, demonstrate a surprising level of income inequality in the villages. The most prosperous households are generally those that receive rural retirement pensions from the government, or that earn income from employment in the school or the health team. In families that lack these sources of revenue, Bolsa Família complements a varying mixture of other resources, including production in one's own field, money sent by relatives in the city, and day-labor jobs. Even among Bolsa Família beneficiaries, therefore, overall income varies widely.[7]

But to its recipients, what does this money mean? This question calls for a look at the "moral structure of the backland home" (Pires 2009: 2), foregrounding its surprising capacity to assimilate and transform resources from the world outside.

Mapping the Backlands Home

At Maracujá and Rio Branco, the household can be understood as a *centerpoint of circulations*. Beans circulate from the field to the house, where a part is sold, a part is saved in plastic soft drink bottles so it can be planted the following year, and a part is prepared and consumed, nourishing those who will work in the fields again. Money does the same: it enters, gets divided, multiplies itself, and leaves. People also circulate, traveling to work in the city and returning under the force of attraction of the family's land. The household appears as a symbolic axis that orients all of these circulations—circulations of objects, money, plants, animals, and humans—around a single point.

The circulations do not all operate on identical temporalities. Some of the circulations function on a short-term basis (the corn that is harvested in three months); others cycle more slowly (the pig that takes fifteen months to mature); still others operate over the long run (the calf that is fed for five years).[8]

To understand the calibration of these unequal circulations, I return to the classic notion of *conversion* (Bohannan and Bohannan 1968). A conversion is a process through which a person manages to exchange common objects for a prestige good. At once economic and ethical, conversions serve as a leap from a mundane sphere to an elevated one.

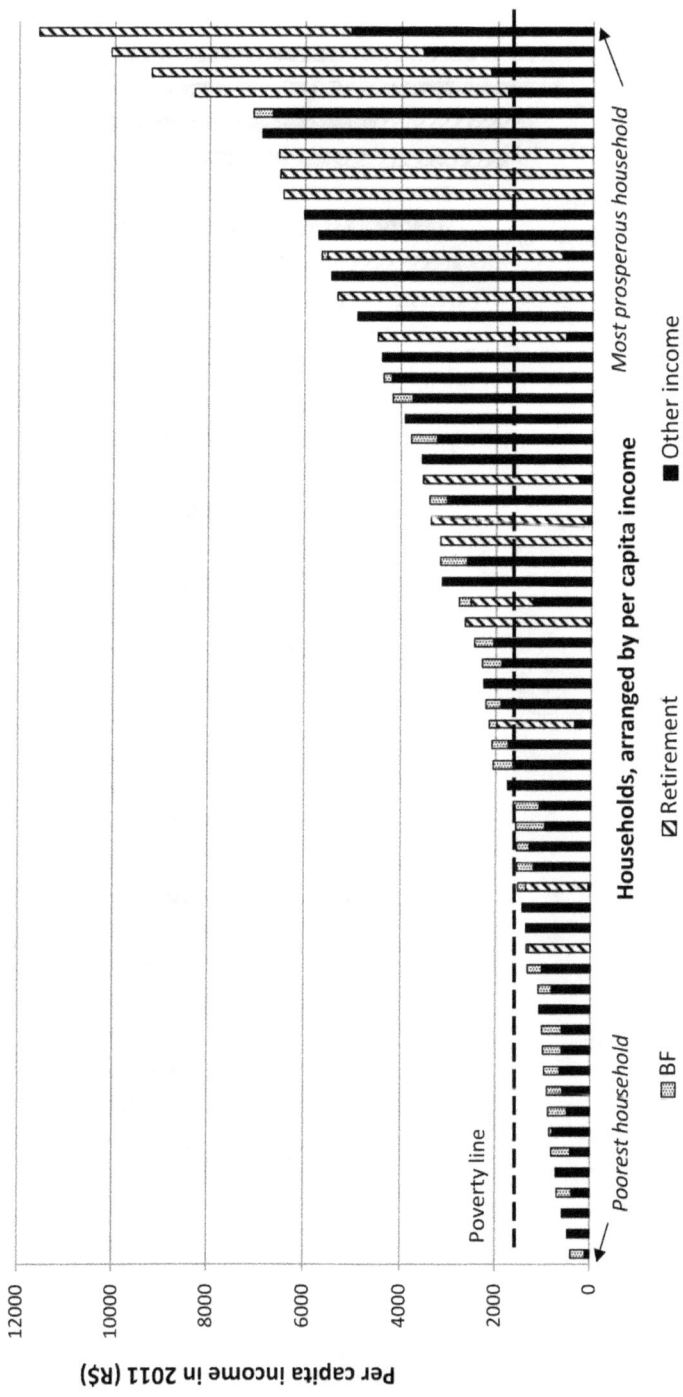

Figure 3.1 Per capita income, 2011, whole year, for households in Assentamento Maracujà

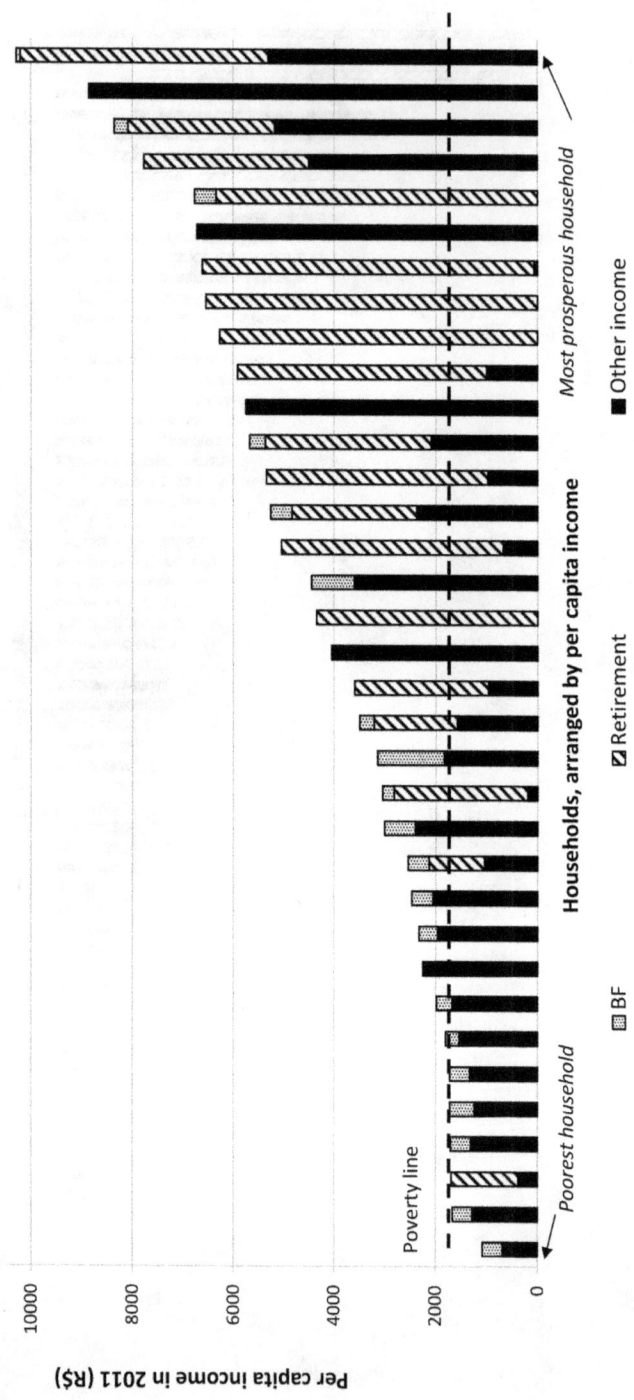

Figure 3.2 Per capita income, 2011, whole year, for households in Rio Branco

In our model of the backlands home, the central conversion is the transformation of shorter-term circulations into longer-term ones. Chickens, which lay eggs quickly, make it possible to buy pigs, who can take a year or more to mature; the results of pig production get invested in cattle, raised in a cycle that can take five years or longer. Inside the house, the circulation of food, a daily activity, is carefully restricted ("taking food out of the mouth," in the common local phrase) so that it is possible to buy clothes, which run in a six-month circuit and renew themselves during the two great purchasing seasons, the June Festivals and Christmas.

The mark of a prosperous household is its capacity to hold (*segurar*) the long-term circulations. Everything happens as if the inhabitants of the household wished to transform everyday objects into eternity. The circulations prolong themselves until they exit time altogether, seeming to confirm Weiner's hypothesis, according to which the objects most crucial to the construction of a collective identity are those that get taken out of the cycle of exchanges to become "inalienable" (Weiner 1985; 1992; also see Palmeira 1976; Sigaud 1976; Sigaud 2007: 137).

In the conversion from short-term circulation to long-term circulation, women and men contribute differently. The man's main tool is cattle. Men reinvest agricultural earnings from a variety of sources by buying cattle. Cows incarnate the specifically masculine power, enacted through the work of caring for a herd, to fix prosperity in bovine form (Ferguson 1985; Comaroff and Comaroff 2005).

But women also have a tool for carrying out conversions. That tool is payment on credit. In rural Brazil, virtually all household items can be bought on credit. The item is delivered immediately, and the household continues to make monthly payments for an extended period of time. At Maracujá and Rio Branco, villagers typically buy from *mascates*, itinerant salespeople who drive around the countryside in impossibly dusty vehicles stuffed with merchandise, each *mascate* cultivating relationships with a chain of villages that she or he visits monthly.[9] *Mascates* do not run formal credit checks; they come to people's houses each month to collect the money, and they tolerate almost constant changes in payment practices from month to month. Women take primary responsibility for deals and payments involving the *mascate*.

Women carefully plan out their purchases from *mascates*, and when women make these plans, they will often chart out a long-term map of the durable goods that they aim to obtain. This map might begin with a sofa, and then a gas stove, and later a new mattress. And so the furniture and appliances inside a house bear witness to an extended project. They are the signs of the woman's capacity to transform Bolsa Família money into assets, to turn a monthly circulation into an object that endures.

So we can identify two kinds of objects that circulate in long-term cycles: cattle and household goods. And inside a household, it is these long-term objects that tend to be owned on an individual basis. All of the relatives will know how to name the owner of each head of cattle. The furniture and the appliances can sometimes belong to a specific person; if not, usually everyone remembers who bought the item and when.

If cattle and furniture circulate in slow, long-term cycles, there is a different kind of object that iconizes rapid circulation par excellence. It is food. With its daily circuit, food enters and leaves the house in a rush, and during its trajectory, it recreates the most basic domestic relationships.

Food has a number of special qualities. In contrast to long-term objects, food cannot be individually owned: there are strong norms that rigidly prohibit food from becoming alienable property. No one may withhold food from another who requests it. The mandatory sharing of food is obvious as a core practice in the everyday ethics of the region, a practice on display at lunchtime, when everyone nearby is called to come inside and eat, and even in the purchases made by children, who buy more than one piece of candy at a time, knowing that when they enjoy a sweet they will need to share with their companions.

Food, not being the exclusive possession of anyone, remains the responsibility of a specific person: the man. According to the common phrase, the man must "put food inside the house" (botar comida dentro de casa). Food expenses are his special obligation, and they define his role as a man, in opposition to the woman, who transforms the purchased or harvested food into edible nourishment. Gift of the father, prepared by the mother, food weaves the relations between the genders and produces one of the sides of the backlands home, the side that is most shared, most public, most mobile, and most quotidian, the side where the household becomes most equal to all of the others.

Enter Bolsa Família

When I conducted my first interview with Dalia, she was dreaming of a sofa. Dalia was seventeen years old and the mother of a small girl. Despite several attempts to register, she did not receive Bolsa Família.[10] She and her husband had great difficulties in finding day-labor jobs in the fields, and sometimes they spent the week with not even beans in their home, making do by eating with relatives who lived nearby. Dalia told me that she had never had a sofa, and that was what she really wanted.

Ten months and many interviews later, Dalia's situation had changed. She was the mother of a second girl. Her husband had found temporary work, which increased the family's disposable income. Helped by the special privileges granted to expecting mothers, Dalia had finally started getting Bolsa Família. And one day she gracefully invited me into her house, smiling a proud smile, asking me to have a seat on a soft brown couch that still smelled like a furniture store.

When Bolsa Família money enters the backlands home, it generates a challenge: how will the family convert this resource into an object that circulates over the long term? Bolsa Família is paid out on a monthly cycle—a temporality that is rare in rural areas, where incomes tend to follow the rhythm of the harvests. This monthly sum must get converted; it must be transformed into acculturated wealth inside of the household. As it turns out, the conversion is carried out in one manner by the poorer villagers and in a different manner by their more prosperous neighbors.

In the poorest households, the money is often used to cover expenses related to food, and perhaps electricity, medicine, some clothes, or school supplies. These expenses are described as "little consumption" (comsumozinho).[11]

[Woman, 37 years old:] I use it more for food in the home.	[Mulher, 37 anos:] Eu uso mais para alimentação de casa.
[Woman, 61 years old:] I would buy things to eat, things for the child . . . anything for inside the house . . . it wasn't enough for a big thing, not at all. It was really just for little consumption.	[Mulher, 61 anos:] Comprava coisas para comer, coisas para a criança . . . qualquer coisa para dentro de casa . . . não dava para coisa grande não. Era mesmo para consumozinho.

In the poorest households, then, Bolsa Família money circulates almost exclusively along short-term circuits.

In more prosperous households, Bolsa Família has a quite different destiny. A woman will save a sum each month to make the credit payment for a piece of furniture or an appliance. She will carefully plan this conversion, with an exact calculation of the monthly installment that the family can afford.

Martina explained to me that she always set aside part of the Bolsa Família money for a main credit payment on a large object. Over ten years, she had managed to buy a television, a blender, a gas stove, and a sofa.

Martina: Bolsa Família isn't enough for you to buy things, only if you put together money from several months, you know?	Martina: A Bolsa Família não dá para você comprar, só se você for juntando várias meses, né?
Duff: Mm-hm.	Duff: Mm-hm.

Martina: Then you can get something
together. But if you don't have a
financial situation that lets you get the
money together, then you buy on credit.
I myself, I always buy something like
that, something that costs around fifty
reais.

Martina: Aí você pode ajuntar. Mas
quem não tem condições de ajuntar,
você faz uma prestação. Eu mesma,
eu sempre compro uma coisa assim,
no valor de cinquenta reais

In more prosperous households, through this careful, premeditated conversion, a sum that circulates monthly gets transformed into a long-term object.

Families, Differences

When Dalia finally started getting Bolsa Família, in the first days after the benefit arrived she bought the sofa on credit. She also went food shopping with her husband, Natan, at a discount store on the outskirts of the city. To carry their purchases from the store to the bus stop, they needed a taxi. "That we divided," Dalia remembered, "Natan and I" (Aí a gente dividia. Eu e Natan). Dalia and Natan each paid for half of the taxi. And it wasn't only the taxi that they divided. Dalia started to make the credit payments for the couch; Natan paid for food. When it came time to buy clothes, "Then, the sandals was me. Natan bought a dress" (Aí a sandália fui eu. Natan comprou um vestido). With the arrival of Bolsa Família, almost without noticing the difference, Dalia and Natan had created a divided budget: the Bolsa Família money, in their understanding, belonged to her, and the wages from his work belonged to him. These separate income sources would buy separate items. Bolsa Família had helped to mark a division.

If Dalia and Natan managed to divide the household's budget, this was, in part, because he had obtained a job and they had quickly become a relatively prosperous family. In the poorest households, a divided budget normally did not exist. This does not mean that the poorest households owned all of their income in common. What got unified in the poorest households was not income; it was expenditures. In the words of a perceptive farmer at Maracujá, father in one of the poorest households,

Her money is hers, mine is mine. It's just
at the time when we buy that we buy
everything together.

O dinheiro dela é dela, o meu é meu.
É só na hora de comprar que nós
compra tudo juntos.

So the poorest households unite not their money, but their purchases. This union of purchases can be understood more easily when we remember that the poorest households spend the majority of their resources on objects that circulate rapidly and, in particular, on food. Food being an obligatorily shared substance; the poorest households are devoting most of their money to precisely the item that cannot be divided.

Food has no owner, but food is the responsibility of a particular figure, the man. And so the unified expenses are associated with the man. In the poorest households, then, the money from Bolsa Família does not necessarily appear as the woman's money. There is a process of double separation here. In the first place, Bolsa Família money becomes a resource for collective consumption, not a form of wealth owned by the woman. And in the second place, this collective consumption is consumption of the object that the man is obligated to provide. So here, what Bolsa Família does is help the man to carry out his own paradigmatic gendered task — to acquire food.

This is the context that helps us to understand the domestic strife that arises around some Bolsa Família expenditures. Politicians have often imagined that families fight over the money supposedly spent on masculine luxuries. But here we can see that what really provokes conflict is rice and beans. Listen to this fight over Bolsa Família, as described by a woman whom Suárez and Libardoni (2007: 145) interviewed:

My husband doesn't give anything for inside the house. According to him, the Bolsa money is just to buy food, but I don't think so. I buy other things. I invest in the house. I decide.	Meu marido não dá nada para dentro de casa. Para ele o dinheiro do Bolsa é só para comprar alimentos, mas eu não acho. Compro outras coisas. Invisto na casa. Eu decido.

I heard the same story from Francisca:

Men don't know how to manage money, like this one here. . . . He wants to go shopping right away, buy beans and rice. . . . The woman thinks about buying some sandals.	O homem não sabe administrar o dinheiro, tipo esse. . . . Ele quer logo fazer compras, comprar feijão e arroz. . . . A mulher já pensa de comprar umas sandálias.

In these conflicts, the men think about using Bolsa Família primarily to fulfill the man's responsibility to obtain food. How can women push against this? How can they find the space to "invest in the house"? Or "to buy some sandals"? The women who manage to save some money for these other purchases are generally the women who live in the more prosperous households. In these households, after the food has been purchased, there still remains some money that can be carefully converted into objects that circulate over the long term. And these long-term objects are the objects that have owners. Everyone remembers who bought the television. Once a couple starts accumulating these objects that can be assigned to separate owners, then it seems easy to divide the household budget. In the first month after Bolsa Família arrived, Dalia and Natan had already started the division.

The practice of dividing the budget seems to produce an individualizing effect, an ease in speaking from the position of the I.

[Woman, 30 years old:] Then this Bolsa Família came for me.

[Mulher, 30 anos:] Aí que veio esse Bolsa Família para mim.

[Woman, 44 years old:] My Bolsa Família, I use it to buy something for myself. . . . I make a credit payment . . . and then I buy something that's really for myself.

[Mulher, 44 anos:] Meu Bolsa Família, eu compro alguma coisa para mim. . . . pago uma prestação . . . e depois compro alguma coisa para mim mesma.

But individualization, here, did not just mean individualization of women. When there was some Bolsa Família money left over at the end of the month, several women told me that they also had to balance out the personal needs of each child. They had use Bolsa Família to individualize their children, too.

[Woman, 30 years old:] [After finishing with the credit payments for the fridge,] now I myself don't want to spend on a big thing, nope. . . . I'm thinking that the children need shoes—and clothes. . . . I'm going to spend on them . . . and on the new school supplies.

[Mulher, 30 anos:] [Depois de terminar a prestação da geladeira,] agora eu mesma quero gastar com coisa grande agora não. . . . Estou pensando que os meninos estão precisando de calçado, de roupa. . . . Vou gastar com eles . . . e os materiais novos para a escola.

[Woman, 54 years old:] One day I give some little thing to one of them, and one month I give to another one. . . . Their father, he's different. What he earns, what he puts inside the house, it's just for the family.

[Mulher, 54 anos:] Um dia eu dou uma coisinha para um, um mês eu dou para outro . . . O pai já é diferente. O que ele ganha, o que ele bota dentro de casa, é só para a família.

The woman, here, hit the nail on the head. The man thinks of food, the object that he "puts inside the house." As she expresses it, he spends money "for the family." The mother, by contrast, thinks not of the family but of each child's individual needs.

We can witness here an ironic inversion. According to Pires (2009: 8), Bolsa Família's administrative ideology paints the woman as the incarnation of the entire family, while the man, with his supposed luxury expenses, gets cast as the figure of individualism. Mariana and Carloto (2009: 904) make the same observation.

But if such a model inspires the program's administrative planners, a different symbolism is at work inside the backlands home. Here, it is the man who represents the totality of the household. That which is shared, the collective resource, has been set aside as his responsibility, and it serves as a fundamental pillar for sexist power. The wishes and projects of the man appear as general wishes and general projects of the family. The women's projects, in order to become visible and comprehensible, must be represented as the particular interests of some person—either as her own or as those of a child.

More than a few women managed to express themselves to me, and even to become inspired, inside of this particularistic grammar, by the language of the I and its interests:

[Woman, 44 years old:] Before, I depended on asking to be able to buy things. Now, thank God, I have my own. [She explains that she used to plant an individual field in order to have her own money.] Today I don't have to do all of that any more in order for me to buy something for myself.

[Mulher, 44 anos:] Antes, eu dependia de estar pedindo para comprar as coisas. Hoje, graças a Deus, tenho o meu. [Relata que antigamente ela fazia uma roça individual para ter dinheiro próprio.] Hoje eu já não preciso fazer tudo isso para mim comprar uma coisa para mim.

[Woman, 27 years old:] I'm happy when my money comes.

[Mulher, 27 anos:] Tou alegre quando chega meu dinheiro.

Nor are women the only ones. Marta told me about children who claimed the money as theirs:

Because there are children who say, "Yeah, whatever. Mom got the money and she gobbled it all up. And the money is from my Bolsa Escola."

Que tem filho que fala, "Kwa, não é nada. Mãe recebe o dinheiro, comeu o dinheiro todo. E o dinheiro é do meu Bolsa Escola."

One night at Dona Luca's house, I saw this logic in action. The family was dozing around the TV set, and William, Luca's teenaged son, was envisioning the soccer cleats he had been wanting. Suddenly he shouted out, "Hey Mom! How much do you get from Bolsa Família?" (Ó Mãe! A Senhora recebe quanto da Bolsa Família?).

A long pause ensued. Finally Dona Luca answered him in a weary voice: "Seventy."

"Hey!" William exclaimed. "That would have been enough to buy my cleats in one month." (Uai! Dava para comprar minha chuteira em um mês). (See the insightful commentary in Pires 2014: 143; and Pires and Silva Jardim 2014: 105).

What does individualization mean? Is there is a vision of autonomy here? If there is, then the autonomy in question is about using objects to change relationships between people. I got a sense for the power of this autonomy when I asked a man if Bolsa Família had changed the situation of women.

That happens, because the woman gets kind of bold . . . she starts throwing it in the husband's face. If she buys something, she's like, "I've got this thing here because of the Bolsa Família money" . . . just like an independent woman who works. If anything happens, she's all, "I work, I don't need you."	Acontece, porque a mulher fica meio ousada . . . fica jogando na cara do marido. Se comprar alguma coisa, é, "Eu tenho isso por causa do dinheiro do Bolsa Família" . . . que nem mulher independente que trabalha. Qualquer coisa, "Eu trabalho, não preciso de você."

The man here has identified a critical moment, a turning point for gendered power. And the critical moment revolves around the purchased object. The woman's imagined declaration—*I've got this thing here*—implies the act of pointing at something. What matters for autonomy, here, is therefore not the money, nor is it the Bolsa Família program in general. What matters is, in a specific way, the thing: the man understands the woman's autonomy *through the object*, in other words, through the concrete form in which wealth was fixed inside the household. *I've got this thing here*: in order to be able to make such a declaration, the woman must have in the house a culturally recognized object toward which she can point. And not any object will do. As we have already seen, some items, like food, cannot be perceived as someone's property. Others, circulating over the long term, can be clearly and permanently identified with a person. In this context, these long-term objects are the objects that make autonomy possible. One can only imagine how many mattresses and refrigerators have stood in the middle of this kind of argument.

The Logic of the Secret

If women in more prosperous households convert Bolsa Família money into objects that circulate over the long term, this does not mean that poorer women do not also try to use the money to create forms of permanence. Living in a difficult situation, one in which everyone recognizes the necessity of dedicating resources toward food, the woman may find it hard to initiate the visible and regular project of buying an object on credit. She can, sometimes, use the secret.

At Rio Branco, in one of the poorest households, I heard about a way to hide money:

Fernanda: I—if I counted, if I counted on my husband, there wouldn't be anything. . . . Money in his hand is the same thing as water, the way he spends. [Duff laughs.] To be spending like that— the situation here is difficult already. If you keep spending like water, then— [she explains that she saves money.] . . . I don't have a bank account, no I don't.

Duff: But your brother-in-law does.

Fernanda: . . . But my husband doesn't know. Duff. No way.

Duff: He doesn't know?

Fernanda. Nope. No way.

Duff: Then how do you do it?

Fernanda: I send the money to my brother-in-law.

Duff: Wow!!

Fernanda: I tell Jacobo [Fernanda's husband], "Look, this is going there for your brother. He's going to help out." And my brother-in-law knows to put it in his bank account. Because otherwise, he'll spend it. . . . Sometimes it's fifty, sometimes less. . . . You've got to save, right? . . . Otherwise, you're never going to have anything. So it'll help. I go along getting it together, getting it together. Out of the little bit that we have, it ends up being a lot. . . .

Duff: That money that you have there is going to be for what?

Fernanda: Ah, Duff. I think about so many things—I don't know. I think about something like this, to gather and gather to pay for college for the children when they get older. Because today, as hard as the situation is, if you don't start saving right now to pay for college for your children—I myself, since I don't work, what's going to happen, then? That's what I think.

Duff: That's great.

Fernanda: Eu— dependendo, dependendo do meu marido, não tem nada. . . . Dinheiro na mão dele é a mesma coisa de água, do jeito que ele gasta. [Duff dá risada.] Estar gastando assim— já é difícil a situação aqui. Se ficar gastando como água, ai—[Ela relata que ela guarda dinheiro.] . . . Eu não tenho conta não.

Duff: Mas o cunhado tem.

Fernanda: . . . Mas meu marido não sabe não. Duff.

Duff: Ele não sabe?

Fernanda: Não sabe não.

Duff: Mas como é que faz?

Fernanda: Eu mando para meu cunhado.

Duff: É mesmo!!

Fernanda: Eu falo para Jacobo [marido], "Ô, é lá para seu irmão, ele vai ajudar." E meu cunhado sabe que põe na conta dele. Que se não, ele gasta. . . . Às vezes cinquenta, às vezes diminui. . . . Tem que economizar, não é verdade? . . . Se não for assim, você nunca vai ter alguma coisa. Então vai ajudar. Vou juntando e juntando—do pouco que a gente tem, um tanto. . . .

Duff: Aquele dinheiro que você tem lá vai ser para fazer o que?

Fernanda: Ah, Duff. Tantas coisas que eu penso—sei não. Eu penso assim, ajuntar e ajuntar para pagar uma faculdade para as crianças quando crescer. Porque hoje em dia, como a situação está difícil, se você não começar a ajuntar de agora para pagar uma faculdade para os filhos— eu mesma que não trabalho, como vai ser então? Eu penso.

Duff: Gostei.

Fernanda: What I didn't have, I want them to have. For them to have a place to study—this, that, the other. I said, "My daughter, the day that I die, you won't study any more. But as long as I'm alive, I want to see you all graduate."

Fernanda: O que eu não tive, eu quero que eles tenham. Eles têm um lugar para estudar, isso, aquilo. Eu falei, minha filha, o dia que eu morrer, você não vai estudar mais. Mas enquanto eu tiver vida, eu quero formar vocês.

Duff: Really, that's great.

Duff: Realmente, eu gostei.

Fernanda: It's a good thing. . . . Isn't it through struggle that we obtain ourselves?

Fernanda: É bom. . . . Não é lutando que a gente se consegue?

Fernanda did not create an object that was immediately visible to the public, much less to her husband. Nonetheless, she managed to convert the monthly government benefit into an entity that circulated over the long term, in the circuit of the planned dream. And it was quite a dream: Fernanda herself had never finished sixth grade. The college education did not represent today's permanence; rather, it stood for change. It differed from furniture or cattle, the lasting goods that attempted to preserve the current situation forever and thus eliminate time. Among the least prosperous families, secret money tries to transform an intolerable present state by means of a rupture between the present and the future. Fernanda's project was to weaken the now in order to build something new.

Conclusions

Ethnographic analysis, attuned to social diversities, has a specific role to play in the evaluation of public policy. Often, a new policy proposal does not affect everyone involved in a program. It affects only a margin: for example, the people who earn just a little above the eligibility limit, or the poor households still unregistered for the benefit. Ethnography is sensitive to the differences between groups of people. And so ethnography can inform these decisions about how to make change at the margins. Ethnography can help us understand who, exactly, will be affected and why.

Based on ethnography, I want to make two claims about policy. First, when policymakers tighten the income limit for Bolsa Família, they are reducing the program's power to promote gender equality. Second, policymakers need to think about Bolsa Família not only as an income program, but also as a wealth program.

Let me turn to the first claim. Over the last two years, legislators and journalists alike have advocated for the stricter enforcement of Bolsa

Família's income limit, in order to prevent fraud or waste.[12] And, indeed, administrators have started following the limits more strictly. Since 2003, three million families have had their benefits cut (Ministério de Desenvolvimento Social 2015). But other policymakers disagree with the focus on enforcement. Instead, they think, the income limit should be raised and Bolsa Família should be opened up for more Brazilians.[13]

These are not just two policy proposals. They correspond to two altogether different visions about what social assistance means. And these are two visions that have accompanied Bolsa Família from the start.

In the first vision, Bolsa Família is understood as a short-term social program. It needs to operate flexibly in order to avoid misuse of resources. In particular, Bolsa Família has to prioritize access by the neediest.

By contrast, the second vision sees Bolsa Família as a new social right. Here, the program is understood as a stepping-stone toward a universal basic income guarantee for all Brazilians. This view has been strongly supported, since the 1990s, by Workers' Party senator Eduardo Suplicy (Weissheimer 2006: 26–31; see also Brazil's Law 10835/2004, championed by Suplicy).

This debate should be informed by an understanding of what Bolsa Família's money means to women who live just around the poverty line—the women who would be most immediately affected by any raising or lowering of the income eligibility line. I have argued that Bolsa Família money has great importance to families that live right around the program's income limit. And for that reason, strict enforcement comes with an unanticipated cost. As the government cuts off beneficiaries who are close to the income limit or just above it, the households that get excluded are precisely those households where gender relations have changed the most. Francisca came from a household less poor than some of her neighbors. But she had never done shopping before Bolsa Família. Her situation returns us to the feminist insight that all women who lack control over money suffer from a certain form of poverty.[14]

My second claim expands on the first. If Bolsa Família is an attempt to transform gendered injustice in the home, then program administrators need to pay attention not only to income but also to wealth. They need to pay attention to women's capacity to build long-term assets. We need to ask an important question: do women have access to permanence? Or, to pose the question another way, how much responsibility can women take for that feeling that is so deeply desired in a household, the feeling of durability? Do women own permanent assets? Can women point to these assets? In the case of the poorest women, like Fernanda, who hid money for her children's college, Bolsa Família may not be nearly enough to create permanence.

I have made two claims: first, strict income limits may hinder the gendered effects of Bolsa Família; and, second, policymakers should focus not only on income but also on wealth. What unites these two claims is the notion of the social right. Or, more precisely, the absence of this notion. Throughout Latin America, conditional cash transfers are not cast as rights—they are understood as social programs. An administrator can cut off a beneficiary's money at will. And, similarly, the legislature could eliminate the program at any time. This is a foundational difference that separates CCTs from an earlier generation of social policies. CCTs are not rights. Or, perhaps, not yet rights.

Because CCTs are not rights, the women who receive Bolsa Família often find their benefit frozen or eliminated because of bureaucratic difficulties—and these shocks have the harshest impact on the poorest recipients. In the villages where I conducted research, it was very common for beneficiaries to lose Bolsa Família for months at a time as a result of bureaucratic problems.[15] Moreover, first-time applicants were not guaranteed to get Bolsa Família, even if they fulfilled all of the program requirements: a limited number of Bolsa Família slots were available in each municipality, meaning that some applicants waited months or years until a slot opened up. Bolsa Família was, quite clearly, not a right that one could demand, but rather a program for which one might be selected.

Bolsa Família's uncertainties—from a beneficiary's point of view— have been discussed elsewhere (see Morton 2014; 2015: 1292–1295; for an interesting US comparison, see Dickinson 2014). Perhaps one example here will suffice. The day before I submitted the initial version of this chapter, I went to Dalia's house to show her the manuscript and admire her couch. "This week," she informed me, "a tragedy happened to me." In a cruel irony, her Bolsa Família had been cut off after only three months; Natan's wages were fifteen reais ($7.50 US) per month above the income limit. When Natan had been unemployed, she had waited more than a year to obtain the benefit. After being cut off, she did not know if she would have to return the sofa to the *mascate* to whom she still owed the credit payments.

What possible public policies can promote Dalia and Fernanda in their search for permanent forms of wealth? We can highlight, in passing, the importance of the rural Maternity Salary program (Salário Maternidade rural), which is supposed to guarantee a one-time lump sum payment to rural workers who become pregnant. In further work, I hope to interrogate this program. It is worth noting immediately, though, that at my current field site, the households that receive this benefit usually use the money to acquire a durable good that creates a flow of income—like cattle, for instance—and that becomes individually identified with the mother or with the child. Thus, rural Maternity Salaries have the potential to change the dynamic of permanent wealth inside the household.

Bolsa Família also raises questions that go beyond the immediacies of policy change. When Francisca said that every woman wishes "to be independent . . . to be there with no one to be ordering you," I identified her words with the concept of autonomy, a concept so frequently invoked in the literature on conditional cash transfers. In the backland home, what are the qualities of this autonomy? Here, autonomy does not appear as a primordial separation between people, but rather as a position inside a cultural system (Comaroff and Comaroff 1987: 197). In the region I have investigated, a person gains autonomy to the extent that she becomes the source and owner of objects that circulate over the long term, objects that build the eternity of the house. In the context of this home, autonomy does not stand outside of culture, but instead the cultural system itself always already defines the meaning of "autonomy," setting aside a particular autonomous space that a person can come to occupy. Autonomy is not separation from others; it is a specific kind of position in relation to others. From this position, one can speak in the language of "I" and "my"; one can "be there with no one to be ordering you"; one can answer male commands with the phrase "I've got this thing here," "just like an independent woman."

It was at the end of 2011 that Clara said to me, "A woman, really, she doesn't do anything." A year later, I went back to ask once again about Bolsa Família. Clara had found a temporary job cleaning houses. She remembered how she had used the Bolsa Família payment back when she still had no work: "Before, it was just a few things. It wasn't even enough to get through the month" (Antes, era só pouco de coisas. Não deu nem para passar o mês.) Now, with her cleaning job, the house was transformed and she was proud; she had bought a set of kitchen cabinets, a closet, and shelves for the television, gray with a little bit of black. These objects would probably last longer than the job. Fruit of careful savings, they had the incredible power of prolonging today into the future, getting through more than the month, more than the insecure gig.

We have seen that permanent family wealth is not collective wealth in any simple sense. It matters very much *how* this permanent wealth gets created inside the household. An object can seem like the collective property of the household—and at the same time, inside the household, it may be the individual property of someone. As women slow down the Bolsa Família money, they stretch out its circulation time, fixing the rapid cash into more and more stable forms. Thus even without the certainty of a right, they hold onto kitchen tables and gas stoves and bank accounts, the markers of their autonomy. Markers not of their separateness but rather of a particular kind of relationship, a relationship to their families, their nation, and the world, a world whose wealth has entered, in some small but significant way, into their own hands.

Postscript

Over the years since 2014, Brazil has undergone an extraordinary national crisis. A business slowdown was followed by a prolonged recession. In 2016, in the middle of this recession, President Dilma Rousseff was impeached by Congress and removed from office. Rousseff belonged to the Workers' Party and had associated herself closely with efforts to expand access to Bolsa Família. Her impeachment seemed to represent— at least for the moment—a turn away from the particular form of welfare-state growth that Brazil's federal government had been pursuing since the 2002 election of Lula, and, more broadly, a weakening of the Workers' Party project for Brazilian social democracy. Bolsa Família was up for grabs.

As it turned out, however, Bolsa Família could not be grabbed so easily. In the proposal for the 2016 budget, issued during the impeach-ment drama, conservative deputy Ricardo Barros proposed to slash Bolsa Família expenditures by discontinuing new enrollments in the pro-gram (Jungblut 2015a). Weeks of controversy ensued. The proposal was ultimately defeated in parliamentary committee, where the center-left Workers' Party and the center-right Brazilian Social Democratic Party (PSDB) both threw their support behind Bolsa Família (Jungblut 2015b). Bolsa Família, like Progesa/Oportunidades/Prospera in Mexico, seemed to enjoy support across party lines.

Bolsa Família's survival was secured, at least for the moment. But the program's meaning remained uncertain. Was Bolsa Família an incipient universal right? Or was it a short-term social intervention to assist the poorest of the poor? This debate revived with the ascendency of Michel Temer, Rousseff's vice president, who took power after the impeach-ment and promptly assembled a right-wing governing coalition to sup-port an austerity agenda. Temer did not attack Bolsa Família directly, as Barros had done in the budget proposal. In fact, shortly after the impeach-ment, Temer increased the amount of the Bolsa Família benefit more than Rousseff had proposed to increase it (Cruz and Uribe 2016). He later proposed further increases (iG São Paulo 2017) and created a credit pro-gram to help Bolsa Família recipients become entrepreneurs (Hirabahasi and Cury 2017). At the same time, Temer's government implemented a "fine-toothed comb operation" that suspended or canceled the benefit for

nearly two million beneficiaries. One-and-a-half million of these beneficiaries, according to the federal government, were suspected of having
per capita incomes between R$170 and R$477 per month (Peduzzi 2018).
In other words, these beneficiaries were believed to be earning slightly
more than the eligibility limit. They would have to redo their registration
for Bolsa Família. Temer was aiming to tighten eligibility at the edge—to
put women like Francisca under the microscope.

This chapter has argued that when Bolsa Família is strictly policed
at the income limit, the families that get excluded are precisely those in
which the benefit has had the most success at changing gender relations.[16]
The strict policing implies a stance about the nature of the social program.
For the advocates of the "fine-toothed comb," Bolsa Família is a targeted
intervention to be directed only at a small subpopulation of the neediest
people. For proponents of a different view, Bolsa Família is a right, a gesture of universalism, and a step toward a basic income guaranteed to all
Brazilians. This debate is, indeed, the crucial ambiguity in Bolsa Família,
the existential argument that remained unresolved at the program's
founding. Today, the struggle for the soul of Bolsa Família continues.

Gregory Duff Morton is an economic anthropologist. He studies the
movements of money through northeastern Brazil. He engages with the
reverse migrations of agricultural laborers, the wanderings of itinerant
merchants, and the payouts that come from the world's largest national
cash welfare program. Morton serves as an assistant professor at Bard
College, and he has published on welfare dilemmas for social movements
(*Anthropological Quarterly* and *Journal of Peasant Studies*), on the peculiarities of the modern meeting (*American Ethnologist*), and on the intersection
between Donald Trump and Uber drivers in the twilight of the neoliberal
era (*Dialectical Anthropology*).

Notes

This text overlaps in many areas with Morton 2013 and with chapter 3 from my dissertation; it reproduces and translates significant portions of those two earlier publications, but
it is identical to neither one. Morton 2013 can be accessed on the *Política e Trabalho* website
at http://periodicos.ufpb.br/index.php/politicaetrabalho/article/view/14360. Many thanks to
editors for their permissions. That article is part of a special issue of ethnographies that
reflect on the tenth anniversary of Bolsa Família, Brazil's conditional cash transfer. The
present text reports on research that was conducted with the assistance of a Tinker grant
from the Center for Latin American Studies at the University of Chicago, a Grassroots
Development Fellowship from the Inter-American Foundation, and a dissertation fellowship from the Social Science Research Council. All are gratefully acknowledged. Even more

gratefully acknowledged is the generosity of people at the field site. This chapter is dedicated to the memory of Renan Souza and to his children.

1. Because I take a close look at language use, the Portuguese-language transcript is
    included side by side with English translations, so that readers can consider speech in
    detail.
2. For overall results, see, for example, the important work by researchers in AIBF-1 and -2,
    reported in Vaitsman et al. 2007 and DeBrauw et al. 2010. Also see Rasella et al. 2013.
3. See also the entire special issue that contains Pires 2013; it features ethnographic analy-
    ses of Bolsa Família.
4. See Wallerstein's notion of "semiproletarianization" ([1983] 2003:26) and compatible
    analyses by Burawoy 1976 and Meillassoux [1975] 1981, especially part II, ch. 5. Special
    thanks go to Jean-Pierre Olivier de Sardan for pointing out this important connection.
5. During research in the villages in 2011, I found that among fifty-one receiving house-
    holds, the benefit amount ranged from R$38 ($20 US) to R$226 ($122 US) per household
    per month, with a mean payment of R$117 ($63 US) per household per month (SD =
    42.7, median = 102). For comparison, the minimum wage in Brazil in 2011 was R$540
    per month ($290 US). When a household registers for Bolsa Família, the registering
    officials request that a woman from the household register as the beneficiary, although
    a man can register if there are good reasons. The beneficiary receives the payment in
    the form of a direct deposit every month, via a debit card. Not every eligible family
    that registers will receive Bolsa Família; the federal government caps the number of
    beneficiaries per municipal area. The caps are based on statistical information about
    the poverty rate in the municipality. When the number of applicants exceeds the cap,
    municipalities can create a waiting list. Generally, a household will continue receiving
    Bolsa Família until its income increases, its members fail to comply with the conditions,
    its composition changes, or a bureaucratic obstacle occurs (such as difficulty with the
    biannual re-registration, a very frequent source of problems in the villages where I car-
    ried out field work). See Morton 2014 and Morton 2015 for more details.
6. My decision, here, runs the unfortunate risk of stereotypically taking heterosexual cou-
    pling to be the default normal.
7. An emphatic caution: we cannot conclude, based on the graphs, that some households
    receive Bolsa Família despite having incomes above the eligibility limit. This is for
    three reasons: (1) our method for calculating income diverges, in some details, from
    the PNAD (Brazil's household survey), since we carefully record agricultural income;
    (2) the household units defined in our research may differ from the household units
    registered in CadÚnico, Bolsa Família's application system; (3) here we present income
    for the year as a whole. Income can vary over the course of a year, and after several
    months of prosperity, a family may run into difficulties and request Bolsa Família. The
    poverty line here corresponds to R$140 per person per month, and the absolute poverty
    line corresponds to R$70 per person per month, the standards used by the Bolsa Família
    Program at the time of study.
8. The argument here parallels, in some regards, the thesis advanced by Parry and Bloch
    (1989: 2), according to which economic systems can be divided into two cycles, the
    cycle of transient, short-term individual exchanges and the cycle of abiding, long-term
    reproductive exchanges. But unlike Parry and Bloch's model, my argument emphasizes
    a range of possible temporalities, from faster to slower, and I focus on the struggle to
    slow a cycle down.
9. The term "mascate" apparently has its origins in the trading city of Muscat, in Oman,
    on the Arabian Sea.
10. For more on problems in receiving Bolsa Família, see Morton 2015.
11. Also see Pires 2011: 3 and 2013: 126–127n4.

12. For one example, see the recent statements of Deputy Ricardo Barros (in Frota 2015).
13. See, for example, the arguments outlined in Weissheimer 2006: 26–31. Also see Peck and Theodore 2015, chs. 3 and 4.
14. I owe this observation to the teaching of Jessica Cattelino.
15. In one memorable case, a family with four children was left without Bolsa Família for eleven months because their caseworker wrote down the family information on a piece of paper, from which it was apparently never transferred to the computer. The family's mother had to make repeated trips to the Bolsa Família office in the city—each trip taking twelve hours and costing a full day's wages in bus fare—in order to get to the bottom of the problem.
16. Also excluded, of course, are very poor families swept up because of mistakes or paperwork problems. Due to their extreme poverty, these families may have particular difficulties in providing extra documents, attending multiple appointments at the welfare office, and satisfying repeated audits. In the villages where field work was performed, for example, a trip to the welfare office required taking the day off of work and buying a bus ticket that cost the equivalent of a day's wages. Enforcement policies can thus claim to be prioritizing the poorest, while in fact perversely excluding the poorest by putting up the kind of bureaucratic roadblocks that the poorest are often least able to overcome.

References

Ballard, Richard. 2013. "Geographies of Development II: Cash Transfers and the Reinvention of Development for the Poor." *Progress in Human Geography* 37(6): 811–821.
Bohannan, Linda, and Paul Bohannan. 1968. *Tiv Economy*. Evanston, IL: Northwestern University Press.
Burawoy, Michael. 1976. "The Functions and Reproduction of Migrant Labor: Comparative Material from Southern Africa and the United States." *American Journal of Sociology* 81(5): 1050–1087.
Comaroff, Jean, and John L. Comaroff. 1987. "The Madman and the Migrant: Work and Labor in the Historical Consciousness of a South African People." *American Ethnologist* 14(2): 191–209.
———. 2005. "Beasts, Banknotes and the Colour of Money in Colonial South Africa." *Archaeological Dialogues* 12(2): 107–132.
Cruz, Valdo, and Gustavo Uribe. 2016. "Temer Dá Aumento Maior do que Prometido por Dilma para Bolsa Família." *Folha de São Paulo*. 29 June 2016. Accessed 5 January 2018. http://www1.folha.uol.com.br/poder/2016/06/1786804-temer-da-aumento-para-bolsa-familia-prometido-por-dilma.shtml.
De Brauw, Alan, Daniel O. Gilligan, John Hoddinott, Vanessa Moreira, and Shalini Roy. 2010. *Avaliação do Impacto do Bolsa Família 2: Implementation, Attrition, Operations Results, and Description of Child, Maternal, and Household Welfare*. Washington, DC: International Food Policy Research Institute.
Dickinson, Maggie. 2014. "Women, Welfare and Food Insecurity." In *Women Redefining the Experience of Food Insecurity: Life off the Edge of the Table*, edited by Janet Page-Reeves, 65–84. Lanham, MD: Lexington Books.

Ferguson, James. 1985. "The Bovine Mystique: Power, Property and Livestock in Rural Lesotho." *Man* 20(4): 647–674.

Frota, Marcel. 2015. "'Há Muita Fraude no Bolsa Família,' Afirma Relator-Geral do Orçamento." iG Brasília. 18 November 2015. Accessed 29 February 2016. http://ultimosegundo.ig.com.br/politica/2015-11-18/ha-muita-fraude-no-bolsa-familia-afirma-relator-geral-do-orcamento.html.

Gomes, Simone. 2011. "Notas Preliminares de uma Crítica Feminista aos Programas de Transferência Direta de Renda – O Caso do Bolsa Família no Brasil." *Textos & Contextos (Porto Alegre)* 10(1): 69–81.

Hirabahasi, Gabriel, and Teo Cury. 2017. "Temer Anuncia Crédito de R$3 Bilhões a Beneficiários do Bolsa Família." *Poder 360.* 26 September 2017. Accessed 5 January 2018. https://www.poder360.com.br/governo/temer-anuncia-credito-de-r-3-bilhoes-a-beneficiarios-do-bolsa-familia/.

iG São Paulo. 2017. "Bolsa Família Deve Aumentar Mais do que a Inflação em 2018, Diz Ministro." *Último Segundo.* 13 November 2017. Accessed 5 January 2018. http://ultimosegundo.ig.com.br/politica/2017-11-13/bolsa-familia-2018-aumento-acima-inflacao.html.

Jungblut, Cristiane. 2015a. "Relator do Orçamento Quer Cortar R$10bi do Bolsa Família." *O Globo.* 20 October 2015. Accessed 5 January 2017. https://oglobo.globo.com/brasil/relator-do-orcamento-quer-cortar-10-bi-do-bolsa-familia-17825157.

———. 2015b. "Comissão Aprova Recomposição do Bolsa Família no Orçamento de 2016." *O Globo.* 16 December 2015. Accessed 5 January 2017. https://oglobo.globo.com/economia/comissao-aprova-recomposicao-do-bolsa-familia-no-orcamento-de-2016-18312775.

Lavinas, Lena, and Marcelo Nicoll. 2006. "Pobreza, Transferências de Renda e Desigualdades de Gênero: Conexões Diversas." *Parcerias Estratégicas* 11(22): 39–76.

Mariana, Silvana Aparecida, and Cássia Maria Carloto. 2009. "Gênero e Combate à Pobreza: Programa Bolsa Família." *Estudos Feministas (Florianópolis)* 17(3): 901–908.

Meillassoux, Claude. (1975) 1981. *Maidens, Meal, and Money: Capitalism and the Domestic Community.* Cambridge: Cambridge University Press.

Ministério de Desenvolvimento Social. 2015. "Mais de 3 Milhões de Famílias Saíram Voluntariamente do Programa." 30 April 2015. Accessed 29 February 2016. http://mds.gov.br/area-de-imprensa/noticias/2015/abril/mais-de-3-1-milhoes-de-familias-sairam-voluntariamente-do-programa.

Molyneux, Maxine. 2009. "Conditional Cash Transfers: A Pathway to Women's Empowerment?" *Pathways Brief* 5.

Morton, Gregory Duff. 2013. "Acesso à Permanência: Diferenças Econômicas e Práticas de Gênero em Domicílios que Recebem Bolsa Família no Sertão Baiano." *Política e Trabalho* 38: 43–67.

———. 2014. "Protest before the Protests: The Unheard Politics of a Welfare Panic in Brazil." *Anthropological Quarterly* 87(3): 925–933.

———. 2015. "Managing Transience: Bolsa Família and Its Subjects in an MST Landless Settlement." *Journal of Peasant Studies* 42(6): 1283–1305.

Palmeira, Moacir. 1976. "Casa e Trabalho: Nota Sobre as Relações Sociais na 'Plantation' Tradicional." *Actes Du XLIIème Congrès International Des*

Américanistes 1: 205–315 (Republished in *Camponeses Brasileiros: Leituras e Interpretações Clássicas*, edited by Clifford A. Welch, Edgard Malagodi, Josefa S. B. Cavalcanti, and Nazareth B. Wanderley, 203–216. São Paulo: UNESP, 2009).

Parry, Jonathan, and Maurice Bloch, eds. 1989. *Money and the Morality of Exchange.* Cambridge: Cambridge University Press.

Peck, Jaime, and Nik Theodore. 2015. *Fast Policy: Experimental Statecraft at the Thresholds of Neoliberalism.* Minneapolis, MN: Minnesota University Press.

Peduzzi, Pedro. 2018. "Bolsa Família: Problema em Cadastro Bloqueia ou Cancela 2 Milhões de Benefícios." *EBC Agência Brasil.* 4 January 2018. Accessed 5 January 2018. http://agenciabrasil.ebc.com.br/geral/noticia/2018-01/ bolsa-familia-problema-em-cadastro-bloqueia-ou-cancela-2-milhoes-de-beneficios.

Pires, Flávia. 2009. "A Casa Sertaneja e o Programa Bolsa-Família: Questões para Pesquisa." *Política e Trabalho* 27: 1–15.

———. 2011. "Do Ponto de Vista das Crianças: Os Efeitos do Programa Bolsa Família no Semi-Árido Nordestino." 28 Congresso Internacional da Associação Latino-Americana de Sociologia, Recife, 6 September 2011. Recife: Associação Latino-Americana de Sociologia.

———. 2013. "Comida de Criança e o Programa Bolsa Família: Moralidade Materna e Consumo Alimentar no Semiárido." *Política e Trabalho* 38: 123–35.

———. 2014. "Child as Family Sponsor: An Unforeseen Effect of Programa Bolsa Família in Northeastern Brazil." *Childhood* 21(1): 134–147.

Pires, Flávia Ferreira, and George Ardilles da Silva Jardim. 2014. "Geração Bolsa Família: Escolarização, Trabalho Infantil e Consumo na Casa Sertaneja (Catingueira/PB)." *Revista Brasileira de Ciências Sociais* 29(85): 99–112.

Queijo, Diego. 2018. "MDS repassa R$2,4 bilhões aos beneficiários do Bolsa Família em abril." 17 April. Accessed 24 April 2018. http://mds.gov.br/area-de-imprensa/noticias/2018/abril/ mds-repassa-r-2-4-bilhoes-aos-beneficiarios-do-bolsa-familia-em-abril.

Rasella, Davide, Rosana Aquino, Carlos A. T. Santos, Rômulo Paes-Sousa, and Mauricio L. Barreto. 2013. "Effect of a Conditional Cash Transfer Programme on Childhood Mortality: A Nationwide Analysis of Brazilian Municipalities." *Lancet* 382(9886): 57–64.

Rego, Walquiria Leão. 2008. "Aspectos Teóricos das Políticas de Cidadania: Uma Aproximação ao Bolsa Família." *Lua Nova: Revista de Cultura e Política* 73: 147–85.

Rego, Walquiria Leão, and Alessandro Pinzani. 2013. *Vozes do Bolsa Família: Autonomia, Dinheiro e Cidadania.* São Paulo: Editora UNESP.

Sigaud, Lygia. 1976. "A Percepção do Salário entre Trabalhadores Rurais no Nordeste do Brasil." *Actes Du XLIIème Congrès International Des Américanistes* 1: 317–330 (Republished in *Capital e Trabalho no Campo*, edited by Paul Israel Singer and Jaime Pinsky, 49–68. São Paulo: HUCITEC, 1977).

———. 2007. "'Se Eu Soubesse': Os Dons, as Dívidas e Suas Equivalências." *Ruris. Revista do Centro de Estudos Rurais* 1(2): 123–153.

Suárez, Mireya, and Marlene Libardoni. 2007. "The Impact of the Bolsa Família Program: Changes and Continuities in the Social Status of Women." In

Evaluation of MDS Policies and Programs. Results 2, edited by Jeni Vaitsman and Rômulo Paes-Sousa, 117–160. Brasília/DF: Ministério do Desenvolvimento Social e Combate à Fome.

Vaitsman, Jeni, and Rômulo Paes-Sousa, eds. 2007. *Evaluation of MDS Policies and Programs. Results 2*. Vol. 2: *Bolsa Família e Assistência Social*. Brasília/DF: Ministério do Desenvolvimento Social e Combate à Fome.

Valencia Lomelí, Enrique. 2008. "Conditional Cash Transfers as Social Policy in Latin America: An Assessment of Their Contributions and Limitations." *Annual Review of Sociology* 34: 475–499.

Wallerstein, Immanuel. (1983) 2003. *Historical Capitalism with Capitalist Civilization*. London: Verso.

Weiner, Annette B. 1985. "Inalienable Wealth." *American Ethnologist* 12(2): 210–227.

——. 1992. *Inalienable Possessions: The Paradox of Keeping-While-Giving*. Berkeley, CA: University of California Press.

Weissheimer, Marco Aurélio. 2006. *Bolsa Família: Avanços, Limites, e Possibilidades do Programa que Está Transformando a Vida de Milhões de Famílias no Brasil*. São Paulo: Editora Fundação Perseu Abramo.

Chapter 4

Queuing in the Sun
The Salience of Implementation Practices in Recipients' Experience of a Conditional Cash Transfer

Maria Elisa Balen

Montes de María is a 6,317–square kilometer region on Colombia's Atlantic coast. At least until 2008, more than half of its population of mixed European, African, and Indigenous descent were living in rural areas. Montes de María has long been the center of land disputes, beginning with social protests about land possession in the 1930s and land takeovers in the early 1970s. At the end of that decade, guerrilla groups began to appear in the area, and a heavy expansion of paramilitary groups fighting the guerrillas began in the late 1990s. Montes de María would then be the site of some of the most notorious paramilitary massacres in the country—landmarks of terror such as El Salado, Chengue, and Macayepo—as well as big changes in the distribution of land. In a country with one of the highest homicide rates in the world (UNdata 2011), there were years in which the homicide rate in some municipalities of Montes de María was triple the national average. Year after year (until 2013, when it was surpassed by Syria), Colombia registered the largest internally displaced population in the world, according to the Internal Displacement Monitoring Centre (IDMC), with Montes de María being one of the country's hot spots of forced displacement. This short overview helps to explain why this region became the focus of different types of regional, national, and international programs and interventions.

It was not by chance that I, too, ended up going to Montes de María in 2011, enquiring about what had been happening there, for what was to become my Ph.D. research. Among the myriad programs trying to deal with the effects of the conflict and ongoing challenges of reconstruction (I was also interested in government programs related to security issues and human rights), there was one program that, to my surprise, people were particularly interested in talking about: a conditional cash transfer (CCT) called Familias en Acción. This CCT was not something people were usually asked about, but it had a tremendous impact on their everyday lives. Gradually shedding the skepticism that for many colleagues prevented further engagement with this program, as it was often associated with aid in a pejorative sense (*asistencialismo*), for the next two years I followed the controversies surrounding this CCT. Traveling between Montes de María and Bogotá, I analyzed this phenomenon in terms of action at a distance (Balen 2014).

This chapter is based on conversations with functionaries, recipients, and onlookers of the CCT, my observations, and a series of endeavors (including the production of videos, photographs, and theatrical plays) in what was a joint effort with CCT recipients to reflect upon their experience, and help make their experiences known to others. Many CCTs include monitoring mechanisms that enable impact measurements using large databases. Based on these, CCT reports are often teeming with numbers as the impact of the program on one dimension or another is quantitatively evaluated. Interposed measurement apparatuses allow for a database vision of CCTs that can be accessed in different centers of calculation, not only in Washington or London, but in the multiple places in which these interventions are discussed, including conferences in Turkey or Kenya, as well as policy briefings in Ecuador or the Philippines. This chapter's entry point is not the specific (rather than universal) view of one such database, but the view of recipients of a conditional cash transfer in a place that is at a considerable distance from such centers of calculation. While some of the issues that will be presented are specific to that setting, the argument this chapter seeks to make is much broader in its concern with the sort of things that escape from engagements based solely on the database view of CCTs. These include recipients' experiences of the program, how they contrast (as is the case here) with CCTs' ostensible claims, and, crucially, how such divergences or differences of view are dealt with.

Familias en Acción, the largest CCT implemented in Colombia, was introduced in 2001 as a temporary intervention to counter the effects of economic recession, yet has constantly expanded in terms of geography and population, with the year 2012 marking both the program's redesign (it now goes by the name Más Familias en Acción) and its enshrinement into national law. The cash transfer, given to mothers of poor households on the condition that their children attend school and medical check-ups, is accompanied by a series of activities and materials through which program functionaries seek to influence cultural practice. These are carried out in the meetings of the program's network, which connects over 2.5 million families nationwide through municipal nodes composed of smaller groups led by representatives among recipients who are known as "leader mothers."

There are a series of issues that stand out once one changes the viewpoint from centers of calculation to locations at a distance from them, such as Montes de María. Queues, in particular, come into view: the first section of this chapter expands on this phenomenon, which has become one of the main symbols of the CCT. The second section addresses the importance of the CCT for its recipients—why have they agreed to be subjected to the queue treatment to begin with?—before delving into problematic issues they have faced in which queues play an important role: shame, humiliation, and stigmatization. The chapter concludes with a contrast between the CCT's ostensible claims of women's empowerment and the interactions surrounding the queuing phenomenon in order to argue that different viewpoints, apart from database views, are worth taking into account.

Queuing

> Since the program started, what one sees are those terribly long queues, it hurts to see the families . . . under such sun! In the street the motorcycles pass by, cars pass by, there are fights, from there come all sorts of things. Tools must be sought in the municipalities in order to attend the families with some dignity.
> —Teacher, El Carmen de Bolívar, in *Voces Encontradas*, 2012

> If we get heated up by the sun and we get heated up inside! . . . No. I left my small ranch alone, so anyone can come in. Here we came to lose time, yes. But now let's do it: patience.
> —Woman in the payment queue, San Juan, 23 February 2012

The long queues are perhaps the most striking feature of Familias en Acción; the most commented on, the most visible, the most impressive. Some people in the region referred to the program as "families under the sun" precisely because of this. In El Carmen, a central municipality in Montes de María, daytime temperatures can reach 40 degrees Celsius (104 degrees Fahrenheit), and lack of an aqueduct means that water can be expensive, especially during the summer periods. The above quote came from a woman from nearby San Juan who was in a queue of perhaps fifty people. San Juan, touted by a regional functionary as an example of how well the program works, has around 4,700 registered families, in comparison to El Carmen's 12,300-plus registered families (program functionary, Cartagena, 13 July 2011). Every two months, when payment periods are declared open, all the beneficiaries in a municipality go to the bank or payment point to get their money. At the time of my research (2011–2012), the overall procedure (whose specifics could vary) included checking the identity of the beneficiary, checking in the computer how much money had arrived for her, and recording it on a slip of paper, which the beneficiary then took to another bank functionary in order to receive the money. This itinerary was followed by thousands of beneficiaries attended to by fewer than a handful of functionaries. Crashes of the information system, as well as problems with the arrival of the money to be distributed, could cause further delays. These were the overall conditions, but it requires a strain on the imagination to conceive what these payment queues were like.

Queues have changed over the years. In El Carmen, at the beginning, payments were made in the office of the only remaining commercial bank in town, Banco de Bogotá. Many beneficiaries still remember the mistreatment they received in those days. After a national tender process, Banco Agrario became in charge of delivering the money. Not having any office in town, this second bank set up shop for a few days every two months or so and operated from the main patio of the mayor's office. Later on, the option of other commercial sites became available, where women could take out the transfer money in exchange for a negotiable fee. Even then, I witnessed a couple of the remaining "short" queues in which people waiting since 8:00 A.M. (others, who had not lost the habit, waiting since 3:00 A.M.) were still waiting at 2:00 P.M. for money that had not come, and that would be processed by only three cashiers that had gone out for lunch. "They just have to wait," was the disdainful answer I got from the man in charge, who was the one responsible for saying payments would start at 9:00 A.M. Queues were a key issue of mobilization from early on:

> One of the reasons we established ourselves as a citizen oversight group was because of the way beneficiaries were mistreated. They were mistreated in the most terrible way. From the moment you see a pregnant woman in a queue under the sun, and treated like anybody else, there is mistreatment. On top of that, what we called "los mochileros" arrived. "Give me your identification card and a percentage." There is mistreatment right there. Because they are taking advantage of the need of those people standing in the sun who want to go home because their children are alone. I do not blame them; if one of those mochileros asks me for 5,000 pesos, I have to think about those 5,000 pesos because they mean a meal for my children. "But seño," she says, "my children are alone back home, the worst thing is that they are alone, something can happen to them." See? That is putting a beneficiary against the wall. . . . With the children being alone, I have to go. I'd better pay the 5,000 pesos and go and take care of them. (Olga,[1] El Carmen, 27 July 2011)

Not only have queues been a strain on beneficiaries' bodies and minds, standing hour after hour under the sun and sometimes under the rain, they have also been opportunities. *Mochileros*, bank functionaries, and sometimes leader mothers themselves took groups of identification cards and, for a fee, helped beneficiaries jump the queue. At the height of their splendor, queues had epic proportions:

> D: In those banks, people came at dawn, yes? And the bank could take up to a month in paying them. By letters, by numbers, however it was, it lasted a lot of time. And those people, if it was only a month that was being paid, they came for 15,000 pesos.

> S: And the people from the *veredas* [rural areas], those from the *veredas* have always had a priority here in El Carmen. Because those people are already paying for transport, you have few days. They always had a priority. When it was payment period, we did a flow chart. But the [bank] authorities here said: no, that does not go. It is on a first-come first-served basis. . . . they do not care. These people, sometimes they stayed three and four days here. It was a situation . . . if it was like this here in El Carmen, leaving the kids alone, those mothers from rural areas came and left the kids alone over there for two or three days. It was critical, and we sometimes suffered with them. "Seño, look at this . . ." but what could we do? (focus group, El Carmen, 27 July 2011)

It is no wonder, then, that when asked what about their experience with Familias en Acción they would want other people to be aware of, one of the three things a group of women in the urban center of El Carmen mentioned were the queues (22 June 2012). During a similar exercise, this time in one of the *veredas*, a group of beneficiaries chose to make up a short theatre play in which they made fun of themselves in the queue: pushing, fainting, someone's foot being run over by a car. As part of the staging, they muddied their feet. Other members of the group, who wanted to paint, also chose the mud. They drew a broken-down car in the middle of a very big and long, muddy road. Sometimes, when the rain had wrecked the roads, they had to walk six to seven hours only to arrive in town and start queuing (see next page).

There are other places where mothers had to queue: at school when asking for attendance certificates, at the hospital, and at the program office when seeking information or handing in paperwork. Some sorts of informal arrangements could be made in these cases. Standing at 4:00 A.M. in front of the municipal office in December 2011, I saw that people queuing for Familias en Acción and SISBEN (the national system registering beneficiaries of social policies) had small pieces of cardboard with numbers on them. The new arrivals were pointed toward a young man, part of the queue, who was writing the two sets of numbers (a set for each program's queue) on a large piece of cardboard someone had brought and tearing

Recreating the Queue Drama

(Vereda Caracolicito, 6 July 2012)

Walking for hours in the mud . . .

. . . to arrive at the troublesome queue . . .

. . . and faint under the heat, even . . .

. . . to not get money anyways . . .

. . . or get less, without an explanation . . .

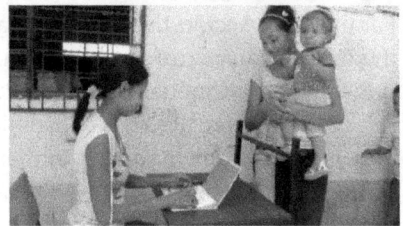

. . . sometimes receiving what is expected . . .

. . . before the well-known "system is down, come back tomorrow"; leaving them with no money, after having skipped breakfast and lunch, and borrowed for the bus fee.

Figures 4.1–4.8 Stills from a video of a theater play, recorded in El Carmen De Bolívar (Colombia). The video is now lost and these small stills are the only images of the play available. Screenshots taken by the author.

the pieces while he waited. This allowed for people to chat in circles, walk about, sit somewhere, and come back. Yet as the wait time and queues lengthen, such solutions become untenable.

Sometime after daybreak, a young policeman approached us, asking whether we were queuing or not. The others broke from the circle in which we were chatting in order to take their place in the line. I stayed and talked with the agent, who told me there were five or six of them assigned to the queue. So I decided to approach the police station and interview the commander in charge of this queue operation. The commander was considerate enough to turn on the air conditioner for our interview, in which he quoted the Colombian constitution and criticized the *costeños* [people from the Caribbean coast] for living off the state and for not being passive enough. They had been giving trouble from before, he said: one day, the exact date he did not remember, they even blocked the road in protest. "And the police have to keep order, always." I pointed out to him, through the window, how impressive the queue looked. "And when the sun comes out . . . there is going to be a brawl," he said.

When certain leader mothers were around, their word was sometimes enough to let those with priority go through. Others, though, such as government functionaries and teachers (who are not supposed to be in the program anyway) used their influence to jump the queue, a practice others complained about: "I am not a revolutionary only because I am not going to let the wife of a council member, all perfumed and fresh out of the shower, be attended before those who have been queuing" (CCT recipient, El Carmen, 14 March 2012).

It is hard to believe such queues have actually taken place. How can such a thing become normal? One is tempted to say the queues had become invisible to the bank functionary, the policeman, the individual using his connections in order to "skip it," etc. The aspects of suffering in the queue are quite human and easy to understand: standing for hours under the sun, with her body tired and overheated, often hungry and dehydrated, hardly any chance of going to the bathroom, her mind worrying about the house and the children left behind, the chores not being done, trying to pass the time through conversations with the people closest in the queue, which does not take away the feeling of uselessness and waste. So why endure the queues in the first place? Why not reject the CCT?

The Importance of Familias en Acción

Many social leaders in the region of Montes de María were critical of the myriad projects in their territory; a lot of money was being spent on the salaries of desk functionaries, on workshops and refreshments, and on covering the travel costs of participants, with comparatively little money arriving to the communities themselves. There were two dimensions to which this critique applied. On the one hand, there was the political economy of NGO interventions and the perception that other people were thriving on the back of their miseries. On the other hand, many social leaders spent their days going from one place to another, from one meeting to the next, using up their mobile phone minutes while missing work and wages that could help support them and their families. It was not only that their work and time were comparatively undervalued, but that many needed money to solve their most pressing needs, whether food on the table or a family member's medical bills. This was not only a matter of unpaid local leaders and participants spending days in one NGO or government workshop after another.[2] The cash subsidies became prominent in a context in which different issues intersected: changes in the life of forcibly displaced populations moving from rural to urban areas, the dynamics of an informal economy in a context of high vulnerability, and issues of trust.

On the one hand, monetization marks an important change in the life of many displaced people coming from rural areas:

> The displaced, returned or not, insist that in the rural world they lived in their own houses, they could provide themselves with food from the crops they cultivated in their plots and from domestic or wild animals, and that they could rely on their neighbors in case of need: money was not a resource on which wellbeing depended so critically, nor did it pervade everyday life; it circulated but it did not impose a total monetization. In the urban world, on the other hand, everything had to be paid for: rent and food, without taking into account the emergence of new expenses such as transportation that could invade many activities of the everyday life, plus expenses in education and health. (GMH 2009: 50, my translation).

Even for those who have been living in towns for a while, getting their hands on some money is not easy. As a leader mother put it, referring to Familias en Acción: "Assistencialism? Yes, it is assistencialism. But when you don't have a stable job, when each day you wake up without a coin in your pocket and have to go out and hope you will make enough to buy food for that day, that small amount of money becomes an important safety net" (Olga, El Carmen, 30 November 2011). The cash transfer, in a context of high rates of unemployment and a population scraping out a living with informal jobs, was worth defending.

The amount of money a family was entitled to changed depending on the number of children in the family, their age and school level, and whether they had fulfilled all the Familias en Acción requirements. The average, though, was around 12.6 percent of the official minimum salary.[3] The subsidy money was not enough to live on, but it mattered. I heard of a wide variety of ways in which women spent it. Some used part of it for food, and others saved it, little by little, to buy school uniforms. Or they used all of it to buy the school uniform for one of their children, and with the next payment they would buy the uniform of another one, and so on. That is without counting the notebooks, the books, and internet service. Others invested the subsidy in a crop or their own business, so that they would have more money for expenses throughout the year (this was referred to as "strengthening" the subsidy). Others invested in a farm animal that would be "owned" by the child, or little by little saved the money and, complementing it with other loans (*pagadiario*), bought a small plot of land or a house for their children. Some used it to improve their housing conditions, and others used it to give their children a treat they could not otherwise afford. There were those who already had incurred debts for their everyday maintenance, and when the subsidy arrived, it went straight to pay these amounts plus the substantial interest rates. In some cases, the husband simply came and took it away. In other cases, it was the mother who used the money on herself, whether on clothes or alcohol. And in what was the most shocking of cases for those telling the stories, some women took the money and abandoned their children.

School headmasters, themselves struggling with scarce resources, argued that if the money was given to them, they would make sure it was spent on uniforms or school supplies (meeting of school headmasters, El Carmen, 21 July 2011). But who better than the mothers, argued Olga, to know what is it that the child lacks most: food, clothes, a bicycle for getting to school, or a bed to sleep on?

There was an unresolved tension regarding what the best use or investment of government funds would be. This included not only Familias en Acción but other social programs: if a community kitchen for the elderly was not using fresh vegetables, was the best solution to dissolve it and divide the funds individually, or to press for a better service? These different options were traversed not only by a vision of the state (and state institutions) versus civil society (and individuals through the market) as the most appropriate allocator of goods, but by issues regarding trust in others: could the community kitchen be expected to be run by concerned as opposed to negligent individuals, or cliques seeking to take advantage? And from the opposite shore, could families be trusted to be competent users of government grants?

It was not only a matter of the difficulty in trusting others, one of the most persistent legacies of the violence that has taken place in the region, but of a context of high vulnerability:

Us, our fight, and the anguish and the desperation and the yearning to succeed is when as leader you enter the last little house on the street that really has nothing. Maybe she lives in the last home but maybe she lives nowhere. On top of not having anything, the only thing she earns is to pay one of those rents. She does not have . . . if we add the issue of there being no electricity, no gas, no water, which is the most important thing, then that lady, that family anxiously expects that subsidy. That is what one defends. The neighborhoods, because as a leader, one gets to know the family in depth. And maybe a person behind a desk can simply be based on what I am going to tell. But does not give herself the task of going there, looking and seeing whether what I am saying is the reality. (Olga, 27 July 2011)

These conditional cash transfers were not going to take them out of poverty; many were conscious of this and put it forward quite openly. But they could affect their world-making abilities, their capacity to have an influence in their world, and expand it: this was something that strongly drew my attention during fieldwork. The relevance of cash transfers also pointed to the struggle of different members of the population to have choices and autonomy over what to do, other than errands and posing for pictures in a context of high NGO intervention. This in a context in which certain options—such as fighting for the land that was taken away—were still kept off the table by way of intimidation, threats, and assassinations.

If I have highlighted the importance of Familias en Acción, it is not because this conditional cash transfer is the ultimate solution. It is only because this was the backstage upon which considerable problems were played out. CCT designers and adapters in Bogotá had sought to mobilize notions about autonomy and ethics, about the caring and creation of the self (see Atuesta 2008), and there were traces of this legacy here and there. But the issues my interlocutors kept coming back to were mainly three: the queues, stigmatization, humiliation, and what seemed like the random logic of entering and disappearing from the list of Familias en Acción beneficiaries. The next section addresses the second of these issues (for a discussion of the CCTs' information system, see Balen 2014). It is worth noting the relevance of money in these arrangements: on the one hand, its association with autonomy makes it particularly valued for CCT recipients. On the other hand, though, there is a question that emerges for many: is it wise to give money to poor people, just like that?

Shame, Humiliation, and Stigma

Many functionaries saw the queue situation as an apparently acceptable or unimportant fixture of the CCT. Yet why was there the attitude that "they just have to wait," as in the quote from section one? It is as if a symbolic boundary was established between "us" and "them," an underlying system of classification that made "them" a group apart, a group that must somehow deal with conditions one would find unacceptable for a member of one's own group. What would be the basis to draw this line between "us" and "them"? The need for marking group boundaries, limits for solidarity and responsibility, and distinctions to help make sense of one's identity can be matters for a lengthy discussion. With regard to poverty in particular, others have pointed out how "poverty has long been viewed as a sign of social failure, with welfare recipients singled out for special scorn" (Murray 2000: 39). Shame and humiliation appear so often as central aspects in the descriptions given by persons in a situation of poverty regarding what it means to be poor (Narayan 2000), that there are now attempts to measure shame and humiliation in order to take them into account within public policies that combat poverty (Zavaleta 2011). In his study on queuing in Argentina, Auyero (2011) highlights how social program recipients' experiences of waiting teach them the need to be patient and comply. What I will be arguing here is that it doesn't stop there: queues play an important role in processes of humiliation and shaming. Humiliation and shaming can serve various social purposes, and in this section, three of these will be addressed: their use as an instrument to avoid leakages in the sense of the subsidy going to the undeserving; as tool of pressure regarding the way in which the cash is spent; and as part of the stigmatization of program beneficiaries.

The issue of eligibility offers a good example of the use of shaming as social control. During my study (and still today), eligibility for Familias en Acción was based on databases that were known to have irregularities, and people with jobs or in economic situations that were more comfortable than the ones specified, but who had influence in the local administrations, often ended up being included in the list. This was seen as a problem by program functionaries but also by beneficiaries, many of whom I heard complaining about lousy targeting and demanding better control by the state. An idea of justice deeply traverses this: in one of the interviews, a young school graduate said she was thankful for Familias en Acción, without which she could not have graduated, but started disliking it when she began working alongside a functionary in the mayor's office and realized the sort of people that were receiving the subsidy (San Onofre, 28 February 2012). Three Bogotá functionaries that had taken part in the initial program registrations recalled how shocked they were to see well-dressed women signing in. As one of them recalled,

When you started seeing that the mayor's wife, his mother, the mayor's father, the school teacher, the one working at the mayor's office lived off the SISBEN . . . we were in the processes of registration and often when a person came, and we saw her, we would tell her: aren't you ashamed, don't you feel pity signing yourself up for this program when you are taking the chance away from others who really need it? Some we would not let register. I mean, we could not tell them "do not get registered," but at least we questioned them, and they got ashamed and left. Others did not care . . . not at all. (Program functionary, Bogotá, 3 February 2012)

Shaming was, in this case, a way of sanctioning what were considered inappropriate behaviors. Another arena in which shame was used to influence behavior was the way in which the subsidy money was spent, which was a hotly debated topic. The link between money and autonomy has already been touched on when discussing the importance of Familias en Acción for many of its beneficiaries; money has been signaled as particularly valuable due to its exchangeability and even neutrality in so far as it is independent from restrictions. In principle, people can use it for whatever they want (Simmel [1900] 2011). But this can also be seen as problematic:

Some institutions say they will not lose time with it: that Familias en Acción is shameful [*una sinvergüenzura*], that they do not want to collaborate with it in any way. Because that [money] is to show off [*tirar lujo*], to buy a cell phone, to do who knows what, they invent all sorts of things. And we tell them: not all year long is for buying school supplies; they also need other shoes, different from the ones they wear to school. They need other clothes, different also. Equally, what the kids getting the nutrition subsidy need is nourishment, a balanced nourishment that can strengthen them. (Rosa, 3 December 2011)

If, before, it was the schools who sometimes got uniforms and notebooks and were the ones in charge of distributing them among students, they now faced a situation in which the decisions were made by the families themselves, in ways they did not agree with. Some of the subsequent attempts to control or at least influence the way in which the subsidies were spent involved the children directly; others, their parents. CCT recipients referred to, for example, how students were singled out at the school entrance. It went more or less like this: an institutional representative (it could be the security guard or a teacher) would stop the student and, while others passed by, point at her clothes or lack of shoes, ask her why didn't she have the school uniform, and instruct her to tell her parents to use the CCT subsidy to buy her the uniforms, for that was not the proper way to attend school. Sometimes the intervention stopped there, but other times it was accompanied by the vague (and unconstitutional) threat that other actions could follow, such as denying entrance in the future. Understandably, such singling out could be deeply felt by the children, but did not necessarily result in their being bought the school uniform. Thus, sometimes parents themselves were singled out at school meetings in which those who were beneficiaries of the CCT were set apart and told off for not using the subsidy to buy uniforms and school materials. Such public reinforcements of their economic situation and failure in regard to institutional standards was denounced by the following interviewee:

> It is not fair to endure so much for so little. You endure so many things through this . . . for example when there is a school meeting: Who are the beneficiaries of Familias en Acción? And at the entrance, if the children do not wear shoes every day, they will not let them in. All the work we have done, well, the ones that are from Familias en Acción are put apart. And they are always putting it in them: you do not have the physical education uniform; you do not have . . . because they think they get millions of pesos. (Rosa, 3 December 2011)

Shame, here, was used as a tool of pressure, and a painful tool it is, when you consider what it can imply, as noted in the following summary of psychosocial research, which contrasts it with the feeling of guilt:

> Shame, on the other hand, is a much more global, painful, and devastating experience in which the self, not just behavior, is painfully scrutinized and negatively evaluated (Lindsay-Hartz 1984; Tangney 1989; Wicker et al. 1983). This global, negative affect is often accompanied by a sense of shrinking and being small, and by a sense of worthlessness and powerlessness (Lindsay-Hartz 1984; Tangney 1989; Wicker et al. 1983). Phenomenological data also suggest that shame is likely to be accompanied by a desire to hide or to escape from the interpersonal situation in question (Lindsay-Hartz 1984; Tangney 1989; Wicker et al. 1983). (Tangney 1991: 599, citations in the original).

There is a certain introversion to shame, an acceptance of having failed to reach recognizable standards (Zavaleta 2011). This is instilled in children quite early on, as well as in their parents; when a mother is yelled at by the municipal functionary for smelling badly, told to go have a shower and come back, shame can ensue. But this can also be taken as a case of humiliation, a feeling of being unfairly treated, if one takes into account the scarcity of water, for example. Queues, in particular, can be examined precisely in these terms of unfair treatment: they are a telling instance, just like the previous examples, of people being submitted to procedures that hurt their pride and dignity. In queues, though, this is done on a systematically large scale. There are various instances in which shaming and humiliation take place, including not only at schools but also at health centers and municipal offices, in which mother recipients asking questions or looking for certificates have been told to wait, to move out of the way, and by various means made to feel their presence is an unwanted obstruction, yet it was the banks that recipients associated with the worst mistreatment. The fact that they were receiving a payment for processing the distribution of the cash transfers did not stop banks from treating recipients as a nuisance, as second-class citizens set apart while other "normal" clients were let through, as pointed out by another interviewee.

What the Bogotá functionary was resorting to in shaming relatively affluent women can be an important mechanism for reducing targeting leakages through self-selection: if shame and inconvenience are attached to a procedure, only those who really need it will undergo it. There is a step from what she recalls to accepting shaming as a more or less systematic benefit of queues, but it is a fairly more acceptable reasoning when it is argued that people that do not need that money would not stand such queues (hence the implied self-selection through opting out). Undergoing such queues implies learning the cost of being poor, of the valuelessness of one's time and comfort. Furthermore, the queues are powerful markers. Those people standing in the payment queues have accepted a price for their suffering, and are willing to undergo it every two months. "Is the queue humiliating?" was not one of my interview questions, but was often evident in the attitudes of those surrounding it: from bystanders disapproving in silence, to the drunkard who spent a whole morning cursing in front of the queue and who at some point spat on it.

Yet, is not this humiliation reading too much into a queue? After all, it could be seen as a mere operational difficulty: a large demand and not enough services. There have even been improvements in the services offered, as with the introduction of debit cards. Yet this is not the view pursued here: far from mere bureaucratic procedures, the queues can and do work as degradation ceremonies. H. Garfinkel (1956: 140) defined a degradation ceremony as "any communicative work between persons, whereby the public identity of an actor is transformed into something looked on as lower in the local scheme of social types." A beggar, queuing for a handout: that is the treatment these beneficiaries seemed willing to accept. As one person put it: "the fact of making queues to receive [the CCT] is an inhuman and even humiliating attitude" (*Voces Encontradas* 2012). Who does the humiliating, though?

In Garfinkel's degradation ceremonies, there is a verbal labeling and a denunciator. This case falls rather on what Murray (2000: 40) has termed "deniable degradation": "here the ceremony's official purpose is instrumental; however, the latent symbolic message is degrading. Officials can deny there is any labelling while still achieving degradation in practice." In bureaucratic settings, there can be a diffusion of responsibility: is it the fault of the cold-blooded bank functionary, the apathetic municipal functionary, planners in Bogotá who do not enforce agreements at the municipal level, or complaint schemes within the tender process with banks at the national level? Independently of attributions, shame and humiliation are on their own relevant issues of concern because they are hurtful, because they can have consequences in people's lives, because they can influence people's actions, generate poverty traps, and prevent public policies against poverty from achieving their expected results (Zavaleta 2011). On the one hand, then, these queues can be deemed as lousy public policy practice. On the other hand, though, can't they be instrumental in and of themselves? Tapping into the failure to comply with social norms is also useful in establishing and reinforcing social distinctions. Whether the queues are a case of deniable degradation or an open reinforcement of symbolic boundaries, these implications can be contested, at least this is how I interpret these women's wish for the queue situation to be known.

Yet the problem with the queues does not stop in the queues themselves: they conflate with other practices of discrimination, of humiliation on account of individuals belonging to a group (Zavaleta 2011). I have already given examples of Familias en Acción beneficiaries being set apart; stereotyping further traverses many of the discussions regarding the cash transfers:

> M: There are others who have had the largest troubles in the world, the minute they get the subsidy the parents go— [drinking]. That is another problem that arises with institutions because institutions always see the bad part. They don't see the good. So "all children go without shoes, children . . ." It is not all cases but they generalize.
>
> S: Those cases make damage. From one hundred, three or four. It is not everyone.
>
> (joint interview with CCT recipients, El Carmen, 27 July 2011)

Stigmatization, shame, and humiliation can turn into disadvantages. Not all people are equally prone to shame, or susceptible to humiliation. Yet these feelings are particularly relevant in contexts of poverty. They can directly affect the functioning of a program like Familias en Acción in terms of participant withdrawal because of shame, as well as outbursts of rage on account of repeated humiliation. Discussing the effect of similar CCT policies in Bolivia, Perú, and Ecuador, Molyneux and Thomson (2011) note "mistreatment affects women's self-image (accused of being lazy, having children to get benefits etc. . . .)," and that new social stigmas and stereotypes are being generated, with no positive messages being

generated by the program about the beneficiaries who, similarly to what
has happened in El Carmen, "are treated badly in the banks (told to wash
their feet before they can enter; that they smell bad; that they cannot sign
in; or that they are not in the system)" (Molyneux and Thomson 2011:
38). Not all of this branding can be traced back and explained away on
account of CCT programs exclusively. Yet it is worth considering how
these problems beneficiaries encounter are not seen as important by CCT
policy designers and evaluators.

Developments in the CCT's information system, such as the crossing of
databases between the program and the education sector, brought about
disruption in 2013, when many were left without the cash transfer, but
as they stabilized resulted in less work (and queuing) for the mothers,
who in most cases were no longer in charge of presenting education certificates each period (such improvements have not been possible with the
health sector). The expansion of the financial system and introduction of
new instruments, such as mobile money and the aforementioned debit
cards, have also multiplied possible transaction sites, which has somewhat diminished the concentration of recipients that produced the largest queues. Yet not only did the queuing phenomenon continue, officials
kept downplaying its importance. The director of Familias en Acción at
the time of the redesign, complaining about the sensationalism attached
to queues nationwide, stated that for those signing up for the new version of the program, queues were unnecessary since no one would be left
without a slot (Angulo 2012). In Cartagena in particular, five months after
Angulo's words, "a human chain surrounding the coliseum in which the
paperwork was being received" lasted ten days and even then, even after
an extra day was appointed, many were not able to enter the coliseum,
complaining about the injustice of spending days in a queue and not being
able to submit the paperwork (Fernández 2012). Queues could qualify as
unintended effects only if one ignores the fact that these are not one-off
transactions but periodic, ongoing interactions.

Conclusion

This chapter has introduced, to varying degrees, some of the main problems CCT recipients have faced: the queues, humiliation, and stigmatization. Along with the cash—which particularly interested them—these
experiences or complications would mark not only the ways in which
the program was often perceived in the municipalities—as humiliating,
a hand out—but the challenges participants faced and attempted to overcome. While supporters of conditional cash transfers sometimes point out

the potential of these programs in terms of requiring women to get out of the house, such experience outside the house can be marked primarily by things such as queuing under the sun. Leaders within the program have various suggestions regarding the queue situation, including proposals regarding the periodicity and distribution of the subsidy as well as infrastructure in order to properly attend CCT recipients (see Balen 2014). Yet it took more than a decade for improvements to start to materialize, in the meantime none of their suggestions for amelioration were taken into account, and, even after the program's redesign, some incredibly long queues continued to take place.

Once one steps away from the database view, it is evident that the practice of distributing these cash subsidies includes specific arrangements and interactions. The distinctive features of an intervention can change depending on where one stands, with the characteristic queues, for instance, going by unremarked in the renderings of experts looking at their databases in centers of calculation.

Postscript

The issue of the extent to which CCT queues' shaming effects have been intentional, or a mere by-product of insufficient government infrastructure deemed not important enough to be addressed, currently faces a somewhat altered context of justification. In the years after 2012, payment methods for disbursing these cash transfers moved from debit cards to mobile banking, following the global trend of making financial inclusion a policy goal and using mobile banking as a way to leapfrog southern countries' limited financial infrastructures (see AFI 2010; Campos and Coricelli 2010). In Colombia as elsewhere, a "ladder of financial inclusion" is predicated upon the harvesting of payments' digital traces, with the idea that the creation of banking histories is the first step toward access to other financial services, including savings, credit, and insurance, as well as formalization of the economy (Balen 2016). Retrospectively, it can be claimed that a decade of complaints about queues and high transaction costs is being addressed through technological innovation. The difference, though, was not made by these complaints on their own but by the promise of new, government-enabling mechanisms linked to financial inclusion. In places like El Carmen, queues have indeed shortened. In others, deficient government infrastructure goes a significant way in explaining not only persistent queues, but poor adoption rates (Balen 2017).

Maria Elisa Balen is associate researcher of the Grupo de Protección Social at the Universidad Nacional de Colombia. Relevant publications include "Policy Translation: An Invitation to Revisit the Work of Latour, Star and Marres," cowritten with Cristian Leyton (in *Global Discourse: An Interdisciplinary Journal of Current Affairs and Applied Contemporary Thought*, 2015), and the book *Money from the Government in Latin America: Conditional Cash Transfer Programmes and Rural Lives*, coedited with Martin Fotta (Routledge, forthcoming).

Notes

1. While most interviewees are only identified by place and date, or with a letter for ease of the narrative, there are two leader mothers that are important characters in this story, and appear with pseudonyms: "Olga" and "Rosa."
2. Typical workshops address issues such as human rights, empowerment, hygiene, savings, and agricultural techniques, among others.
3. This calculation is based on Acción Social (2008), which states that the average payment is of 116,338 Colombian pesos (COP) every two months. The minimum payment could be as low as 30,000 COP (around $15 [US] at the time) every two months: this would be 3.2 percent of the official minimum salary in 2008. The director of Familias en Acción would speak in 2012 of an increase in the average subsidy "in the most peripheral regions of the country" from 95,000 to 125,000 COP (Angulo 2012).

References

Acción Social. 2008. "Contratación de servicio de pago de subsidios y bancarización," 26 November 2008. PowerPoint presentation.

Alliance for Financial Inclusion (AFI). 2010. "Mobile Financial Services: Regulatory Approaches to Enable Access." Accessed 9 May 2018. https://www.afi-global.org/sites/default/files/publications/afi_policynote_mobile_financial_service_en.pdf.

Angulo, Roberto. 2012. "Más Familias en Acción." *Razón Pública*, 11 November 2012.

Atuesta, Delio. 2008. "Gestión de riesgos y Cuidado de sí: Dispositivos de la resistencia de la vida en el programa Familias en Acción." M.Sc. dissertation. Universidad de Los Andes, Centro Interdisciplinario para el Desarrollo–CIDER.

Auyero, Javier. 2011. "Patients of the State: An Ethnographic Account of Poor People's Waiting." *Latin American Research Review* 46(1): 5–29.

Balen, Maria Elisa. 2014. "Queuing in the Sun, Action at a Distance: The Social Politics of a Conditional Cash Transfer in Colombia." Ph.D. dissertation. School of Sociology, Politics and International Relations (SPAIS) at the University of Bristol.

———. 2016. "Dinero electrónico y regulación de banca móvil en Colombia y Bolivia: el resultado de diferentes apuestas por la inclusión financiera". Working paper, Grupo de Protección Social, Universidad Nacional de Colombia.

———. 2017. "The Mobile Money Revolution That Has Not Come." Working paper, IMTFI, Irvine, CA. Accessed 30 March 2018. https://www.imtfi.uci.edu/files/docs/2017/Maria%20Balen%20-%20Final%20report%20-%20v2.pdf.

Campos, Nauro, and Fabrizio Coricelli. 2010. "How to Maximise the Development Impact of Social Protection Policies in Africa? The Role of Financial Development." Background Paper to the European Report on Development 2010. Accessed 30 March 2012. http://erd.eui.eu/publications/erd-2010-publications/background-papers/how-to-maximize-the-development-impact-of-social-protection-policies-in-africa/.

Colectivo Narrar para Transformar, and Maria Elisa Balen. 2012. Stills from theater play during workshop in Vereda Caracolisito, El Carmen de Bolívar, Colombia, on 6 July 2012.

Fernández, Paulo. 2012. "Terminaron las filas por Más Familias en Acción." *El Universal*, 27 October 2012.

Garfinkel, Harold. 1956. "Conditions of Successful Degradation Ceremonies." *American Journal of Sociology* 61(5): 420–424.

Molyneux, Maxine, and Marilyn Thomson. 2011. "CCT Progammes and Women's Empowerment in Perú, Bolivia and Ecuador." CARE International Policy Paper, London.

Murray, Harry. 2000. "Deniable Degradation: The Finger-Imaging of Welfare Recipients." *Sociological Forum* 15(1): 39–63.

Narayan, Deepa, Raj Patel, Kai Schafft, Anne Rademacher, and Sarah Koch-Schulte. 2000. *Voices of the Poor*. Vol. 1: *Can Anyone Hear Us?* New York: Oxford University Press.

Simmel, Georg. (1900) 2011. *The Philosophy of Money*. London: Routledge.

Tangney, June. 1991. "Moral Affect: The Good, the Bad, and the Ugly." *Journal of Personality and Social Psychology* 61(4): 598–607.

UNdata. 2011. "International Homicide Data." Accessed 2 June 2011. http://data.un.org/Data.aspx?d=UNODC&f=tableCode%3a1.

Voces encontradas. 2012. A video of Colectivo Narrar para Transformar, El Carmen de Bolívar, Colombia.

Zavaleta, Diego. 2011. "Pobreza, vergüenza y humillación: una propuesta de medición." Accessed 10 October 2012. http://www.ophi.org.uk/wp-content/uploads/Verguenza1.pdf. /.

Chapter 5

Conditional Cash Transfer Program Implementation and Effects in Peruvian Indigenous Contexts

Norma Correa Aste, Terry Roopnaraine, and Amy Margolies

Introduction

Launched as a pilot in September 2005 by the Peruvian Government, the National Program of Direct Support to the Poorest (Programa Nacional de Apoyo Directo a los más Pobres)—commonly known as Programa Juntos—has become a prominent component of the Peruvian social protection system. The CCT traveling model (Olivier de Sardan, chapter 1 in this volume) was translated in Peru as a temporary antipoverty program directed to poor rural households, which was presented by the government as a departure from assistentialism (Correa 2007). More than a decade after its creation, Juntos has expanded its coverage across the country, but remains mostly concentrated in rural areas. At the end of 2017, the number of households included in the program was 763,367, which represented 1,640,606 beneficiaries, including pregnant women, children, and youth up to nineteen years old (Programa Juntos 2017).[1]

The findings presented in this chapter form part of a broader dialogue with a significant body of existing research carried out on the intensively studied Programa Juntos in Peru (Monge and Campana 2012; Sánchez and Rodríguez 2016; Herrera and Cozzubo 2017). Among the topics engaged by this literature are childhood poverty and changes in intra- and inter-household dynamics (Jones, Vargas, and Villar 2006; Jones 2009;

Notes for this chapter begin on page 180.

Vargas 2010; Streuli 2012); understanding of program aims, behavior change, and associated tensions (Díaz et al. 2009; Huber et al. 2009); and changes in food consumption patterns and investments in productive activities (Arroyo 2010a). Particularly relevant to the research we present here, Huber et al. (2009) and Escobal and Benites (2012b) documented the existence of requirements that are misinterpreted as program conditionalities. Trivelli, Montenegro, and Gutiérrez (2011) explored women's savings, while empowerment and gender representations associated with the program have been analyzed by Nagels (2014) and Alcázar (2015). Local economy effects have been studied by Del Pozo and Guzmán (2011) and Segovia (2011). Apocalyptic and mythical interpretations related to the program have been explored in Andean communities by Piccoli (2014). Particular mention should be made of the Young Lives project,[2] within which a number of studies of Programa Juntos have been carried out. Sanchez and Jaramillo (2012), for example, showed the positive effect of the program on reducing childhood malnutrition, while Escobal and Benites (2012a and b) discussed unexpected program effects at the household and individual level.

However, a pending issue in the CCT research agenda is to explore whether the characteristics and central assumptions of its design and implementation are always appropriate in contexts with high sociocultural diversity, especially in those with a presence of ethnically differentiated populations in situations of poverty and vulnerability. Although there are numerous evaluations of the results of CCTs in Latin America, their implementation and impacts on indigenous populations have received very limited attention in the literature and remain largely unexplored. There is a need to broaden the understanding of how and why CCTs operate in these contexts, as well as the intended and unintended effects they may create. Our research project was designed to respond to this gap in the specialized literature on social protection and poverty alleviation. This study is to date the largest comparative qualitative exploration of CCT implementation and impacts in Peruvian indigenous contexts, including Amazonian and Andean communities.

Our research is based on extensive case study data gathered using ethnographic approaches among beneficiaries and nonbeneficiaries in six Peruvian indigenous communities—located in Andean and Amazonian regions—from January to July 2012. The study sample included communities where the Programa Juntos was present for at least five years. The study design was somewhat atypical in the context of CCT research, which has tended to be dominated by econometric impact evaluations and randomized controlled trials (RCTs). Where qualitative approaches have been used in CCT research, they have tended to (1) play a supporting role, illustrating or at best corroborating survey findings, and (2) be constrained by fairly brief fieldwork periods and a limited methodological repertoire based on focus group discussions. These tendencies have been challenged over the years by a small number of social research specialists, but have generally maintained the methodological orthodoxy.[3] In our study, we were given considerable freedom in research design.[4] We worked closely with a small team of three Peruvian researchers, each trained to at least bachelor's level in anthropology in an excellent department.[5] Working together, we developed an extensive question list designed to guide the in-depth interviews that formed the backbone of the research. Each researcher then spent eight weeks in each of the six villages, living full time in the communities. This design, combined with the unusually high-level anthropological qualifications of the field team, allowed us to build a significant and meaningful rapport with residents of the study communities; as we will show in this chapter, one of the strengths of this nuanced, in-depth, ethnographic approach is the foregrounding of culture and social dynamics. The salient positioning of these concepts in the research agenda, together with the extended periods of community-based fieldwork, allowed our research team access and insights into aspects of the relationship between the program, local actors, and the community that are notoriously opaque and difficult to explore. These aspects included the role of different interest groups and the shape and effect of various kinds of power relations in program implementation; the study thus also contributes to debates on the political economy of social protection.[6] Finally, we would note that the comparatively extended periods of residential fieldwork, together with the developed anthropological awareness of the researchers, encouraged a particularly reflexive consciousness about observation and positionality, which is often missing in social protection research.

Arrival and Establishment: Myths, Local Interpretations, and Targeting in Programa Juntos

Arrival and Incorporation

Households across the study communities associated the launch of Juntos in their communities with the arrival of census agents from the National Institute of Statistics (Instituto Nacional de Estadística); the agents had come to identify potential beneficiaries. Informants noted that most census agents arrived in the communities without any advance notification, and that it was not always possible to summon the whole community together—especially those families living far away. Entering the community space in this unannounced manner was regarded, especially in the Amazonian communities in the study, as a breach of the norms of courtesy that should ideally be obeyed by visitors.

In all study communities, problems with the census and registration process were reported; these in turn negatively affected the perceived transparency of the program's incorporation procedures. For example, when the data collection activity took place in the center of the community, some people were not contacted because they lived far away or were in their fields or managing their livestock. Cases were also reported of census agents not making the effort to visit communities that they considered too remote. Other problems concerned the recording of names for the issuance of national identity cards (Documento Nacional de Identidad, DNI): indigenous names were difficult for census agents to spell correctly. In the view of indigenous households in the study communities, these problems explain why some deserving households were not selected as Juntos beneficiaries.

Accounts from residents of the six study communities reveal that the process of arrival and incorporation of Programa Juntos was regarded as long, confusing, difficult, often discourteous, and very bureaucratic. At times, the process also required paperwork that could only be done in towns (requiring the expense of travel and lost work time), as well as other expenses, which made it particularly challenging for extremely poor families.

Fears and Myths Associated with Programa Juntos

Programa Juntos has been operating continuously since its arrival in the study communities in 2006–2007. It is important to understand that for residents of the indigenous communities studied, the program is not simply a neutral social protection initiative, but also a site for cultural elaboration and interpretation: its presence in the communities has, over time, been associated with a range of fears and myths. These issues were generally found to be more present in the Amazonian communities in the sample, where they were deployed as interpretations of the program's intentions. While this interpretive tendency was also found in Andean communities, it should be noted that in these settlements it was associated more with the earlier stages of the program's presence; over time, trust in the program has increased. It is also important to register that the fears and myths associated with Juntos now coexist with a generally favorable interpretation of the program as offering an important development opportunity. Findings presented here are broadly congruent with those presented in earlier studies (for example, Huber et al. 2009), although some new interpretations were also identified.

These fears reflected interpretations of threats based in religion and mythology, as well as ambivalence about encroaching economic development in the region. The most common fears related to the program in Amazonian and Andean communities were associated with two principal themes: (1) variants on the myth of the *Pishtaco* and (2) apocalyptic religious interpretations.[7] An example of the former motif was the belief that the Juntos beneficiary lists were being used by *Pishtacos* to identify potential child-victims within the communities. A key instrument for program transparency—the public beneficiary list—was thus cast as a potential threat to children's safety. An example of the latter was the interpretation of the program's arrival as an indicator of the impending end of the world; photographs and fingerprints taken for national identity cards were considered to be the "mark of the Devil". An important new finding to emerge from our field research was the association of Programa Juntos with the penetration of extractive industries into indigenous homelands. It follows that the benefits offered by the program are regarded as a palliative offered by the government to facilitate the exploitation of natural resources.

While these fears and interpretations support the call for better program communications and marketing, it is also important to understand that they emerge from a cultural and ethnohistorical context in which external actors have consistently been associated with abuse, exploitation, and discrimination. The fear of loss underlying these interpretations is associated with the most valued possessions of indigenous families: their children and their lands. In turn, this fear is linked to their vulnerability in the face of possible abuse as well as their concern for the very continuity of lifeways and sociality of their communities. This idea of a credible "interpretive critique" of the state in service to an expanding extractive front resonates with Michael Taussig's (1980) now classic theorization of processes of proletarianization in Colombia's Cauca valley and Andean mining communities of Bolivia.

Our data also reveals that the actual payment of the cash transfers was a key nexus of suspicion. As one Aymara beneficiary father from a household case study in Sicta asked rhetorically, "Where have you seen a state that gives away money? In the countryside, we're forgotten. Where are they going to get all that money?"[8] People were concerned about the *real* aims of the state: in all the study communities, some informants believed that signing the Commitment Agreement upon joining the program (known as the "contract") meant that they were selling their children to the state. From this perspective, the state might at any moment arrive to claim and seize these children. As the transfer is seen as investment, the state could send their children to war or sell them abroad to recoup this investment. Extending this logic, some informants also glossed the receipt of cash transfers (for buying food) as a form of eating their children.

These interpretations were spread by various actors within the communities, including program beneficiaries. That said, it should be noted that two groups were particularly active disseminators: (1) nonbeneficiaries and (2) religious pastors. Over the course of fieldwork, it was observed that new religious movements (as opposed to established Catholicism and Adventism) were intensely active in five of the six study communities. The pastors leading these movements often exhorted their congregations to reject social programs and public health campaigns on the grounds that they could threaten families or traditional gender roles. The actual effects of these movements on social program participation was beyond the scope of the current study, but certainly warrants further research.

In what ways have these local interpretations affected the implementation of Programa Juntos in these communities? Possible effects map out along three main axes: (1) families that chose to delay their applications to the program until they had a better understanding of its real intentions; (2) beneficiary families that did not collect the first transfer they were entitled to out of fear; and (3) mistrust or even expulsion of Programa Juntos personnel. In the Aymara community of Sicta, the program field staff was expelled because the residents did not want to "sell the village." As described above, the community associated the program with extractivist companies carrying out actual exploration in the area. In the Asháninka community of Betania, some program field staff (known as *gestores*)[9] were publicly questioned about whether the transfers were in any way related to the gas exploration underway in the neighboring community of Poyeni.

Mothers recalled that after the census and community validation process, they received a beneficiary identification document. With the arrival of the local program representatives, the initial distrust began to diminish, but it never completely disappeared. The first few transfers were interpreted as proof of the government's commitment, while subsequent continuity of the transfers lent further support to this notion. Moreover, families saw that their children were not being kidnapped, and that the state was not going to take them away. Visits from program field staff, as well as learning about the experiences of other families and communities, also helped smooth the way for program rollout and expansion. By the time field research was carried out for this project, community confidence in the program had improved significantly.

Targeting

Programa Juntos employed geographical targeting at a national level, followed by household targeting at the community level. Household targeting is further validated at various stages of the process. Although it was generally understood in all the study communities that the program is directed at poor families, there nonetheless existed local interpretations about inclusion and exclusion criteria. These criteria were not restricted to economic indicators, but also included variables such as parental occupation, place of residence, and the family's social capital. In some Amazonian communities, it was felt that Juntos should only include the indigenous people of the area, excluding poor mestizos living in these communities.

In the study communities, there was a lack of available information about Juntos' selection processes. For example, a significant number of households in the communities of Achoaga, Sarhua, and Betania felt that the beneficiary lists were created by random lottery, either in the communities or nationwide. Thus, anyone who had not been chosen for the program believed they should keep applying until selected. It was also observed during fieldwork that some program field staff told mothers that the program's system would determine who joined Juntos; mothers were also told that this decision would be made in Lima. However, in the view of household informants, the program field staff had some influence over this decision.

Aspects of targeting that generated particular confusion in study communities included the following:

Age limit for participating children: although some program field staff and the local authorities informed people that the age cutoff for program participation was fourteen, some families believed it to be nineteen or twenty. Other households expected that the program would support university study, believing that the Beca 18 program was a continuation of Juntos.[10]

Household economic selection criteria: in various communities there were nonbeneficiary families that were considered to be poor and deserving by other community members. Community members felt that they should have been included, and these situations were regarded as unfair.

Perceptions that Juntos punishes or excludes families that engage in economic ventures: beneficiaries in all six communities felt that they could be expelled from the program if they launched any kind of economic enterprise because their neighbors and the program field staff would no longer consider them to be deserving cases. Among interviewees, the social appraisal of poverty was considered to be important: people needed to be perceived as poor by their neighbors. Beneficiaries feared that if their status changed, they would be denounced to the program local staff. Envy was a strong social control mechanism in these communities, and the participation in Juntos was perceived as a limited good only accessible to few households selected by the government. Such interpretations may have a negative effect on women-led enterprise development in extreme poverty contexts. It is important to point out that our evidence does not suggest that Juntos is promoting passive attitudes toward poverty in indigenous contexts. Families understood that Juntos is a temporary program and therefore expressed strong interest in participating in productive projects that would allow them to generate autonomous income.

Over the course of fieldwork, it was also observed that some households employed strategies based on kinship with the aim of joining the program (or extending their eligibility). These included the following:

Inclusion of grandmothers: in the Amazonian communities it was observed that some Juntos beneficiaries handed over the custody of one child to a grandparent, at which point the grandparent became eligible for the program. It is worth noting here that it is a cultural norm in any case for a granddaughter to go and live with her grandparents for a time, helping them to look after the house, and in turn receiving instruction on traditional female activities. Under the current circumstances, this practice has been redeployed as a strategy for extending the beneficiary circle in a given family. It should not be confused with cases of children who live with their grandparents out of necessity.

Lending children: this practice was identified in the Aymara community of Sicta. Beneficiaries with children of fourteen years, or those whose children were about to finish secondary school (and thus graduate from the program), tried to take charge of a younger child so as to be able to maintain their beneficiary status. As there were few children of the target age in Sicta due to migration, children were sought in more distant communities.

Since we carried out fieldwork throughout the first semester of 2012, there has been a major change in the targeting criteria used by social programs operating in the Amazon region. The Ministry of Development and Social Inclusion (MIDIS) published a decree in 2014 (227-2014-MIDIS) that established a new targeting mechanism to facilitate the access of Amazonian indigenous peoples to Programa Juntos and to other social programs.[11] The decree defines the forty-two Amazonian indigenous groups included in the official database of the Ministry of Culture as extremely poor. This classification ensures automatic prioritization in the official Targeting System for Households (Sistema de Focalización de Hogares—SISFOH). As a result, all the indigenous households meeting the beneficiary criteria are entitled to join the program. It is expected that this change will increase the number of indigenous beneficiaries of cash transfers in Peru; however, its effects have not yet been evaluated. Finally, it should be pointed out that this is one of the few public policy instruments created by the Peruvian state to specifically respond to the poverty and exclusion dynamics that affect indigenous communities in the Amazon.

Conditionality

Local Interpretations and Understandings of the Concept of Conditionality

Conditional cash transfer programs are designed around a logic of rights and obligations expressed through the notion of co-responsibility.[12] Within this framework, the state and the beneficiaries enter a pact designed to break intergenerational cycles of poverty. The cash transfer is designed to incentivize or stimulate demand for public services, particularly health and education. The state offers public services to the public as a right by investing in the supply side dimension of these services and proffering them to beneficiaries as an obligation. It is thus obligatory for beneficiaries to use the health and education services, the idea being that incentivizing uptake should lead to habituation and positive long-term behavior change.

In the six communities in this study, however, participation in Juntos was not generally interpreted in terms of rights and duties, but rather as an obligation to the state in exchange for receipt of the transfer. For example, in the context of questions about the rights of program beneficiaries, one Asháninka father from Betania explained, "Yes, they [beneficiaries] have the right to comply with what the program demands. They have to do everything the program requires. If they don't comply, they get cut out." Within this idiom, the transfer is not necessarily understood as an incentive for behavior change, or even as a right. Rather, it is understood as a gift in the Maussian sense, around which an exchange relationship is created and renewed with a powerful external actor: the Peruvian state (Mauss [1925] 2000). Having received their cash transfers, households must, under this logic, continue to reciprocate by complying with the established conditionalities. The cycle of reciprocity is broken if either the household or the state fails, in a given moment, to comply with its side of the bargain.

In all study communities, the conceptual basis and technical rationality of the CCT program were reconfigured and reinterpreted within an indigenous moral logic. The Peruvian state—incarnate in Programa Juntos—established a relationship with indigenous beneficiaries. The relationship was mediated by a series of actors: the program field staff (known as *gestores*), local authorities, health and education personnel—all possessing a significant degree of influence over how the aims, objectives, and conditionalities of the program was understood at a local level. The transfer could be interpreted as a salary, as an allowance, as a support, or as a debt to the state. Within these perspectives, how was compliance with

conditionalities actually interpreted? Three principal corresponding interpretations emerged from our data: (1) as an obligation; (2) as gratitude to
the state for the support received; or (3) as a way of settling a debt with
the state. Additionally, in Betania, a community with a high proportion
of Adventist adherents, some informants compared the compliance with
conditionalities to obeying the Christian commandments. This compliance was not perceived as an obligation, but rather as a means to attaining
virtue. Interestingly, it was also observed over the course of fieldwork that
the *gestores* did not possess a common discourse on co-responsibilities,
but often presented them as obligations or demands instead of duties or
commitments. The moral logic of the program is illustrated in figure 5.1.

Finally, while it is clear that the indigenous respondents in this study
understood that suspension or expulsion from the program was a consequence of noncompliance with their commitments as beneficiaries, it is
worth noting that they also interpreted such sanctions as a punishment
applied by the government, or as revenge on the part of the *gestor* or
local authorities or even resulting from the envy of neighbors acting as a
kind of social control. The program thus acquired a somewhat punitive
character based on these sanctions. However, the notion of punishment
was valued as a teaching method in both households and schools in all
the study communities. Likewise, punishment imposed by the program
was seen as a way of teaching mothers that they must take better care
of their children. That said, we should also note that Juntos sanctions
produced feelings of fear and embarrassment, especially (but not only)
among women. In the Amazonian communities, researchers encountered
cases of husbands who said that they felt humiliated when their wives
were sanctioned by the program—so much so that they preferred that
their wives not participate in the program, thus avoiding criticism from
the *gestor* and other local actors.

Official Conditionalities in Indigenous Communities

In 2007, four key conditionalities were defined for Programa Juntos.
Additionally, a list of complementary activities was added to these conditionalities. Complementary activities were nonobligatory activities that
were to be actively promoted by the program.

In the six study communities, it was found that neither household
informants nor local actors associated with Juntos had a very clear notion
of the official conditionalities of the program. It was also found that the
complementary activities were regarded as obligatory, and furthermore,
that local actors (*gestores*, local authorities, and health and education personnel) had in fact elaborated their own series of unofficial requirements.

Transfer understood as:
Salary, support, gratuity,
debt to the State

Mediators:
Programa Juntos *field staff ("gestor")*
Health personnel
Education personnel
Local authorities

State

Beneficiaries

Compliance with conditionalities
understood as:
Obligation
Responsibility
Gratitude
Reciprocity
Recognition of debt to State

Yes

Comply

No

Official conditionalities understood as:
Good
Fair
Obeying commandments
Source of virtue and life improvement

Suspension or expulsion
from *Juntos*:
Punishment
Embarrassment
Vengeance of a mediator
Envy and accusations

Extra-official conditionalities understood as:
Obligation, coercion related to:
Use of contraceptives
Donation of money to school
Contribution of labor in collective work
Handicraft making
Home improvements
Attendance at civic events (food
preparation, parades)

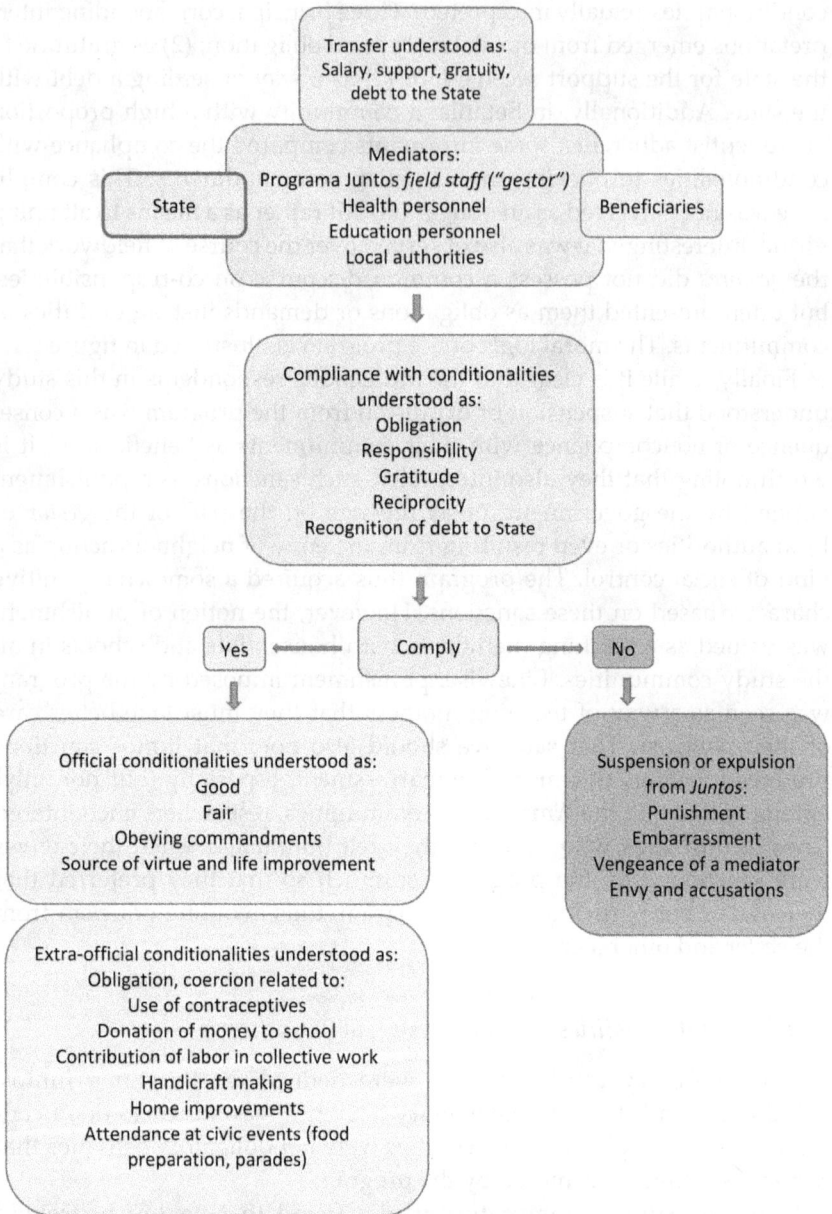

Figure 5.1 Moral system of conditional cash transfers in indigenous communities. Figure created by the authors.

Table 5.1 Official conditionalities and complementary activities at the time of fieldwork

Official Conditionalities	Complementary Activities
• Ensure attendance of children aged 0–5 years at integrated health and nutrition services according to Ministry of Health protocols • Women of childbearing age, especially pregnant women, must receive their integrated health services per Ministry of Health protocols • Enroll and ensure attendance of children aged 6–14 years in school • Apply for children's national identity card	• Participate in trainings for the improvement of kitchen facilities • Participate in women's literacy programs • Participate in health and nutrition training • Participate in latrine building training • Participate in productive activity training • Participate in programs of early childhood education for children aged 0–5 years

Note: In mid-2013, Juntos conditionalities were refined, redefined, and updated as part of a systematic reform of the program associated with its transfer to the Ministry of Development and Social Inclusion (MIDIS). Overall, program reform focused on improving verification of conditionality compliance, improving access to services, and clearly defining the role of gestores, as well as on strengthening support for families that have difficulty complying with the conditionalities (Resolución de la Dirección Ejecutiva No. 42-2013-MIDIS/ PNADP-DE del 11 de junio de 2013). In the Spanish-language publication based on this study (Correa and Roopnaraine 2014), more than twenty recommendations were offered to the government of Peru as a contribution to these debates over Programa Juntos' implementation.

A particularly worrying example was the definition of contraceptive use as a Juntos conditionality, with women who did not comply being threatened with suspension or expulsion.

In table 5.2, we list all conditionalities perceived as obligatory by households in our study communities. In the list appear official conditionalities, unofficial conditionalities as described above, and complementary activities redeployed by local actors as conditionalities. These findings are in line with those of other qualitative studies that have documented similar confusion about conditionalities in rural areas, as well as the existence of requirements imposed by *gestores* and other local actors in relation to agriculture, livestock, community clean-ups, handicrafts, or home improvements (Huber et al. 2009; Streuli 2012). The Young Lives survey also demonstrated the existence of unofficial conditionalities, such as livestock rearing, homestead gardening, and cleaning of public spaces. That survey

Table 5.2 Conditionalities perceived as obligatory

Area	Conditionalities perceived as obligatory by study households
Education	• School attendance from the age of 6 years • Purchase of materials required by the teacher • Purchase of school uniforms • Children to be sent to school with snacks, including fruit • Support for the school: donations for the purchase of materials and for activities, according to the requests of school directors • Communal work activities: school cleaning, construction, repair, painting, cultivation of school gardens, in accordance with the director's requests
Health and Nutrition	• Food purchasing: in Amazonian communities, noodles, meat, eggs, fish, and other groceries; in Andean communities, fruit, vegetables, meat, and groceries • Attendance at growth monitoring and development checks for children aged 0–5 years • Attendance at medical checkups for children • Provision of baby porridge • Ensure that children grow and put on weight • Toilet training of children • Attendance at prenatal and postnatal checkups for pregnant and postpartum women • Use of contraceptives: implants or pills • Vaccination of children • Provision of vitamins and micronutrient sprinkles to children as long as these are available at the health center • Attendance at trainings • Communal work: cleaning of health center and repairs according to health personnel requests
Identity	• Mothers and children must obtain a national identity card
Other	• Participation in the Local Juntos Committee: attend meetings, pay fines and collaborate with activities of the committee • Participation in communal work activities organized by the local authorities for program beneficiaries (typically street and public space cleaning) • Purchase of children's clothing • Home improvements and repairs: kitchen improvements, cupboards, latrines, separate bedrooms for adults and children • Cleanliness and order in the home • Needlework and weaving • Cultivation of an organic garden or greenhouse • Raising animals for household consumption • Saving for business investment

also found that 15 percent of beneficiary mothers interviewed had been pressured by *gestores* or local authorities to pay expenses of Programa Juntos (Escobal y Benites 2012b).

During fieldwork, it was observed that households went to great lengths to comply with what they perceived as conditionalities associated with the program. Cases were also observed of mothers who became discouraged at the thought of joining Juntos because they felt the program would be too demanding. Indigenous households also tended to elaborate a hierarchy of conditionalities, based on their positive or negative character.

Positive and Negative Conditionalities

Indigenous households in our study tended to regard program requirements related to health, nutrition, documentation, and training as positive for their families and communities, given that they generally improved quality of life and increased the possibility of transitioning out of poverty. However, as discussed above, what is considered to be a conditionality in health or education may well not be an official Juntos conditionality. For example, when discussing education conditionalities, people referred to academic performance, proper clothing, and cleanliness of children in addition to the actual conditionality of school attendance. Similarly, in regards to health, achieving increases in weight and height were considered to be as much a conditionality as attendance at medical checkups.

A number of perceived conditionalities that are interpreted by beneficiaries as negative or even abusive are intermingled with the official conditionalities, complementary activities, and unofficial non-Juntos requirements imposed by local actors. These are described below. It should be noted than none of these requirements is an official program conditionality.

Contraception: although the majority of women value access to contraception for family planning purposes, they feel that obligatory use of contraception is wrong. During fieldwork, it was found that various household informants believed that contraceptive use was a conditionality of the program. Respondents alluded to recent or past experiences, and also to rumors originating from other communities. Researchers found that health personnel obliged or strongly suggested that beneficiaries — including girls as young as twelve—use contraception. In two Amazonian communities, health personnel explicitly used *Juntos* as a means of forcing women to use contraceptives, indicating that they would not sign their attendance cards and threatening to inform the *gestor* if the women did not comply.

Free labor: the traditional *faena,* or communal work activity, has been redefined as a Juntos conditionality in all the study communities. Mothers attend these activities because they are afraid of punishment by the program. These demands are socially accepted because the beneficiaries of the program are (as described above) considered to be receiving a salary, donation, or support from the state, which in turn needs to be reciprocated. Work demands typically include cleaning of public spaces but can also extend to building repair and construction work. Given that the *faena* is a traditional institution both in Andean and Amazonian communities, program beneficiaries were inclined to participate, but questioned why they were assigned arduous tasks and threatened with being denounced to the *gestores.*

Demands for donations on the part of schools: in all the study communities, it was found that education personnel requested donations and support from the beneficiary families. These requested contributions included payment for services, the purchase of classroom materials, and the obligatory acquisition of "activity cards" for fundraising activities such as raffles and sales of prepared meals. Beneficiaries in all the communities explained that demands had increased because the teachers knew who was receiving cash transfers and would thus have some financial liquidity every two months. In the view of teachers, the transfer was supposed to be for education, so such demands on beneficiary families were perfectly legitimate. This viewpoint was perhaps unsurprisingly shared by nonbeneficiaries in all the study communities.

Transfers

Understandings and Uses of the Transfers

Cash transfers were highly valued as a source of liquidity among beneficiary families. Transfers also constituted a cushion in the face of economic shocks such as bad harvests or a lack of seasonal work. In the poorest households, the cash transfer was at times the only source of regular income. However, in all the communities, the transfer was considered to be insufficient for families with several children and was always considered to be a complementary contribution to the domestic economy.

How was the transfer used in the study communities? Observations carried out in homes and markets on paydays revealed that beneficiaries used most of their transfers to buy food, clothing, cleaning supplies, and school materials for children. Observed purchases included fresh meat and fish, tinned tuna, fruit, vegetables, noodles, soap, detergent, and matches. The transfer also permitted families to buy items that are not normally part of the basic basket of foodstuffs: fruit and vegetables in the case of Andean communities, and legumes, meat, and condiments in the case of Amazonian areas. Purchases of treats such as sweets, ice creams, and sodas in community shops were also made on paydays. In the majority of study households, foodstuffs purchased with the transfers lasted between one and two weeks. A common discourse existed about appropriate use of the transfers, in which the purchase of alcoholic beverages, coca leaves, or luxury items such as cellphones or radios was scrutinized. Tensions over the use of the money did arise, particularly between wives and husbands or with their adolescent children. In all the communities, there was a perception that traders increased the prices of their higher-demand goods on paydays in order to take advantage of the captive clientele. Numerous testimonies to this price effect were collected over the course of research, and the phenomenon was also confirmed by direct observation in our research.

When the transfer was used for educational purposes, the purchase of school materials and uniforms was prioritized. As noted above, education expenses also included contributions for teaching materials and to the Parents Association (Asociación de Padres de Familia—APAFA). In all communities, requests for such contributions were said to have increased since the arrival of Juntos. Even where these contributions were small, they were said to be frequent and of a cumulative nature according to the number of children in the household. Three other main uses of the transfer were identified:

Payment of expenses associated with program participation: these costs were generally associated with photocopies, transport to payment locations, fees or fines demanded by the local Juntos committee, and the purchase of materials need to engage in the complementary activities related to the program.

Saving: beneficiaries used two main strategies for saving: (1) emergency funds, usually used to handle sudden illnesses of family members or to respond to demands made by the APAFA or the school, and (2) productive savings targeted at purchases of small animals (guinea pigs or pigs), cattle, and for motors or fishing boats, in the case of Amazonian communities. Most households found it very difficult to save regularly. However, when they managed to do so, they prioritized emergency funds. Productive saving was found to be much less common, and examples were generally found in households with only one or two children.

Payment of debts: debts were found to be of two types. The most frequent were related to the purchase of foodstuffs and medicines on credit terms within the home communities, a very common practice in the Amazonian communities. Beneficiaries requested credit in local shops to buy noodles, tuna, eggs, rice, matches, soap, and candles, as well as black market medicines. A second type of debt payment was connected to microfinance credit. This situation was only encountered in Sicta, where researchers found, on the one hand, confusions about the conditions of the loans, and, on the other, that some beneficiaries felt obliged by the program (through the *gestores*) to participate in microfinance programs in spite of the interest charged on loans.

Discussion

Programa Juntos was introduced in indigenous communities in Peru with a less than auspicious launch characterized by distrust and skepticism. Since then, Juntos has acquired legitimacy through the fulfillment of its commitment to provide cash transfers, and, as the experiences of different communities have become better known, relationships between *gestores*, families, and local authorities have grown stronger. The program's continuous presence for at least five years in all the study communities has been a key factor in achieving this legitimacy.

These findings suggest that Programa Juntos can be regarded as an important instrument for building social inclusion in indigenous contexts similar to those in this study: possessing economic systems that combine monetization with traditional exchange systems such as barter, sufficient connections to the market, and access to health and education services. Note that they do not imply that Juntos would necessarily serve as a successful social protection instrument in indigenous contexts where these criteria are not met.

That said, challenges remain for the program. Many of these problems relate to the issue of communications: Juntos personnel must clarify not only the main program aims and objectives, but also clearly specify practices that do not support the program or its goals, and which in fact undermine the achievement of positive outcomes, such as the imposition of unofficial conditionalities. This strategy goes beyond simply communicating which conditionalities are official requirements of the program. It is equally important to understand the context in which the concept of conditionality can be appropriated by local actors—who may then redeploy it strategically in order to help them achieve goals unrelated to those of the program. Key to this context is the interpretation of compliance with conditionalities. This compliance is understood not within the framework of rights and duties that is central to the design of Juntos and other CCT programs, but rather as the discharge of obligation, gratitude,

or debt payment within an indigenous framework of reciprocity relations with the state. It is critical that the framework of rights and duties,
within which conditionalities can be refigured as co-responsibilities, be
communicated in terms appropriate to indigenous communities. It is
also of pressing importance to terminate the imposition of extra-official
conditionalities by local actors. Better communication around the issue
of conditionality should be accompanied by clearly understood systems
for registering complaints and reports of abuse. *Gestores*, leader mothers, and indigenous organizations should be sensitized about official
conditionalities of the program so that they can be alert to abuses and
manipulation.

A key aim of CCT programs is to improve beneficiary households'
access to nutritious foods: while the transfer is supposed to incentivize
uptake of health and education services, it is also supposed to make a
positive contribution to the domestic economy. In this study, we found
that the transfers appeared to have had a positive influence on household
dietary behaviors—by increasing the purchase of diverse foods and the
incorporation of these foods into the diet—in all communities. We would
note, however, that there are a number of factors that have the effect of
limiting the transfer's impact on household nutrition. The first of these
factors is that foods bought with the transfer only last between one and
two weeks. The second is that the transfers cannot be invested as fully as
they might be in food purchases given the increase in program-related
expenses, the increasing financial demands emanating from schools,
and—to a lesser extent—the opportunistic price manipulation at local
markets on paydays.

An area of frequent misunderstanding and confusion is beneficiary
selection and eligibility. As explained in this chapter, while residents of
study communities recognized a common experience of poverty based
around lack and inadequacy, they also make distinctions between levels
of poverty. These distinctions are based on criteria not typically used in
social protection program targeting, such as social capital, access to natural resources, family structure, or position in the local political economy.
Moreover, a common fear expressed by indigenous informants was not
appearing "poor enough" in the eyes of the broader community. This
fear can have potentially negative effects on beneficiary/nonbeneficiary
relations, as well as obscuring the central program objective of breaking
the cycle of intergenerational transmission of poverty. One approach to
making targeting and beneficiary selection more readily comprehensible
at the local level would be to mobilize the above-mentioned indigenous
conceptions of poverty gradation as a set of criteria complementing the
official poverty assessment program indicators.

A final point related to the question of eligibility concerns the perception that the program excludes or punishes families that manage to launch productive enterprises. This viewpoint is, in a sense, the logical extension of the preceding issue: launching an economic enterprise can have the effect of undermining the assessment of a given household as poor by their peers. This perception could constitute an important barrier to the development and implementation of program graduation strategies. It is therefore very important to promote beneficiary household participation in productive activities—both for the economic benefit of the households, and also to demonstrate clearly that Juntos supports and encourages such participation. However, as it is demonstrated in this study, indigenous families understood that Juntos is a temporary program and most of them expressed interest in participating in productive projects that would allow them to generate autonomous income to improve their quality of life, particularly to invest in their children's education. Here lies an important arena for policy innovation for Peru and Latin America, since existing productive development policies have not been adequately adapted for indigenous contexts. These adaptations should include sociocultural and political dimensions, but also be grounded on a sound understanding of the implications that climate change and the expansion of market economy have in indigenous livelihoods.

Postscript

The persistence of indigenous poverty is one of the main public policy challenges in Peru. Social protection and, specifically, cash transfer programs have been among the main instruments of the Peruvian State to respond to poverty and indigenous vulnerability. Since 2010, social programs have experienced a remarkable expansion of coverage in the Amazon, which has been accelerated by a regulatory change made in September 2014 on the targeting of beneficiaries in Amazonian indigenous communities (Ministerial Resolution 227-2014-MIDIS). This regulation, promoted by the Ministry of Development and Social Inclusion, created a new targeting mechanism to facilitate access to social programs and subsidies for residents of Amazonian indigenous communities. To this end, this regulation grants the socio-economic classification of "extreme poor" to all residents of Amazonian indigenous communities, using geographical targeting criteria. Therefore, all residents of Amazonian indigenous communities are eligible for social programs directed at their age group. As a result, the two cash transfer programs present in Peru have expanded throughout the Amazon, including border areas: Program Juntos directed at households in poverty with children under 19 and the non-contributory pension program "Pension 65" directed at adults over 65 years of age living in poverty. Likewise, the coverage of other social programs has been expanded (school feeding, children's early development, adult economic inclusion). The effects of the greater presence of the State through social programs in indigenous contexts has not been evaluated systematically.

Five years after the culmination of our field work in the regions of Amazonas, Ayacucho, Junín, Huancavelica, Loreto, and Puno, we observe that Programa Juntos has improved its operational processes, especially those related to the selection of beneficiaries, monitoring compliance of conditionalities and its transfer payment system, for which it obtained an international quality management system certificate (ISO 9001) in 2015. Despite these improvements, several challenges persist. Firstly, it is necessary to move beyond a logic of extending coverage to improving the supply, quality, and cultural pertinence of education and health services, on which the conditionalities of the Peruvian CCT are based. This implies sustained intersectoral work among social ministries, otherwise there is a high risk of deepening inequalities due to poor quality of public services, where—as our study documents—there may be situations of mistreatment and discrimination against indigenous citizens. Secondly, it is urgent to abandon the "one size fits all" model in Peruvian social policy to promote the adaptation of the supply of existing social programs to the cultural, social, economic, and geographical peculiarities of indigenous communities, especially in the Amazon. Finally, thirteen years after its creation, Programa Juntos faces the challenge of providing better opportunities for overcoming poverty. To this end, the Peruvian State has been promoting the participation of Juntos beneficiaries in Haku Wiñay/Noa Jayatai, an economic inclusion social program which develops productive capacities and promotes small-scale entrepreneurship oriented toward the generation of autonomous income. This productive social program has also experienced an important expansion in indigenous contexts as a consequence of the normative change referred to at the beginning of this note. However, current interventions undertaken by the Peruvian State are still insufficient to respond to the causes of indigenous poverty, for which a larger scale and multi-sectorial effort is required to ensure food security, access to productive assets, and fair articulation with the market, as well as to protect the environment on which the livelihoods of indigenous communities depend.

Norma Correa Aste is a professor of anthropology at Pontificia Universidad Católica del Perú (PUCP). Her work focuses on public policy, anthropology of development, poverty, and social innovation. She has extensive experience as a senior researcher, project director, and evaluator for international organizations, public sector institutions, and think tanks in Latin America. Correa Aste holds a master's degree in social policy from the London School of Economics and a professional title in anthropology from PUCP. As a Huiracocha and TRANDES fellow, Norma is currently a doctoral candidate at PUCP. Her doctoral thesis studies the expansion of poverty alleviation interventions in the Amazon. She coauthored *Pueblos indígenas y Programas de Transferencias Condicionadas* with Terry Roopnaraine (BID, 2014) and has contributed to various edited volumes, including Peru's *Human Development Report* (UNDP, 2010).

Terry Roopnaraine is currently Senior Consultant in Social Development at Oxford Policy Management. At the time of research, he was a consultant working under contract for the International Food Policy Research Institute. Roopnaraine has been carrying out research on cash transfers and social protection programming since 2003. Key publications include "Understanding Use of Health Services in Conditional Cash Transfer Programs: Insights from Qualitative Research in Latin America and Turkey" (with Michelle Adato, 2012, *Social Science and Medicine* 22: 12); "Programming for Citizenship: The Conditional Cash Transfer Programme in El Salvador" (with Michelle Adato and Oscar Morales Barahona, 2016, *Journal of Development Studies* 52: 8); and with Norma Correa Aste, *Pueblos indígenas y Programas de Transferencias Condicionadas* (BID, 2014).

Amy Margolies is currently a doctoral candidate at the Johns Hopkins Bloomberg School of Public Health. Amy holds a master's degree from the Fletcher School at Tufts University. At the time of research, Amy was working for the International Food Policy Research Institute (IFPRI). As a Mickey Leland International Hunger Fellow, Amy also worked with the Brazilian government on their National School Meals Program. Key publications include "Costing Alternative Transfer Modalities" (with John Hoddinott, 2015, *Journal of Development Effectiveness*); "Cash, Food, or Vouchers? Evidence from a Randomized Experiment in Northern Ecuador" (with Hidrobo, Hoddinott, Peterman et al., 2014, *Journal of Development Economics*).

Notes

1. Per year, Programa Juntos provides six bimonthly installments using a flat fee of 200 soles ($62 US), which are paid to beneficiary families through the public bank (Banco de la Nación). By 2017, the minimum monthly wage in Peru was $257 (US).

2. Known as Niños del Milenio in Spanish.
3. See, for examples of more sophisticated qualitative approaches to CCT research, Adato and Hoddinott 2010.
4. This chapter presents a selection of findings from a wider study produced as a result of an institutional cooperation agreement between the International Food Policy Research Institute (IFPRI) and Pontifical Catholic University of Peru (PUCP). The research was funded by the Gender and Diversity Unit of the Inter-American Development Bank (IDB) as part of the project implemented by IFPRI: Enhancing the Effectiveness and Addressing the Sociocultural Impacts of Conditional Cash Transfers in Indigenous Contexts. The results, interpretations, and conclusions expressed in this document are the sole responsibility of the authors.
5. Anthropologists Mariella Gonzáles Jacinto, María del Pilar Ego-Aguirre Rodríguez, and Romina Seminario Luna from Pontificia Universidad Católica del Perú.
6. A detailed description of the methodological approach used in this study is published in Correa and Roopnaraine 2014.
7. The myth of the *Pishtaco* or *Nakaq* originated in colonial times and is particularly common in Andean and Amazonian communities. Also known as *saca-ojos* or *saca-grasa* (eye-snatcher or fat-snatcher), the *Pishtaco* is always an outsider to the community—and generally a foreigner—who wants to kidnap victims in order to steal or extract body parts. As a myth, it alludes to unequal power relations and serves as an interpretive motif in times of acute change or crisis (Ansión 1989).
8. As a response to these types of concerns, some *gestores* simply explained that the transfer money came from taxes collected from food sales.
9. Juntos field staff, known as *gestores*, are the most important intermediaries between the program, communities, and households. Their main responsibility is to verify the compliance of program conditionalities by beneficiary households, a process that requires coordination with local teachers and health personnel.
10. Beca 18 is a Ministry of Education program. The program funds qualified but poor students to continue tertiary education.
11. The Ministry of Development and Social Inclusion (MIDIS for its acronym in Spanish) is the governing body for social protection and poverty policies in Peru.
12. Note that Programa Juntos uses the Spanish term "corresponsabilidad," which translates best as "co-responsibility." However, in this chapter, we usually opt for the term "conditionality" because this is the standard English term used in most CCT program documentation and literature.

References

Adato, M., and J. Hoddinott. 2010. *Conditional Cash Transfers in Latin America.* Baltimore, MD: Johns Hopkins University Press.

Ansión, J. 1989. *Pishtacos: De verdugos a sacaojos.* Lima: Tarea.

Arroyo, J. 2010a. *Estudio cualitativo de los efectos del Programa Juntos en los cambios de comportamiento de los hogares beneficiarios en el distrito de Chuschi: Avances y Evidencias.* Lima: Ministerio de la Mujer y Poblaciones Vulnerables.

Alcázar, L., and K. Espinoza. 2015. "Impacts of the Peruvian Conditional Cash Transfer Programme on Women's Empowerment: A Quantitative and Qualitative Approach." *Policy in Focus Brasilia: IPG-IG* 32: 33–36.

Correa, N. 2007. "Exploring the Adoption and Adaptation of a Conditional-Cash Transfer Program in Peru: The Case of Programa Juntos." M.Sc. dissertation, London School of Economics and Political Science.

Correa, N., and T. Roopnaraine. 2014. *Pueblos indígenas y programas de transferencias condicionadas: Estudio etnográfico sobre la implementación y los efectos socioculturales del Programa Juntos en seis comunidades andinas y amazónicas de Perú.* Washington DC/Lima: IADB, PUCP, and IFPRI.

Del Pozo, C., and E. Sánchez. 2011. *Efectos de las transferencias monetarias condicionadas en la inversión productiva de los hogares rurales en el Perú.* Proyecto Breve PB-014-2010. Informe Final. Lima: Consorcio de Investigación Económica y Social.

Díaz, R., L. Huber, O. Madalengoitia, R. Saldaña, C. Trivelli, R. Vargas, and X. Salazar. 2009. *Análisis de la implementación del Programa Juntos en las regiones de Apurímac, Huancavelica y Huánuco.* Lima: Consorcio de Investigación Económica y Social y CARE, Programa de Derechos en Salud.

Escobal, J., and S. Benites. 2012b. "Transferencias y Condiciones: Efectos no previstos del Programa *Juntos*." Lima: Proyecto Niños del Milenio. *Boletín de políticas públicas sobre infancia 7.*

———. 2012a. "Algunos impactos del programa *Juntos* en el bienestar de los niños: Evidencia basada en el estudio Niños del Milenio." Lima: Proyecto Niños del Milenio. *Boletín de políticas públicas sobre infancia 5.*

Herrera, J., and A. Cozzubo. 2017. *Pobreza, desigualdad y políticas sociales: Balance 2011–2016 y Agenda de Investigación 2017–2021.* Diagnóstica y Propuesta 54. Lima: Consorcio de Investigación Económica y Social

Huber, L., P. Zárate, A. Durand, O. Madalengoitia, and J. Morel. 2009. *Programa Juntos: certezas y malentendidos en torno a las transferencias condicionadas. Estudio de caso de seis distritos rurales del Perú.* Lima: Instituto de Estudios Peruanos, UNICEF, and UNFPA.

Jones, N. 2009. "Cash Transfers to Tackle Childhood Poverty and Vulnerability: An Analysis of Peru's *Juntos* Programme." *Environment and Urbanization* 20(1): 255–273.

Jones, N., R. Vargas, and E. Villar. 2006. *Conditional Cash Transfers in Peru: Tackling the Multi-dimensionality of Poverty and Vulnerability* (draft). Young Lives Project, funded by the United Kingdom Department for International Development, Oxford.

Mauss, M. (1925) 2000. *The Gift: The Form and Reason for Exchange in Archaic Societies.* London: W.W. Norton & Co.

Monge A., and Y. Campana. 2012. *Pobreza, distribución del ingreso y programas sociales.* In *La investigación económica y social en el Perú. Balance 2007–2011 y Agenda 2012–2016, Chapter 9,* edited by Consorcio de Investigación Económica y Social, 325–380. Lima: Consorcio de Investigación Económica y Social.

Nagels, N. 2014. "The Social Investment Perspective, Gender and the Conditional Cash Transfer Programs in Peru and Bolivia." In *Analysing Public Policies in Latin America: A Cognitive Approach,* edited by Maria Rocha Lukic and Carla Tomazini, 1–24. Newcastle upon Tyne: Cambridge Scholars Publishing.

Piccoli, E. 2014. "Dicen que los cien soles son del Diablo: L´interprétation apocalyptique et mytique du Programa *Juntos* dans les communautés andines de Cajamarca (Pérou) et la critique populaire des programmes sociaux." *Social Compass* 61: 328–347.

Sánchez, A., and M. Rodríguez. 2016. *Diez años Juntos: un balance de la investigación del impacto del programa de transferencias condicionadas del Perú sobre el capital humano.* In *Investigación para el Desarrollo en el Perú: Once Balances,* edited by Grupo de Análisis para el Desarrollo – GRADE, 207–250. Lima: GRADE.

Sánchez A., and M. Jaramillo. 2012. *Impacto del Programa Juntos sobre nutrición temprana.* Banco Central de la Reserva del Perú. Serie de documento de trabajo. Accessed 5 December 2017 http://www.bcrp.gob.pe/docs/ Publicaciones/Documentos-de-Trabajo/2012/documento-de-trabajo-01-2012. pdf.

Segovia, G. 2011. *Efectos del Programa Juntos en la economía local de las zonas rurales a cinco años de intervención en las regiones de Apurímac, Huancavelica y Huánuco.* Lima: Programa Nacional de Apoyo Directo a los más pobres.

Streuli, N. 2012. *Children´s Experiences of Juntos, a Conditional Cash Transfer Scheme in Peru.* Working Paper 78. Young Lives, Oxford.

Taussig, M. 1980. *The Devil and Commodity Fetishism in South America.* Chapel Hill, NC: University of North Carolina Press.

Trivelli, C., J. Montenegro, and M. C. Gutiérrez. 2011. "Un año ahorrando: Primeros resultados del Programa Piloto 'Promocion del ahorro en Familias Juntos.'" Documento de Trabajo 159. *Serie Economía* no. 51. Lima: Instituto de Estudios Peruanos.

Vargas, R. 2010. *Gendered Risks, Poverty and Vulnerability in Peru: A Case Study of the Juntos Programme.* London: Overseas Development Institute. Available at http://www.odi.org.uk/sites/odi.org.uk/files/odi-assets/publications-opinion-files/6246.pdf.

Chapter 6

Making Good Mothers

Conditions, Coercion, and Local Reactions in the Juntos Program in Peru

Emmanuelle Piccoli and Bronwen Gillespie

Introduction

The Juntos conditional cash transfer (CCT) program in Peru has greatly increased poor rural women's encounters with the state and has shaped their relationships with state workers, helping to cement recommended parenting and nutrition practices as "normal." This chapter aims to explore the implications of the conditional aspects of the cash transfer program, in particular the way in which it is used to impose certain behavior on women, and the way it operates within and reproduces existing social hierarchies.

The Peruvian CCT program is similar to the Mexican version (see Agudo Sanchiz, chapter 2 in this book) in terms of the importance of conditionality. Under this program, mothers living in poverty or extreme poverty, with children under eighteen years of age, receive financial support (equivalent to about $30 [US] per month) on the condition that they bring their young children to public health checkups, and once they are school age, ensure that they regularly attend preschool, primary school, and high school. Participants must also have valid state-issued identity documents. The financial support is paid bimonthly, generally at the closest bank.

Set up in 2005, the program expanded to include 807,552 families by 2014, when it was present in 1143 of the 1844 districts of the country. The Humala administration (2011–2016) included Juntos within the newly

---

created Ministry of Development and Social Inclusion (MIDIS), which has a vision to "eradicate extreme poverty and chronic child malnutrition, that children of all the national territory receive quality universal health-care and education," and aims to "break the historic intergenerational transmission of poverty and social exclusion."[1]

As we will describe, various extralegal (i.e., unofficial) conditions have been added to the two central conditions, varying from region to region, with the common factor of inducing women to carry out activities in areas related to public health, education, public representation, and domestic life, far beyond the legal framework of the program (see also Correa Aste, Roopnaire, and Margolies, chapter 5 in this book). We will demonstrate that the imposition of extralegal conditions has been part of how Juntos exists at the local level, that this overlaps with discriminatory views of rural Andean life, and that both are part of the way motherhood "best practices" are promoted to villagers. How women react—from resistance and opposition to the adoption of Juntos discourses—will be described. We will see not only how the disciplinary nature of the program is han-dled by state workers, but also how it is utilized by village mothers to carve out distinctions among themselves.

This chapter is based on two ethnographic investigations in the rural Peruvian Andes. One took place in Cajamarca, in the first years of the program (2008–2013 by Piccoli), and the observations on Juntos were part of a Ph.D. and postdoctoral project on local politics and peasant institutions. The other took place later on in Ayacucho (2012–2013 by Gillespie). This chapter is a result of the dialogue between these two distinct realities and the historical shifts in the application of the Juntos Program. This allows us to provide a reflection on state policies at the local level and highlight some of the consequences of the use of conditions for the women and communities involved.

Programa Juntos: Conditions and Impositions

From the outset of the program, as well as the two central pillars of nutrition appointments and school attendance, a variety of additional requirements were communicated, not officially published as part of the program, but locally presented as obligations. This was also observed by Correa, Roopnaire, and Margolies (in this volume), demonstrating that these extralegal practices became generalized and cannot therefore be dismissed as "local exceptions."

For instance, between 2008 and 2011, field observation in a peasant community in Cajamarca revealed that, in practice, women had to fulfill three extralegal requirements on top of the official conditions in order to receive their subsidy. The first requirement related to kitchens. According to women in the village, the local Juntos coordinator had insisted that women have so-called "improved" stoves, that is, brick stoves with a chimney. Moreover, the kitchen could no longer be a living space for guinea pigs (a common source of food for the household): they had to be raised in cages. The second condition related to personal hygiene: all houses had to be equipped with latrines and a *ricón de aseo*, a personal care area, with access to water, soap, and toothbrushes. The third extralegal condition was to put up signs with the program logo and the slogan *Programa Juntos, para salir adelante* (Juntos Program, let's move forward), at the entrance, on the latrines, and in the personal care area.

In Ayacucho, in the initial years of the program, women were told, as in Cajamarca, to remove their guinea pigs from the kitchen, cook indoors on improved stoves, and construct latrines, and also to create ecological refrigerators and food-storage shelves, to grow vegetable gardens, and ensure homes had separate bedrooms for children and parents. In Ayacucho, the Juntos coordinator at that time (pre-2011) was said to have come to visit the day after the payment and snoop in the cupboards to see what food had been purchased. The Juntos official in a neighboring province was reported to have gone over to the pot on the stove, lifted the lid, and said, "This is what you are cooking? No wonder your children have malnutrition." These domestic recommendations were widely understood to be compulsory: even a local nurse was heard to ask why one of her patients was not cut from the program, noting that she did not have a latrine.

The household visit (tellingly referred to at the village level as "inspection") was phased out by the end of 2012 and the domestic practices, though still recommended, were no longer subject to regular observation, though women still appeared to expect surprise visits to occur. Juntos coordinators continued to use the threat of withdrawing aid, not so much to make domestic changes, but rather to incite women to participate in additional state programs and events, often not direct Juntos activities but seen to coincide with program interests. The type of conditionality shifted, yet the principal remained the same. For example, district-level coordinators of various MIDIS programs have interpreted, along with Juntos, the mandate to work together for social inclusion as a license to present MIDIS programs as obligatory for Juntos participants. With the Juntos program, the aim is to "kill two birds with one stone" and use the conditionality to ensure participation in other government initiatives. Both in Cajamarca and Ayacucho, in the 2012–2013 period, the Cuna Mas (often translated as "Cradle Plus") infant daycare program was insinuated as mandatory for Juntos members. "We use this as a strategy in order for women to take part," agreed Maria,[2] the local Juntos coordinator. In Cajamarca, during Juntos assemblies, terms such as "conditions," "requirements," or "suggested activities" were used interchangeably in discourse, which allowed the extralegal conditions to seem compulsory. The regional coordinator in Cajamarca confirmed that this confusion was created voluntarily. For instance, when asked how women could differentiate between "official conditions" and other requests, she explained that "these are not conditions, they are requirements" (*no son condiciones, son obligaciones*). When asked whether women were aware of the subtle difference she inferred between requirement (optional) and condition (compulsory) she replied, "No, women do not know this. This is part of the awareness raising: they need to learn what their duties are." In her opinion, their duties included putting their child under the care of the state in Cuna Mas daycares; there is an underlying assumption that children will inevitably benefit from better attention and nutrition in centers than with their families.

In Ayacucho, women were told that the new Cuna Mas Family Accompaniment program (involving home visits to educate mothers on the importance of guided play) was linked to Juntos in a strategy to increase local participation. The phrase "we will share the list" was commonly used as an indirect threat by the Juntos coordinator and other officials, suggesting that they would compare the names of women registered for Juntos with those on the other program's attendance sheet, effectively presenting it as compulsory. This was used, for example, to get women to attend a Qali Warma lunch program cooking demonstration (also a MIDIS program).

Not only MIDIS programs, but municipal authorities, health workers, teachers, and even local community authorities used Juntos to ensure participation in their own events. Although the increased use of public services (health and education) is an official program goal, this affiliation between Juntos and public services was taken a step further to meet the interests of other agendas. For example, in Cajamarca, health workers threatened to remove women from the program if they did not take part in extra workshops. Also, inasmuch as schools, with their limited budgets, are concerned, there is a strong temptation for teachers to perceive of Juntos as "manna" (Olivier de Sardan 2014: 211) to finance teachers' initiatives. Considerable involvement is already expected from families—and mothers—from the start: teacher-parent meetings, preparing meals for children, and organizing and taking part in school fairs. With the arrival of Juntos, some teachers have been documented to significantly increase their demands for parents to pay for additional materials and activities for the school. The school director in a village in Ayacucho was observed to have called upon the Juntos recipients to carry out a day of school grounds maintenance, even though some women's children did not even attend school yet. In Ayacucho, nurses made use of the fear of being cut from the program to chastise mothers who they deemed as failing to follow their nutrition advice. As Lena complained, "I went to the post[3] and the nurse got angry with me: 'your boy needs more food, liver, fish, he's not gaining weight! I will tell Juntos to cut you off!' she yelled. I tried to explain it was because he had a cough, then diarrhea." Moral reprimand regarding parenting permeated the fabric of the program, and the conditions tied women to the health center, where they often received verbal abuse.

Political use of the Juntos program as a means to obtain votes has been observed but is strongly monitored by the program. We did not hear of any cases during our fieldwork, although Juntos was nonetheless commonly used to ensure citizen participation in public activities such as flag-raisings and parades. This demand could come from government officials (such as governors and mayors, and even village-level authorities) and had been part of the visibility of the program since the outset. "Marching, checkups, meetings," Olga, from Ayacucho, listed the burdens of Juntos and half-laughed, "Juntos will be with us, even as we die!" At a meeting the week before National Flag day, the Juntos coordinator told the village Juntos representatives, "Yes, we are marching.... There will be a fine if no one comes from your village." Weeks later, during the next monthly meeting, she was angry: "I saw that on Flag Day the women wore any clothes they wanted. They didn't wear what we agreed upon.... Well go like that if you want, but I'm not going to note your names as present." Juntos was also used as a forum to organize the Healthy Communities municipal program in numerous communities in a district of Ayacucho. Juntos members complained that they were required to pick up litter, make public play areas, improve their houses, and attend training sessions, while government workers, on top of their salaries, received new jackets and other materials for individual use as part of the program budget. It appeared to them as a kind of corruption, that as mothers they were taught "what we already know" and made to work, while professionals were seen to benefit.

Even at the village level, the program was subject to abuse. However, village-level attempts to cash in on the program were generally more contested. For instance, at an assembly in a Cajamarca community, it was decided that the village fair would be funded with money from the program. This gave rise to a conflict, as many people argued that the money was meant for families and children, not for the community as a whole. Finally it was decided that financial contributions would be made on a voluntary basis. Tensions were also noted in Ayacucho, when Juntos was used by other actors to further the duties of participating mothers. As Leonor explained, "In the community when something has to be done, like cleaning the school or community hall, people say, 'Oh, those mothers can do it, they receive money.'"

Imposing these extralegal conditions is possible because Juntos coordinators have tended to monopolize information on the details of program functioning. Women's fear of losing the payment, combined with challenges of objectively measuring poverty and assessing some of the conditional requirements (such as failure to attend school due to illness), can appear to give a rather arbitrary power to the coordinators. Importantly, Juntos coordinators relied on maintaining a working relationship with district, provincial, and regional government officials (in order to gain access to census lists, office space, and other practical concerns), as well as with health centers and schools, from which they rely on attendance lists to ensure program compliance, so program use and abuse by various agents to push women to act in a certain way was tolerated. Although no one was actually cut from the program when extralegal conditions were not met, the repetition of the threats and lack of alternative information had the effect of making it true. As well, the threat of fines, as mentioned above, worked to enforce participation, at both the community and the district level, despite not being part of the official Juntos system. Women marked absent at events linked to Juntos would either pay a small fee or be sent to represent the village when required.

If CCTs have been described as "manna" for recipients (Olivier de Sardan 2014: 211), in the Peruvian case, we can see that the program also serves as a "manna" for state agents, used for their own agendas. The practice of giving out 100 soles (around $30 [US]) each month (in bimonthly payments), officially tied to health and education, has created an instrument of coercion, permitting a much larger collection of health-related activities and behaviors to be tied to the program, in the interest of state workers and other authorities. In this sense, we ask whether the Juntos program can be seen to be indirectly financing other policies and projects, improving overall indicators, such as participation numbers, that would have weak performance if they had to rely on quality rather than coercion in order to gain attendance.

Toward the end of the research period, Juntos officials at the central government level attempted to reduce the misuse of the program: in 2013 the government issued a resolution to clarify that the only legal program conditions are school attendance, and for those under school age, nutrition checkups at the health center. The information started to trickle down to rural communities. In October 2013, in Ayacucho, Juanita said that her husband had heard on television that Juntos cannot "obligate things anymore . . . or make us paint the sign on our doors, they can't do that to the poor." People were pleased. Another woman commented, "It's good because before they were saying, 'There is a *faena*[4] in the school, now everyone has to go or we will tell Juntos,' or if you are late, you have to pay a fee, and they also said we have to march. . . . Maybe these words arrived to the government and now they are changing it." Despite the new declaration, women erred on the side of caution, waiting over an hour for a state-run cooking demonstration to take place (although no one ever arrived), as they remained unsure of the position of local state workers regarding the new information, and had heard that, as always, "the list would be passed" for Juntos. The well-intentioned clarifications regarding misuse still seemed far removed from women's everyday lives. The extent to which operational changes actually take place remains to be seen—interviews at regional level in both Cajamarca and Ayacucho suggest a purposeful policy of lack of clarity, as regional officials felt that despite the intentions of respecting the poor, following the full implications of the legal resolution would cause disruption in the coordination of the program in the field.

Remaking the Andean Mother

The program has been active in disseminating ideas of what it is to be a "good mother." Both Juntos employees and other state workers (primarily public health) understand their mandate as one of being sent to ensure rural people change their lifestyles. We will look at how these messages overlap with the stigma of being an Andean peasant.

The encounter with the health center is central to the Juntos experience: previous to its inception, visits to the health center were few and far between (predominant use was for giving birth, a result of concerted efforts to reduce maternal mortality). Although the government has made a significant effort to offer universal health coverage, and rural populations recognize the benefits of increased access to medical care (Del Pino et al. 2012), public health is still subject to criticism for low-quality service and discriminatory treatment, as has already been documented in the rural Andes (Diez Canseco 2003). An underlying philosophy of the Juntos program was to link the cash transfer to the use of state services, in this sense "activating demand" for public health services. In our experience, descriptions of the healthcare service demonstrate a tendency toward improvement. Even so, in our research in Ayacucho, while most women insisted that they themselves were not usually yelled at, almost everyone had a complaint to voice, having received criticism such as "you people reproduce like guinea pigs"; they knew to avoid certain "angry" staff members more liable to deliver verbal abuse, and were prepared to have to wait long hours for attention.

Similarly, the Juntos coordinator in place while this research was carried out was described as "kindly," yet the discriminatory actions of the previous one were fresh on everyone's minds: "The last Juntos woman was very mean. She never had patience for questions. Luckily she didn't inspect much here. But they said she went to every house in Corugata and said, 'How can you live like this, like a pig!'" Clara demonstrated how the previous coordinator would greet her by holding her hand out, pointing it downward, so just to offer her wrist to shake, implying that Clara's hand was too dirty to touch.

As well as increasing the encounters with Juntos and health-system staff, the program puts women into contact with other visiting professionals, who make use of the Juntos forum to present other programs. As observed in the Ayacucho region, one engineer proclaimed, during his presentation in a Juntos meeting: "Poverty and health problems are not the problems of the Juntos coordinator; they are the problems of the beneficiaries. Why are there so many hospitals in Peru? It is because there are a lot of sick people, and this is because mothers do not feed their children well and they live in dirtiness. The illnesses come from the dirty conditions."

Measures to fight poverty and ill-health can be seen to inadvertently stigmatize or undermine Andean lifestyles and identity. Houses are to be made hygienic in a Westernization of local household habits and body positions. Although several studies did indeed reveal a link between traditional kitchens (which lack a chimney) and lung disease (Silva Serrano and Zeña Giraldo 2007), the "improved" stove projects (as well as the introduction of tables and insistence on indoor food preparation and cooking) promoted the standing position as the appropriate position to prepare a meal, rather than the usual Andean sitting position, and pushed aside the customary family gathering around the open fire. This implies significant symbolic violence. In the same way, prohibiting the presence of guinea pigs prioritizes a hygienist vision of the household at the expense of traditional guinea pig breeding practices. It follows a logic based on the separation of human and animal spaces, introducing a specific notion of impurity foreign to Andean people, all the more because the presence of guinea pigs near the hearth is due to practical necessity: these creatures need warmth, and protection from predators; and the freedom to range free, outside cages, is seen to make them more robust and strong.

Furthermore, the program requirement to display the flag and slogan on and inside the house (as observed in Cajamarca) allows the program to penetrate people's private space and makes the presence of the state visible in the intimacy of their own homes. Moreover, these symbols reveal the family's economic situation to the whole community and to visitors passing by, subjecting the family to the associations this labeling may bring: they are in Juntos, they are "the poor," according to the criteria officially established.

Obviously, this type of discriminatory language and the social stigma facing Andean populations did not originate with Juntos, nor did the state's interest in hygiene and nutrition, which had been the subject to much earlier interventions (Wilson 2004; Ewig 2010). Juntos formalized these encounters, so that they became an everyday part of women's lives. In Peru, poverty and malnutrition indicators overlap significantly with rural and indigenous language speaking areas (Benavides et al. 2010). This, combined with the way in which malnutrition and poverty are presented as individualized problems to be combatted with lifestyle changes, means that state workers, in efforts to ingrain "responsibility," have ample opportunity to slip these prejudices into their daily interactions with local mothers as almost intrinsic to the way public health and Juntos work, based on assumptions of the need to "fix up" the rural Andean rural mother. In this sense, the state appears to be inadvertently legitimizing problematic language and treatment used within public services.

Reacting and Resisting

Initially, women were suspicious of the program. Trina, from Ayacucho, recalled, "At first we were scared, we didn't understand. Someone said that if they were giving us money, it was to later take our kids and sell them to foreigners. But then a doctor came and told us, 'No, why would they want your kids? They want special kids, not ones like these!' And so we laughed and realized it was true." In Cajamarca, some women said they rejected the program fearing its links with the devil, in line with their evangelical beliefs. The region has experienced a growing predominance of evangelical churches, with their apocalyptic prophecies (Piccoli 2014). Others made reference to the historical deeply feared Andean figure of the *Pishtaco*—a child thief who kills humans for their fat (see Correa Aste, Roopnaire, Margolies in this book; Ansion and Szeminski 1982; Gose 1986; Weismantel 2001) who in a modern-day version makes use of Juntos coordinators as a sort of kidnapping service (Piccoli 2014). These types of discourse surrounding the program are widespread and numerous, and should not be put aside but merit being seen as "a manner to represent, using fantasy . . . anger and reciprocal aggression in the face of a dominant repression" (Scott 2000: 64).

Women express their frustrations with the demands of the program in a variety of ways. Slowness and a lack of will to comply is one way women maneuver in response to the extralegal demands. For instance, in 2009, Doña Elsa told us in confidence, alone in her house, "I will not make the flag. She can get angry all she likes. There will be no such thing in my house." In this way, she will promise to comply, and she will not oppose the coordinator upfront nor give voice to her indignation, but by being very slow to act, she will hinder the orders and ultimately completely avoid them. Such slowness, which generally irritates coordinators, also expresses discontent. In this community, the coordinator was none the wiser and became angry, as did other Juntos workers before her, at the peasants' supposed apathy, and she did not realize she had triggered this reaction herself by imposing unilaterally unwanted practices.

Another form of resistance is to be found in the interrelationship between peasants and their animals, in which the animals themselves play a role in this resistance. For example, one night, some of Tilia's guinea pigs were indeed in cages, but others were roaming free in the kitchen because "they got out, that's all." Both humans and nonhumans appear to be revolting against the conditions. Tilia could say she complied with the demands, putting her animals in cages, yet at the same time, the animals remained free, as they themselves escaped and she had not taken part. Here, the responsibility is placed on the animals. This, too, was noted in Maria's house, her guinea pigs had "escaped," and she let them enjoy their freedom from the formally prescribed spaces. Despite social programs' recommendations, animals rebelling against hygienist programs are not promptly put back in their place (Piccoli 2015).

Women in Ayacucho actually took a more public stance of resistance, complaining to local authorities about the verbal abuse they received from the Juntos coordinator, who was in turn removed from her post. They described it in victorious terms. Maura laughed and said, "They say they sent her to work far away, where cars don't even arrive!," and her husband added "On what *puna*[5] is she now, where did they send her, for being bad?" The new coordinator has earned women's trust and they have begun to experiment with voicing their complaints. Regarding the Healthy Community program, mentioned above, one woman told the coordinator, "They scare us with Juntos. They told us that if we don't participate, they will cut us from Juntos. Sometimes I think it would be better to leave"; the coordinator in turn advised them to make their protests heard at the regional office.

Adopting Juntos

Despite the coercive aspects, the discriminatory discourse, and frustrations with the program, these challenges do not tell the whole story. In fact, a widespread normalization of some Juntos-promoted behaviors were observed. Over time, the program had come to reflect not coercion but rather a generalized acceptance of the Juntos recommendations and a high level of participation. Juntos was frequent in conversation as a marker of "before and after," with women commenting that before Juntos "we didn't know" about nutrition, or "with Juntos" the latrines arrived. Most significantly, after seven years of the program in Ayacucho, nutrition checkups became normalized, an activity carried out not only by those participating in the Juntos program, but by other mothers who did not have any official obligation, just to see if their baby was fine. Through Juntos, the health system managed to introduce new measures for what "fine" means, so that height, weight and malnutrition have come to represent significant concerns for mothers. Mothers also linked the practice of hand washing, the tendency to save choice bits of meat and fruit for toddlers and the increased preparation of solid meals (rice and beans) as compared to traditional soup, to the Juntos program.

We suggest that Juntos ideals have come to fit into a vision of the future shared by local women and that, by taking up Juntos recommendations, certain women aim to maneuver past the low-status category within which Juntos has located them. Juntos recommendations have been sold as an investment in the future: ensuring nutrition and education (diet in infant years is linked to brain development) is their children's ticket out of rural poverty. This sales pitch was observed (and recorded in field notes) in a village-level Juntos meeting in Ayacucho in March 2013:

> Seated in a long row on big stones and temporary benches in the dusty, half-finished community hall in the village, women listened to the visiting Juntos social program coordinator, as she finished her brief visit to the village: "Please, dedicate yourselves to your children," she urged. She went on to describe how her own mother, in a remote district, with six children, left alone with her land and animals, worked hard and made it happen. "All of us have become professionals. It's about sacrifice. Sacrifice yourself so you at least have your one last child as a professional. . . . We are lucky those of us who have a child under three, they have a chance! Those above three, there is not much we can do if they had malnutrition."

Juntos is taken up in part due to the way in which it aligns with women's hopes for an urban professional future. When Eustavio left his village in

Ayacucho for the jungle, to work in the coca harvest, his wife explained, "That's why I want my children to be professional, so they don't have to worry about money—how much it costs to send kids to school and their transport and food and have them living far away. Then they can have a regular salary and not be so worried about money. You can't afford education just by farming." Various authors have noted this conviction, that education will allow one's children to leave rural suffering and low status behind (Boyden 2013; Hill 2013). Those of rural, indigenous language–speaking backgrounds come to believe that with education, they can escape the discrimination facing the "Andean farmer" category. De la Cadena (2000: 5) has written about the shift from racial discrimination in Peru to one based on education and economic success, and says that individuals "deny the existence of insurmountable hierarchies and immanent cultural differences—those that would place them in absolute inferior positions—and at the same time acquiesce to the legitimacy of social differences created by educational achievements." Rural people have to take responsibility for overcoming their own low position. They choose to be a responsible Juntos mother, and have an educated child—goals that the government promotes, and that families themselves see as the likely path to a better life, one of less sweat and more money.

Positioning Oneself

In Ayacucho, it was found that in more recent years (2012–2013) women had begun to describe Juntos as "easy," or in similar terms. This can be seen as part of an image that women prefer to cultivate. Ana said, "It's no problem for me. . . . It's only a problem for those who don't understand. For those women it's difficult." Later on, the previous village Juntos president, Vera, said that in fact Ana was actually one of the few women whose payments were cut: "She was often suspended for not fulfilling requirements. Her boy was off pasturing animals. She wanted to just receive the money. She did not invest in education."

Several times, in conversations about the Juntos-related workload, women would comment, "But it's for our own good!" Irena made this comment on various occasions, pointing out the improvements she made in her house. These types of statements appeared to be about presenting oneself in a certain pro-Juntos, responsible light. Many women shared stories with us about how they had overcome poverty, suffering, and food scarcity. Some also described a "before and after" in terms of parenting style, demonstrating how they had taken up new values compared to their parents. Rene recalled her own childhood:

My grandmother sent us to school only with *canchita* (roasted corn kernels), and was always asking us to work in the *chakra*. I say to my grandfather, "They didn't educate me. That's why I'm here suffering in the *chakra*." Before, they didn't worry about education. I went with one notebook, divided in half for two courses. It makes me feel bad when I think about my education. Maybe I would have been something. . . . I tell my daughter, "In my time do you think there was food waiting when I got home from school? Do you think there was food ready in the morning before I went to school?" So I tell her, "Take advantage "

These recollections serve to exemplify that the negligent rural Andean parents, so alive in the nation's imagination, are a thing of the past, that parents aim to show themselves to be "other" than that category that Juntos targets. In this case, their narratives of overcoming help women make a place for the descriptions of dirty or lazy mothers that reach them through those who are sent to improve conditions for poor rural children. They use them to frame their own past against which they demonstrate their difference, or progress, often using criteria learned from external, mostly state, actors to position themselves as responsible self-made mothers.

Juntos and the health system have served in some cases to enable women to gain recognition and to differentiate themselves from the rest. After her visit to the health center, Belinda reported, "They congratulated me. Diana is fine, in weight, height and hemoglobin. I was happy all the way home. They said I am the only one who cares." Vera spoke of being one of the "masses," at the very beginning of the program, and how that changed as she gained leadership and status by serving as Juntos president. "In the post they looked down on us. For three days I went to wait with my baby. I was humble, quiet. I went at 2:00 in the morning; I waited. At the start, four hundred women at a time had to go.[6] My husband said, 'Don't keep going!' Because I was humble and quiet, they take advantage!" Vera described how they were crowded into the center, but they weren't called in for appointments, and after they waited for hours, the nurse would close the door saying that they would not attend any more women that day. Vera contrasted those early days with her later years as Juntos president: "Later the doctor would say 'oh how are you, my dear,' and to others she would say 'just wait!'" Vera imitated the switch from a sweet to a gruff voice. She went on, "Now they are very nice to me. . . . Now Dr. Sonia respects me. She saw me speak when we went on the field trip with Juntos."

Taking up Juntos nutrition-related recommendations and a leadership role appears to be a way to distinguish oneself from the mass of poor indigenous women targeted by the program. One's own progress is more visible if it can be contrasted with others' failures. Women in Ayacucho have begun to use Juntos nutrition recommendations to describe a hierarchy.

As Vera pointed out, "Rene has an improved stove, shelves and all, but still she is cooking outside and her kids are touching dirt and eating with dirty hands." She contrasted this with another neighbor: "Maureen is good, she is always feeding them lentils, and salad." This noting of difference has taken a further step, in which women at the local level create a replica of the Juntos policing role. On several occasions I heard women suggest that others be "punished through Juntos" for different misdemeanors, such as not bringing children to preschool, or failing to attend the health center nutrition demonstrations. Trina commented, "There are women who do not obey, they do not comply; there should be sanctions."

Some women are seen to be in need of reprimanding. Juli told me, "Last time we went for Juntos, Leonor went to get the money and went directly to the bus, so I told her, 'At least buy food for your kids,' and she went and bought one sol of mandarins and one sol of oranges.[7] She didn't buy meat or anything. . . . Her kids are used to not eating at midday because she goes to work and leaves them there. . . . Leonor sells the eggs she has, doesn't give them to her kids." Leonor, one of the poorest women in the village, has come to serve as a sort of scapegoat, a nutrition failure against which others can measure themselves.

As a result of Juntos, nutrition checkups and recommendations became a regular part of life, and so did the dynamic of inspection, normalizing the intrusion of the state into the private domain of the family. Although home visits have been phased out, inspection remains very alive in people's imagination. Women have been observed to surreptitiously and frantically sweep floors, clean tables, and kick animals out of the kitchen before any visitors are called in. Others want to show off their homes as a matter of personal pride. In fact, in Ayacucho several women actually proposed a house contest and invited district authorities and health workers to tour their homes, demonstrating vegetable gardens, storage shelves, and other achievements. In this sense then, Juntos has contributed to a public view of what is a good mother, which is used to gain status on the local level. As we mentioned above, problems of hygiene and behavior were insinuated to occur along racial lines. Rural Andean women realize this and make use of it, presenting a responsible self, in a conscious manner, moving themselves out of the low-status category by aligning themselves with the state-recommended norms.

Conclusion

The legal and extralegal conditions of the Juntos program thus enable the state to promote a wide politic of parenthood, using the coercive power of the CCT program and the subsequent normalization of the behavior required. Juntos thus also became "manna" for the Peruvian state to generate "good mothers" out of indigenous and peasant populations, targeted as poor and vulnerable (and with high rates of malnutrition), so that state workers meet the requirement of their own mandate to improve ways of living they find backward.

The way the program seeks to culturally integrate a rural, indigenous population has to be highlighted. The messages regarding the way homes are to be arranged, which types of meals are consumed and how they are prepared, and the use of healthcare and daycare centers, for example, all send an implicit assertion that state institutions know more about parenting than mothers themselves. The program is directed at poor and underserved populations, which in practice, due to the nature of inequality along racial lines, means that indigenous people are the main targets of the behavior recommendations, implying that state health workers and Juntos are given free range to work to transform Andean practices to an externally envisioned public health model, in encounters that reproduce the power dynamics of the stigma of poverty and rurality in a very hierarchical society, but in the name of social services, or most recently, under the slogan of "social inclusion." The culturally loaded nature of this exchange remains politically implicit, nondebatable, and accepted at many levels as for their "own good," as many elements are either extralegal and not necessarily traceable to policy, and at the same time implemented within a social hierarchy along racial lines, which is largely unacknowledged at the official level.

We touched briefly on a whole range of reactions to the program's various demands. Many women have resisted, but many others have incorporated the discourses and try to appear as a "good mother." Poor women in the Andes are conscious of what it actually means to be treated as rural and indigenous. The "responsible mother" category is not only handled by state workers, but is also passed into the hands of village mothers, who start to manage the exclusionary categories themselves. This could be read as the work of a governance strategy in which citizens are "made complicit" in the workings of power; however, we lean toward a more conscious or willful version of women's agency: women go along with Juntos in part because it reflects their own hopes for an urban professional future for their children.

This raises important reflections about the nature of conditionality. To what extent does the state need to pay women to make use of state services and mold behavior, if mothers themselves are uniquely motivated to do their best for their family's future? Rather than recourse to conditionality or coercion, investing in good quality health and education services would very likely greatly increase families' use of said services, given that women's own self-defined best interests respond to a vision of progress that has come to coincide in many ways with the goals of the state.

Postscript

Four years after the last of our main fieldwork was carried out, we can observe that MIDIS, created as a ministry in 2011, continues to consolidate and extend its functions, continuing beyond the Humala presidency to remain active under Kuczynski, with a string of programs including Juntos, Cuna Mas (early childhood development), a school lunch program, FONCODES (economic development for poor rural regions), and including implementation of a new cash transfer program, Pension 65, designed to help elderly people living in poverty. MIDIS approved the program at the end of 2011, and about 300,000 people had received support by 2013, figures which rose to 540,000 in 2017. The transfer is about $37 (US) per person per month. The cash transfer model is thus extending its scope within Peru, with similar mechanisms applied to new categories of the population. In this case, the program includes an initiative called Saberes productivos (productive knowledge), with an aim to collect elderly people's wisdom in order to pass it along to children.

Toward the end of 2017 Juntos officials began to evaluate whether to include mandatory blood tests for pregnant women and for children under three years of age, in line with a national priority to reduce high levels of anemia.[8] Since our fieldwork was carried out, a nutrition monitoring center has been set up in one of the villages in Ayacucho, and some of the mothers in the village have been active in promoting iron-rich recipes as part of Ministry of Health and nongovernment organization education campaigns to reduce childhood anemia. They were even celebrated in a national newspaper in 2017 for their success in reducing anemia, using traditional knowledge to prepare iron-rich foods. One of the mother leaders describes her son as the best student in first grade in the village school.

While extralegal conditions distance some women from the Juntos program and cause frustrations among many, other mothers, who have the time and the opportunity to take on leadership roles, manage to make use of these initiatives that arrive from the state, when and if these activities make sense in accordance with their own goals. While the new requirement of blood tests for Juntos participants may not represent a surprise for mothers in Ayacucho who have had the chance to be involved in this pilot work on reducing anemia, it remains to be seen how this conditionality will be received by Juntos mothers across the country. Our fieldwork in Ayacucho also found mixed reactions to blood tests for children—for the most vulnerable families, whose children were suffering from anemia, it represented another moment to be judged and found wanting as a mother.

Emmanuelle Piccoli is an assistant professor in development studies at the Université Catholique de Louvain (UCL). She previously benefitted from a doctoral and postdoctoral grant from the National Fund for Scientific Research (FNRS) in Belgium. During those mandates, she was an associate researcher at the Instituto Francés de Estudios Andinos, at the Pontificia Universidad Católica del Perú, at the Université de Laval in Québec, and at the University of Michigan. She published a book titled _Les Rondes paysannes: Vigilance, politique et justice dans les Andes péruviennes_ (Academia, 2011), as well as numerous papers about the Peruvian Andes.

Bronwen Gillespie has a Ph.D. in social anthropology from the University of Sussex. Her research draws on Quechua-speaking women's experience as recipients of state programs and services in the rural Andes to explore contradictions in public health and social policy. Recent publications include "Negotiating Nutrition: Sprinkles and the State in the Peruvian Andes" in _Women's Studies International Forum_. Affiliated with CORTH (Centre for Cultures of Reproduction, Technologies and Health) at the University of Sussex, she is currently working as an independent researcher in the areas of public health and social programs, primarily in Latin America.

Notes

1. Authors' translation from "Quiénes somos?" (About us), MIDIS website, accessed 20 May 2015, http://www.midis.gob.pe/index.php/es/nuestra-institucion/sobre-midis/quienes-somos.
2. All names have been changed to protect anonymity.
3. Health center, which is locally referred to in Spanish as "_posta_" (or _posta médica_).
4. Community work day.
5. Remote high altitude Andean grasslands.
6. She is making mention of the initiation of the Juntos program, when large numbers of women were being registered in the system for the first time.
7. Equivalent to a few cents worth, or a small bag of each fruit.
8. "Juntos inicia en enero verificación del tamizaje de anemia en hogares con gestantes y menores de tres años," Juntos website, 26 December 2017 (date posted), accessed 17 April 2018, http://www.juntos.gob.pe/noticia/index/id/113/title/juntos_inicia_en_enero_verificacion_del_tamizaje_de_anemia_en_hogares_con_gestantes_y_menores_de_tres_anios?t=wJAr7Acgmc.

References

Ansión, Juan, and Jan Szeminski. 1982. "Dioses y hombres de Huamanga." *Allpanchis* 19: 187–233.

Benavides, Martín, Magrith Mena, and Carmen Ponce. 2010. *Estado del Niñez Indígena en el Perú.* Lima: UNICEF and INEI.

Boyden, Jo. 2013. "'We're Not Going to Suffer Like This in the Mud': Educational Aspirations, Social Mobility and Independent Child Migration among Populations Living in Poverty." *Compare: A Journal of Comparative and International Education* 43: 580–600.

De la Cadena, Marisol. 2000. *The Politics of Race and Culture in Cuzco, Peru.* Durham, NC: Duke University Press.

del Pino, Ponciano, M. Mena, S. Torrejón, E. del Pino, M. Arones, and T. Portugal. 2012. *Repensar la desnutrición.* Lima: IEP.

Diez Canseco, Lupe Camino. 2003. *Exploratory Study to Develop an Intercultural Approach and to Improve the Quality of Health Services in the Departments of Huancavelica, Ayacucho and Andahuaylas in the Framework of the Program for Modernizing the Health Sector.* PER B7-310/97/209, Lima.

Ewig, Christina. 2010. *Second-Wave Neoliberalism: Gender, Race and Health Sector Reform in Peru.* University Park, PA: Penn State University Press.

Hill, Michael D. 2013. "Growing Up Quechua: Ethnic Identity, Narrative, and the Cultural Politics of Childhood Migration in Cusco, Peru." *Childhood* 20: 383–397.

Olivier de Sardan, Jean-Pierre. 2014. "La manne, les normes et les soupçons: Les contradictions de l'aide vue d'en bas." *Revue Tiers Monde* 3:197–215.

Piccoli, Emmanuelle. 2014. "'Dicen que los cien soles son del Diablo': L'interprétation apocalyptique etmythique du Programa Juntos dans les communautés andines de Cajamarca (Pérou) et la critique populaire des programmes sociaux." *Social Compass* 61: 328–347.

Piccoli, Emmanuelle. 2015. "Entre créateurs d'alliance et marchandises: les cochons d'Inde dans les Andes péruviennes à l'heure des projets d'élevage." *Religiologiques* 32: 267–297.

Scott, James. 2000. *Los dominados y el arte de la Resistencia, Discursos ocultos.* Mexico: Ediciones Era.

Silva Serrano, H., and S. A. Zeña Giraldo. 2007. *Efectos de las cocinas tradicionales y las cocinas mejoradas en zonas de friaje y en cuatro localidades de extrema pobreza de las zonas altoandinas del departamento de Cusco.* Rapport pour l'Organisation mondiale de la santé. Accessed 17 February 2014. http://www.paho.org/per/index.php?option=com_content&view=article&id=660&catid=862:noticias-2007&Itemid=900.

Weismantel, M. 2001. *Cholas and Pishtacos: Tales of Race and Sex in the Andes.* Chicago, IL: University of Chicago Press.

Wilson, Fiona. 2004. "Indian Citizenship and the Discourse of Hygiene/Disease in Nineteenth-Century Peru." *Bulletin of Latin American Research* 23: 165–180

Chapter 7

Expectations beyond Development

Toward a Prospective Chronology of Cash Transfers from Mexico to Argentina

Andrés Dapuez and Sabrina Gavigan

Introduction

Conditional Cash Transfer development programs (CCTs) are now ubiquitous in Latin America, and evaluations of their effects, particularly in the case of Mexico's Progresa-Oportunidades program, fuel much of the literature concerning their perceived success or failure.[1] Based on the stated and unstated objectives of Progresa-Oportunidades-Prospera (1997–)[2] and Argentina's Asignación Universal por Hijo (2009–) and Progresar (2014–) this chapter suggests that these programs can be examined not strictly according to their measurable effects on the health, education, and consumption of their beneficiaries, but by the fictional expectations they created. In short, this chapter entails a short history of the future, as it has been expressed and anticipated by cash transfer policies.

However, CCTs do not indicate a shift away from long-established economic monetarist policies in the region; rather they re-create ideals of market inclusion for their beneficiaries and portend the emergence of an ideal type of citizen. Despite having references to many elements of their respective national welfare systems and the repertoire of populist ideologies in which they emerged (Cardenismo and Peronismo, in Mexico and Argentina respectively), CCTs do not seem to radically differ from the social services associated with mid-twentieth century Euro-American welfare systems. Moreover, it is worth mentioning that CCTs were not

---

Notes for this chapter begin on page 220.

alien to Euro-American economics. On the contrary, such transfers have emerged from a natural progression within this specific area of knowledge and policy making. In this sense, CCTs can be considered a mobile technology for global governance that can be traced back to the emergence of the post–World War II welfare state (for cash transfers as mobile technology, see Dapuez 2016 [after Ong 2007]).

In the global south, however, cash transfers do not work as a compensation for transitory unemployment, nor are they "in any simple way socialist, or necessarily subversive of dominant capitalist forms of economic organization" (Ferguson 2015: 16). Nowadays, Mexican and Argentinian governments explicitly aim for their CCT programs to contribute to national development. To become full-fledged development instruments, CCT programs should include the principal objectives of unhinging the "poverty trap" or interrupting the "auto-reproductive cycle of poverty" to impact national development. To that end, we consider this goal to be an important criterion for our classification of the trajectory of the implementational intent in the two major Latin American cash transfers we discuss, in an ongoing "CCT wave" (Fiszbein and Schady 2009) across Latin America.

Conceptual Repertoire for Objectifying Cash Transfers Goals

We propose that there have been three waves of cash transfers implementation based on changing goals and extending time frames. Regardless of whether or not these programs attain their goals, we argue that they have projected three imagined futures or fictional expectations (Beckert 2013) that frame each of these three "waves" of CCT implementation. We consider intentional aims to be fundamental for policy implementation and analysis. To that end, we describe and analyze the prospective contexts of Mexico's (Procampo 1993; Progresa 1997; Oportunidades 2002; and Prospera 2014) and Argentina's (Asignación Universal por Hijo 2009) cash transfer programs with a specific emphasis on the formation of what are known as "imagined futures" or, interchangeably, the "fictional expectations of the economy" (Beckert 2013). These mental representations of the future, such as the eventual breakdown of a self-reproductive cycle of poverty, are taken for granted in economic thinking and cannot be calculated rationally or empirically; As Jens Beckert (2013: 220) points out, the imagined futures are relevant "fictional expectations" in all spheres of human action, but are essential for economic decision-making. Assuming that some decisions in economic situations are characterized by fundamental uncertainty, Beckert suggests that "the decisions of intentionally rational actors" are based on "fictions." Fictions are "images of some future state of the world or course of events [that] are cognitively accessible through this mental representation" (Beckert 2013: 220). As long as they constitute an anticipation of a future that is impossible to calculate a priori, "fictional expectations" cannot be considered fraudulent. Their "fictionality" lies, instead, in the simulation for describing a future reality and for suggesting decisions "based on nothing more than assumptions" or on "*as if* futures" (Beckert 2013: 228). In this sense, the main argument of this chapter is that cash transfers have anticipated different futures and have been accommodated to changing realities and diverse national challenges in the last twenty years.

In the late 1990s, constituting the first wave, the Mexican government implemented cash transfers to manage the short- and mid-term structural adjustment consequences of market liberalization and the privatization of state enterprises. Earlier, in 1993, Mexico devised and implemented Procampo (N.d.; 1994), an unconditional cash transfer, to mitigate the effects of the structural adjustment of the Mexican agricultural sector. Later, in 1997, the Mexican government created Progresa (1997). Both programs were instruments to attain the foreseen market benefits promised by the North American Free Trade Agreement (NAFTA) and to reduce the country's rural peasant populations.

A second wave of cash transfers can be demarcated based on the clearly enunciated and universal goal of human capital accumulation, which, in turn, was expected to break the cycle of poverty reproduction. Derived from expert knowledge originating in the United States, this CCT objective has been widely promoted by officials from the Mexican government and the Inter-American Development Bank (IDB) and the World Bank. This is, still, often the most enunciated objective in the CCT literature, regardless of political-economic context. In its transformational scheme, economists and development officials regard cash transfer effects in terms of "impacts," today represented as a recurring "future past" (Koselleck [1979] 2004). These hoped-for "impacts" often vary according to the contexts in which the CCT is implemented. In Mexico, for instance, the hope was to increase human capital in poor children to encourage their move from rural areas to urban centers for employment. Regardless of any distinct national goals—social, political, or economic—the CCT schema was implemented in different national contexts with only minor attention paid to the local context, but with inclusions of populist repertoires. The important factor, in line with expert knowledge, is the supposed universality of the CCT goal: human capital accumulation.

Finally, we propose that a third, more recent and ongoing, wave of CCT programs emerged when CCT researchers and functionaries (Levy 2008; Hanlon et al. 2010; Alemán 2014) came to the realization that they could not calculate the achievement of "breaking the vicious cycle of poverty" in

advance, neither rationally nor empirically, and that, without deep structural changes in the economy, beneficiaries could not access the desired
goal of formal employment (Levy 2008: 229). According to the new realization of these limited prospects, cash transfers are currently better understood as a permanent right (as in the case of Argentina's AUH) in a new,
incoming economic system of redistribution (Ferguson 2015).

Localities and Object of the Research

During his Ph.D. research, Andrés Dapuez conducted interviews with
Procampo and Oportunidades officials, among other research errands,
between 2003 and 2011. Drawing on a total of twenty-six months of ethnographic fieldwork, archival research, and in-depth interviews, he explored
how conditional and unconditional cash transfers relate to ritual exchange
in a Mayan-speaking village in Eastern Yucatan (Dapuez 2013). In this village, he concentrated on how people model their reception of cash transfer
on their ritual practice of requesting from powerful lords of nature (Dapuez
2011; 2013). In Valladolid, Mérida, Mexico City, and the Inter-American
Development Bank in Washington, D.C., he researched the effects cash
transfers were devised to provoke. In Argentina, where he now works
as a full-time researcher in its National Research Council, he conducted
interviews with government officials and Asignación Universal por Hijo
(AUH) and Progresar recipients in 2013–2015. In 2014, Sabrina Gavigan
also worked in this research team[3]. She carried out nine months of fieldwork in 2014–2015 in Concordia, Entre Ríos, where she interviewed local
social workers and health providers concerning their interpretations of the
AUH cash transfer uses and impacts. In Concordia, she primarily interviewed and conducted participant observation with AUH recipients who
were also beneficiaries of a local development program that targeted the
informally employed. Her research focused on program participation as a
bureaucratic process through which parents were encouraged to imagine
different futures for their children in relation to the state.

While we have read and interpreted policy papers looking for rationales and a chronology of policy, we also found that speaking with cash
transfer policy makers for insight into their intentions was fundamental
to understanding how these polices "make sense" to different actors. In
many interviews, we asked them not only about the emergence of this
particular form of intervention through cash but also how they envision
the future for the transfer recipients. Although we abstractly classify cash
transfers according to three intentional categories, these categories stem
from an ethnography of policy making and from Dapuez's conversations

with development officials, promoters, and beneficiaries concerning the Procampo program at the Inter-American Development Bank (IDB) in Washington, D.C.; at the Mexican Secretary of Agriculture and Fishery (SAGARPA) in Mexico; and with Oportunidades' promoters and recipients in Eastern Yucatán. With his research, Andrés Dapuez intended to expand the tasks of doing an "anthropology of policy" beyond textual analysis of policy documents (Shore and Wright 1997) by taking into account the technical and political practices that have defined and continue to redefine definitive senses of cash transfer policies' prospects.

In short, this chapter focuses on the expansion of successive communities of expectations regarding the cash transferred through cash transfer programs. Therefore, in this particular case, we focus on a transnational "closed epistemic" community's set of practices, which has further developed into national policy networks of consultant experts, consensus formation, and transfers of expert knowledge (Mosse 2005: 132–156), by ethnographically investigating cash transfer policies beyond their textual semantics in two very different localities. One is a Mayan-speaking eastern Yucatec village in which the mistrust of government, white Mexicans, and foreigners stems back at least to the Caste Wars of 1857. There, half of the eligible landowners and eligible agriculturalists receive Procampo (around 400), while almost 80 percent of families are beneficiaries of the Oportunidades program in some form. There are approximately 250 thousand inhabitants in Paraná and 150 thousand in Concordia, Entre Ríos, Argentina. Beneficiaries of AUH and, since 2014, of Progresar (a cash transfer program that allows unemployed youth to further their education) in both cities primarily reside in suburban areas with high rates of unemployment and public employment. Therefore, the data presented here should not be directly expanded to understand Mexico or Argentina without paying close attention to the locales' particularities.

First Wave: Coping with Structural Adjustment

Today in Ixán, a village of around two thousand in Mexico's Eastern Yucatan state, the most important commodity that some people produce is honey. However, many remember the good days when they exchanged maize for money, around "thirty years ago." The purposeful isolation of local crop markets peaked with the implementation of NAFTA treaties, and almost none of them still exist today. In this sense, the only completely local conversion of maize into money takes place at the village mills, where people go to grind their soaked maize grains, paying a percentage, or to buy the maize paste to make tortillas.

Structural adjustment aimed toward integrating Mexico with the North American Free Trade zone necessitated a new generation of development programs in Mexico in the early 1990s. In this political context, Procampo (1994) and Progresa (later called Oportunidades, 1997) emerged. According to the first article of the presidential bill of its creation, Procampo was introduced as an unconditional cash transfer program mandated "to transfer resources to support the rural producers economy" (Procampo 1994). Procampo support is given to older farmers, an immense majority of whom entered the program in 1994. This rural cash transfer was ideated not to promote productiveness but to support the switch toward a context in which "prices were determined by the market, based on their international references" (Procampo n.d.: 3). Three years after the unconditional Procampo was implemented, the Mexican state began to distribute conditional cash transfers to poor mothers through Progresa. While Procampo did not require the same conditionalities as Progresa, namely tracking the vaccination, education, and health of poor children, both cash transfers were implemented as a response to economic turmoil. Piester (1997: 471) argues, "For these governments [grappling with the political costs of economic restructuring,] targeted social programs were viewed as the most effective instrument available to reduce the likelihood of mass mobilization against austerity and market reforms."

Procampo (1994) and Progresa (1997) made a clear-cut switch from in-kind transfers and services (agricultural consultancies, development of new products, implementation of irrigation, marketing of crops, agricultural schools, etc.) to financial services (securitization) and monetary transfers. Although their implementations were sensitive to election calendars, national and state news, and other events, their main aims were the preparation of new generations for a different labor market, while concomitantly reducing the rural populations.

According to workers in a dependency of the Agricultural Secretary (SAGARPA), in Mérida, Yucatán, agriculture is thought to exclude other economic activity and, thus, development. Andrés Dapuez asked an official in the office, a man who managed Procampo and related insurance programs, why he thinks people in Ixán continue with their agricultural work. The official explained that "their religion" was the most difficult impediment for reaching development. He explicitly mentioned the need to "get rid of the peasants" to achieve better living conditions in the so-called countryside. This long-term transformation of "peasants into more productive laborers" has been occluded, he continued, because the people sponsor cargo rituals that coincide with the agricultural cycle (see Dapuez 2011 on harvest ritual propitiations and Procampo). Ritual and religion, for him, justify an economic activity that does not provide sustainable economic returns or a long-term future for the cash transfer recipients in Yucatan.

While there are some differences between CCT programs implemented around the world, most justify their schemes on the Progresa (1997–2002) model, the first CCT implemented on a massive scale. Progresa is also among the most rigorously studied, evaluated, and reformulated CCTs, first by the Mexican government and then by multilateral agencies. Unlike similar programs in other countries, the documentation of Progresa-Oportunidades-Prospera's objectives and results is largely open access, clearly expressed, and with relatively reliable data. Nevertheless, Progresa (1997) was unexceptional in its initial formulation and in its aims.

In this sense, Progresa's objectives were not extraordinary or necessarily groundbreaking. In fact, in an interview in 2009, an IDB economist said that Progresa was derived from the US food stamp system. This revelation partially challenges the current appreciation of cash transfers as a "development revolution from the global South" (Hanlon et al. 2010; Ferguson 2015:16). Not only does this open up potential new inquiries into the history of welfare in the United States, it also reveals that the prospect of a new politics of distribution (Ferguson 2015) is, at least in part, precariously based on a well-known economy's horizons. It is not our intention to offer a comprehensive examination of the relationship between the North American welfare systems and cash transfers elsewhere, but it would be useful to situate the former in the context of CCTs.

The total discontinuation of agricultural assistance to the countryside following Procampo's implementation, along with Oportunidades' implicit mandate that children and women should abandon the fields to—in the short term—fulfill school and health duties, indicates both the financialization and monetization of rural development in the long term. For instance, rather than distributing fertilizers, crops, and technical assistance to agriculturalists as they had done in the past, SAGARPA promoters started to offer them new forms of J.P. Morgan crop securitization programs (mainly for maize) to stabilize crop prices in the marketplace of futures. In conclusion, cash transfers were introduced in the context of economic turmoil to alleviate the effects of changing horizons on the poor in the short term so that the state might avoid potential social turmoil in the face of economic restructuring, while in the very long term people living in the countryside were expected to switch to urban-based economic activities.

Second Wave: Breaking the Poverty Trap

Within a decade of their emergence in Mexico, cash transfers underwent continuous evaluation. Between 1998 and 2000, the positive effects of the program were mainly established through quasi-experimental evaluations (based on randomized controlled trials)[4] primarily conducted by the International Food Policy Research Institute (Skoufias, Davis, and Behrman 1999; Skoufias and McClafferty 2001). These positive evaluations, in turn, promised a different future for Progresa's beneficiaries: "The research results show that after just three years, the poor children of the rural communities of Mexico where Progresa operates are attending school longer, eating more diversified diets, improving their health, and learning that the future may look quite different from the past" (Skoufias and McClafferty 2001: 1).

These Progresa evaluations inspired a rethinking of the program's objectives, which became more ambitious and extended to the longer term. These changes brought about the second CCT wave, in which program objectives postponed fulfillment to future generations. After having managed the effects of the 1994–1995 crisis, the Mexican state then used Progresa for a different purpose: to project an imaginary future in which the children of the impoverished peasantry would find formal employment in NAFTA markets after, of course, they had accumulated sufficient "human capital" through education and health. If the first CCT wave constituted pushing the poor away from certain economic practices, the second wave meant redirecting them toward an idealized future through long-term investment in their children. These children would be, according to the implicit and explicit rationale of policies, the generation that breaks, finally, the self-reproductive poverty cycle. In this sense, the characterization of poverty as a self-reproducing phenomenon is practically the same in all CCT programs. In its last reformulation, CCTs regard poverty as

a social phenomenon that is easily reproduced and transmitted from generation to generation in those cases in which there is no intervention specifically aimed at these three shortcomings that have already been mentioned. This vicious cycle of intergenerational transmission of poverty shows that poverty eradication demands action combined and simultaneous with intersectoral interventions. One, aimed at improving poor households' disposable income and its members' access to their rights for social development; another associated with increased accumulation of human capital in younger members of these households to increase the probability of access to permanent sources of income; and a third to consolidate the greatest accumulation of human capital achieved in these younger members through activities that facilitate their integration into productive activities. (Prospera 2014, our translation).

In what is considered to be the second historical CCT moment in Mexico, Progresa-Oportunidades was attributed with the capacity to support a definitive break with the self-reproductive cycle of poverty. Through incentives and conditionalities related to education and health, it seeks to achieve the accumulation of human capital in its beneficiaries. However, in line with Amayrta Sen's philosophy of development, the terms of the "human capital" objectives of Progresa-Oportunidades were partially modified and, in 2005, the stated objective of "human capital" accumulation was partially replaced with a focus on developing what Nussbaum (2000) and Sen (1985; 1999) have called "human capabilities"[5] (Agudo Sanchíz 2011).

In her analysis of the widespread implementation of CCTs in Latin America, Sugiyama (2011: 262) suggests that initial positive reports concerning Bolsa Família and Oportunidades in Brazil and Mexico, respectively, contributed to the adoption of the CCT program scheme as the "new professional norm within the development community." The fact that these first reports could not possibly evaluate the extent to which either program met its long-term goal of human capital development did not hinder their support by international development practitioners. In turn, as the new development norm, CCT programs were also more likely to be funded by international financial institutions, consequently incentivizing countries to adopt the schemes and further reinforcing them as the international norm. As Sugiyama (2011: 264) succinctly puts it, "funding and norm-creation work in tandem."

In the case of CCTs, however, the objective of "breaking the cycle of poverty" has not and, perhaps, cannot be definitely proven.[6] Subsequent changes in rates and patterns of education, health, and consumption in a generation of recipients, however, have been measured and recorded. When faced with the potential or observed failure of cash transfers to meet their key objectives, then, cash transfer proponents do not question the CCT schema, but rather suggest the following as potential impediments to its success:

1. Saturated labor markets. The market has no demand for the number of available workers.
2. The "accumulation" of human capital takes time. The benefits of cash transfers can take more than one generation to be apparent, perhaps due to shortcomings in health and education services provided by the state.
3. The benefits of human capital and of accumulated capabilities alone are not sufficient for individuals to achieve formal employment and get out of poverty.

IDB economists, along with Mexican government officials, are well aware of the above-mentioned impediments. While Gammage (2010) finds the inherent ambiguity of capabilities to be a strength of Sen's approach, these ambiguities have also created fictional expectations for CCT beneficiaries and promoters. If increased education does not seem to affect the intergenerational "transmission" of poverty, for instance, then CCT proponents can choose instead to focus on health as the most important driving factor. This potential process of revising evaluation to maintain faith in the efficacy of CCTs falls in line with what Beckert (after Merton 1948) refers to as the "self-fulfilling prophecy" of agreed-upon fictions. As Beckert (2011: 8) points out, "If the fictional story is disappointed, expectations will eventually be revised. This points to an experimental process in which stories are open to 'revision and modification as new data and new interpretative insights become available' (Holmes 2009: 401)." The objective of "breaking the cycle of poverty" through CCT, whether through an accumulation of human capital or the development of human capabilities, has thus been repeatedly rewritten and yet this second wave of cash transfers still promises the same conclusion: a future without poverty and with formal employment for beneficiaries.

Supporting Expectations

In 2009, while conducting fieldwork in Ixán, Dapuez noted that Mayan-speaking cash transfer recipients never spoke of Oportunidades or Procampo, or of their effects, using the programs' terms of "development," the "capacity approach," or "human capital accumulation." The women and men, instead, conceptualized cash transfers as a "support" (or *apoyo*) from the government for the livelihoods of "peasants." The villagers, however, did not all agree over which future livelihoods were best. Their relationship to agriculture—and expectations for their children's futures—also differed across generations.

In line with the Oportunidades program, younger parents (those in their 20s, 30s, and early 40s) identified the need for their children to receive an education and health services so that in the future they would be better equipped for higher-paying jobs in urban economies, most often in the tourism sector. The older generation of parents, however, maintained that traditional peasantry —ritualized slash and burn agriculture—was the best way to develop an "even," tranquil, if not prosperous, life course and to overcome poverty and hunger. All the cash transfer recipients we spoke with, despite their hopes and expectations for the future of their families and children, stressed that the cash transfer support they received, and the expectations it implied, were insufficient and incongruent. Although economic activities have multiplied in this eastern Yucatan village, with a swift increase in the number of food stores, the majority of people wonder "if we all become shopkeepers, who is going to buy?"

Despite the CCT programs' expected impacts on their long-term futures, the older inhabitants of the village view the cash transfers in a shorter context, related to their subsistence. Romeo, for instance, negatively evaluates Procampo and the other cash transfer programs when he explicitly points out that he did not need such support some years ago. Nowadays, however, he has no other option but to complete all the paperwork required for a new cash transfer program for people over the age of seventy, called 70 y Más, launched by the government of Felipe Calderon in 2007. With the help of a state representative from the Partido Revolucionario Institucional (PRI) in 2009, Romeo asked the government to incorporate him into the program, but he especially complains about the discretional distribution of cash transfers. Procampo money, Romeo says, "does not help me at all. $1300 [MXN] each hectare is not enough for anything. I could not even buy fertilizer this year." Producers like him later became beneficiaries of the "insufficient government support" of Procampo "for doing nothing," as Romeo and other agriculturalists put it. Moreover, most of the older male agriculturalists deduce that Procampo and other cash transfers are tokens of government corruption.

In Romeo's own words, the state "supports deviate," that is, are syphoned off somehow, "on the way to the village":

> They do not arrive to us intact. Supports remain on the way to here . . . they make announcements in the newspapers but in Mérida and in Valladolid supports deviate for other things. . . . This is what happened with last year's help for the drought . . . this is what is happening with Oportunidades . . . people should get MXN $650 but they are just receiving in the village MXN $330, just half. As a village authority, I am writing letters to the government for getting the support in entirety.

Oportunidades beneficiaries, for their part, pointed out that the extenuating tasks the program imposes on them only added to the burden of their daily work. These developmental tasks, along with the conditionalities of the program, rest solely on the women receivers. In Ixán, these women must attend regular Oportunidades meetings, from Monday to Friday. In these meeting, promoters stress women's responsibilities regarding their children's transitions toward better lives. In these spaces, promoters indicate another form of normalcy women should attain in the long term. While designers of the program propose that mothers should transform the received money into "human capital" in the long run—through doing physical exercise; modifying their daily consumption of maize with meat, vegetables, and fruits; using contraceptives; involving themselves in school-related activities; and participating in the village decision making, among other advice they receive—these beneficiaries focus on the very short term and complain that, besides attending these tiresome meetings, they are also expected to take care of their children and complete menial tasks in their households and backyard orchards.

This program takes for granted that as mothers fulfill their *compromisos* (a term locally used to refer to the program's "co-responsibilities"), the children will embody human capital in three main forms: through state health, formal education, and household food. Alimentary support will provide the basis for the moral leap that women are "co-responsible" for, or are "obliged" to make for, their children. The long-term accumulation of capacities demarcates a universal and moral imperative of human development. By law, these women are truly situated as intergenerational links between the state and their children's future. Therefore, Oportunidades discourse perpetuates their situatedness as well. For this program, the Mexican state avoids references to the "social prestations" it owes to Mexican citizens. Instead, it uses a language of "co-responsibilities."

The Oportunidades program rhetoric prevents discussion of the Mexican state as the provider of social, economic, and medical "prestations." Instead of "prestaciones sociales, médicas y económicas," the state provides mothers with regular transfers of cash. A hypostatization is performed when the Oportunidades documents avoid even mentioning state prestations and exclusively focus on specific effects of the monetary support. Phrased in quasi-contractual terms, the documents and promoters not only treat the mother as a mere "conduit of policy" (Molyneux 2006: 439) but also do violence to the complexity of the mother-child relationship that would generate the preferred adult capacities. Assuming that it is not necessary to consider the complexity of the mother-child relationship, and avoiding even mentioning the father-child relationship as a capability enabler, developers prefer to express and legislate mothers' behaviors in quasi-contracts, which do not have legal effects but instead refer to moral tropes of "obligations" and "co-responsibilities."

As regular sources of money, however, most families count on cash transfers to buy maize for consumption. As a "little help" that to some extent, once again, "supports" the people, the Procampo and Oportunidades cash transfers reveal that the programs' objectives imply a moral construction unrelated to Ixán's concrete forms of poverty. None of the cash transfer recipients of Procampo or Oportunidades, neither men nor women, have entertained the idea that poverty is an intergenerational phenomenon that can be overcome once and for all. Instead, poverty seems to be a day-by-day development for which harvests and labor migrations represent a mid-term mitigation. However, both programs' money directly relates to people's practices and ideas of normalcy when they express the moral necessity of support from the government. The insufficiency of this required support materializes in the amount transferred, which most of the recipients consider "meagre."

Third Wave: Toward a New Redistributive Economy

In the third, current CCT wave, the state programs appear limited to establishing "responsibility schemes [between the executive state and transfer-manager mothers] that enable families to improve their living conditions and ensure the enjoyment of their social rights and access to social development and equal opportunity" (Prospera 2014). Although Argentina's Asignación Universal por Hijo (2009) and Progresar (2014) programs were partly financed with loans from international organizations,[7] their beneficiaries assume that they are fully funded and allocated by the National Social Security Agency (ANSES). This assumption is, in large part, based on the understanding of the transfers as a new "right," not necessarily as a tool of development.

President Cristina Fernández de Kirchner announced AUH in late 2009, after the 2008 economic crisis negatively impacted Argentina's economy as well as her own popularity (Catterberg and Palanza 2012). In the words of its architects, AUH is "a social inclusion program without precedent in the history of [the] country" (ANSES 2013: 9).[8] The beneficiaries of this noncontributory cash allowance are Argentine children under the age of eighteen, disabled children, and, more recently, pregnant women. Initially Fernandez referred to AUH as a compensation for those most negatively impacted by Argentina's neoliberal past, clarifying in her presidential bill that the program "does not necessarily imply the end of poverty but it undeniably offers a restorative response to a population that has been punished by neoliberal economic policies" (Asignación Universal por Hijo 2009). In this sense, at least during its first year, AUH was intended as a transitory measure until more employment opportunities were available in Argentina's formal labor markets.

In terms of its target and its permanency, AUH eventually diverged from existing social benefits in Argentina. Plan Jefes y Jefas de Hogar Deocupados (JJH), an unemployment benefit initiated by the Duhalde administration in 2002, for instance, targeted individual unemployed adults according to a framework of temporary need. AUH, which also began as a transitory measure, soon became a seemingly permanent fixture. This contrast is made explicit in World Bank AUH funding documents, which note that previous social assistance programs in Argentina, including JJH, were "created as a response to the economic crisis in 2001–2002," but the Family Allowance program, on the contrary, was "a permanent, non-emergency related transfer program" (59201-AR) and promoted as a program that "pursues broader goals in the longer term" (ANSES 2012:17). While JJH, a benefit that targeted adults, was meant to address current unemployment, AUH, in contrast, focuses on children and, in that sense, postpones its effects to a long-term future but maintains the national goal of full employment.

AUH was widely considered to be one of President Cristina Fernández's greatest successes, to the extent that no opposing political party has dared propose ending the policy. Its popularity resulted in AUH abandoning its role as a transitional measure (whether it be for coping with negative effects or promoting the economic development in the children of the under- or unemployed) and has transformed, popularly and politically, into a full-fledged welfare "right." Fernandez de Kirchner confirmed the benefit's seemingly permanent position when she explicitly assured citizens that AUH benefits "do not constitute a gift, but a right'" (Mustafa 2010).

In contrast to the Mexican case, AUH program beneficiaries and its state administrators make only minimal references to the goal of accumulation of human capital. In our 2014 interviews with health and social workers in Paraná and Concordia, Entre Rios, for instance, we were told that the education and health requirements of the benefit were inconsequential for the program's continuation. In fact, they were rarely mentioned in conversations about the benefit, unless prompted, and even then brushed aside as secondary aspects of the program. In short, based on current interviews with ANSES state officials and other government functionaries, it appears that the transformative process of developing "capabilities" or "human capital accumulation" are less crucial to AUH support. Functionaries from Argentina's National Social Security Agency (ANSES) also avoid using the terms "cash transfers," or "*transferencias monetarias*" in Spanish, opting instead to refer to the program benefit as "family allowances" or "income transfers" (*asignaciones familiares* or *transferencias de ingresos*). ANSES functionaries at different dependencies expressed this assumption to us, alleging that AUH proposes a sort of distributive justice wherein those who have formal jobs are contributing to the child allowances distributed to those who do not. The state strategically stressed AUH's equalizing effects among children of both populations. More commonly, people argue for children's right to receive monetary allowances regardless of their parents' employment status (formal, informal, or unemployed) as a normative universal ideal.

However, this new permanency of the cash transfer benefit as a "right" does not directly reflect what Ferguson (2015: 12) has described as a distributive regime decoupled from labor. At least in Argentina's official AUH discourse, the program has evolved into a more ambitious program that would subsume existing social benefits toward the very long-term goal of full employment. Despite clear distinctions between their policies and those of a "neoliberal" past, the Kirchner-Fernandez administrations expressly aimed to increase the monetary base and promote virtuous consumption among recipients to move toward an ideal situation of full employment.[9] In the Argentinean case, at least, the envisioned multidimensional image of "inclusion" has never strayed from its final objective of producing formal laborers. A fictional future with demanding labor markets and plenty of opportunities still functions as the main expectation behind the implementation of Argentina's cash transfer programs (both AUH and Progresar), while politicians praise them for their effects in the present. Beneficiaries who are in contact with the labor market know that their incorporation in the formal sector would be a difficult ideal but, along with the majority of the people interviewed in Ixán (around sixty), beneficiaries still prioritize this possibility for their children's futures.

Unlike the United States' New Deal's 3Rs (relief, recovery, and reform), and the Peronist ideology behind AUH and Progresar, nowadays Mexican cash transfers' "pro-spenders" have limited expectations that their beneficiaries will achieve gainful wage labor as an escape from poverty. In Santiago Levy's (2008) book, interestingly titled *Good Intentions, Bad Outcomes*, Levy describes a definitive turn in cash transfer policies. Levy writes of his realization that firms do not necessarily want to hire more laborers, implying a necessary turning point for all similar program designs. While the permanence or transitoriness of cash transfer programs depends on structural conditions that are beyond the scope of developmental economists' modifications, Mexico has postponed the conditional cash transfer treatment of its poor population from one generation (twenty years) to one-and-a-half generations (thirty years).

This ongoing wave or period of CCT expectations, we argue, could be extraordinary if its policy makers were to clarify their anticipations. One particularly powerful anticipation, for instance, is that the conditions that necessitated the creation of CCTs—especially the lack of a gainful, permanent wage labor for the majority — will be the normal state of affairs in their envisioned long-term future. Ferguson (2015: 11–12; see also Seekings and Nattrass 2005; Li 2010; Marais 2011), once again, referred to this possibility in his summation of research results:

> The suffering of the poor and marginalized appears as functionally isolated from a production system that simply no longer has any use for them. And if such people increasingly receive social payments, this cannot plausibly be understood as part of a vital and necessary functional logic of reproducing a workforce, for there is simply no demand for the kind of labor such payments might plausibly "reproduce." On the contrary, insofar as today's social protection programs do support a sort of social reproduction, it is the reproduction of precisely that class of people who have increasingly slim prospects of ever entering the labor market at all.

However, even when Ferguson clearly sees a radical disconnection of global capital reproduction from social reproduction, especially when the former does not necessitate the reproduction of a large labor force, we do not presuppose that cash transfers will abandon all their formal labor teleology, at least in Argentina, as the current transfer wave progresses.

In the Argentinean cases of CCTs, ANSES, which helps fund the program, is responsible for a considerable amount of the existing AUH research in Argentina, despite the Fernandez government's claim that the policy approval stems from independent university research. In one of these institutional papers, researchers provide data obtained from different AUH assessments. Only highlighting the public policy's positive outcomes, one such report on AUH's effects on schooling and family life, written only two years after the program was implemented, concludes that the "poverty trap of the intergenerational reproduction of poverty has been overcome for those sectors most severely condemned by the effects of the previous neoliberal model" (Scarponetti et al. 2011: 125, our translation). This premature celebration, challenged by our fieldwork interviews with ANSES officials and by official and unofficial data on poverty (for 2014, the Argentinean Statistic Research Institute, INDEC, reports those in poverty as 20.4 percent of the total population and those in extreme poverty as 5.1 percent; the Catholic University of Argentina reports different data for that same year: 28.7 percent for poverty and 6.4 percent for extreme poverty), shows that formal labor teleology infusing the program has been much stronger than reality. To explain why formal labor and laborism has not extended to the whole society, Peronist officials stress the "lack" of purposeful "culture" rather than the structural conditions of the national economy.

Conclusions

Ordering cash transfers according to three expectational waves has allowed us to highlight a particular economic justification for these policies. The initial justifications for cash transfers (addressing structural changes in the Mexican economy and responding to financial crises) were immediate. The second group of justifications—to break, once and for all, the repro-duction of poverty through human capital accumulation and develop capabilities in children—were not only exceptional but also extended fur-ther into the future. However, whether identified as a silent developmen-tal "revolution from the global South" or simply the application of a more familiar form of welfare in new locales, cash transfers have always been initially implemented as a temporary compensation for unwanted price variations (Procampo in the Mexican case, due to market liberalization), structural adjustments, the negative effects of "neoliberal policies" (as the presidential bill that created the Argentinean Asignación Universal por Hijo states), or the more well-known temporary unemployment.

Ideals and practices of money in Ixán, Mexico, and in Concordia and Paraná, Argentina, confront and, at times, clash with CCT imagi-nary futures. Recipients have relocated CCT money beyond the scope prescribed by economic experts' discourses. Money's new capacities for subject-building were either reframed in terms of promises made by government officials in Ixán, or directly ignored. Meanwhile, all the vari-ants of Peronism have established that labor should be a universal right in Argentina. In that national context, then, a future national economy with no potential escape from poverty through formal labor has been mostly equated with gambling and dissipated life courses. In both places, cash transfers are given significance and framed according to different, precise monetary ideologies and future expectations. While religious practices and ritual promising in Ixan establish a common ground for pact-making and a commercial understanding of money, the distribution of cash trans-fer money in Argentina is framed by a commonsensical laborism.

However, with the third justification, or wave, of CCTs, we came to envision, at least according to Ferguson (2015), a great transition, one that could entail a new global politics of distribution. Whether Ferguson's fic-tional expectations would be fulfilled or not in the years to come in each if not all of their implementations, cash transfers have been considered, first, to be a transitory measure for coping with undesirable circumstances, and, later, a tool to end poverty once and for all. In their third wave, CCTs are presented as a super long-term tool for a new redistributive economy (2009–) and recharacterized as a permanent right of a more distributive society. In such a society, however, the role of marketing labor is highly disputed. Whether it no longer assures the end of poverty or not, money has become the only carrier and producer of expectations.

In this sense, we still need to explore to what extent cash transfers are animated by monetarist ideals and practices all over the world to know if we are truly facing, as James Ferguson (2015: 94) recently suggested, a new system of distribution as well as a new "system of distributed livelihoods." These radical redefinitions of money as a social good do not only discharge expectations for the state's responsibilities to the poor, through discourses of opportunities for the development and accumulation of human capital or capabilities, but also collide to any ideal of laborism, as we have shown in the Argentinean case. Marked by the monetization of family life as well as of state services, CCTs stand as examples of the creation of more monetarily accountable citizens, but they cannot easily foreclose or reframe long-lasting monetary ideologies. Beyond fueling development expectations, cash transfers are now being used as a means of producing morally autonomous subjects. Nevertheless, CCTs have not yet been able to end the Mexican "religious" commitment to maize agriculture or the "political" value of labor in Argentina. On the other hand, experts' expectations for this money do not portend anything concrete. Instead, they may be working as expectations of expectations: expectations of the emergence of new individuals with their own expectations. Thus, we believe, it is crucial to investigate whether or not cash transfers as the meaningful decommodification of money merits further study.

Postscript

While our research in the Argentinian context is ongoing and reflects the current implementation of AUH, much of the Oportunidades research informing this chapter was completed in 2011. In the ensuing six years, the Mexican government has revised Oportunidades to broaden its scope. Renamed Prospera in 2014, the CCT program has added measures in an attempt to increase beneficiary access to higher education and formal employment. Prospera, according to the World Bank,

> promotes the linkage of beneficiaries with complementary social and productive programs, expands education services to youth through scholarships for vocational training and favors their access to formal employment through the National Employment Service. Additionally, it promotes financial inclusion through beneficiaries' increased access to savings, microcredit and insurance. (World Bank 2014).

Comparing Prospera to Argentina's Progresar program, also implemented in 2014, suggests an alignment of both nations' concerns for "inclusion" fueled by labor. Progresar is a "new right" that targets unemployed or underemployed young adults between the ages of eighteen and twenty-four, offering cash transfer support as they advance through an educational or vocational program. Interestingly, these programs are moving toward the same, or very similar, goals: higher education and inclusion in formal labor. The impacts of these changes remain to be seen. Extending the scope of cash transfers to young adulthood indicates a further postponement of the cash transfer effects, and the continued expansion of CCTs' targets and goals suggest that new CCT waves are in our future.

Andrés Dapuez is a researcher of the National Research Council of Argentina (CONICET). He teaches at the National University of Entre Ríos, Argentina. He received his Ph.D. and M.A. in sociocultural anthropology from Johns Hopkins University. He has published in the *Journal of Latin American and Caribbean Anthropology*, *Research in Economic Anthropology*, and *Anthropologica*, among others journals. His research has been funded by the National Science Council, the Fulbright Commission, and CONICET.

Sabrina Gavigan is currently completing her Juris Doctor at the University of Maryland, Baltimore. She received her M.A. in public anthropology from American University. She has published in the *Journal of International and Global Studies* and *Research in Economic Anthropology*.

Notes

1. For a broader assessment of the results of conditional and unconditional transfers worldwide, see Hanlon et al. 2010 and Lavinas 2013. For a more empirical and situated approach on the interplay of Procampo and Oportunidades, in this case in the Mexican Countryside, see Fox and Haight 2010.
2. In 2002, the Vicente Fox regime changed the name of Progresa to Oportunidades. On 4 September 2014 President Peña Nieto again modified the program, which is now called Prospera. In Argentina, perhaps because many analysts consider Asignación Universal por Hijo (2009) and Progresar (2014) to be "universal" and highly idiosyncratic programs, comparative studies are scarce.
3. Brian Ferrero and Andrés Dapuez are the co-principal investigators of the project Naturalezas en desarrollo: análisis de las apropiaciones de la Asignación Universal por Hijo y programas de desarrollo sustentable en dos regiones de la Provincia de Entre Ríos. The research team includes María Kendziur, Laura Raffo, Juan Sabogal, Patricia Fassano, Graciela Mingo, Carolina Gómez, Mercedes Gomítolo, and César Sione. This project

has been funded by the Argentinean Research Council (CONICET) and the National University of Entre Ríos.

4. For a critique of the application of Randomized Controlled Trial methodology to CCTs, see Dapuez 2016.

5. In her exploration of Sen's "capability approach," Sarah Gammage (2010: 76) points out the seemingly infinite ways in which these capabilities can be measured and, subsequently, evaluated: "There is no single list of capabilities nor a unique array of spheres or dimensions that describe these capabilities, nor techniques to combine these spheres that can be relevant in all circumstances. As a result, one of the strengths of a capability approach is that the researchers can employ multiple analytical techniques and measurements of poverty, selecting those that appear to be most relevant for the analysis they wish to undertake."

6. According to official statistics, the indexes imply that the reproductive cycle of poverty has not been broken. CEPAL established that poverty increased in 2014 to 37.1 percent and extreme poverty to 14.2 percent (CEPAL 2015). The National Council for Evaluation of Social Development indicated the poor made up the following percentages of the population for the years 2010, 2012, and 2014; 46.1 percent, 45.5 percent, and 46.2 percent respectively (CONEVAL 2015). The World Bank itself admits that poverty in Mexico remains almost unchanged from the period before Progresa (2009) was implemented.

7. These include the World Bank and the Inter-American Development Bank, in the following distribution: WB loans: P120622 for $480 (US) million in 2011, and P115183 for $450 (US) million in 2009. IDB loans: AR-L1098 for $850 (US) in 2009.

8. AUH, however, is not the first CCT administered by the Argentine government. A similar program, Plan Familia por la Inclusión Social (PFI), was implemented in 2004 under the guidance of Alicia Kirchner, minister of social development. AUH was promoted as an expansion of these programs by incorporating more beneficiaries and distributing larger cash transfers (ANSES 2012:16).

9. This concern could stem from strong ties to Laborism, in particular with the ideology of Peronism, the political movement from which both presidents Kirchner and Fernández de Kirchner began their careers.

References

Agudo Sanchíz, Alejandro. 2011. "Mejoras Privadas, Beneficios Colectivos: La Producción y Subversión de Regímenes Globales de Política Social en Chiapas." In *(Trans) Formaciones del Estado en los Márgenes de Latinoamérica. Imaginarios Alternativos, Aparatos Inacabados y Espacios Transnacionales*, edited by A. Agudo Sanchíz and M. Estrada Saavedra, 231–283. México: El Colegio de México-Universidad Iberoamericana.

———. 2012. "Consultorías (Pos) Modernas: La Mímica del Positivismo y la Construcción del Conocimiento en la Evaluación de Programas Sociales." *Estudios Sociológicos* 30: 88.

Alemán, Vanessa. 2014. "Oportunidades no Acabo con la Pobreza: Robles." Quadratin Morelos. 23 September 2014. Accessed 20 May 2016. https://morelos.quadratin.com.mx/Oportunidades-acabo-con-la-pobreza-Robles/.

ANSES. 2013. "La Asignación Universal por Hijo Cumple 4 Anos." Observatorio de la Seguridad Social. 30 October 2013. Accessed

1 September 2015. http://observatorio.anses.gob.ar/noticia/
la-asignacion-universal-por-hijo-cumple-anos-202.
Asignacion Universal por Hijo. 2009. "Decreto del Poder Ejecutivo Nacional
1602/2009." InfoLEG. 29 October 2009. Accessed 1 September 2015. http://
www.infoleg.gov.ar/infolegInternet/anexos/155000-159999/159466/norma.
htm.
Beckert, Jens. 2013. "Imagined Futures: Fictional Expectation in the Economy."
Theory and Society 42(3): 219–240.
Catterberg, Gabriela, and Valeria Palanza. 2012. "Argentina: Dispersión de la
Oposición y al Auge de Cristina Fernández de Kirchner." *Revista de Ciencia
Política* (Santiago) 32(1): 3–30.
CONEVAL. 2015. "Anexo Estadístico 2010–2014." Accessed 1 August 2015. http://
interwp.cepal.org/sisgen/ConsultaIntegrada.asp?idIndicador=2268&idioma=e;
www.coneval.gob.mx/Medicion/MP/Paginas/AE_Pobreza-2014.aspx.
Dapuez, Andrés. 2011. "Promesas rituales y compromisos de libre mercado.
Regímenes de futuro en un pueblo de Yucatán." *Cuicuilco* 18(51): 181–202.
———. 2013. "Promissory Prestations: A Yucatec Village between Ritual Exchange
and Development Cash Transfer." Ph.D. dissertation. Johns Hopkins
University, Baltimore, MD.
———. 2016. "Políticas de Transferencias Monetarias: Exportando Expectativas en
Desarrollo." *Runa* (online) 37(1): 53–69. Accessed 12 October 2017. http://www
.scielo.org.ar/scielo.php?script=sci_arttext&pid=S1851-96282016000100004&lng
=es&nrm=iso.
———. 2016. "Supporting a Counterfactual Futurity: Cash Transfers and the
Interface between Multilateral Banks, the Mexican State, and Its People."
Journal of Latin American and Caribbean Anthropology 21(3): 560–583.
Ferguson, James. 2015. *Give a Man a Fish: Reflections on the New Politics of
Distribution*. Durham, NC: Duke University Press.
Fiszbein, Ariel, and Norbert Schady. 2009. *Conditional Cash Transfers: Reducing
Present and Future Poverty*. World Bank Policy Research Report. Washington,
DC: World Bank.
Fox, Jonathan, and Libby Haight, eds. 2010. *Subsidizing Inequality: Mexican Corn
Policy since NAFTA*. Washington, DC, and Santa Cruz: Woodrow Wilson
International Center for Scholars, Centro de Investigaciones y Docencia
Económicas, and University of California, Santa Cruz.
Gammage, Sarah. 2010. "Gender, Time Poverty and Amartya Sen's Capability
Approach: Evidence from Guatemala." In *The International Handbook of
Gender and Poverty: Concepts, Research, Policy*, edited by Sylvia Chant, 71–76.
Cheltenham: Edward Elgar Publishers.
Hanlon, John, Armando Barrientos, and David Hulme. 2010. *Just Give Money
to the Poor: The Development Revolution from the Global South*. Sterling, VA:
Kumarian Press.
Inter-American Development Bank (IDB). 2012. "About Us." Accessed 12
January 2012. https://www.iadb.org/en/about-us/about-the-inter-american-
development-bank%2C5995.html.
Keane, Webb. 2007. *Christian Moderns: Freedom and Fetish in the Mission Encounter*.
Berkeley, CA: University of California Press.

Koselleck, Reinhart. (1979) 2004. *Futures Past: On the Semantics of Historical Time.* New York: Columbia University Press.

Lavinas, Lena. 2013. "21st Century Welfare." *New Left Review* 84 (Nov/Dec): 5–40.

Levy, Santiago. 2006. *Progress against Poverty: Sustaining Mexico's Progresa-Oportunidades Program.* Washington, DC: Brookings Institution Press.

———. 2008. *Good Intentions, Bad Outcomes: Social Policy, Informality, and Economic Growth in Mexico.* Washington, DC: Brookings Institution Press.

Li, Tania. 2010. "To Make Live or Let Die? Rural Dispossession and the Protection of Surplus Populations." *Antipode* 41: 66–93.

Molyneux, Maxine. 2006. "Mothers at the Service of the New Poverty Agenda: Progresa/Oportunidades, Mexico's Conditional Transfer Programme." *Social Policy & Administration* 40(4): 425–449.

Mosse, David. 2005. *Cultivating Development: An Ethnography of Aid Policy and Practice.* London: Pluto Press.

Marais, Hein. 2011. *South Africa Pushed to the Limit: The Political Economy of Change.* Claremont: UCT Press.

Nussbaum, Martha. 2000. *Women and Human Development: The Capabilities Approach.* Cambridge: Cambridge University Press.

Ong, Aisha. 2007. "Neoliberalism as a Mobile Technology." *Transactions of the Institute of British Geographers* 32(1): 3–8.

Oportunidades. 2010. "Reglas de Operación del Programa de Desarrollo Humano Oportunidades para el ejercicio fiscal 2012." *Diario Oficial* (Tercera Sección), 30 December 2010. México: Diario Oficial de la Unión.

Piester, Kerianne. 1997. "Targeting the Poor: The Politics of Social Policy Reform in Mexico." In *The New Politics of Inequality in Latin America: Rethinking Participation and Representation,* edited by Douglas A. Chalmers, Carlos M. Vilas, Katherine Hite, Scott B. Martin, Kerianne Piester, and Monique Segarra, 469–488. Oxford: Oxford University Press.

Procampo. 1994. "Decreto de Creación del Procampo. Decreto que Regula el Programa de Apoyos Directos al Campo Denominado Procampo." *El Diario Oficial de la Federación,* 25 July 1994. México DF: Diario Oficial de la Federación.

———. N.d. "Vamos al Grano para Progresar." México: Secretaría de Agricultura y recursos Hidráulicos.

Progresa. 1997. "Decreto de Creación del Programa de Educación, Salud y Alimentación: Decreto que Regula el Programa de Educación, Salud y Alimentación Denominado Progresa." *El Diario Oficial de la Federación,* 8 August 1997. México DF: Diario Oficial de la Federación.

Prospera. 2014. "Decreto por el que se crea la Coordinación Nacional Prospera Programa de Inclusión Social." Prospera website. Accessed 1 September 2015. https://www.prospera.gob.mx/Portal/work/Web20132/documentos/05092014_DOF_Decreto_de_Creacion_Prospera.pdf.

Sanz, Ernesto. 2010. "La asignación universal por hijo se va en droga y juego." La Política Online. Accessed 14 December 2017. http://www.lapoliticaonline.com/nota/44397/.

Scarponetti, Patricia, Silvia Mabres, and Zenaida Garay Reyna. 2011. "Proyecto: Evaluación socioeducativa de la Asignación Universal por Hijo para la

Protección Social. Los sentidos de la educación. Estudios de casos urbanos y rurales en Córdoba y San Juan." In *Análisis y evaluación de los aspectos educativos de la Asignación Universal por Hijo (AUH)*, edited by Marta Castro, 107–126. Buenos Aires: Ministerio de Educación-Presidencia de la Nación.

Seekings, Jeremy, and Nicoli Nattrass. 2005. *Class, Race, and Inequality in South Africa*. New Haven, CT: Yale University Press.

Sen, Amartya K. 1985. *Commodities and Capabilities*. Oxford: Oxford University Press.

———. 1999. *Development as Freedom*. New York: Knopf.

Shore, Cris, and Susan Wright. 1997. "Policy: A New Field of Anthropology." In *Anthropology of Policy: Critical Perspectives on Governance and Power*, edited by Cris Shore and Susan Wright, 3–39. London: Routledge.

Skoufias, Emmanuel, B. Davis, and J. Behrman. 1999. *Final Report: An Evaluation of the Selection of Beneficiary Households in the Education, Health, and Nutrition Program (PROGRESA) of Mexico*. Washington, DC: International Food Policy Research Institute.

Skoufias, Emmanuel, and Bonnie McClafferty. 2001. "Is Progresa Working? Summary of the Results of an Evaluation by IFPRI." FCND discussion paper no. 118. Washington, DC: Food Consumption and Nutrition Division. International Food Policy Research Institute.

Sugiyama, Natasha Borges. 2011. "The Diffusion of Conditional Cash Transfer Programs in the Americas." *Global Social Policy* 11(2/3): 250–278.

World Bank. 2014. "A Model from Mexico for the World." The World Bank website. 19 November 2014. Accessed 14 December 2017. http://www.worldbank.org/en/news/feature/2014/11/19/un-modelo-de-mexico-para-el-mundo.

Chapter 8

Conditional Cash Transfer and Gender, Class, and Ethnic Domination
The Case of Bolivia

Nora Nagels

Introduction

Conditional cash transfer (CCT) programs have been spreading in Latin America as the answer to the widespread realization that the neoliberal model failed to generate economic growth and to reduce poverty. In the region, policy makers sought a more global approach for social policy than the prevalent methods. CCT programs filled the gap they identified. In the development scene, they are considered one of the major changes in social development policy in Latin America in the last twenty years. One of its consequences is the general consensus on the CCT program as being the "best practice" to reduce poverty, not only by financial institutions but also in the United Nations, think tanks, and academies (e.g., Rawling 2004; Fiszbein et al. 2009).

However, in Latin America, CCTs were not imposed by the international development community but appropriated—not only by national political regimes (Nagels 2014) but also in the local implementation. The study of such local implementation in Bolivia—of the Bono programs—mitigates the mainstream positive understanding of CCT as the best practice to reduce poverty. The main argument developed here maintains that CCT blindness to the weak quality of health services delivery reinforced preexisting class, gender, and ethnic inequalities. While they were elaborated under the administration of the first "indigenous" president in Bolivia—which claimed the decolonization and the depatriarchalization

Notes for this chapter begin on page 240.

of the state—the CCTs reproduced old features of Latin American social policies: maternalism and indigenous stigmatization.

This argument is based on the socioanthropological approach of development. This approach is, empirical, and fundamental but not normative. Development is an object (and not a theory) of academic anthropology. The goal is not to save or condemn the development but to understand complex social practices. In the words of Olivier de Sardan (2001: 731),

> development is indeed nothing but the set of actions of all kinds who claim to be near or far to it (from the "developer" as well as from the "developed") in the diversity of their assumptions, meanings, and practices. The existence of a "developmentist configuration"—the complex set of institutions, flows and actors for whom development is a resource, a job, a market, an issue, or strategy—is enough to justify the existence of a socioanthropology that takes development as an object of study or as an "input."[1]

This approach analyzes the interactions between developers and developed. It is based on methodological interactionism where social interactions are considered "privileged empirical 'input' while refusing to make it an object in itself, i.e. without being limited to it or trapped by it" (Oliver de Sardan 2001: 742).

While, historically, development referred to interventions made by Northern actors in the South, development studies gradually overcome this historical context and acquire thereby a more general nature. This allows focusing on new items, such as the conditional cash transfers (Beaulieu and Rousseau 2011: 5). While Bolivian CCT programs are assistance policies financed by state treasuries, international development organizations are very active in the monitoring and the diffusion of these programs. Additionally, we can speak about the existence of a developmentist configuration in which the socioanthropology of development is more and more linked to a socioanthropology of changes. Development policies are tangled with local public policies, and to separate the developmentist configuration and the everyday state is complicated (Oliver de Sardan 2001: 746).

This approach is close to the field and based on a qualitative method aiming to understand the sense giving by the actors to their actions. In this chapter, the developmentist configuration of Bolivian CCT is analyzed through a qualitative analysis of discourse. The chapter draws on fieldwork conducted during my Ph.D. studies (Nagels 2013), research that was supported by the Swiss National Science Foundation via its National Centre of Competence in Research North–South (NCCR N/S). Between 2008 and 2010, about fifty interviews were carried out with policy makers and CCT recipients in La Paz and El Alto.[2] Access to interviewees was easier with policy makers and medical staff than with recipients, whom I met mostly in health centers. This could reveal the mistrust of indigenous poor women to a young Western scholar. At the outset of my fieldwork, my assumptions might have led me to underestimate recipients' agency. In particular, as I started from a materialist feminist standpoint —which later evolved—it was difficult to discern the strategic dynamisms of respondents' actions in relation to CCT's management. The study of interactions between developers and developed was based on the analysis of the perceptions and representations of policy makers and recipients about each other. The mobilized quotes illustrate massive discourses that are not marginal. The use of discourse analysis on these interviews provided access to the social representations of gender and racial relations constructed by Bolivian CCT programs' stakeholders.

This chapter shows unpredicted results on the targeted population and the gaps between CCT and local norms. It is divided into three parts. First, the Bolivian context of adoption of CCT programs is described. Second, consensus about gender representations is analyzed. Third, gaps, tensions, bypass strategies, and unpredicted results are considered. I will conclude by discussing how the socioanthropologic approach is useful to understand these gaps.

The Bonos

The Bonos—the Bono Dignidad, the Bono Juancito Pinto (BJP), and the Bono Juana Azurduy (BJA)—were presented by the Bolivian president Evo Morales (2005–) as the pillars of a new and universalistic social policy (Nagels 2014). This chapter focuses only on the BJP and BJA because they are conditional cash transfers, whereas the Bono Dignidad is a noncontributory pension for elderly after the age of sixty-five.

The programs are implemented in a context of strong inequalities. Aware of bias in the construction of statistical indicators, we could cite the Gini coefficient, which is one of the highest in the world with 0.56 in 2007 (CEPAL 2010). In 2007, the income distribution was such that 20 percent of the total population held 60 percent of the national income, more unequal than it was in 1970 (Paz 2010: 58). Moreover, in 2004, 69 percent autodetermined indigenous households were poor (Molina 2005: 126).

In this context, based on the principal claims of the social movements that brought the Movimiento al Socialismo (MAS) to power, the first reforms of the Evo Morales government were the hydrocarbons nationalization[3] and the new Plurinational State of Bolivia's constitution. The first one aims to break the state dependence on international aid and to finance public policies, including the Bonos (Gray Molina 2007). On the other hand, the Plurinational State of Bolivia's constitution recognizes a new political subject: "indigenous, native and peasant."[4] From this constitution surged in 2006 the National Development Plan: Bolivia Worthy, Sovereign and Productive, to Live Well[5] (PND), which underlined that one of the first goals of the Evo Morales administration was "to dismantle colonialism and neoliberalism in order to build a pluri-cultural and communitarian state" (Ministerío de Planificación del Desarrollo 2006: xv–2).

The PND had a broad approach to development, including long-term social policy priorities. Only short-term programs of the plan (i.e., the Bonos) have materialized, however. The Bonos were hastily constructed in order to expedite the redistribution of resources resulting from the nationalization of hydrocarbons. Both BJP and BJA are entirely funded by the additional capital generated by this nationalization. They also were a response to pressures from many social groups for visible material gains and for a direct impact in their daily lives of the new form of resource management (Canavire-Bacarreza 2010: 36).

The Bono Juancito Pinto (BJP) was established in October 2006[6] with three objectives: increase school enrollment, reduce the dropout rate, and diminish the intergenerational transmission of poverty (Estado Plurinacional de Bolivia 2006). This program emerged hastily in response to a specific request from President Evo Morales. Under the BJP, all children may receive Bolivianos 200 (around $30 [US][7]) yearly upon meeting two conditions: (1) enrollment in a public school and (2) maintenance of a minimum 80 percent rate of school attendance (Unidad Ejecutora 2008: 1). Since 2006, the program has been expanded to all the grade levels of the public school system. Cecchini and Madariaga (2011) estimate that in 2010 this program reached 17.5 percent of Bolivia's total population, 32.4 percent of its poor, and 59.7 percent of the country's extreme poor.

The Bono Juana Azurduy (BJA)[8] originated from other social policies imagined, but not realized, by the Evo Morales government. The majority of social policy projects developed under the new constitution, and the PND included among their instruments a mother-child stipend whose objective was to reduce maternal and child mortality and child malnutrition. The BJA was launched in May 2009 and was the extension of a mother-child stipend that targeted the fifty-two poorest municipalities in the country. The president decided to extend it to all pregnant and breastfeeding women, as well as those with children under two years of age, who do not have another form of healthcare insurance. The BJA is a cash transfer with conditions focused on healthcare. In order to receive the benefit ($260 [US] equivalent[9]) over a period of thirty-three months, mothers are required (1) to have a formal form of identification for themselves and their children, (2) to attend prenatal health checkups, and (3) to commit to giving birth in a medical institution and follow through with postnatal checkups. They receive a different amount of money for each condition fulfilled. In 2010, the BJA benefited 3.5 percent of Bolivia's total population, 6.4 percent of the country's poor, and 10 percent of its extreme poor (Cecchini and Madariaga 2011). Between 2009 and 2012, 33 percent of pregnant women who qualified for the BJA received it, and 50 percent of children under the age of two (Vidal Fuertes et al. 2015: 87, 88).

This chapter will analyze the recipients and policy makers' perception of gender relations and their representation of conditions.

Maternalist Consensus

A consensual element of CCT is to target women (and not men) as recipients of the cash transfer. Built in the late 1990s, in a post-Beijing and gender-sensitive world that was becoming concerned with the specific problems of women in poverty, CCT programs are gender aware (Molyneux 2009: 22). They were based on the assumption that giving money to women empowered them. Nevertheless, this allusion to gender empowerment was rhetorical, and the discourse finds a clear maternalist frame. It is based on a longstanding belief that providing benefits to mothers will benefit children more than transfers or income going to fathers or "the household" in general. Maternalism is grounded in Latin American social norms and is based on the reduction of women's roles solely to motherhood, and linked to moral values such as sacrifice and altruism (Jelin 1990). Rather than fight gender inequalities, CCT reinforced a traditional gender role and maternalism.

Two underlying conceptions of gender differences were used to justify this social maternalist norm. First, program managers assumed the existence of a clear difference between women and men as well as mothers and fathers in relationship to children, and cited the "cost-effectiveness" of paying the CCT to the mother. Program managers worked with this instrumental approach, as illustrated by a statement of the BJA operative chief: "Generally in Bolivia . . . the important person for health, it is the mother more than the father. The mother has more relationship with the child to go to health checkups; this is not the case with dad. And the aim is to strengthen this aspect, that is to say, the power that the mother has in [children's] health." Women recipients accept this role of intermediary precisely because they also represent themselves exclusively as mothers in charge of their children. For example, one recipient of the BJP reiterated that it should be granted to mothers because they spend in the interest of children: "Because we, women, we can manage it and if we receive it we will spend for our children and buy what they need."

To this efficient argument another was added, the second underlying conception of gender difference. It attributed moral value to the sexes. In the strict and dichotomous view of men and women, vice was associated with the former, and virtue with the latter. Men are described as likely to spend the subsidy for personal ends or on failings, such as alcohol. There was a clear justification for excluding men from CCT programs. A former male director of the BJA expressed this mistrust of men: "We were not able to be 100 percent sure that the fathers were not going to spend their money on drinks at the traditional bachelors' Friday night outings taking place all over the country." This view was shared by the BJA coordinator for La Paz: "If they [men] receive money for their children, they say 'celebrate first': two small beers, then 4, 8, 10, 12 . . . and at 6:00 the next morning, there is no more money for the baby. . . . Because the idiosyncrasies of our people are that the man who receives the money will . . . squander it on alcoholic beverages." Moreover, women CCT recipients share these negative representations of men. For example, the director of an informal workers organization in La Paz spoke about the men's tradition to celebrate: "Some fathers who requested Juancito Pinto Friday reappeared on Tuesday penniless. . . . If it is the man who receives it, he goes to the bar and after six beers, he forgets Bono Juancito Pinto."

It should be emphasized that all actors, across every levels of the CCT programs, share and never question this representation of men. What emerges is an overwhelming vision of men as irresponsible and selfish, focused on leisure and most often alcohol. While these representations have negative effects for men, they most importantly reinforce social norms that assign women responsibility for maintaining the household, whether they have employment or not.

By transferring income to women, CCT programs can have some positive effects on intrahousehold gender relations (Nagels 2011; Martinez and Voorend 2012). These programs nonetheless rely largely on the unpaid care work of women in order to improve children's wellbeing. Indeed, a single representation of gender relations strikingly dominated the discourse of every stakeholder: women are mothers. CCTs reinforce preexisting maternalism and the sexual division of labor. Because CCT programs discourage men from assuming care work and because of their conditional feature, they overburden women. This extra work reinforces gender inequalities. As Molyneux (2009: 37) highlighted, "Women's position within the social division of labour is not only reinforced by confirming their customary caregiving roles, but the program depend to a significant degree upon their carrying out this work without any direct financial compensation for their time and, indeed, exist in tension with any income generating activities that they may undertake."

Tensions about Conditions

As seen above, the Bonos official norms, which are explicit and written in the *Decreto Supremo*, linked the conditions to the improvement of health and education of children and pregnant women. Moreover, the Bonos are integrated in higher official norms—such as the plurinational constitution—that explicitly promoted indigenous rights and practices. However, the blindness to poor quality health services delivery meant that the Bonos' implementation remained strongly shaped by practical norms that stigmatize the indigenous population. According to Olivier de Sardan (2015: 8), practical norms are "the various informal, de facto, tacit or latent norms that underlie the practices of actors which diverge from the official (or social norms)." In the implementation process, local managers overlap the official norms with practical norms independent of social norms (e.g. religions, culture, tradition) and official norms (law, rules, etc.).

Beyond the official norms' objective to familiarize poor and indigenous populations with health institutions, the conditionalities are clearly oriented to modifying the behavior of the indigenous poor women, dismissing their knowledge and practices. Here, conflicts emerge between CCT officials and women recipients. While the former estimate that the conditions of the programs should modify recipients' mentalities and practices, the latter question the conditions.

The Respect of Conditions

The on-the-ground operation of the BJA carried normative practical prescriptions about appropriate maternal behavior that derived from the rejection of indigenous family and reproductive practices, as well as a more generalized dismissal of the capacity of indigenous women.

First, the discourses of CCT policy makers were based on the assumption that women were ignorant of the proper way to feed and care for their children, and were perpetuating bad practices. According to program officials, recipients did not have sufficient knowledge to practice good motherhood. Although the problem clearly arose because of both packaging and delivery of health services, a doctor in charge of children's health complained about recipients' lack of comprehension of how to be a good mother:

> People in this region were given granules as a nutritional complement: 60 bags . . . one bag every day to add to their diet. . . . Unfortunately the mothers did not always use them since they did not taste good and the children did not want to eat them. They left the bags on the side, pretending "their children

did not want to eat them," not realizing the impact of these granules on their children's health.

Second, in the data, only a few quotations explicitly referred to ethnicity or indigeneity as an explanation for ignorance, but the derogative use of terms such as "community," "idiosyncrasy," "myths," and "beliefs" were codes for the same idea. They revealed cultural and ethnic hierarchies. Myths, for instance, were perceived as obstacles to accessing healthcare centers, as explained by a doctor implementing the BJA: "It could be then concluded that women did not go to healthcare centers because of the myths that doctors did not provide good care, mistreating or causing more suffering to their patients." Similarly, a doctor in charge of BJA used idiosyncrasy to explain the low rate of vaccination among the children's population: "Mothers would use the same idiosyncrasy when they pretended that vaccination could kill children. 'You came to kill one of my children because I have many and you want to kill one of them.' Therefore, it became difficult to attract the women to the healthcare centers." Confronted with what they saw as ignorance, BJA officials judged that the conditions set by the programs were important because via their application they would be able to modify mentalities and recipients' behaviors. Explicitly, the Bonos served to educate the population, as expressed by a BJA agent: "The hardest part was to educate the population." The education concerned hygiene, nutrition, and feeding. One initiator of BJA in UDAPE[10] explained, "While the child was given a health checkup, the mother was provided with information about hygiene and health, such as how to wash their hands and treat food." Specifically, these doctors saw themselves as invested with a mission to teach mothers how to breastfeed and properly feed their children: "Additionally, we advised mothers on how to feed, how to breastfeed, what was to be done. . . . We educated them, we met with them to watch and monitor the improvements . . . we provided them with explanations but they did not understand quickly . . . we had then to repeat the explanations."

This kind of attitude is at odds with respect for the myths and idiosyncrasies of indigenous people, the Andean worldview and social norms. But it is also at odds with official norms of medicine which teaches respect of the patient. As elsewhere, they are practical norms and "reflect the widespread view subscribed by the majority of healthcare workers that patients are ignorant" (Olivier de Sardan 2015: 7).

The educational mission of several local BJA workers was so hard that they eventually used the cash transfers as leverage to impose extralegal conditions. For example, a doctor in charge of the BJA said that she intimidated recipients by threatening to withdraw them from the program if their children did not gain weight: "If their child's weight decreased, they were then told, 'Madame, if your child has not gained weight by next month, you will not have Bono.'" This was an additional requirement not substantiated by any legal provision to link the inclusion in the BJA to improvement in the health condition of the children. This example illustrates the agency of CCT local promoters, who have margins of maneuvering and creativity in the implementation process. In a repertory of various norms, doctors choose practical norms in order to operationalize the Bonos objectives (improvement in child malnutrition). This kind of extra-condition seems to be part of "adaptive practical norms" that are tolerated by the administration because they are in the spirit of the rule (Olivier de Sardan 2015: 27).

This propensity on the part of the agents responsible for the implementation of Bonos to support and even force development on the poor could be explained by their personal experience. For those with often modest and indigenous origins, becoming a professor or a medical doctor—in other words acquiring a higher education and social status—demanded great sacrifices, and they tended to consider cash handouts by the state as inappropriate. Hence they increased the counterparts (Rousseau 2009). The developmentist logic was shared by local implementers who opposed any type of assistancialism.

Nevertheless, the focus on hygiene and education constructed representations of these populations as irresponsible and dirty. In large part, these representations of ignorance and the need to intervene in household behavior arose from CCT program officers' refusal to recognize knowledge derived from experience and cultural practice. Conflicts over medical practices, pregnancy, and childbirth frequently brought the issues to the foreground.

Biomedicine versus Ethno-medicine

While biomedicine refers to knowledge from the West, Andean medicine refers to the Andean worldviews. Where the first sets dichotomous items (health versus disease; body versus reason; culture versus nature), the second reflects values and holistic knowledge systems based on principles of reciprocity and complementarity (Arnold and Yapita 1999). In the practices of Andean populations, both systems are neither impermeable nor exclusive. The patients incorporate elements of both sets and implement flexible and creative negotiation processes (Miles and Leatherman 2003). Since 1986, Bolivia was one of the few countries in the world to legalize traditional medicine. Moreover, in the National Development Plan (2006), a chapter was dedicated to the decolonization of health (NDP 2006: 37–43). Articles 35, 37, and 39 of the new Constitution of 2009 of the Plurinational State of Bolivia retained the same principles. However, the role of ethno-medicine was only lightly respected and recognized in the practices of medical staff (Rozee 2007: 5). Health policy advocated biomedicine, and tended to impose it over ethno-medicine. Biomedicine was seen as more scientific and better than ethno-medicine.

Health practitioners did not intend to reject traditional medicine but to promote institutional biomedicine. Even if ethno-medicine practices were accepted in households, they were seen as complementary to bio-medicine, which was the kind of medicine privileged in health centers, as explained by a BJA doctor: "Of course, the women, mothers, some-times have a different opinion: they treat certain pathologies with differ-ent home methods. Most are not bad, they do not hurt, but they should be a complement to medical care."

The problem is not so much the promotion of biomedicine in itself, but the rejection of ethno-medicine even while the indigenous women patients value and combine both. According to the women, biomedicine and ethno-medicine save lives, whereas medical staff believed this is only true of bio-medicine. These tensions between biomedicine and ethno-medicine were reflected in childbirth. Briefly, ethnomedical birth refers to rituals and manipulations that correspond to Andean holistic representations of the body, health, and individuals. During the ethnomedical birth, women are related to the *Pachamama*, the mother earth. Then she needs to push down, hence the vertical positions. The midwife, the future father, and other trusted persons accompany the parturient, hence the collective qualifica-tion of childbirth. Childbirth is considered an important rite of passage in the lives of women and newborns. The institutional delivery goes against it. Even if it considerably reduces maternal mortality, the ways in which it is implemented do not respect childbirth as an essential rite of passage. For example, it meets the criteria of biomedicine and is accompanied by Western cultural norms and gynecological tables, without the presence of family or relatives. The medicalization of childbirth gives primary place to the therapist, who steals the protagonist role of the woman and her power to give birth. It reproduces, therefore, ethnic, class, and gender domination between practitioner and parturient (La Riva Gonzalez 2000).

According to legal standards and official norms of intercultural health, traditional childbirth should be possible in Bolivia. Nevertheless, in real-ity, vertical childbirth was not practiced in health centers where fieldwork was carried out. A doctor in charge of the BJA recognized that verti-cal childbirth was not allowed: "We still do not meet this requirement.

As I said, mainly [because] our infrastructure is not adequate." Other investigations showed that personal health staff considered traditional birth dangerous and unsuitable. Crouching was perceived to cause injury to the baby, and delivery rooms were considered too small to host the family (Platt 2006; Rozée 2007). Childbirth reflected the debate between traditional medicine and biomedicine: health staff accepted the incorporation of elements of traditional medicine only when they did not involve changes in their practices or representations of biomedicine, considered the unique, valid medical science. In universities, biomedicine was hegemonic, while ethno-medicine was absent or marginalized and depreciated (Uriburu 2006: 176). Therefore, "a significant proportion of doctors was not prepared to attend deliveries in traditional positions, by lack of training and by an authoritarian attitude of non-acceptance of expectations and cultural traditions" (Rozee 2007: 7).

The health interculturalism official norms advocated by the government remained in the limbo of official palaver. Bonos implementers still believed that indigenous practices and culture were responsible for poor health indicators, and that culture was still a barrier to biomedicine, the modern and only path to good health. The Bonos' blindness to poor health services delivery reinforced preexisting practical norms of health institutions. The problem was not the promotion of behavior changes in accordance to biomedicine per se—hygiene and nutrition practices improved health indicators—but the denigration by medical staff of ethno-medicine and actors who supported it: indigenous women. Changes were promoted only in patient populations and not in health personal. Indigenous culture remained invoked as a fatality, responsible for all ills even while this causation was unproven (Rozee 2007: 7–8). The instrumentalization of culture to explain the problems related to health services access "transformed in cultural terms prejudices with strong racist connotations" (Fassin 2001: 9). The focus was only on recipients' culture and practices. Practitioners' and institutional actors' culture was absent. Therefore, the relations of domination between the two groups—preexisting to the Bonos—were denied. The power relationship between, on the one hand, BJA policy makers, experts, and practitioners—mostly male and considered or auto-identified as white, mestizo, and middle class—and, on the other hand, the poor indigenous women, was reinforced.

Recipients' Reactions

Confronted with these CCT norms and practices, the recipients developed their agency in order to adapt themselves and to maximize their own interest and first priority: to survive. As seen above, they share the maternalist social norm that assign them solely to their reproductive and care role. Additionally, they share the goals of the program: improving the wellbeing of children,[11] as expressed by one of them: "The money is used for my little one, buy food, clothing, etc." Women positively evaluate the programs and greatly appreciate the help that the Bonos represent in their daily lives, as expressed by one of the BJP recipients: "Wow, yes! It has changed a lot for us! It is a joy because we support our children. . . . This Bono Juana Azurduy is also a motivation for there to be more care in health centers. . . . It helps us a lot."

These positive comments relate only to the money transfer. The women appreciated the incentive of the Bonos; at the same time, they are critical of the quality of health services delivery. First, the recipients report health service supply issues, such as their insufficient number and geographical spread. The distance between places of residence and institutions related to BJA is a problem for women assigned to other productive tasks, as explained by a BJP recipient: "There are always difficulties. If we could establish banks in the provinces, it would be better, right? That way, at any time when the mom has some time, she will get the money, because otherwise it takes two days." Moreover, recipients criticized the amount of money received as insufficient to feed their children: "The money is not enough: 125 bolivianos only buy two cartons of milk." Another BJA recipient shared this opinion, considering it senseless to attend workshops and learn how to improve children's diets, since she was financially unable to obtain more protein- or vitamin-rich food: "The problem is that we give what we have at home. I do not see why I should go to these meetings [about how to fight malnutrition] because I cannot buy more fruits, vegetables, or chicken."

This kind of criticism is structural: the programs do not consider the social conditions in which the recipients are struggling. In other words, women recipients highlighted the Bonos' blindness to weak quality of health services delivery. Furthermore, they noted that programs do not meet their own obligations in terms of family planning and traditional birth.[12] The access to modernity, through access to occidental maternity in which personal accomplishment takes precedence, cannot cope with the lack of contraceptive methods. While the CCT program affirms the use of, and disseminates information about, contraceptives, it is not enough. A recipient of the BJA explained it as follows: "I calculated. They told me to come after the birth and the return of my period to ask questions [but] the problem is that doctors do not have time to answer our questions." Before the consultation, she expressed her desire to ask how she could plan her pregnancies, but during the consultation, she would not ask the question. She explained her attitude as follows: "The problem is that doctors do not have the time to answer our questions." As indicated by Dibbits (2003:

151), women's submission to public officials could be functional, a means of self-protection without acceptance of their social inferiority. No talk and no questions prevented doctors' further intrusion into their privacy. Interesting to note is that these women, judged as premodern indigenous, share claims more generally associated with feminist white and middle-class women: birth control. This kind of attitude could be interpreted as complying with their first priority: to secure their life. Still, on the subject of sexual and reproductive rights, the vertical childbirth or squatting is not allowed, as explained by a recipient of the BJA: "I gave birth here; they do not respect traditional childbirth, but my husband was able to go into the room. Childbirth is better at home because it takes care of us for seven days." By claiming information about family planning or the right to be able to give birth as at home, recipients seize the program commitments and official norms to denounce it (Faya Robles 2008). They appropriate institutional requirements (contraception and respectful institutional delivery) to construct margins of maneuvering and agency in order to improve their life condition, maintaining their identity as indigenous women.

Beyond the institutional and structural problems, recipients denounce the abuse they are subject to in the health centers. The behaviors of health workers are disrespectful, discriminatory, sexist, and abusive. They are absent, make them wait, laugh at them, and do not respect them. One recipient of the BJA complained, "I've been here since 7:40 and it is 12:00. Sometimes I wait all day." The inability to access health centers exists, and it is especially problematic when health centers are at great distances from recipients' homes, as explained by a BJA's recipient: "Doctors do not honor their commitments. Sometimes it's far away and they make us come for nothing."

The critiques and the adaptive strategies become explicit when women develop bypass strategies to the CCT requirements while continuing to benefit. One of them concerns medical pluralism, combining biomedical and ethno-medicine, as explained by a recipient of BJA: "I also use traditional medicines." The use of medical pluralism by the recipient allows resisting the imposition of the prescribed biomedicine by the program. Therefore, women who go to the health centers and meet the program requirements fall under a nonexclusive pragmatism. This is confirmed by two recipients of BJA. A first recipient recognized, while snickering, that if it were not for the financial attractiveness, she would not go to health centers: "[Hee hee], yes indeed, without Bono I would not come." Another recipient in El Alto was at the same time in favor of the improvement of her child, but did not seem overly concerned that her daughter was in a state of malnutrition: "No, I do not care because my other children were also too small but they recovered. . . . My baby is too small and not very big but she is in the process of recovering." Women are very well aware what they must say to stay in the program (for example, about the improvement of child nutrition) while continuing their own fundamental strategy: survive. Women indigenous recipients adopted adaptive strategies in order to stay in the program, improving their life conditions, reducing their costs, and maintaining their own meaning system—about health, for example. Their attitudes followed the first logic of development in the interaction of every development configuration: the logic of the search for security (Olivier de Sardan 1995: 134–136).

Conclusion

The socioanthropology approach of development allows one to highlight and understand features of social policies implemented by the first indigenous government of Bolivia that seemed paradoxical. Analyzing social and development policies as an object of research by studying the interactions between developers and developed allows one to clarify implementation gaps between official norms of the Plurinational State and the Bonos on the one hand, and practical norms of local implementers on the other. While the Plurinational State, from the new constitution to ministerial rules, promoted the depatriarchalization and the decolonization of the state, its public actions involved representations that reproduced both the maternalism and indigenous stigmatization.

The continuation of indigenous stigmatization in the era of state decolonization claimed by Evo Morales's administration seemed contradictory. This contradiction could be explained by the supremacy of the developmentist logic inside the government over the "wellbeing" perspective present at the beginning of Morales's administration and in the new Plurinational State constitution. Originating in the Economic Commission for Latin America and the Caribbean (ECLAC), the developmentist logic advocated a strong state as an agent of development through huge infrastructure projects (Lavaud 2009). Whatever the nuances, this developmentist model advocated the exploitation of natural resources and productivity policies. In contrast, the "wellbeing" perspective was structured by socioenvironmentalist discourses and based on social, legal, economic, and political ethnic pluralism. Again, whatever its nuances, it was reluctant to endorse productivist projects and the exploitation of natural resources. The power relationship between both development models, sustained by different social forces, weighed in favor of the developmentist logic which reproduced neocolonialism and understood modernity solely as Western concept.

Moreover, these implementation gaps can be explained not only by tensions within the Morales government but also by the fact that development and its policies, following the socioanthropological approach to development, are strategies and resources for their stakeholders. Medical staff and recipients of the Bonos used them according to their interests and representations of what constituted development. The blindness of the Bonos to the poor delivery health service left plenty of space for practical norms impregnated by maternalism and indigenous stigmatization.

Postscript

This research was carried out in 2008–2010. Since then, the institutional design of the BJA and the BJP has not changed. The conditions — school attendance for the BJP and healthcare for the BJA — and the amount transferred — around $20 (US) once per year for the BJP and around $260 (US) over a period of thirty-three months for the BJA — have remained the same. The number of BJA recipients — around 33 percent of women and 50 percent of children qualified for the BJA — has been stable. So far, no ethnographic research has attempted to explain why two-thirds of the women who qualify for the BJA have not used it. However, quantitative research by Vidal et al. (2015: 92) about the impacts of BJA stresses that about 30 percent of women qualifying for BJA have not been enrolled in it due to lack of information and the perceptions of very long queues and very long administrative procedures. Moreover, around 20 percent of enrolled women have not attended all the medical checkups (for them or their children). The stated reasons for this are that they had to work or care for their children, but also because of the poor quality of health service delivery and because of abuses from the medical staff (Vidal et al. 2015: 94). These results are aligned with the ones presented in this chapter. They show Bonos' institutional design is also maladapted to the experiences of poor indigenous women.

Nora Nagels is an assistant professor in political science at the Université de Québec à Montréal (UQAM). Her research is concerned with gender, citizenship, and social policies in Latin America. She has recently published on comparative politics, conditional cash transfers, development, citizenship, and gender in leading journals such as *Social Policy and Administration, Social Policy and Society, Revue internationale de politique comparée,* and *Lien social et Politiques.*

Notes

1. All translations are by the author.
2. All these interviews are analyzed in Nagels 2013. During the research, informants received a guarantee of anonymity in order to avoid any risks (such as job loss) associated with their agreement to be interviewed.
3. It was more a negotiation of taxes with transnational corporations than an expropriation of corporations.
4. Article 30 of the Plurinational State constitution created a new category of "indigenous, native and peasant nation and people" who are a "whole human community that shares cultural identity, language, historical tradition, institutions, territoriality and worldview, whose existence predated the Spanish colonial invasion."
5. *Plan Nacional de Desarrollo Bolivia Digna, Soberana Productiva Democrática y para Vivir Bien.*
6. By the Decreto Supremo no. 28899, 26 October 2006.
7. The national minimum monthly salary was Bs 500 in 2006 and Bs 2000 in 2017, whereas the BJP amount have remained at Bs 200.
8. Launched by the Decreto Supremo no. 0066, 3 April 2009.
9. This amount represents between 1 and 5 percent of the household consumption in 2014 (Vidal et al. 2015: 91).
10. Unidad de Análisis de Políticas Sociales y Económicas (Social and Economic Policy Analysis Unit), research center of the Development Planification Minister.
11. This is related to the internalization and reproduction by the recipients of the Marianist stereotype, who see themselves primarily as mothers responsible for their children (Nagels 2011).
12. According to their guidelines, the BJA should provide family planning information and traditional birth.

References

Albó, X. 2004. "Interculturidad y salud." In *Salud e interculturalidad en América Latina: Perspectivas antropológicas*, edited by G. Fernandez Juárez, 65–74. Quito: Ahya-Yela, Universitad de Castilla de la Mancha.

Arnold, D., and J. Dios Yapita. 1999. *Vocabulario aymara del parto y de la vida reproductiva de la mujer*. La Paz: ILCA, Family Health International.

Beaulieu, E., and S. Rousseau. 2011. "Évolution historique de la pensée féministe sur le développement de 1970 à 2011." *Recherches féministes* 24(2): 1–19.

Canavire-Bacarreza, G., and M.-M. Ayaviri. 2010. *Políticas macroeconómicas, choques externos y protección social en Bolivia*. La Paz: UDAPE.

Cecchini, S., and A. Madariaga. 2011. *Programas de transferencias condicionadas: Balance de la experiencia reciente en América latina y el Caribe*. Santiago de Chile: CEPAL, ASDI.

Dibbits, I. 2003. *Uno de los dos: el involucramiento de los hombres en la atención de la salud perinatal, revelaciones desde Santa Rosa Pampa, el Alto, Bolivia*. La Paz: Tahimapu.

Faya Robles, A. 2008. "L'humanisation de l'accouchement et de la naissance au Brésil: de nouveaux dispositifs de régulation des femmes pauvres?" *Lien social et politiques. Corps et politiques: entre l'individuel et le collectif* 59: 115–124.

Fiszbein, A., N. Schady, F. Ferreira, M. Grosh, N. Keleher, P. Olintro, and E. Skoufias. 2009. *Conditional Cash Transfers: Reducing Present and Future Poverty.* Washington, DC: World Bank.

Gautier, A., and A. Quesnel. 1993. *Politique de population, médiateurs institutionnels et régulation de la fécondité au Yucatan (Mexique).* Paris: Institut francais de recherche scientifique pour le développement en coopération, El colegio de Mexico.

La Riva Gonzalez, P. 2000. "Le Walthana Hampi ou la reconstruction du corps, conception de la grossesse dans les Andes du Sud du Pérou." *Journal de la Société des Américanistes* 86: 169–184.

Lautier, B. 2009. "Gouvernement moral des pauvres et dépolitisation des politiques publiques en Amérique latine." In *Penser le politique en Amérique latine: La recréation des espaces et des formes du politique,* edited by N. Borgeaud-Garciandía, B. Lautier, R. Peñafiel, and A. Tizziani, 19–36. Paris: Karthala.

Lavaud, J.-P. 2009. "Indianisme et écologie dans les pays andins: dispositif légal, discours officiels et mobilisations." *Problèmes d'Amérique latine* 76: 97–117.

Martínez Franzoni, J., and K. Voorend. 2012. "Blacks, Whites, or Grays? Conditional Transfers and Gender Equality in Latin America." *Social Politics* 19(3): 383–407.

Miles, A., and T. Leatherman. 2003. "Perspectives on Medical Anthropology in the Andes." In *Medical Pluralism in the Andes: Theory and Practices in Medical Anthropology and International Health,* edited by J. D. Koss-Chioino, T. Leatherman, and C. Greenway, 3–15. London: Routledge.

Ministerio de Planificación del Desarrollo. 2006. *Plan Nacional de Desarrollo: Bolivia digna, soberana, productiva y democrática para Vivir Bien.* La Paz: Ministerio de Planificación del Desarrollo.

Molyneux, M. 2009. "Conditional Cash Transfers: A 'Pathway to Women's Empowerment'?" Pathways of Empowerment Working Paper 5. Pathways Brief 5. London: UK Dept. for International Development.

Nagels, N. 2011. "Les représentations des rapports sociaux de sexe au sein des politiques de lutte contre la pauvreté au Pérou." *Recherches féministes* 24(2): 115–134.

———. 2013. "Genre et politiques de lutte contre la pauvreté au Pérou et en Bolivie: quels enjeux de citoyenneté?" Ph.D. dissertation, Graduate Institute, Geneva.

Olivier de Sardan, J.-P. 2001. "Les trois approches en anthropologie du développement." *Tiers-Monde* 42(168): 729–754.

———. "Les transferts monétaires au Niger: la manne et les soupcons. Synthèse des recherches menées par le LASDEL." *Études et travaux* 108. Niamey: LASDEL.

Platt, T. 2006. "El feto agresivo. Parto, formación de la persona y mito-historia en los Andes." In *Salud e interculturidad en América Latina: Antropología de la salud y crítica intercultural,* edited by G. Fernandez Juárez, 145–172. Quito: Ahya-Yela, Universidad de Castilla de la Mancha.

Quijano, A. 1980. *Dominación y cultura: Los cholos y el conflicto cultural en el Perú.* Lima: Mosca Azul Editores.

——. 2000. "Colonialidad del poder, eurocentrismo y América Latina."
In *La colonialidad del saber: eurocentrismo y ciencias sociales. Perspectivas latinoamericanas*, edited by E. Lander, 201–246. Buenos Aires: CLASCO.

Ramírez Hita, S. 2009. *Calidad de atención en salud: Práticas y representaciones sociales en la población quechua e amayará del altiplano boliviano*. La Paz: OPS, OMS.

Rawlings, L. 2004. *A New Approach to Social Assistance: Latin America's Experience with Conditional Cash Transfer Programmes*. Washington, DC: World Bank.

Rousseau, S. 2009. "Genre et ethnicité racialisée en Bolivie: pour une étude intersectionnelle des mouvements sociaux." *Sociologie et sociétés* 41(2): 135–160.

Rozée, V. 2007. "Les patrons culturels du comportement reproductif et sexuel dans les Andes Boliviennes." *Cuestiones del tiempo presente* 7: 1–13.

Unidad Ejecutora del Bono Juancito Pinto. 2008. *Informe de cierre preliminar del Bono Juancito Pinto al 31 de diciembre 2008*. La Paz: Ministerio de Educación y de Cultura.

Uriburu, G. 2006. "Mortalidad materna en Bolivia: ¿Que hacer para evitar tantas muertes de mujeres?" In *Salud e interculturidad en América latina. Antropología de la salud y critica intercultural*, edited by G. Fernandez Juárez, 173–227. Quito: Ahya-Yela, Universitad de Castilla de la Mancha.

Vidal Fuertes, C., S. Martínez, P. Celhay and S. Claros Gómez. 2015. *Evaluación de Impacto del Programa de Salud Materno Infantil "Bono Juana Azurduy."* La Paz: Unidad de Análisis de Políticas Sociales y Económicas, BID.

Chapter 9

Behind the Official Story
The Unintended Effects of Social Transfer Programs in
Conflict-Affected Contexts

Fiona Samuels and Nicola Jones

Introduction

Cash transfers, a widely used form of social transfer to poor households,
have been heralded as a recent success story in international development.
However, measures of their success have been narrow and have tended
to focus on improving economic and human capital outcomes. Less is
known about how beneficiaries and communities view cash transfers and
how they affect broader wellbeing, often unintentionally, at the individual level and in relation to others, both at the community level as well as
in more distant relationships with implementers and the state.

To address this gap in knowledge, this chapter draws on findings from
a multicountry study, using qualitative and participatory approaches,
of unconditional cash transfer programs of considerable longevity,
which allows us to tease out broader wellbeing effects. For the purposes
of this chapter we focus on the conflict-affected/postconflict settings of
Mozambique, Palestine (both Gaza and the West Bank), and Yemen.

Toward an Analytical Framework

To situate our findings, in this first section we briefly explore recent theories of wellbeing, then broaden our discussion to look at relationships

between citizens and the state in order to develop an analytical framework for discussing our study findings in subsequent sections.

Development theorists are increasingly emphasizing that not only are nonmonetary dimensions critical when exploring progress (see, e.g., Sen 1999), but that people's own experiences and subjective assessments of what matters in their lives need also to be taken into account. When asked to describe what poverty means to them, people invariably mention feelings of frustration, shame, humiliation, lack of dignity and confidence, and hopelessness (Narayan et al. 2000b; Walker et al. 2013). Similarly, when they are asked what wellbeing means, peace of mind and confidence in the future, autonomy, self-respect and dignity, and the ability to fulfill social expectations and participate in community life are common themes in participatory poverty assessments (Narayan et al. 2000a).

The concept of wellbeing is not challenge-free, with ways of defining and understanding it varying both among social scientists and among experts from other disciplines (economists, psychologists, and mental health practitioners) (Patel and Kleinman 2003; Lund et al. 2011; Helliwell et al. 2013), and ways of measuring it being mostly restricted to quantitative approaches, with research mostly conducted in high-income Western countries. We nevertheless argue that it is a useful concept for framing our findings. Work emerging from the University of Bath (White 2013) on psychological wellbeing in developing country contexts has developed a model to explore subjective perceptions of wellbeing, emphasizing also the importance of the particular context and the relational aspect of wellbeing. Developing the concept of "inner wellbeing," or what people think and feel they can be and do, scholars in this tradition stress that "wellbeing is not the property of an individual, it emerges in relationship" (White 2013: 4). They propose a focus on seven distinct but closely interrelated domains through which to view wellbeing: economic confidence, agency and participation, social connections, close relationships, physical and mental health, competence and self-worth, and values and meaning (White 2013). As will be seen in the analysis of our findings, many of these themes emerged in discussions with cash transfer beneficiaries.

For the effects of individual wellbeing and community relationships to be harnessed and channeled into social action, strengthening relationships between citizens and state actors is essential. Here we turn to explore a more anthropological perspective on governance relations—that is, the micropatterning of state-citizen relations—a level of analysis that is often overlooked in more mainstream state building and governance literature (Mooij 2007). In this vein, Corbridge et al. (2005: 5) emphasize the importance of a more nuanced understanding of how the poor "see the state" because "states are best thought of as bundles of everyday institutions and forms of rule." It is, therefore, critical to explore how poor and excluded citizens understand citizenship, how they practice it, and the barriers they face when interacting with the state. In particular, Corbridge et al. (2005) highlight the need to better understand how marginalized populations visualize the state and with whom in their day-to-day interactions they engage.

Mindful of these limitations of state-citizen engagement in many developing country contexts, proponents of good governance are increasingly promoting interventions that seek to enhance so-called "social accountability." Social accountability refers to the wide range of citizen and civil society organization actions to hold the state to account, as well as actions on the part of government and the media (McNeil and Malena 2010). While the sanctions imposed by social accountability remain informal, primarily through reputational and political costs, the sustained efforts of a well-informed, critical mass intent on reform can "offer a sharper, more targeted form of accountability" (Unsworth 2010: 41; see also Hickey and Mohan 2008; Ringold et al. 2012). Moreover, because outcomes rather than processes are key, social accountability can focus on "best fit" rather than "best practices," which means that it can use lenses that are culturally sensitive and attuned to local political dynamics (Unsworth 2010; Bukenya et al. 2012; Tembo 2013), as well as deploy a wide range of methods to achieve its objectives, including prospective information campaigns, budget analysis, retrospective social audits, and "contentious actions" (Bukenya et al. 2012: 28).

Whether and how public programs are designed to encourage social accountability—and in order to bring these discrete bodies of thinking together—we argue that it is helpful to situate them within a broader ecological framework, and within that, linkages between individual, community, and state-level relationships. Using White's (2013) wellbeing conceptual framework as a starting point, we not only include linkages with state actors, but also present possible pathways through which these interactions can be cemented. Figure 9.1 highlights the effects of cash transfer programs on different dimensions of individual wellbeing, as well as their relationships with community members, program implementers, and state actors more broadly. Often these linkages—which can be beneficial and deleterious—are unplanned for and unintended; nevertheless, our contention is that they are a critical component of program efficacy, without which poverty alleviation and wellbeing goals are unlikely to be met and sustained (Hunter and Sugiyama 2014).

Research Methodology

This chapter draws on primary qualitative and participatory research in three countries—Mozambique, Palestine, and Yemen—undertaken in

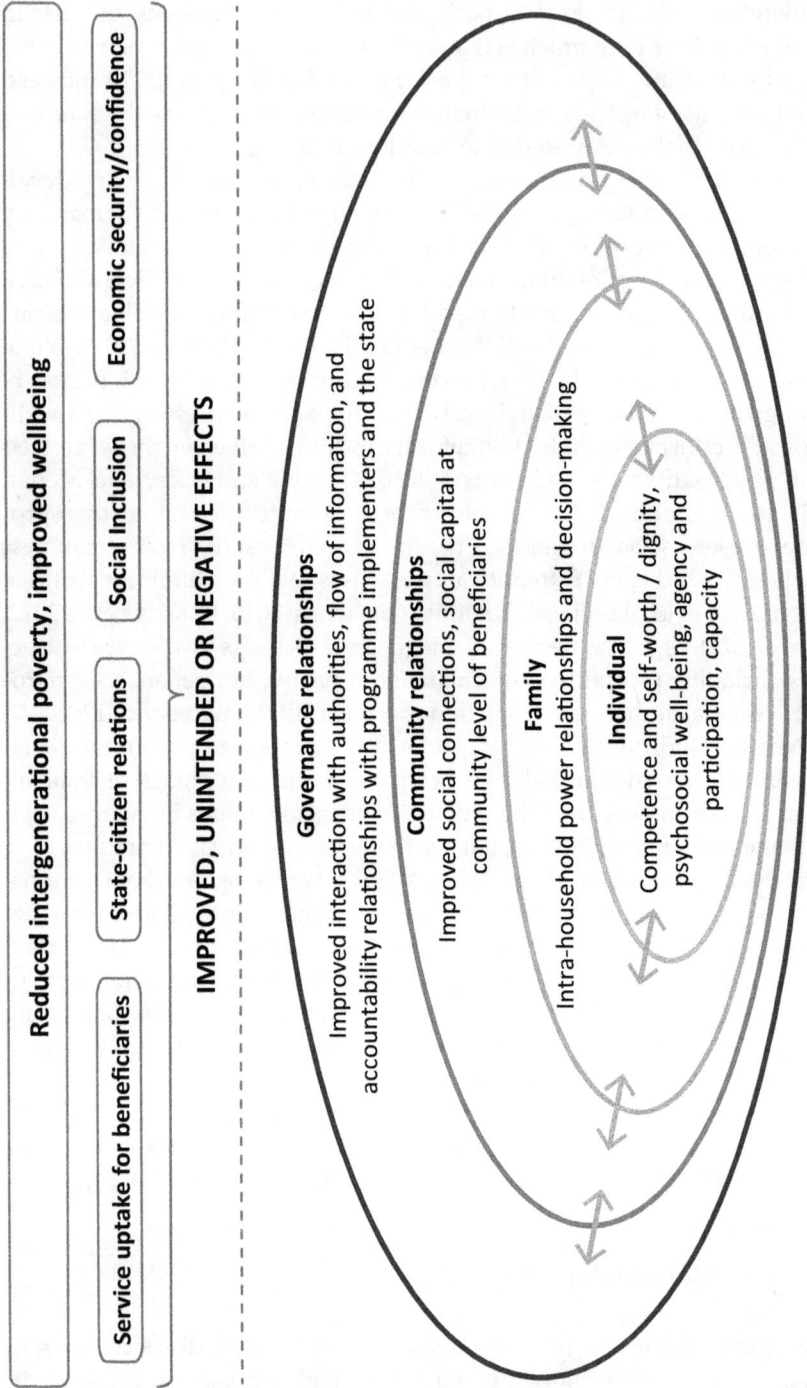

Reduced intergenerational poverty, improved wellbeing

| Service uptake for beneficiaries | State-citizen relations | Social Inclusion | Economic security/confidence |

IMPROVED, UNINTENDED OR NEGATIVE EFFECTS

Governance relationships
Improved interaction with authorities, flow of information, and accountability relationships with programme implementers and the state

Community relationships
Improved social connections, social capital at community level of beneficiaries

Family
Intra-household power relationships and decision-making

Individual
Competence and self-worth / dignity, psychosocial well-being, agency and participation, capacity

Figure 9.1 Individual, community, and state-citizen relationship pathways. Figure created by the authors.

2012 and 2013, which explored beneficiary perceptions of unconditional cash transfers (see table 9.1). The three country case studies were carried out by researchers based at the Overseas Development Institute in the United Kingdom in partnership with national researchers from independent research organizations who led the in-country research. National-level training workshops were held in each country to adapt the research instruments to local context realities and to familiarize the teams with the research conceptual framework, research questions, and data collection instruments. Team members from the different countries came from diverse disciplinary backgrounds, including anthropology, political science, and public health. As such, the different theoretical and conceptual paradigms underlying these disciplines were brought to this study and no doubt influenced the study process, ranging from the development of the tools to the analysis and interpretation, as well as in the framing of the final reports and recommendations. National researchers' knowledge of their country contexts, as well as political realities and priorities, also no doubt influenced the ways in findings were discussed and presented.

Although members of the research team brought their own experiences, opinions, and beliefs to the research process, it was stressed during the training sessions that researchers had to remain as neutral as possible during the process, not ask leading questions, and not pass judgment. From the perspective of the respondents, as is often the case with qualitative and participatory approaches, community members generally welcomed the opportunity to speak about their experiences regarding the cash transfer programs, with the open-endedness of the tools as well as the relative distance of the researchers allowing for a level of candidness not always possible with closed questionnaires. The study teams in all countries also ensured that the process of entry into the community (e.g., through headmen or elders) followed expected protocols, and thus data collection in all countries proceeded smoothly.

In selecting the country case studies, we employed a comparative case study approach. Our starting point was that, whereas individual case studies can illuminate local complexities in terms of the implementation of poverty reduction and human capital development initiatives, a comparative case study approach can help to "construct more general understandings which transcend individual research sites" (Yin 2003, quoted in Campbell and Cornish 2010: 3). We draw on George and Bennett (2005), who argue that while case studies share a similar epistemological logic with statistical methods and formal modeling in so far as they attempt to develop logically consistent theories, their added value includes their ability to test hypotheses and build theory. In this case, our comparative case study methodology, informed by the different cash transfer program

Table 9.1 Overview of social transfer programs in case study countries

Country	Occupied Palestinian Territories		Yemen	Mozambique
	West Bank	Gaza		
Name / start date	Palestinian National Cash Transfer Program (PNCTP); 2010 in West Bank; 2011 in Gaza.		Social Welfare Fund (SWF); 1996.	Basic Social Subsidy Program (PSSB*); 1992.
Transfer amount / frequency	From 750 to 1,800 NIS ($195–468 US); quarterly payments.		Maximum benefit of YER 4,000 ($20 US) for a family of six people, per month; quarterly payments.	130mzn (approx. $4.50 US) to 380mzn ($13 US). Increments of 50mzn ($1.80 US) for each dependent in the household. Monthly payments.
Program target group	Focus on extremely poor households; and to specific vulnerable groups, including female-headed households, people with disabilities, people with chronic illnesses, and older people.		Since 2008 program targets all people living below the poverty line, using a proxy means test, with a plan to gradually phase out those who met vulnerability targeting but not PMT targeting.	Permanently labor-constrained, extremely poor households. Also households headed by older people with no dependents or with dependents unable to work; households with members with chronic degenerative illnesses; and households headed by a disabled person with no household members capable of work.
Program reach	Approx. 99,000 families with an aim to reach a target of 120,000 households by the end of 2013.	Approx. 48,000 families.	Approx. 1,500,000 beneficiaries.	261,519 (169,542 female direct beneficiaries and 91,977 male direct beneficiaries) as of 2012, of which 13,125 were households with people with disabilities.

Research site characteristics	Hebron and Jenin governorates were selected due to high poverty, unemployment, and conflict-affected histories.	Beit Lahia, in the north near the Israeli border, and Rafah, in the south near Egypt, were selected due to very high unemployment, extreme poverty, and large refugee populations.	Al-Qahira and Zabid districts are in West Yemen, both primarily urban and peri-urban. Al-Qahira is part of Taiz City, the third largest in Yemen; Zabid is located in a fertile flood plain.	Chokwe and Chibuto districts in southern Mozambique. Both are sparsely populated, rural and arid with high dependence on agriculture. One in four adults are HIV+.

* The PSSB refers in Portuguese to Programa Subsidio Social Basico, which in English translates as the Basic Social Subsidy Program.

designs and country contexts, as well as existing literature (Holmes and Jones 2013; Hickey 2014; Hunter and Sugiyama 2014), allows us to explore a number of hypotheses about underlying dynamics and mechanisms which shape program outcomes at multiple levels.

- At the individual and family levels, we anticipated that the Palestinian cash transfer program, which offers beneficiaries an integrated package of services (e.g., educational stipends, health insurance) in addition to the cash transfer, would afford beneficiaries a greater level of individual wellbeing than the programs in Mozambique and Yemen, which only address economic vulnerabilities.
- At the community level, given the involvement of community committees in program targeting in Palestine and Yemen, we anticipated greater positive effects on community cohesion and social capital.
- In terms of citizen-state relationships, we hypothesized that the Mozambique and Yemen programs, because of the mediating role of community facilitators, would be more likely to engender strengthened understandings of citizenship.

These hypotheses underpinned our empirical work and are explicitly revisited in the discussion section.

A range of qualitative and participatory data-collection instruments were used, including community mappings, focus group discussions, individual interviews, and observational case studies of the program beneficiary-implementer interface (see table 9.2). Sample size was determined by a combination of resource parameters, the importance of triangulating findings across diverse informants, and the principle of research saturation—that is, reaching a point where no new insights were being garnered by additional interviews. After obtaining informed consent from research participants, interviews were recorded, transcribed, and translated. The analysis was thematically based, using a common thematic matrix, but with scope for country-specific subthemes to emerge.

The Unintended Effects of Cash Transfers: Findings from the Field

Individual/Community Relational Aspects

Drawing on the wellbeing domains discussed above, below we present how the cash transfers in our studies address and interact with psychosocial vulnerabilities faced by program beneficiaries. To situate our findings

Table 9.2 Research sites, instrument type, and respondent numbers

	Occupied Palestinian Territories (OPT)		Yemen	Mozambique
	West Bank	Gaza		
Study sites	Hebron	Bethlehia	Hodeidah	Chokwe
	Jenin	Rafah	Taiz	Chibuto
Qualitative and participatory research tools				
Community mapping (vulnerability, institutional, historical)	4	4	4	4
In-depth interviews	31	31	14	22
Focus group discussions	17	16	8	9
Key informant interviews	32	18	16	19
Observations	6	6	5	6
Life histories/case studies	8	8	11	20

within cash transfer debates, it is useful however to first briefly discuss literature that explores nonmaterial effects of cash transfers. While it is increasingly acknowledged that cash transfers can have often unintended and mostly positive nonmaterial effects on people's lives, and in particular on their psychosocial wellbeing (e.g., Devereux et al. 2013), most of the evidence comes from a quantitative and medical paradigm and has measured the effects of cash transfers on mental health issues such as stress, anxiety, and depression, mostly using self-reported questionnaires.[1] A limited number of qualitative studies have adopted a more relational focus and explored the social effects of cash transfer programs, including their psychosocial wellbeing effects.[2] These qualitative studies are more in line with the current study as they take into account not only contextual factors, but also beneficiary perceptions of wellbeing and the role that relationships with others play in this, aspects which are missing in the quantitative and medicalized approaches. We argue, along with others (e.g., White 2013), that such dimensions are critical in understanding and conceptualizing broader wellbeing. We now turn to our fieldwork findings.

Improved Financial Security Reducing Stress and Anxiety (Economic Confidence/Mental Health)

Lack of income and resources, inadequate food, education, and healthcare, or poor living conditions, usually as a result of the particular situation in which they were living (the international blockade and ongoing violence in Gaza and West Bank, limited prospects for the future in Yemen), were daily stressors felt by people in the study countries. Respondents also spoke about feelings of stress, anxiety, helplessness, and low self-esteem, often due to lack of employment and the subsequent inability to fulfill both their social obligations and their traditional breadwinner role: "I feel helpless when my wife demands money or food for the family" (man, Beit Lahia); "As a father, I would say that the hardest thing is when I see my child sick and I can't help; it breaks my heart" (man, Jenin).

Although the cash transfer was insufficient to cover all needs, it did help its recipients to cope with daily challenges and cover food, medical, and education costs, or even pay their debts. In Gaza, for instance, respondents spoke about the transfer allowing them to "breathe again." Its regularity and predictability also provided a sense of financial security and allowed people to plan ahead in Mozambique, in turn resulting in a reduction of individual and familial stress and anxiety.

Reduced Dependency Leading to Increased Control over Lives (Economic Confidence/Agency)

Linked to the above, being dependent on others as a result of poverty (and/ or disability in the case of Mozambique) was seen as extremely humiliating, leading to loss of dignity, isolation, and feelings of powerlessness. The cash transfers were therefore able to reduce people's dependency on others. Given the unconditional nature of the cash transfer, beneficiaries were able to spend it as they saw fit, thus also allowing them to reestablish some control over their lives. In Gaza, for instance, people commented that the cash allowed them to meet their own priorities compared to other forms of assistance. In Mozambique, disabled and older beneficiaries found that the transfer reduced their dependency on their families and gave them the chance to set their own priorities and spend money according to their own needs: "Among the positive effects of the program is that I'm now able to contribute to some basic household expenses" (female beneficiary, Chokwe).

Improved Household Relationships (Close Relationships)

Lack of resources and other household-level stresses put a strain on close relationships, and thus our findings highlighted people's concerns that they were being disrespected and abandoned, and that they were a burden on other family members. Although the cash is given to one individual, it is usually shared with other household members, and often has a positive effect on intrahousehold relationships. In the West Bank, people observed increased collaboration among family members and reduced tension and violence due to lower stress levels. In Yemen, a young man similarly explained, "When coming to the house with money, family members will like you, the wife will be happy and everything is OK. Money is the main source of happiness." Relationships between parents and children were also seen to improve: in the West Bank the ability of a father to fulfill his breadwinner role reduced his stress and improved his relationship with his children: "I feel closer to my kids when the payment comes. I can meet their needs. Other times when they ask for money I become angry." In Yemen, a father noted that the transfer enabled the purchase of food that improved his image in front of the children. This domain clearly relates to wellbeing in terms of relationships with others and in this case close relationships, or those within a household.

Decreasing Social Isolation and Increasing Integration (Social Connections/Agency and Participation)
Isolation and feelings of exclusion are key dimensions of poverty faced by people in all three case study countries. The cash transfers were seen to counter these feelings, and many respondents spoke about the transfer enabling them to break their isolation and feel more integrated in their communities, and thus less vulnerable. Some recipients also used part of the transfer to contribute to religious ceremonies, festivals, and community activities, which gave them "personal fulfillment." Payment days also provide opportunities to socialize and feel part of a community: in Palestine during these days, beneficiaries were able to meet and share experiences and problems, increasing their knowledge about assistance channels but also communicating with and feeling closer to others facing similar challenges.

Restored Dignity and Self-Esteem (Competence and Self-Worth)
Loss of dignity and self-esteem are key nonmaterial dimensions of poverty. According to women in the West Bank, the transfer accorded them greater respect and helped them to feel more confident: "People respect us more for having some money, unlike when we didn't have anything" (female beneficiary, West Bank). In Mozambique, the transfer improved the social status of its elderly recipients: "Before I received the help [transfer] my life was not going well. . . . With the help, many things have improved. My relationship with other people has improved. Before, nobody wanted to have anything to do with me. Now, nobody looks down on me" (male beneficiary, Chokwe). Disabled beneficiaries in Mozambique also reported improved self-confidence: "It means I can cook for myself for the first time in a long time. Before, I hardly ate anything—just when it was given to me" (male beneficiary, Chokwe). While this domain appears to emphasize

more individual aspects of wellbeing, relationships with others are critical in being able to feel dignity and self-esteem.

This being said, cash transfers can also have some limitations in terms of their effects on psychosocial wellbeing. In some cases, cash transfers have increased household tensions and domestic violence, as well as tensions between beneficiaries and nonbeneficiaries, leading to stigma, envy, resentment, and reduced informal support (MacAuslan and Riemenschneider 2011; Molyneux and Thomson 2011; Devereux et al. 2013). These unintended negative effects of cash transfers on psychosocial wellbeing were also found in our research.

Thus cash transfers were found to trigger or exacerbate preexisting intrahousehold and community tensions. In the West Bank, violent husbands or sons demanded female recipients to hand over the cash to buy alcohol or drugs, and in Yemen not only did some men use it to purchase drugs, but tensions arose between recipients and family members that typically control cash—that is, husbands and parents. Similarly, in the West Bank, envious in-laws sabotaged the possibility of certain family members participating in the program, and in other cases relatives stopped supporting beneficiaries.

At an individual level, in Palestine some respondents felt that accepting the transfer was seen as a humiliating act and that the transfer increased dependency, with some children feeling stigmatized that their mothers were beneficiaries: "My oldest son shouted at me and tried to prevent me from becoming a beneficiary of the cash transfer because, he said, 'my peers said your mother is a beggar and also a servant and cleaner of houses' so he tried to stop me and also to stop me working" (female beneficiary, Jenin). In Gaza, people also spoke about increased dependency on assistance with negative impact on their psychosocial wellbeing: "We are losing our dignity. I wish all support ends and we have jobs instead" (female beneficiary, Beit Lahia).

Finally, findings also provide some useful insights into how the delivery of cash transfer programs can impact beneficiaries' psychosocial wellbeing. In West Bank, respondents complained that social workers coming once a year to assess their economic situation did not have time to talk with beneficiaries about their problems, let alone provide any support; some respondents in Gaza described the social workers as disrespectful. Similarly, some respondents in both Gaza and West Bank also complained of being treated in a disrespectful way by bank employees: "[they] are mean and sometimes they call us beggars" (male beneficiary, Hebron). And a number of respondents in Mozambique and Yemen also complained of being treated by program staff members with inadequate sensitivity to their particular vulnerabilities and "with no respect."

Individual-State Relations

We now turn to a discussion of how social protection programs are, in unintended ways, promoting stronger state-citizen relations. We look at the strengths and weaknesses of three social accountability mechanisms embedded in the three unconditional cash transfer programs: information flows between program implementers and citizens, spaces for state-citizen interaction and feedback within the program context, and grievance mechanisms.

Program Information Flows

Social transfer programs implemented in resource-poor settings often have complex institutional arrangements. Proactively providing beneficiaries and the wider community with information about the institutional actors involved, about rules, and about entitlements is therefore a critical building block in any social accountability system.

This is especially so when programs undergo reforms, as has been the case with the Palestinian National Cash Transfer Program since 2010, when it amalgamated several predecessor programs into a more streamlined and poverty-targeted approach. Key informant interviews indicated that community-based organizations (CBOs), nongovernment organizations (NGOs), and community leadership were neither consulted about this reform nor informed about it. While there were efforts to broadcast information about the changes and registration process through Palestinian National TV, staff from the Ministry of Social Affairs (MoSA, the implementing agency) were inadequately prepared to manage the process and still have an incomplete understanding of the details of and rationale behind the proxy means test approach, which means they are unable to communicate the reasons for the reforms to beneficiaries and nonbeneficiaries alike. Study respondents highlighted multiple concerns relating to targeting, indicators, transparency, and the formula itself, and expressed a high level of discontent toward the ministry: "What really matters when they [referring to MoSA] select someone is the color of the shirt one wears [referring to green for Hamas and yellow for Fatah supporters]" (man, focus group discussion, Gaza). In the West Bank, while there were fewer complaints along party lines, there were similarly high levels of discontent due to inadequate communication by program implementers: "Even if we were hanging by a rope they would not help us! They don't tell us anything [about other services and entitlements]—only from each other and our neighbors do we learn about our rights" (female beneficiary, West Bank).

In Mozambique, information flows have been similarly limited and uneven. The Basic Social Subsidy Program (PSSB) targets extremely poor households, but our research suggested that there are areas of divergence between the official definitions and community perceptions of eligible households. At inception, the PSSB provided a low-value cash transfer to single-person elderly households. Therefore, communities continue to assume that the PSSB is a grant for older indigent people. There is also an assumption that only individuals, rather than households, are eligible for the transfer. During the fieldwork, it was noted that people in the community focused on the plight of an individual elderly or disabled person as the key to eligibility, without taking into consideration whether the level of dependency on care and support from other household members also rendered households eligible to benefit. This has a number of consequences, including low uptake of the additional money for dependents, and misunderstanding and mistrust of the system in cases where the transfer was suspended due to changes in the status of household members that affected their entitlement (e.g., when a child becomes eighteen years old, or a member of the family marries an able-bodied adult).

The experience with Yemen's Social Welfare Fund (SWF) was not dissimilar. District offices manage the daily operations of the SWF, including registration of potential new beneficiaries. Yet our findings indicated that staff in these offices not only lack authority to make decisions on beneficiary selection, but the community leaders who do have more decision-making authority frequently suffer from limited information about important program details and linkages to other social protection interventions. As one female beneficiary from Zabid noted, "They say it is from the government for the poor people and those who have limited income. . . . All those who receive it deserve it as they are jobless and poor." Accordingly, there is limited capacity to demand accountability from local authorities, particularly as there is a concern among beneficiaries that they might be sanctioned or taken off the list of beneficiaries if they complain, especially in Taiz, an urban and more politicized district.

Feedback Channels and Spaces for Interaction

Institutionalizing regular information provision and feedback channels is an important part of working toward and strengthening the social contract between citizens and state agents. Institutionalized spaces ensure that problems or concerns are detected quickly and help providers gauge community responses to reforms or new features.

Opportunities for information exchange and feedback between citizens and program implementers are relatively constrained in the Palestinian context. Since the 2010 cash transfer program reforms, the primary interaction between social workers and beneficiaries (or unsuccessful applicants) takes place during short (15- to 30-minute) home visits when social workers come to assess whether the household is still eligible according to the proxy means test poverty criteria. Social workers and beneficiaries alike emphasized that there was seldom time to discuss broader vulnerabilities and needs, unless the situation was already very serious. Social workers have been effectively removed from the selection process as eligibility is now determined by the proxy means tested formula (PMTF) alone, rather than taking into account information obtained during social workers' home visits. While this has helped to reduce the potential for clientelistic relationships between social workers and beneficiaries, it has also reduced social workers' sense of professional ownership and buy-in into the program. Social workers reported feeling that they had essentially become data collectors, with the bulk of their work now centered on filling out forms, rather than providing the specialist psychosocial support they have been trained to do. One social worker said, "We feel as if we are machines."

Efforts to institutionalize effective links with community stakeholders in program governance have also proved challenging. In the West Bank, social workers are expected to collaborate with local social protection committees to identify potential beneficiaries and screen those who are eligible. However, in practice, instead of holding regular meetings with a full committee, social workers most often call on individual members as an information resource to discuss particular cases. In Gaza, regional social protection committees have not been established, and thus household eligibility is determined through the proxy means test alone, which is centralized in Ramallah. Moreover, while there is supposed to be a suggestion box in each MoSA office, only a handful of beneficiaries said they had seen them, and during a structured observation in the MoSA office in Rafah, no suggestion box was seen.

In Yemen, formal spaces for information exchange and feedback are similarly weak, and beneficiaries and nonbeneficiaries complained about this dearth of spaces. As in Palestine, there are some informal exchanges among beneficiaries on payment day while queuing at the post office to receive the transfer. Generally, though, beneficiaries emphasized that they are not vocal about their concerns or the lack of spaces to express them, as they fear being taken out of the program. There are, however, some informal approaches being adopted to fill this gap. Beneficiaries emphasized the important role played by local community leaders in information provision, who were deemed to "know more about us" than outsiders, especially in Zabid, where local leaders enjoy considerable legitimacy, while in Taiz views were more tempered due perhaps to a generally more politicized community.

In Mozambique, opportunities for interaction with program implementers are more plentiful, but still of limited quality. Community meetings are the most frequently used medium of communication due to high
levels of illiteracy. Such dialogues are also continued through follow-up
with individual beneficiaries, using community liaison agents who have
been selected by the community to act as brokers between them and
the implementing agency, the National Institute of Social Action (INAS).
These agents are, in theory, accountable to both the community and INAS;
the community can request the agent to be replaced if they are not satisfied, and INAS can also remove the agent if judged not to be performing
satisfactorily. However, this role is not without problems, due to the lack
of formal training and the fact that the person most often selected by the
community is also the government's official representative in the area—a
voluntary post that inevitably wields considerable local power. The lack of
an independent liaison agent and effective checks and balances on power
constrains transparency and social accountability, as does the absence of
written materials to explain procedures for potential beneficiaries.

Grievance Channels

Grievance channels provide a third critical mechanism through which
citizens can engage in program governance and accountability processes.
Among our case studies, we found stark differences in citizen perceptions of their right to complain. In the Occupied Palestinian Territories,
program beneficiaries typically saw their involvement in the PNCTP as
their right rather than a gift or charity—especially in Jenin, in the West
Bank, where there is a strong rights-based culture fostered by a substantial NGO presence: "This is better than a hand-out. It is my right" (older
female beneficiary, Hebron). Complaints about the PNCTP can either be
communicated in writing and posted in local district-office complaints
boxes or made verbally to social workers or NGOs, who in turn record
and communicate them to the Ramallah-based Complaints Unit within
MoSA. Nevertheless, respondents were relatively negative about the
value of utilizing grievance and complaints channels, and expressed low
levels of confidence in the system, especially in Gaza, where there was a
concern that social workers might intercept and manipulate information
presented through grievances: "How can one raise a complaint against the
judge?" (male, middle-aged ex-beneficiary, Beit Lahia, Gaza).

In the case of Yemen, while SWF officials explained that they were open
to receiving complaints from beneficiaries, there was no official grievance
system, and respondents were generally reluctant to complain for fear
of being withdrawn from the program, as reporting is not anonymous.
"There was political intervention in the past, but after the involvement of

the social workers in the process this did not occur so much. But in rural areas there is still a kind of political intervening" (informal community leader, male, Zabid). There were reports, however, of informal action being undertaken to address grievances: in one case in Zabid, following prolonged community and beneficiary complaints about poor treatment during cash distribution at the local post office (where some workers were charging "commission" to make the payment), the manager of the post office was replaced in an effort to minimize abuse of the system.

The experience in Mozambique contrasted sharply with those of the Middle Eastern case studies. In relation to the PSSB, the main constraint does not appear to be the design of the grievance system itself, but rather people's lack of understanding of the underlying principles of social transfer programs. Social transfer programs are based on an agreement on the rights and responsibilities of the participating entities—a social contract between the state and citizens, including vis-à-vis the right of vulnerable citizens to receive the appropriate social transfer on a regular basis. In Mozambique, our findings indicated that people had no sense of entitlement to the PSSB transfer, and viewed the money as a gift provided by a benevolent state. The consequence of this attitude was that people felt they should not complain at all, as to do so would be ungrateful; instead, they should just accept what was offered. As one female beneficiary in Chokwe noted, "Why would I question the type of present I am given?"

Discussion and Conclusions

Our findings from three unconditional cash transfer programs show that such programs can have unintended and usually positive effects on psychosocial wellbeing both at the individual level and in relation to others. Given that such effects are also relatively difficult to measure, it is unlikely that quantitative approaches, mostly used for assessing the effects of cash transfer programs, will uncover these effects. Hence qualitative approaches are critical in exploring in more depth the subjective and relational aspects of broader wellbeing stimulated by cash transfer programs.

By drawing on and extending the wellbeing framework developed by White (2013) and colleagues, we explored the pathways toward wellbeing that cash transfers can impact—directly or indirectly—at the individual, community, and state levels. Returning to the hypothesized outcomes at individual and family levels, we found that, contrary to our expectations, the integrated Palestinian program did not appear to afford beneficiaries a greater level of individual wellbeing. Instead, context variables played a critical role in shaping beneficiary perceptions of program efficacy. More specifically, while appreciating the benefits of the cash transfer, Palestinian beneficiaries were also vocal about the fact that the cash transfer could not address their declining wellbeing over time due to the protracted nature of the Israeli occupation and ensuing economic demise. Additionally, by living in close proximity to Israel, Palestinian respondents were also intensely aware of the contrast in their respective living standards.

Turning to our second hypothesis, which focused on the role of community committees in program targeting, the emerging picture was complex. In both Palestine and Yemen, these committees were not seen as impartial and instead came under heavy criticism for being too often politicized and nepotistic. Moreover, in Palestine the committees in practice did not act as a collective but rather as individual members who were called upon by social workers to provide advice and support for specific cases.

In terms of relationships between cash transfer beneficiaries and state implementers, we hypothesized that the mediating role of community facilitators in the Mozambique and Yemen programs would more likely engender strengthened understandings of citizenship. However, in reality, preexisting understandings and practices of citizenship emerged as critical in shaping beneficiary interactions with program implementers. Whereas in Mozambique and Yemen beneficiaries tended to view the program as a gift from God or the government, Palestinian beneficiaries had a much more robust sense of their rights as citizens, even in the absence of community facilitators. This is in part due to a long history of NGO rights-based programming in both Gaza and the West Bank, and the global framing of the Palestinian-Israeli conflict.

Our findings suggest, therefore, that strengthened state-citizen relations in unconditional cash transfer programs are unlikely to happen organically. Instead, deliberate attempts are needed to generate opportunities for interaction between beneficiaries and program implementers, whether through individual face-to-face consultations, community dialogues, or grievance channels that respond in a timely fashion so as to promote confidence in the process. For many study respondents, receiving regular program information updates and having an opportunity to voice their views about program efficacy and areas for improvement is equated with being treated with dignity, rather than mere subjects of charity or largesse. It is at this third dimension of relational wellbeing that considerably more attention is required if cash transfers are to harness their potential as a tool for strengthening a sense of citizenship and a culture of rights and entitlements.

Fiona Samuels is a senior research fellow in the social development program at the Overseas Development Institute. She is a social anthropologist with extensive research experience crossing the fields of public health and social development in Africa, Asia, and the Middle East. She currently focuses on linkages between health, poverty, risk, and vulnerability, with a particular interest in gender, adolescence, social protection, and psychosocial wellbeing. She has published recently on the effects of cash transfers on psychosocial wellbeing, on mental health and psychosocial wellbeing of adolescent girls in postconflict settings, and on drivers of health systems strengthening.

Nicola Jones, a principal research fellow in the social development program at the Overseas Development Institute, is the director of the UK Department for International Development–funded nine-year global mixed-methods research program, Gender and Adolescence: Global Evidence. Her expertise lies in the intersection of gender, age, social inclusion, and social protection. She has conducted a wide range of policy research projects in East Africa, Asia, and the Middle East, including recent mixed-methods studies on child marriage in Ethiopia, gender-based violence in South Asia, and cash transfers to support Palestinian and Syrian refugees.

Notes

1. These studies mostly conclude that the effects have been positive; the Mexican Oportunidades cash transfer was found to modestly reduce child aggressive behavior (Ozer et al. 2009), reduce child emotional problems (Fernald et al. 2009), and lower child cortisol levels, indicating reduced exposure to stressors (Fernald and Gunnar 2009); in Malawi the cash transfer had a 17 percent reduction in psychological distress among schoolgirls offered the conditional transfer and a 38 percent reduction among those who were offered unconditional cash transfer compared to the control group in both cases (Baird et al. 2011); and in Cambodia the cash transfer was found to have a positive effect on education and adolescent mental health (Filmer and Schady 2009).
2. In India and Nepal, cash transfers allowed people relief from the "worries of daily existence," increased their dignity and self-confidence, and improved their social relationships (HelpAge International 2009a; 2009b); in Malawi, beneficiary children reported an improved sense of psychosocial wellbeing, and the transfer enabled them to buy new clothes and soap, to look better, and to be treated better by their peers and teachers (Miller et al. 2010); and women recipients of a Nicaraguan conditional cash transfer noted the regular source of income reduced their stress levels, increased their self-confidence, and improved their psychosocial wellbeing (Adato and Roopnaraine 2010).

References

Adato, M., and T. Roopnaraine. 2010. "Women's Status, Gender Relations, and Conditional Cash Transfers." In *Conditional Cash Transfers in Latin America*, edited by M. Adato and J. Hoddinott, 284–314. Washington, DC: International Food Policy Research Institute.

Bukenya, B., S. Hickey, and S. King. 2012. *Understanding the Role of Context in Shaping Social Accountability Interventions: Towards an Evidence-Based Approach.* Manchester: Institute for Development Policy and Management, University of Manchester.

Campbell, C., and F. Cornish. 2010. "How Can Community Health Programmes Build Enabling Environments for Transformative Communication? Experiences from India and South Africa." HCD Working Paper. London: London School of Economics and Political Science.

Corbridge, S., G. Williams, M. Srivastava, and R. Véron. 2005. *Seeing the State: Governance and Governmentality in India.* Cambridge: Cambridge University Press.

Devereux, S., K. Roelen, C. Béné, D. Chopra, J. Leavy, and J. A. McGregor. 2013. "Evaluating Outside the Box: An Alternative Framework for Analysing Social Protection Programmes." IDS Working Paper 431. Brighton: Institute of Development Studies.

Fernald, L. C. H., and M. R. Gunnar. 2009. "Poverty-Alleviation Program Participation and Salivary Cortisol in Very Low-Income Children." *Social Science and Medicine* 68(12): 2180–2189.

Fernald, L. C. H., P. Gertler, and L. M. Neufeld. 2009. "10-Year Effect of Oportunidades, Mexico's Conditional Cash Transfer Programme, on Child Growth, Cognition, Language, and Behaviour: A Longitudinal Follow-up Study." *Lancet* 374: 1997–2005.

George, A. L., and A. Bennett. 2005. *Case Studies and Theory Development in the Social Sciences.* Cambridge, MA: MIT Press.

Helliwell, J. F., R. Layard, and J. Sachs, eds. 2013. "World Happiness Report 2013." New York: UN Sustainable Development Solutions Network.

HelpAge International. 2009a. *The Social Pension in India: A Participatory Study on the Poverty Reduction Impact and Role of Monitoring Groups.* London: HelpAge International.

HelpAge International. 2009b. *The Universal Social Pension in Nepal: An Assessment of its Impact on Older People in Tahanun District.* London: HelpAge International.

Hickey, S. 2014. "Relocating Social Protection within a Radical Project of Social Justice." *European Journal of Development Research* 26: 322–337.

Hickey, S., and G. Mohan. 2008. "The Politics of Establishing Pro-poor Accountability: What Can Poverty Reduction Strategies Achieve?" *Review of International Political Economy* 15(2): 234–258.Holmes, R., and N. Jones. 2013. *Gender and Social Protection in the Development World.* London: Zed Books.

Hunter, W., and N. B. Sugiyama. 2014. "Transforming Subjects into Citizens: Insights from Brazil's Bolsa Família." *Perspectives on Politics* 12(4): 829–845.

Lund, C., M. De Silva, S. Plagerson, S. Cooper, D. Chisholm, J. Das, M. Knapp, and V. Patel. 2011. "Poverty and Mental Disorders: Breaking the Cycle in Low-Income and Middle-Income Countries." *Lancet* 378: 1502–1514.

MacAuslan, I., and N. Riemenschneider. 2011. "Richer but Resented: What Do Cash Transfers Do to Social Relations and Does It Matter?" Paper presented at the International Conference "Social Protection for Social Justice," Institute of Development Studies, Brighton.

McNeil, M., and C. Malena, eds. 2010. "Demanding Good Governance: Lessons from Social Accountability Initiatives in Africa." Washington, DC: IBRD/ World Bank.

Miller, C. M., M. Tsoka, K. Reichert, and A. Hussaini. 2010. "Interrupting the Intergenerational Cycle of Poverty with the Malawi Social Cash Transfer." *Vulnerable Children and Youth Studies* 5(2): 108–121.

Molyneux, M., and M. Thomson. 2011. "Cash Transfers, Gender Equity and Women's Empowerment in Peru, Ecuador and Bolivia." *Gender & Development* 19(2): 195–211.

Mooij, J. E. 2007. "Is There an Indian Policy Process: An Investigation into Two Social Policy Processes." *Social Policy and Administration* 14 (4): 323–338.

Narayan, D., R. Chambers, M. K. Shah, and P. Petesch. 2000a. "Voices of the Poor: Crying Out for Change." New York: Oxford University Press for the World Bank.

Narayan, D., with R. Patel, K. Schafft, A. Rademacher, and A. Koch-Schulte. 2000b. "Voices of the Poor: Can Anyone Hear Us?" New York: Oxford University Press for the World Bank.

Ozer, E. J., L. C. H. Fernald, L. G. Manley, and P. J. Gertler. 2009. "Effects of a Conditional Cash Transfer Program on Children's Behavior Problems." *Pediatrics* 123(4): 630–637.

Patel, V., and A. Kleinman. 2003. "Poverty and Common Mental Disorders in Developing Countries." *Bulletin of the World Health Organization* 81(8): 609–615.

Ringold, D., A. Holla, M. Koziol, and S. Srinivasan. 2012. "Citizens and Service Delivery: Assessing the Use of Social Accountability Approaches in Human Development." Washington, DC: International Bank for Reconstruction and Development/World Bank.

Sen, A. 1999. "Development as Freedom." Oxford: Oxford University Press.

Tembo, F. 2013. "Rethinking Social Accountability in Africa: Lessons from the Mwananchi Programme." London: Overseas Development Institute.

Unsworth, S., ed. 2010. *An Upside Down View of Governance.* Sussex: Institute of Development Studies, Centre for the Future State.

Walker, R., G. Bantebya Kyomuhendo, E. Chase, S. Choudhry, E. K. Gubrium, J. N. Nicola, I. Lodemel, L. Mathew, A. Mwiine, S. Pellissery, and Y. Ming. 2013. "Poverty in Global Perspective: Is Shame a Common Denominator?" *Journal of Social Policy* 42(2): 215–233.

White, S. 2013. "An Integrated Approach to Assessing Wellbeing." Wellbeing and Poverty Pathways Briefing no. 1. Bath: University of Bath.

Chapter 10

Are Cash Transfers Rocking or Wrecking the World of Social Workers in Egypt?

Hania Sholkamy

Introduction: Social Policy, Social Workers, and the Egyptian Welfare State

This chapter presents an anthropologist's account of encounters with state agents in the context of a cash transfers program in Egypt. The chapter is not on the cash programs per se but is on the agents and service providers tasked with introducing cash transfer programs to Egypt. These are government employees mandated with implementing social protection schemes and services such as social pensions, microcredit and loans, emergency protection and evacuation, benefit payments, and specialized programs such as care for orphans and juvenile offenders. They are also charged with regulating and overseeing civil society organizations, charities, orphanages, and elderly persons' care homes. Their major responsibility in the area of social pensions is in arbitrating people's eligibility and compliance with various pension rules and regulations. They are the frontline bureaucrats whose work is sometimes ignored and has often been treated as a problem.[1] They are policy mediators and program/service providers.

Social workers are "street level bureaucrats" (as labeled by Lipsky 1980) who implement social programs in accordance with a highly centralized system. Lipsky (1980) described frontline workers in the United States and analyzed their interactions with local populations. Their personal traits,

---

training, ethical practices, and know-how partially but significantly shape the impact of policies, programs, and services on applicants and clients.

Sociological and ethnographic engagement with implementation gaps in service provision and in development interventions points to the importance of understanding field-level constraints and contradictions. Contemplating policy and its practitioners at all their levels of action and practice underscores the importance of the distinctions between center and periphery in the application of programs and services, and the distance between ideal types of bureaucracy and their practical manifestations. Hence the ethnographic worlds of frontline workers become relevant to the study of communities and society (Navaro-Yashin 2002 on the creation of political culture in municipalities of Istanbul; Ferguson and Lohman 2004 on mega development projects; Mitchell 2004 on donor-driven development and the role of experts in Egypt; Hull 2012 on writing and paper communication in Pakistan; Gupta 2012 and 2013 on development in India)

Egypt is perhaps the oldest country of bureaucratic state administration and has been ruled by cadres of scribes and officials since ancient times (Weber 2006: 56). In modern-day Egypt, the rule of officials is still significant, although not in the obvious ways posited by theories of centralized bureaucracy. For the past five years, politicians, activists, journalists, and citizens have noted the political impact of what they call "the deep state." This label by and large references the forces that have resisted the sweep of revolution and made the path to change and transformation both difficult and unclear. The deep state is comprised of the security and administrative apparatuses and the interests and values that they represent and support. They have consistently protected the status quo and created a sclerotic political order that is immune to change.[2]

Despite this critical role in social and political life, bureaucrats and their social and political agency have not been recently problematized or described in Egypt (Nagi n.d.) even though their presence and effect on politics has been amply described in the press and media (Isa 2012). The sheer number of administrators employed by government and public entities at the central and governorate levels gives any observer of the country cause for contemplation. Almost seven million people are employed by the state and together form a block of critical political importance (Sholkamy and Kamaly 2013).

The way that frontline workers adapt to change by resistance, acceptance, or modification is an important facet of any analysis of social policy, and of particular pertinence to a critical engagement with new policies. Although ethnographic engagements with bureaucracy, administration, and development in Africa have recently entered the literatures of anthropology (Bierschenk and Olivier de Sardan 2014), there are few that examine the case of Egypt in general and social policy in particular.

In this chapter, I shall begin by describing the CCT program, which is the context in which my social worker encounters took place. I shall then explain the way previous social pensions were organized and implemented, as they are the reference that social workers use by which to judge their ambivalence or welcome toward the new programs (the conditional cash transfers). Then the chapter considers the motivations, explanations, and implications of the social workers' experiences and dilemmas to social protection and policy in Egypt as a whole and to the cash transfers program specifically. The final section revisits the ethnographic and emic perspective as a key to engaging with development and social change.

Understanding the Old System

The Minister of Social Solidarity in 2008 (and all his successors since) was being urged/encouraged to make social protection provisions more effective and less wasteful. The World Bank organized a high level meeting in 2007 in Luxor in Upper Egypt, in which the whole economic team of ministers in the then cabinet participated, where they introduced these senior policy makers to cash transfers as an alternative to untargeted and expensive subsidies. An interagency assessment mission under the Initiative on Soaring Food Prices (ISFP) by the Egyptian government, World Food Programme, World Bank, and International Fund for Agriculture and Development concluded that existing safety nets were then still not reaching many of the poorest and most vulnerable and that there remained a need to rethink the national social protection strategy.

The social spending of Egypt in 2008 consisted of (and continues to date) expensive energy subsidies, which consume almost one quarter of the government's annual budget, and less expensive but broadly targeted food subsidies that entitle over sixty million Egyptians (out of a population of just under ninety million). There are also programs for social pensions for certain categories of poor people, the most significant of which is known as Damman Igtima'y. This scheme provides monthly cash to applicants who are deemed eligible in accordance with the social pensions law and as identified by social workers. It is a system whereby certain categories of "poor" are covered by pensions. These categories include the chronically sick, the handicapped, the elderly, female heads of households, orphans, divorced or widowed women with children, families of conscripts, and families of convicts who have a sentence that is longer than six months. Social workers ensure that documents that prove the eligibility of applicants, as well as determine the allocation of the pension, are correct.

The system of social pensions of Egypt was a celebrated model of social protection at one point, but had become haggard, ineffective, partial, and on the whole unable to stop rising rates of income poverty. By 2008, one quarter of the population was defined as poor according to international metrics as applied by the World Bank and other international organizations. One quarter of children under the age of fifteen years living in rural Upper Egypt had also become malnourished, and almost 40 percent of the population qualified as near poor (IHSN 2013). These metrics indicated the failure of pensions in particular and of social spending on subsidies in general. Consequently, the state decided to adopt cash transfers, both unconditional and conditional, so as to bolster the impact of its social protection expenditure and to eventually replace the old system with a new one. This decision also corresponded to a desire to create fiscal space for public expenditures other than subsidies, and so Egypt began the long haul from in-kind to cash subsidies.

Little attention, however, had been given to understanding why the old pensions grew ineffective over time. Had these pensions failed because the amount given to each beneficiary was too little, because their procedures were complicated, because they were underfunded by the budget, or because of the manner in which they were targeted and implemented? Was the state in need of new ideas or was it a question of failed capacity? Cash transfers seemed to be the modern, internationally celebrated, well-researched best tool for social protection and redistribution. In this situation of *either* old pension *or* cash transfers, the decision seemed to be clear and in favor of cash transfers. But neither the international community recommending cash transfers nor the decision-makers adopting the recommendations were fully engaged with the history of social welfare in Egypt, with the current capacity of the state to deliver welfare, or with the perceptions and experiences of social service providers. Such a distracted view would not be able to discern between the concepts/design and effect of programs and the capacity of the state to deliver those or any other services.

By the end of 2008, the government of Egypt had committed resources to provide effective social protection for one to three million of the poorest families in Egypt. A conditional cash transfer (CCT) program was suggested as the tool to enable the poor to manage their poverty. The revolution of 2011, however, delayed the implementation of new social programs as state administrators and senior decision makers were rocked by the seismic political events that ensued in January 2011 and which cause near paralysis of state-provided social services, despite the popular call that resounded among protestors in the streets and squares of Egypt demanding social justice and fair redistribution of resources.

Karama and Takaful: The New Social Pensions of Egypt

Karama (dignity) and Takaful (mutual support or welfare) are both statistically targeted cash transfers that aim to increase the consumption of individuals and families living in poverty in Egypt.[3] Karama provides the elderly and the severely handicapped with a monthly stipend of 320 LE (approx. $40 U.S.) per beneficiary. Takaful is for families with children living in poverty and is a conditional cash transfer that is given four times per year to help families provide for their children. Takaful provides a 320 LE (approx. $40 U.S.) base pension with increments per child ranging from 60 LE to 100 LE ($7.50 to $12 U.S.) depending on the age of the child.[4]

Both are targeted benefits that rely on the use of a proxy means testing (PMT) formula that identifies poverty without recourse to questions on income or on expenditure. The Ministry of Finance developed this PMT formula and procedures on the basis of household income expenditure data and on poverty maps in 2014. The benefits are managed by the Ministry of Social Solidarity (MOSS) and rely on its staff and experts for enrollment and registration, validation, supervision, and management of both programs and their valuable databases. Actual dispersal of funds is through ATMs, for which beneficiaries have smart cards issued by a specialized financial services provider.

The Egyptian programs were introduced in 2015 and are designed to provide pensions to 1.5 million families in the poorest parts of Egypt.[5] By January 2016, the conditional cash program had 260,000 families enrolled, and the unconditional program for the elderly and disabled had only 5,000. During this first year, problems developed in the sites where the programs were being introduced, which slowed down the registration procedures. Anxious senior decision makers had hoped that the quick proliferation of the programs would have an immediate and significant impact on poverty and perhaps on rising levels of public frustration. The problems encountered, according to senior officials at the Ministry of Social Solidarity, were due to poor social worker capacity. Social workers had neither the training, know-how, or information to administer these new statistically targeted, centrally allocated, and digitally awarded programs.

The programs rely on digital enrollment using computer tablets, and discourage the use of paper forms. They also eclipse the role of the front-line worker in estimating and approving applicant eligibility as they rely on the automatic application of a proxy means testing formula that is applied by the financial and data manager, a subcontractor to the ministry, the cut-off points for which are decided at the central level and on the basis of statistical approximations of poverty. The programs are also designed so as to circumvent the role of social worker as cash provider, as they pay beneficiaries via a bank card that is issued centrally by the subcontractor and collected by the beneficiary at the local post office. Finally, these programs cross-check enrollment data with other national data sets such as social insurance, school enrollment, and card and land ownership so as to limit fraudulent claims and subvert clientelistic relations at the local level.

These design features strip social workers of any muscle they ever had and give them very little room to flex anything. How then, with such little leeway to impact the programs, can social workers be the reason for its slow penetration? In conversations and committee meetings at the ministry, the questions of bureaucratic resistance were raised, as were the issues pertaining to the centrally precipitated flaws of implementation. The social workers were said to be misinforming applicants and refusing to use the tablets.

The Actual Role of the Social Worker

Resistance should be understood in terms of those doing the resisting. From the social worker point of view, the programs looked less than ideal. Although the Ministry of Social Solidarity is bloated with employees, the majority of these administrators have middle-level desk jobs and few serve in local social units. The programs relied on two methodologies of targeting. The first was geographic targeting whereby villages and neighborhoods were ranked according to the poverty count of individuals and families. Places with more than 70 percent poverty were first in line for receiving the program. The other means of targeting was the PMT mentioned above. So the programs were first introduced in places with many eligible families but relied on an application process that had to be handled by social workers in these locations.

The small numbers of social workers who are in the field and not in remote offices meant that the caseload on each worker was overwhelming. Their inability to master the procedures of digital registration and the poor connectivity in the villages where applicants reside also meant that registration took longer than planned. The social workers were augmented with contracted enumerators whose only job was quick data entry for registration. This became the bulk of the Takaful and Karama work. The crowds storming social units in order to register for the program had casualties. Some social workers were crushed due to unexpected stampedes. An angry applicant in a social unit in Upper Egypt even shot a social worker in the leg; such was the chaos and mayhem that social workers had to endure during the registration procedures. In several instances, social units had to close down so as to stem the tide of applications that they felt was unmanageable.

The contracted enumerators worked quickly and quietly, but social workers were wondering what would happen after the quick registration procedures and who or how would the program be handled in the future. They were right to wonder.

After the families were registered and began to receive their payments, how would the program work? The conditions that were stipulated by Takaful needed implementation, verification, and reporting. Would social workers be tasked with these procedures?

To date, no conditions have been required, and the work of social workers has been reduced to handling lists and appeals. There is no cadre of social workers active in anything but answering enquiries and obeying orders issued by program administrators in Cairo. These orders vary from facilitating the creation of local community representative committees to receiving and guiding enumerators. Some social workers have taken part in registration, and many have received a truncated and rapid training provided by the payment provider so as to learn how to handle tablets and send information, but most are still distanced from the programs. By May 2016, millions had been enrolled in the program, and senior policy makers were celebrating,[6] but field social workers I interviewed remained skeptical.

Old Social Work in the Realm of New Policy

The skepticism may be justified and needs to be understood not in terms of the CCT designs but in the context of social workers' history, experiences, norms, and fears.[7] The problem may lie in the stubborn culture of social assistance in which social workers have been immersed for years. This is the culture of Damman Igtima'y and all its details of targeting, purpose, and scope.

The differences between the Damman Igtima'y and the cash transfers program are multiple. The cash transfers programs rely on proxy means testing, not categorical targeting. They provide more money, as more than one member of a family, if entitled, can take the benefit. So, for example, families with more than one disabled child can claim benefits for each child with a maximum of three persons per family. The Damman Igtima'y is allocated to a family with small increments per family member. The most significant difference between the two schemes concerns the role of social workers.

It is the responsibility/duty of social workers and unit heads to insure that beneficiaries comply with rules of eligibility for any program. The welfare services of the ministry rely almost completely on the abilities of these frontline workers. According to a senior and now retired source from within the ministry,[8] social workers in the past had to be graduates of the higher institute for social services and could only be appointed after a prolonged in-service training period. This is no longer the case.

Social assistance and transfer programs prior to Karama and Takaful were categorically oriented and designed to assist segments of the population where there is a clustering of problems. Examples are the disabled, female-headed households, orphans, families of convicts and conscripts, and those with proven very low incomes. In the old system, social workers were the officials who can both confirm the entitlements of these groups and mediate with other services. Their responsibilities include case finding, keeping centralized records, case management through functional services, and legal and administrative matters; they also provide information about services. To be able to fulfill these tasks they must have a legal mandate, adequate resources, access to information and relevant records, and recourse to other services for support and consultation.

There has been little investment in social workers or in the infrastructure that facilitates and determines their work. Social workers (whoever they are) are criminally liable for any misinformation or misstep that they take in their work. If individuals provide them with fraudulent information upon which they act (even in good faith), they become criminally responsible, and there are rumors of innocents who have been jailed. However, they are in no way culpable or responsible for their inactions. If they register no one for pensions or fail to provide services, they do not have to answer to their superiors or ministry.

This means that there are incentives not to provide services.

A senior manager in the ministry and trainer and supervisor for social workers explained that she has always loved her work but was discouraged from fulfilling her true role as a social worker by the structures of decision-making that preclude social worker discretion and know-how. "The safest thing is to do nothing," she emphasized. The profession of social work has become one of filling forms and obstruction. "The state is poor so we are better advised not to make any commitments or pensions," she said.

The legal procedure to recommend or make transfers or benefits relies on official documents. The proof that poor individuals have to present to prove entitlements is costly and difficult to obtain. A deserted woman has to get an official statement from a local police station, signed by the local police chief, attesting to her desertion. The wife of a convict sentenced to more than three years in jail has to get a copy of the sentence from a courthouse. But this is a complex and costly affair, as she has to prove that the sentence is not under appeal and that the duration of imprisonment will not be reduced. A disabled or sick person has to ratify their condition from a state commission that meets, explained a district head, "when there are enough consultants at the public hospital at the capital of each governorate." A peasant has to get paper proof testifying that he has no landholdings anywhere in Egypt. A person working in the informal sector or an occasional or seasonal worker must prove that they earn less than 40 percent of the estimated minimum wage.

Social workers know that much of this documentation is obtained through forgery or bribery. "But these documents cover our own backs," a trainee social worker explained; "The state has money that it can distribute so as long as I have the right documents I am not worried."

The workers interviewed only have the semilegal mandate to keep files and process applications, but they do not have much else. Their work has become desk-bound and bureaucratic. They are also paid very low salaries, although they do enjoy the social security and other benefits that are part of the reward of public sector and government work.

The on-the-job training that social workers get is usually abstract and not linked to innovations or new programs. Training is a way to qualify for promotion, so it is an end in itself, not a means to new knowledge. Rampant favoritism has meant that the lucky few get to go to training workshops, get some time off work, and also get promoted, while the rest are tied to the daily grind of a dilapidated office.

Another feature of the way social work at the ministry is structured and which seems counterintuitive is that those who work at the ministry headquarters and have no field obligations are automatically paid a higher salary.

To make up for the lack of opportunity and pay, social workers strive to be subcontracted to other jobs. The result is that the less motivated and less qualified ones remain as the frontline workers dealing with the poor and administering state benefits and transfers. These social workers have no opportunities for increasing their income except via working in another more lucrative part of state administration or via bribery.

The Implementation Saga from a Social Worker Perspective

Can Social Workers Handle the New Programs?

The cash transfers programs were designed by teams of national and international experts at both the Ministry of Finance and the Ministry of Social Solidarity.[9] The role of social workers was discussed at length.

Would these administrators implement the programs by taking applications, administering the PMT using a tablet computer, and from there take on the responsibilities of informing applicants of the outcomes, explaining to them next steps, handling grievances, and—in the case of Takaful, the conditional transfer—also oversee compliance with conditions? These social workers are also the same persons responsible for allocation of social pensions or Damman Igtima'y. Would they be able to differentiate between the two systems of social support?

Previous interactions during training of social workers suggest some answers to these questions. Training workshops took place in Upper Egypt in January and February 2012, and included 150 social workers in Assiut and Sohag. The workshops aimed to acquaint the social workers with the objectives and logistics of the pilot CCT program, and to learn from the social workers what terms, conditions, and modes of operation they thought would work in their own context.

The trainees were asked to do a daily evaluation of the workshops. The most striking feedback concerned the novelty of participatory learning. They said that they had learned new things because they could ask what they wanted. Most of the questions, especially at the beginning of the workshops, were about current practices and the dos and don'ts of social work. "How do I fill out this form?" "Do I have to have documentation and proof for refusing a request?" "How do I file this?" "Is it legal to do this or that?" Such basic questions fired at the trainers from the ministry created a degree of honesty that was essential for the sharing of knowledge and experience. An example from the session on poverty targeting will illustrate this point.

A previous project in 2008, in order to develop a means of identifying the poor and develop a PMT, had relied on the social workers to perform home visits. They did so under duress. The targeting project relied on social workers for collecting household survey data under the supervision of academics from the National Centre for Sociological Studies and some participating regional universities. On field visits to Assiut, one of the first governorates to complete the household visits, social workers expressed their anger and disdain for the whole initiative.

"We could not enter houses and ask people to show us their toilets," one young social worker said. He and all others working said that the academics refused to get out of their buses and cars to do the household visits, and asked the social workers (who were supposed to be just guiding them to the right village and confirming the names of families) to administer the questionnaire to heads of households. They admitted to making up answers and to filling in the bits that they did not actually ask on the basis of their own prior knowledge of the families.

Concerns of Social Workers: Dealing with Legal Frameworks?

The social workers who expressed their consternation did so for four reasons:

- their own knowledge of the areas in which they live and work was not taken into account by the targeting project;
- the questionnaires and the postulates upon which they are based were never explained to them;
- the outcomes of this endeavor yielded some wildly inaccurate results;
- the households visited expected some returns, such as pensions or other compensations, as that had been the only way for social workers to access their homes. This had turned out not to be the case.

The law of social pensions drafted in 2010 and designed to facilitate objective targeting for all MOSS programs,[10] and for cash transfers in particular, mandated statistical targeting (proxy means testing) as a new procedure for accepting or rejecting applications for social pensions and transfers. The law also mandated regular household visits to monitor pensioners and the creation of a unified registry of welfare recipients that was to be held by MOSS but include data from all other service-providing ministries. This law 137 of 2010 was passed in October, three months before the revolution. Its administrative and implementation decrees came out in mid-January 2011. One of the first orders issued by senior administrators in the midst of ministerial changes and confusions was to issue an informal, verbally communicated order to freeze the law and use law 33 of 1977 (the old social pensions law).

Social workers interviewed were overjoyed. This new law had been imposed with no provisions made for how to implement it. There was no PMT to be applied, no computers in social units to register applicants, no money to use for public transport to go on home visits, not enough social workers to undertake these visits, no mode of coordination with other ministries, and no communication strategy to explain the law within the ministry or to communities.

When in 2014 a new minister reconvened a group to redraft the law and fix the problems left by the Mubarak era, the senior social workers on this committee wanted to basically recreate the 1977 law. In explanation during interviews, those on the committee explained that the old law was clear and unambiguous. Categories of people were targeted, such as government employees making less than the minimum wage (there had been 1.5 million auxiliaries working in the government sector who could qualify for pensions), widows, orphans, the disabled, and the handicapped.

They knew how to process these cases, how to ask for proof of no income. They even knew how to go through the very complicated requirements of the law whereby people with an income that was below a certain level were given the difference between half of what they make and the upper level of pensions. In most cases these were calculations that would defy logic as the sums were so small. But they had their ways and they liked them. "This is because I don't want to find myself committing a crime," one social worker explained. The term used to refer to this feeling of comfort and work satisfaction is about stacking paper: *Asstif al warak*. For as in any bureaucracy, it is the paper work that counts (Gupta 2012; Hull, 2014).

Should These Concerns Be Addressed?

When policy makers ignore the reality of the conditions of work, the capabilities, the habitus, and the points of view of ground-level workers, they run the risk of spending too much time (and money) developing policies, and then running out of steam and resources and finding that policy has been subverted or just whittled down to an aberration of what it was intended to be. In 2014, there were still not enough ground-level workers or computers, no comprehensive and updated databases, no resources to cover running costs, and no equipped administrative structure to accommodate a new system.

In 2015, the cash transfer programs finally created an enabling environment in which statistical targeting and digital registration could be implemented. The programs are supported by a World Bank grant that facilitates implementation; the transfers themselves, however, are from the national budget of the government of Egypt. Yet social workers are still not comfortable.

During group interviews in late 2015 in Aswan governorate, where the programs were about to be introduced, much consternation was expressed by social workers from four local units. They had heard a variety of rumors, many of which they themselves had started spreading. They thought that the tablet and digital registration was just for show, and that the programs actually were not targeted. They had not been given any information on what targeting is, but only on how to fill the form and upload necessary documents to substantiate the application. They had also not been given any overtime or other incentives, despite the stories that they had heard of huge crowds storming social units so as to register. In Giza, two small children had been killed due to a stampede to register.

They had also heard rumors about the inefficient and wrong targeting of the programs. "Some healthy people have taken them, and others who have land too," said one worker from Kom Ombo. They had not been told that Takaful was income support for poor families, and they assumed that they should enroll only families of widows, the disabled, or orphans, like the old Damman Igtima'y.

Much of the missing information that social workers needed to register people in the new program would sooner or later be supplied, either through more training or by experience, but their initial suspicions and the sense of foreboding that they shared about the cash transfers had an effect. According to the program manager at the ministry, not enough people were getting the program and this must be because of failures at the registration point. The programs were supposed to have reached five hundred thousand families by the first year. As of January 2016, only half that number had applied and been rewarded with cash transfers.[11] It was because of the tensions between a center in a hurry and a periphery too fearful to adopt change that contract enumerators were hired.

Experts Still Trying to Rule

One of the most acrimonious incidents that I experienced while doing this research and work in the ministry of social solidarity concerned the role of economists and experts in the reform of social programs. In 2013–2014, a team of experts had been working in the ministry of finance in what was then called the economic justice unit, so as to develop the proxy means testing formula for the cash transfer programs. This team was financed by a World Bank project but was working closely with the Ministry of Social Solidarity, where the new programs and pensions were being designed.

The experts decided that the effort needed to design a sound means testing formula, draft the form that would be used to compile the applicant information to use this formula, and structure the necessary hardware and software for running it would take too long, and suggested that a better strategy

> may be if we go to the poorest areas [districts/villages] and give cash assistance to whoever applies from these areas. We looked at the leakage ratio of the PMT formula and decided that maybe targeting all the areas with 65 percent plus poverty rate is acceptable. We'll have zero under coverage and a leakage ratio of up to 35 percent. This may lead us to cover up to one million households. In the meantime, the MOSS team will continue to work on the preparation for the implementation of the PMT formula in targeting the poor in other areas. So, geographic targeting can be used only in the first round.

Their idea was to "pretend" to use the PMT but basically give pensions to all applicants, as the likelihood of applicants being poor was higher than the possibility of their claims being fraudulent.

Dubois (2016) illustrated how welfare policy and decisions are based on ideas imported from economics that may be totally disconnected from the ordinary experiences of welfare recipients. However, these decisions impose on people a definition of their own experiences and their lived realities and justify the way they are treated in policy programs. The vision of social and economic problems that prevail at the top echelons of the state is shaped by economics in an abstract, quantitative, and simplified version of economic research. Similarly, the experts who were making this practical suggestion, which is statistically sound, had rarely ventured out of their offices.

Saker el Nour (2012) has described the reality of the geographical poverty maps. He has documented the inaccuracies and fallacies of empirical data on Upper Egyptian villages. For example, census data estimated the area of a subvillage targeted as one of the poorest in Egypt as being 14.54 square kilometers, whereas locals, including an engineer, estimated the total area of the village with all its houses to be one square kilometer. The same census estimated that 66 percent of homes were red or mud brick, when in fact the El Nour's data estimated that, of the four hundred household units that comprised the village, 86 percent were built using concrete cement, making the proportion of brick homes 14 percent. Another fallacy concerned fictitious borders. The plan to add a health unit ignored the easy access that villagers had to a neighboring health facility, which on paper was in another district but which was in walking distance from where they lived.

My own work confirms these observations. Service providers from the governorates where these programs were to be fielded were equally dismayed at what was being proposed, but were too intimidated to speak out. From an implementation point of view, it is political suicide to administer a form and not use its information. From a legal point of view, you cannot give a right/resource or service to someone in one area and deny it to the same person if he/she lives in another area. In other words, you cannot give money to everyone who applies for it regardless of their condition and only on the basis of where they live.

When a Mexican World Bank consultant came to review the new programs being developed at the ministry, I took him to one of the villages that would be targeted because on paper it had more than 70 percent poverty head count. As we walked next to the sparkling marble-clad baroque-style villas of local merchants, and as I pointed out to him the macaroni-making factories that they own and which have made them millionaires, and as we crossed a tiny canal that makes this sprawling peri-urban settlement into two, he could see the madness of asking social workers to award pensions to the villa owners, if they chose to apply, and refuse to do it to the mud house–dwellers living across the canal, as technically their village was less poor and not on the list of places that would get 100 percent coverage.

The senior policy makers in government would have supported the procedure suggested by the experts and ignored the field-level workers had the consultant from Mexico not stopped this madness. He supported the MOSS view after seeing the problem of data quality and the huge discrepancies between statistical facts and empirical ones.

Conclusion

This chapter covers a long period of participant observation during which events took many turns. It is difficult to present a linear narrative when the facts tell a meandering and convoluted story. The work illustrates the disaggregation of policies and programs concerning cash transfers when considered as artifacts from an international discourse on social protection and not as a national policy that needs to articulate with other previous policies and practices. A critical approach to policy, and an engagement with the state as an empirical reality, necessitate an understanding of how the state functions and an appreciation of who are the people who do its work. Far from being a rational authority that is rule bound, Egyptian bureaucracy is a socially and politically constructed collation that merits historical understanding. The rules and idioms that express and constrain it are riddled with contradictions and nuanced by the ways in which they are made operational. Despite a reputation of stability and modernistic predictability, bureaucracies of social services are neither predictable nor overtly rule bound.

The chapter has illustrated the relevance of a historically situated and people-centered account of social services. The cash transfer program may be a good policy option for Egypt, one which is an improvement on the existing social pensions called Damman Igtima'y, as it does away with futile requirements for official documents, and revisits unchanged categories of entitlement long overtaken by economic transformations that have impoverished and made vulnerable millions of Egyptians. But despite the potential these programs have for supporting the income of the very poor in rural areas, their implementation has stumbled on the obstacle of service provider ability, preferences, and culture of work. The problem described in this chapter concerns the tensions between center and periphery that plague the way state services and public goods are organized.

"Modernizing" the delivery of services is easier to contemplate than to implement, especially if it precludes those who will be charged with its on-the-ground implementation. In the absence of consideration of the human content and context of implementation, cash transfers will be yet another development ideal and poverty program that fails to account for reality and for the political economy of poverty as a multifaceted construct in which the state and its bureaucracy play nuanced and important roles. Cash transfers in particular lend themselves to creating such rifts because they are such well-documented and regimented programs that impose a way of implementation that may not be ideal for a setting such as Egypt, where the organization and delivery of social pensions are highly influenced by a rich past of social work.

The ministry has succeeded in upgrading its records and its points of service, and is working toward better and more effective service delivery. But the real challenge is the rift between senior/upper-level management, who may come from a parallel system that pays well and that encourages innovation and risk, and the lower-level administrators and social workers who have had little training and almost no investment in them as human resources, and are subject to extremely rigid structures and administrative decrees and protocols.

More serious is the ahistorical aspect of CCTs. At one level, these can be viewed as technologies of poverty alleviation. They rely on statistical objective targeting, create digitized records, construct unified registries, rely on electronic payments, and, because they are so data rich, are easy to monitor and even, at one level, evaluate. But these programs are also social assistance programs that engage people who serve other people, and as such need to transcend the simplistic, yet technically challenging, task of finding and paying the poor to providing social assistance in a meaningful way and one that takes into account the cultures and complexities of daily life and of inequality and poverty.

Postscript

Karama and Takaful now provide monthly transfers to over nine million Egyptians. In early December 2017, the Egyptian president of the republic handed a Karama and Takaful debit card to the two millionth beneficiary. The speedy registration of beneficiaries was necessitated by a political urgency and enabled by international support. The urgency was due to the liberalization of the exchange rate mechanism (ERM) that pegs the Egyptian pound to the dollar. When left to float on 21 November 2016, the pound lost much of its value (it was eight pounds to the dollar and dropped to twenty pounds to the dollar due to the changes in ERM). Inflation jumped to over 30 percent on average, and most people felt the pinch of these macro-stabilization policies. The political leadership came to value the power of the cash transfer programs to absorb anger and alleviate the impact of rapid impoverishment and lowered consumption.

Meanwhile, Egypt had signed a $400 million (U.S.) loan agreement with the World Bank to finance and fully implement Karama and Takaful. The agreement availed the funds to recruit a cadre of well-qualified professionals and an army of enumerators armed with tablets and with contracts that paid them per application, and so enabled the rapid expansion of the programs but sidelined almost completely the local social workers. The IMF agreement loan of $12 billion (U.S.) to Egypt also mentions the importance of these programs and suggests their sustained expansion.

By 2017, the programs were a familiar part of people's public awareness. Problems of mistargeting and of leakage were being addressed by state-level security regulators, and the programs were acknowledged as an achievement for the current cabinet and political leadership.

An impact evaluation funded by the World Bank and designed by IFPRI (Washington, D.C.) should produce some results by March 2018. So far, the impact of the programs on people has not been understood, despite the programs themselves being a focus for much celebration.

Hania Sholkamy is an Egyptian anthropologist and currently an associate research professor at the Social Research Centre at the American University in Cairo. She trained at the American University in Cairo and at the London School of Economics. She has held academic positions and visiting fellowships at St Anne's College, Oxford University, Arab Gulf University in Bahrain, Yale University, and the American University in Beirut. She has published in the fields of gender, population, and reproductive health. Her recent work has focused on welfare and social policy. She received an honorable mention for the American Anthropological Association's 2017 Prize for Public Anthropology.

Notes

1. Since 2011, there have been frequent attempts to criminalize the activities of civil society by political bodies, and social workers are asked to give testimonies to validate these charges.
2. In 2016, the newly elected parliament of Egypt had to rapidly, and in accordance with the stipulations of the constitution, ratify or reject 340 draft laws in a period of fifteen

days. All the drafts were ratified except a new law for public administration reform that introduced principles of dismissal for poor performance, competition for posts, and job performance reviews as a basis for salary increments and bonuses.

3. My interest in understanding the world of officials and administrators has been a long-standing one. Since 2008, I have been undertaking a multidimensional research and service project to investigate the role of the state in poverty programs and in social provisions. I have done so as a researcher, as a trainer, as a technical advisor, and as an unpaid programs designer and special advisor.

4. The amounts given are periodically reviewed and increased in line with political desires to compensate beneficiaries for soaring rates of food price inflation.

5. Interview with program administrators at the Ministry of Social Solidarity.

6. A celebration was held on 28 May to mark one year of the program and was attended by the Prime Minister and many senior policy makers and legislators.

7. "Social worker" is a rank, not a function or role. The administrative hierarchy of the ministry at the local unit levels has a secretary, social worker, and unit head as the three ranks in ascending order of seniority within the unit. There are also auxiliary staff (cleaners, errand boys, and guards) employed at the unit. Each unit is supervised by one regional district office that also has social worker–rank persons working there.

8. Retired special adviser to the minister in 2009 and previous head of social services.

9. The author designed the two programs but was not involved in developing the PMT used to target them.

10. Including microcredit schemes, emergency aid, child support grants, and in kind distributions.

11. The surge in registration implemented since January 2016 has rapidly increased the numbers of beneficiaries of Takaful. There are almost three-quarters of a million families now registered.

References

Al-Shawarby, S. H., "Egypt's Food Subsidies: Estimation of Leakages." 2010. Research Papers Series 32, Economics Department, Faculty of Economics and Political Science, Cairo University.

Appadurai, A. "Grassroots Globalization and the Research Imagination." *Public Culture* 12(1): 1–19.

Barrientos, A., and J. DeJong. 2006. "Reducing Child Poverty with Cash Transfers: A Sure Thing?" *Development Policy Review* 24(5). Accessed 16 June 2016. http://www.eldis.org/vfile/upload/1/document/0708/doc23659.pdf.

Barrientos, A., and D. Hulme. 2010. *Just Give Money to the Poor: The Developmental Revolution from the South*. West Hartford, CT: Kumarian Press.

Bierschenk, T., and J.-P. Olivier de Sardan. 2014. "Studying the Dynamics to African Bureaucracies: An Introduction to States at Work." In *States at Work: Dynamics of African Bureaucracies*, edited by T. Bierschenk and J.-P. Olivier de Sardan, 3–35. Leiden: Brill.

Dubois, V. 2016. *The Bureaucrat and the Poor: Encounters in French Welfare Office*. Translated by J.-Y. Bart. London: Routledge.

el Nour, S. 2012. "National Geographical Targeting of Poverty in Upper Egypt." In *Marginality and Exclusion in Egypt*, edited by R. Bush and H. Ayyeb, 148–169. London: Zed Books.

Escobar, A. 1995. *Encountering Development: The Making and Unmaking of the Third World*. Princeton, NJ: Princeton University Press.

Ferguson, J., and L. Lohman. 1994. "The Anti-Politics Machine: Development and Bureaucratic Power in Lesotho." *The Ecologist* 24(5): 176–181.

Galal, A. 2003. Social Expenditure and the Poor in Egypt. ECES Working Paper, Publication Number ECESWP89-E. Cairo, Egypt.

Gupta, A. 2012. *Red Tape: Bureaucracy, Structural Violence and Poverty in India*. John Hope Franklin Series. Durham, NC: Duke University Press.

———. 2013. "Messy Bureaucracies." *Journal of Ethnographic Theory* 3(3): 435–440.

Hull, M. 2012 *Government of Paper: The Materiality of Bureaucracy in Urban Pakistan*. Berkeley, CA: University of California Press.

IHSN. 2013. "Egypt Household Income Expenditure Consumption Survey 2012–2013." IHSN Survey Catalog, International Household Survey Network website. Retrieved 20 July 2016 from catalog.IHSN.org.

Issa, I. 2012. *Alwan Yaniar* [January's colors]. Cairo: Dar al-Shorouk.

Jones, N., and R. Holmes. 2010. "Rethinking Social Protection Using a Gender Lens." ODI Working Paper No. 320. Available here: https://www.odi.org/sites/odi.org.uk/files/odi-assets/publications-opinion-files/6273.pdf.

Lipsky, M. 1980. *Street-Level Bureaucracy: Dilemmas of the Individual in Public Services*. New York: Russell Sage Foundation.

Maluccio, J., and R. Flores. 2005. *Impact Evaluation of a CCT Programme: The Nicaraguan Red de Protección Social*. IFPRI Research Report No. 141. Washington, DC: IFPRI.

Mitchell, T. 2004. *Rule of Experts: Egypt, Techno-Politics, Modernity*. Berkeley, CA: University of California Press.

Molyneux, M. 2002. "Gender and the Silences of Social Capital: Lessons from Latin America." *Development and Change* 33(2): 167–188.

———. 2006. "Mothers at the Service of the New Poverty Agenda." Special issue on Latin America, *Journal of Social Policy and Administration* 40(4): 425–449.

———. 2009. "Conditional Cash Transfers: A 'Pathway to Women's Empowerment'?" Pathways of Empowerment Working Paper 5. Accessed 16 June 2016. https://www.gov.uk/dfid-research-outputs/pathways-working-paper-5-conditional-cash-transfers-a-pathway-to-women-s-empowerment.

Nagi, S. (N.d.). *In Pursuit of Progress: An Agenda for Social Development in Egypt*. Report to the Ministry of Insurance and Social Affairs, and the United Nations Development Program (UNDP), Cairo, Egypt.

Navaro-Yashin, Y. 2002. *Faces of the State: Secularism and Public Life in Turkey*. Princeton, NJ: Princeton University Press.

Sabates-Wheeler, R., and N. Kabeer 2003. "Gender Equality and the Extension of Social Protection." ESS Working Paper 16. Geneva: International Labor Organization.

Sharma, A., and A. Gupta, eds. 2006. *The Anthropology of the State: A Reader*. Malden, MA: Wiley-Blackwell.

Sholkamy, H. 1999. "Procreation in Islam: A Reading from Egypt of People and Texts." In *Conceiving Persons*, edited by P. Loizos and P. Heady, 139–159. London School of Economics Monographs on Social Anthropology Series. London: Bloomsbury Academic.

———. 2001. "Being Sickly or Eating Well: Child Health in Upper Egypt." In *Directions of Change in Rural Egypt,* edited by N. Hopkins and K. Westergaard, 203–218. Cairo: AUC Press.

Sholkamy, H., and A. Kamaly. 2013. "Social Spending in Egypt." Report prepared for the Ministry of Planning, commissioned by UNDP, Cairo, Egypt.

Soares, F. 2004. "Conditional Cash Transfer: A Vaccine against Poverty and Inequality?" International Poverty Centre Series 3, UNDP, Brazil. Accessed 11 May 2018. http://www.ipc-undp.org/pub/IPCOnePager3.pdf.

World Bank. 2001. *Brazil: An Assessment of the Bolsa Escola Programs.* Accessed 15 June 2016. http://documents.worldbank.org/curated/en/148031468743736711/Brazil-Assessment-of-the-Bolsa-Escola-Programs.

Yaschine, I. 1999. "The Changing Anti-Poverty Agenda: What Can the Mexican Case Tell Us?" *Institute for Development Studies Bulletin* 2(30): 47–60.

Weber, M. 2006. "Bureaucracy." In *The Anthropology of the State: A Reader,* edited by A. Sharma and A. Gupta, 49–70. Malden, MA: Wiley-Blackwell.

Chapter 11

Juggling between Social Obligations and Personal Benefit in Western Côte d'Ivoire

How Do Ex-combatants Spend Their Cash Allowance?

Magali Chelpi-den Hamer

The use of cash transfers in aid programming has received growing support in recent years despite the fear of misuse and loss of control. There is one sector in particular in which its use has rarely been questioned: in processes dealing with the disarmament, demobilization, and reintegration of ex-combatants (commonly known as DDR). The use of cash has become increasingly widespread in this field, yet few grounded studies systematically document its diversity of impacts. Cash transfers are sometimes used in the disarmament stage to "buy back" weapons, in the hope of reducing the number of guns and ammunition in circulation, and they are also sometimes used in the reinsertion/reintegration stage, with the aim to facilitate ex-combatants' return to civilian life. What lies behind these practices is the assumption that giving money to ex-combatants can have a positive and direct effect on their lives and will prevent them from taking up weapons again. Based on a careful examination of over one hundred individual testimonies collected in western Côte d'Ivoire between December 2006 and July 2007, this chapter examines how the financial incentives distributed in the summer of 2006 to progovernmental demobilized militias were spent, providing an empirical base on the subject.

Notes for this chapter begin on page 298.

Cash Transfers in the Ivorian DDR:
Process and Specificities in a Nutshell

The Ivorian DDR process planned to use cash transfers during the reinsertion stage with the intended aim of facilitating ex-combatants' transitioning from soldiering to civilian life. The process was designed in line with what was agreed upon in Linas-Marcoussis in 2003, which was several times reiterated in follow-up agreements. At the time of my fieldwork, the National DDR Commission (CNDDR) was the governmental institution mandated to implement the Ivorian DDR program with the help of the United Nations peacekeeping mission.[1] Official parties were included in the process (which consisted of the Ivorian army and recognized rebel groups), as well as paramilitary and militia groups, which had been active on both sides. Inclusion in the DDR process was based on lists of recruits provided by the respective chiefs of staff, checked by the CNDDR. In line with the national plan, demobilized combatants were entitled to a financial package of 499,500 CFA francs (equivalent to €760 / $940 US), locally designated as *filet de sécurité* (this term literally means "safety net" and is the term locally used in official wording). The financial package was scheduled to be disbursed in three installments: 25 percent paid upon demobilization, 25 percent paid forty-five days later, and 50 percent paid ninety days after demobilization. It was supposed to cover for ex-combatants' basic expenses for the first six months following their demobilization, helping them face the immediate challenges encountered after their return into their community of origin.

In the summer of 2006 (July–August), after a series of political stalls and false starts, pro-governmental militia members started an official demobilization process that included cash transfers.[2] The cash was handed over in three installments, as initially planned (only the third installment was delayed), in Duékoué, western Côte d'Ivoire, under the supervision of the CNDDR and the UN peacekeeping mission. A peculiarity of the Ivorian situation was that the majority of pro-governmental militias undergoing the process were local recruits and had already spontaneously demobilized in 2004–2005 and resumed personal activity. The bulk of the weapons had in fact been collected by their leaders during the course of 2005, when the military situation had stabilized, for storage in local arsenals, ready for a potential redistribution should the situation deteriorate or for a hand-over in case of sustainable peace. Right before the start of the militias' demobilization in the summer of 2006, militia leaders had surrendered batches of weapons to peacekeeping forces as a sign of goodwill. Most of the weapons collected during the summer demobilization operation, however, were defective, and the ratio of combatant per surrendered weapon/ammo was also very low. This situation led the DDR division of the United Nations Operation in Côte d'Ivoire to suspend the demobilization operation in the beginning of August. Nevertheless, 981 militia members had already been registered and had received financial compensation. Out of those, five hundred could enter a follow-up reinsertion program, run by the German organization GTZ-IS,[3] to benefit from individual advice and socioeconomic support. This chapter specifically analyzes the use of cash of these low-ranked demobilized militia members one year after receiving their financial compensation. One hundred individuals were interviewed using two GTZ-IS reinsertion centers as premises for conducting the meetings. Respondents were not observed in situ, when they received their cash transfers, or when they spent them; instead, they were asked to reconstruct their perceptions of past events by taking their life story as a point of departure.

How Were the Cash Allowances Spent?

Among the interviewed recruits, genuine belief that they had earned the right to compensation was a recurring litany throughout the discussions. "We lost five years of our time." "We've been delayed." There was something intrinsic to these statements, namely, the expression of a certain conception of fairness and the implicit claim that financial compensation was due, regardless of the outcome of the conflict. The majority of militia members emphasized the fact that, despite having been called to fight for their country, they had gained little from it, and they had mainly lost their time in the movement instead of being able to work elsewhere. They were therefore entitled to a proper reward for the services rendered. Some threatened to return to violence if not satisfied, but such claims were mostly rhetorical since most of them had already put down their guns and were no longer armed.

While most low-ranked recruits saw financial compensation as a back-payment for their services, military leaders, and especially the high-ranking ones, had a different perspective: they mainly used it as a carrot—an incentive—to retain their troops, especially after it was institutionalized in the national DDR plan. Indeed, the prospect of getting no financial reward at all would probably have led many recruits to abandon their ranks after a certain time, especially among the western militias, who were in this respect much freer than their rebel counterparts. But the prospect of being on the official demobilization list, hence the prospect of potentially being eligible to receive a cash allowance, had the reverse effect of maintaining some recruits' loyalty.

As already noted above, the financial incentive distributed in the summer of 2006 to the 981 militia members was dispatched in three installments: the first installment was supplied in July 2006, right after their official demobilization (125,000 CFA francs);[4] the second installment (same amount) was dispatched mid-September; and the third installment (249,500 CFA francs)[5] was distributed at the end of November.

The three interview fragments presented below show different examples of use of the financial incentives received:

> The first installment, I shared with my family and my in-laws. I kept a little, but not much. Most of the money was used to pay miscellaneous expenses. The second installment, I gave 50,000 to my wife for her small business. I also set up a *cabine* [local phone booth] for my little brother but he screwed everything up. I used the last installment to invest in my own business, a *maquis* [local eating place] and to improve my home.

> I gave the money to my family, and I also paid for my uncle's medical expenses. I also gave petty cash to friends I had in the militia group, who were not yet demobilized. I also bought a plot of land in Guiglo, near the timber industry for 50,000 CFA francs. I am currently building my own house. I purchased wood from the timber company, to make charcoal, and I opened a bank account at the local post.

> I improved my home. I set up a water tap for 58,000 CFA francs and I purchased an electricity counter at 72,000 CFA francs. I helped my brother start his own hevea field and I gave him 125,000 CFA francs. I also gave petty cash to my family.

As seen in the testimonies, respondents used their safety net very differently, constantly juggling between social obligations and personal benefit. A rough categorization of expenses is presented below. The findings are grouped into five categories of expenses: (1) the reimbursement of creditors, (2) response to familial demands, (3) investments, (4) dealing with social events (such as medical expenses, funerals, home improvements), and (5) reward to the military leader.

Reimbursing Creditors

Reimbursing creditors was not an uncommon answer, and many respondents said that upon receipt of the cash, one of the first things they did was to pay the debts they—or their family—had accumulated during the war period. One respondent had accumulated as much as 325,000 CFA francs in debt since the beginning of the war. He had not paid his house rent for several months (which had put him 25,000 CFA francs in debt every month), not to mention the unpaid utilities bills (electricity/water) that had accumulated over the years. For him, it was important to pay his creditors first since he feared they would have gone to the police to file a formal complaint when they found out that he had received a cash allowance (the official demobilization process had been widely advertised in the local medias so it was difficult to hide having received something). Another respondent explained that even if he had slept most of the war in military camps, he had kept renting a home in town for his wife. Several people mentioned having to buy food on credit during the war because even if they could usually eat in the military camps, their dependents were usually not entitled to free food, so they had to contract loans to have them eat. One respondent contracted a loan to bury his mother while he was in the armed group. His dead parent had remained in the mortuary for a month (which is billed 5,000 CFA francs a day), the coffin cost 50,000 CFA francs, and he had to borrow to pay for the stay of his relatives who had come to attend the funeral. Most of his cash allowance was therefore used to clear this debt.

Responding to Familial Demands

The relationships respondents had with their family after receiving their cash entitlement were quite complex, and the way they managed these ranged from strategies of avoidance to strategies of resignation. How to best manage the burden eventually appeared to be the most standard concern. Several respondents reported difficulties in avoiding relatives' requests. As this interview fragment tells, "People know when you get your cash. The following morning, you see all your relatives in a row in front of your door and you have to give them something. You give 5,000 to your aunt, 5,000 to your cousin, 5,000 to your other cousin, etc." One respondent succeeded in bypassing such an issue by putting all his cash in the local bank and by returning empty-handed to his village. Even when cornered, he was essentially incapable of giving cash to anyone.

A few respondents mentioned having loaned money to a sibling (up to 100,000 CFA francs). While most loans were not yet repaid at the time of the interviews, some had already been bitterly abused. One respondent mentioned he had given his complete first installment to his family, "to be left in peace." He used to be employed as a *katakata* driver before the war (a *katakata* is a sort of bush tractor that transports all kinds of merchandise), and he wanted to save the second and third installment of his cash allowance to buy a *katakata* for himself. Given the second-hand cost of such a vehicle (1.5 million CFA francs), one of his brothers convinced him to entrust him with his money. The plan was to travel to Abidjan to ask their eldest brother to participate in the purchase by paying the remaining million. What eventually happened is that the entrusted brother eventually usurped all the money and claimed to the former militiaman that he had been robbed on the way.

But regardless of these cases of peer abuse, a recurring argument in favor of family support is gratefulness. Close to the front line, villages often played an important role in supplying food to combatants, and complex mechanisms of money collection occurred between armed groups, villagers, and the educated elite in Abidjan who were native to these war-affected areas (the *cadres villageois*). One interview fragment summarized it very well: "You have to be grateful and reward those who fed you during the war." Several respondents therefore felt obliged to reward their benefactors, and these included close relatives who participated in the war effort and who supported them during difficult times, including the times spent in the armed group. Rewards to the spouse and to direct parents (father/mother) were rather standard patterns, and several stories were heard of respondents setting up a farm for their father, or helping their wife to develop her own business.

Investing

Several respondents mentioned that it was not until the last installment that they could do something productive with their money. Western Côte d'Ivoire is particularly conducive to agriculture; some also invested in wood and bought loads from the nearby timber industry to turn into charcoal. Others entered the growing sector of hevea cultivation or expanded the plantation they already had (the hevea sector was especially in vogue in 2006–2007, during the period of fieldwork). Respondents who were already engaged in cultivating hevea before the war bought new plants, and those who were new to the activity purchased land, cleared a field, and/or joined the myriad of private and local humanitarian projects that were then offering incentives to cultivate hevea in the Moyen-Cavally region.

One respondent used his last installment to purchase one hectare of hevea for 180,000 CFA francs.[6] He had used the previous two transfers to give petty cash to his relatives (wife, brothers, and sister), to pay for his son's school boarding expenses (35,000 CFA francs), to buy food (three bags of rice at 36,000 CFA francs), and to purchase agricultural equipment (a pulverizer at 48,500 CFA francs). Another respondent used his third transfer to enter a local project, the Nouvelles Plantations Hévéicoles de l'ouest Montagneux de la Côte d'Ivoire, to benefit from free seedlings. When we met, he had just started contracting workers to clear two hectares of forest to start a hevea plantation.

But respondents did not solely invest in agricultural activities. One used his safety net to purchase a sewing machine, a *Singer-à-tête-noire* (75,000 CFA francs). He was planning to return to tailoring, an activity he was doing before the war, and to run his own workshop. Another had to wait for the third installment to restock his shop with 200,000 CFA francs worth of new merchandise. Another invested in a chicken farm. He bought poultry, food, and vaccines, and resumed his prewar activity. Another used most of his safety net to open a local restaurant. He spent 300,000 CFA francs to purchase a freezer, several chairs, a few tables, the first stock of drinks, and to cover the various costs related to the installation (restoration, rent, and a security deposit). Other types of investments included partial payment to an auto school (in the prospect of getting a driving license to be able to work as a taxi/truck/minivan driver), paying city fees for setting up a market stall or a small business, paying intermediaries to find a job, paying registration fees for being authorized to take national civil service exams, and paying bribes and fees to be allowed to take the ninth- and twelfth-grade exams in the hope that this would open more doors (having these diplomas allows the person to sit civil service entrance exams).

Social Uses

Improving one's home, buying a plot of land (when not for agricultural purposes), building a house, purchasing basic furniture, buying clothes, marrying, or rewarding old men who provided mystic protection during the war (*gris-gris*), all these different uses were cited as common expenses. Being further recognized, within the household and/or the community of belonging, as capable of doing so was also sending important social messages. Notably, a certain number of respondents took advantage of their financial safety net to leave the family home and to settle independently: "Before the war, I used to sleep at my parents. With the safety net, I detached myself. I built a *deux-chambres-salon*."[7] One respondent used his second installment to have his identity papers drawn up. In a country where the lack of documentation often impedes free circulation, this is worth noting. Many respondents also mentioned having spent substantial sums on medical expenses right after receipt of their cash entitlement, either for themselves or for close relatives. Usually, such a use was a major expense, and there was rarely anything left. It is difficult to label such types of expenses unproductive even if, indeed, the money was eventually wasted on social matters. When a serious disease hit them (or their family), respondents preferred to refer to the period as "bad timing."

Perhaps the best statement to illustrate how most respondents felt upon receipt of their cash allowance is the following: "When you are not paid for years, you live one day after the other. This cash we got, we could do nothing good with it."[8] That partly explains why a lot of respondents spent their money quickly, with relatively insignificant personal benefit. Many respondents were also not happy with the fact that the safety net had come in three installments. They would have preferred to receive everything in one go, as smaller cash amounts were easily wasted in their views, in particular by responding to familial demands and by dealing with social events (such as medical expenses, funerals, and home improvements).[9] Payment by installment nevertheless continues to remain the preferred international approach for fear of misuse and mismanagement, while, paradoxically, western Côte d'Ivoire is known for seasonal farming activities, with local people relatively used to circulation of large amounts of cash in one go.

Allocating Money to War Chiefs: Racket or Reward?

Allocating part of the financial safety net to war chiefs—the "chiefs' share," as Olivier de Sardan and Hamani label it, in their chapter on Niger (chapter 12 in this volume)—was also a common feature in western Côte d'Ivoire, which raises the question of the extent to which it should be interpreted as a racket or a reward. If we look at interview fragments, there is plenty of anecdotal evidence suggesting that extortion was real. One account is particularly enlightening: "It was serious in Duékoué.[10] You were obliged to give. If you did not give, you could not get out. The first time, my leader took 30,000 out of my installment as recognition payment. The next two times, he did not get anything. As I was walking out of the compound with the cash in my pockets, he asked me, but I lied to him. I told him that I was still expecting my money and that I just wanted to get out for a drink." Retaliation rarely followed such avoidance strategies, and once the immediate threat had passed, there was usually no follow-up action on the part of war chiefs. Other respondents were less resourceful and could not avoid being shaken down after having received each installment.[11]

If some militia leaders seemed more prone to extorting from recruits, some were also more magnanimous than others, and who really benefited from this money eventually remained vague in many situations. The distinction between war leaders and war leaders' envoys was often blurred on the ground and in the respondents' discourse, and it was not easy to distinguish between organized racketeering orchestrated by militia leaders and simple robbery by higher-ranked recruits who were taking advantage of their position to abuse their peers. Most accounts showed, however, that rather than giving cash directly to their chiefs, recruits were more likely to pay an intermediary, especially if the person was known to have a close relationship with their leader (some even signed receipts!). In addition, there was a certain group dynamic, and after the first demobilized recruits had given money to their chiefs, the others were likely to do the same.

Rewarding war chiefs thus resembled a racket in some cases, but that was not the only pattern, and the informal back payment to warlords varied considerably from one individual to another. Several respondents pointed out that they were not forced to give money. There were even accounts of militia leaders gathering recruits before the first installment was made and telling them that they were not obliged to make any financial contributions.[12]

Some recruits beside did not perceive it as coercion. One respondent reported that he had rewarded his chief by paying for several rounds of drinks, and another militia member mentioned that although his chief had mentioned that he did not want anything in return, he was happy to give him 20,000 out of his last installment. Allocating money to war chiefs therefore seemed strongly connected to social obligation. One has to bear in mind that the majority of recruits were grateful to have been put on the official demobilization list by their militia leaders, which turned out to be the key to being eligible for financial compensation.

A last feature to take into account is also to whom recruits wanted to give. Militias also have their hierarchy, and while some felt more inclined to give to their general leader, others preferred rewarding a war chief who was closer to them in the battlefield and to whom they related more. A few respondents who fought in advanced positions reported being keen on rewarding the chiefs of their section. In their view, he had succeeded in the most important thing: he had preserved their lives during combat. One female recruit liberally praised her local commander: "I really say thank you to Colonel T. because he took good care of us. We did not lose anyone in our group. He watched our back. When he knew the day was not good, he would tell us not to move. That's the way we worked." The social value of reward associated with mystic beliefs must therefore not be downplayed when examining the relationship between war chiefs and recruits.

Has the Spending of Cash Allowances Facilitated Social Acceptance?

Given the well-known controversies associated with using cash transfers in the reinsertion stage of ex-combatants, it is worth questioning the extent to which the financial safety net has been helpful in securing acceptance by the community with whom ex-combatants associated, and whether it played a role in facilitating their transition to civilian life. Examining these questions is particularly relevant since in the western Ivorian context, most low-ranked militias had returned home several months/years before being officially demobilized; hence they eventually faced immediate reinsertion issues upon return without any financial safety net then to help them cope. Return to their home mostly occurred in 2004–2005, after the end of open conflict (2002–2003) and after the end of the encampment period in the military settings of Blolequin, Toulepleu, Zéo, and Zagné (the location where they were based depended on the armed group in which they were integrated). As noted above, the first time any financial compensation was disbursed was in the summer of 2006. Accounts widely varied per respondent. The ones who chose to remain in Guiglo, in the militia leaders' compounds or nearby, were clearly waiting for the official disarmament to start and for the supply of the several-times-announced financial benefits. Some reported having experienced no problems at all upon return and being warmly welcomed by their families: "My folks were told I was dead. They were quite happy to see me back." Others had never severed contacts with their parents during their time in the armed group, so their return was expected. Many local recruits, in fact, appointed near their place of residence, did not need to be resocialized after their military experience since their actual bonds with their prewar network had never been cut.

But how smooth was their return to civilian life? Accounts were rather mixed on this question, and there was no single pattern. While reinsertion problems directly experienced after having demobilized oneself were not often spontaneously mentioned (and unfortunately not systematically probed during interviews), several things came up during the discussions. Shortly after their return, a certain number of militia recruits were feared by the people with whom they usually associated, especially those known to have fought with Liberian mercenaries. The account of this female recruit is particularly enlightening:

> In the beginning, I was scaring everyone. Even my cousins were afraid. Even my mother. When I was angry, I often noticed that people acted different. They were all scared of me. But I said no. What I did [during the war], it is past. But even my friends were scared, and they were saying, "She went to war, she's going to kill you at night." It did not feel good. So I moved on elsewhere for some time. I spent two months in Abidjan. When I came back to Guiglo, I started to sell alloco [fried banana] in front of the Becanti. People were coming to see me out of curiosity, also soldiers. Some were surprised, "Eh, you are here now!" Some did not even want to eat alloco, they just came to see me. It took

some time, but people eventually saw me differently. I had not changed, but their perception did. They saw that I behaved well, and that I did not look for arguments with anybody. Now everything is okay.

Like her, several respondents mentioned having felt the need to work on their image shortly after returning to their prewar lives and having to emphasize their nonviolent attitude. If some respondents could resume their prewar activities relatively quickly, others reported encountering difficulties. Again, there was a multiplicity of patterns, which mostly depended on respondents' individual attitudes, characteristics, and social networks. One respondent could not go back to his previous work because he had a bad reputation. He shared his point of view: "Many things happened during the war. I did not know the face of all rebels, so when the chief suspected someone and said, 'This person is a rebel, he has to be killed,' we obeyed. But this man might have family in Guiglo; and now if I approach someone for work, these people can tell him that I'm not a good person and that it is better to avoid me." In contrast, well-known fighters had no problems resuming their prewar jobs. One respondent who had fought in the front line with the Liberians resumed upon return his work as a building painter, and even if he mentioned getting fewer contracts than before, the main cause was the general decrease in the local economic activity due to the displacement of most of the local middle class, not the fear of dealing with him.

Has financial compensation facilitated social acceptance then? For most demobilized militia recruits, the financial safety net was distributed years after their return to their community. This raises doubts about the extent to which cash allowances facilitated social acceptance. In addition, not every combatant benefited from them. As already mentioned, the demobilization program of the summer of 2006 was only partial and only targeted 981 low-ranked militia recruits. Not everyone appeared on the list for inclusion, and in a single village—even in a single family—some received the cash allowance and others did not, even if they also participated in the war effort. Selection appeared quite arbitrary in some cases, and perhaps the most interesting feature is that those who did not receive financial compensation and who were locally known to have participated in the war effort were mocked by their peers. A posteriori, going to war and getting nothing out of it was perceived locally as ridiculous and as a waste of time. There was, however, a certain tolerance with respect to this unfairness, and although the few militia recruits I interviewed who did not receive compensation indeed expressed their frustration, they seemed to accept their situation.

Conclusion

Respondents used their safety net very differently, constantly juggling between social obligations and personal benefit. Out of the five broad categories of expenses identified—(1) reimbursing creditors, (2) responding to familial demands, (3) investing in one's own business, (4) dealing with social events (such as medical expenses, funerals, home improvements), and (5) allocating money to war chiefs—three would not have existed if no cash allowance had been given to ex-combatants. Creditors would not have rushed to ask for their full payback and would have continued to display the same attitude as toward their other debtors; relatives would not have lined up in front of respondents' doors; and war chiefs and undemobilized friends would not have had a share.

For the two other categories (investing and dealing with social events), the financial compensation was useful but rather limited in time and scope. When discussing investments, a recurring point that came up from the interviews was that the financial safety net should have been given in one go instead of in three installments. Relevant investments usually involve substantial sums of money, and small amounts are easily wasted on day-to-day expenses. With respect to social events, one important contribution that this extra cash has made was in allowing ex-recruits to emancipate, by being able to leave the family home and/or by becoming a short-term provider for their close family.

Given the fact that most local recruits who benefited from DDR-related cash transfers had in fact spontaneously demobilized years before the start of the official process, the financial safety net received had a limited impact on their immediate post-return phase, which is probably when social acceptance was the most challenging. If cash transfers have the potential to curb ex-combatants' dependencies on their direct support structures when they return to their homes, it is likely in this case that ex-combatants' spouses and families were socially and economically affected by their return, more or less adversely depending on individual situations.

This case shows little evidence that individuals used the money unwisely on the so-called "temptation goods," such as drinking alcohol, buying drugs, or gambling. After receiving their safety net, ex-recruits faced a certain number of socioeconomic demands (from creditors, family, and acquaintances made during the war) to which they had to respond, and the range of responses greatly varied from one individual to another. In some instances, the extra cash has helped them face a certain number of social events (such as medical expenses, school fees, or costs associated with marriage, a funeral, or a newborn child), and sometimes it has enabled them to partially invest in a small business. The use of cash transfers in the reinsertion phase has indeed meant a breath a fresh air for ex-combatants, but should not be overrated, as their room to maneuver was eventually limited by the way they individually balanced social obligations with personal benefit. Demobilized militia members did not seem particularly privileged in comparison with the communities they related to, and many ended up probably more exposed to abuse by their direct entourage and by targeted robberies.

Postscript

Ten years after the failed start of the demobilization of pro-governmental militias, it is worth reflecting on how the process evolved. If during the period 2003–2007, DDR progress was very slow to materialize, the dynamics changed in 2007–2009, following the Ouagadougou comprehensive peace agreement. The APO,[13] as it was locally labeled, promoted direct dialogue between the Ivorian government and the rebel forces while reiterating its attachment to the existing National DDR Plan. It created two new structures for dealing with demilitarization issues: the Integrated Command Centre (CCI), which was put in charge of the military component of the process (the disarmament and demobilization phases), and the National Reinsertion and Community Rehabilitation Program (PNRRC), which was empowered to deal with the reinsertion of former combatants. Political appeasement then seemed possible, and a series of symbolic launches of the DDR process were organized in several localities. The dismantling of western militias was quickly announced and scheduled for May 2007. But unlike the 2006 attempt, the 2007 operation was very opaque in terms of cash transfers, and neither the National DDR Commission nor the UN peacekeeping mission were associated with the event. In 2007, the dismantling of militias took the form of a media operation, where 1,026 weapons were collected and handed over to the presidency by several militia leaders in return for a presidential envelope of 280 million CFA, supposed to be distributed to low-ranked recruits. Following that event, an official press release announced the official end of the operation.

The government switched focus afterward, away from the militia issue, which obviously had not been solved by the press release, toward the demilitarization of the official parties, which consisted of reducing the size of the Ivorian army while finding ways to incorporate part of the rebels in the new force. In 2008–2009, some disarmament and reintegration initiatives occurred, but they were very localized and small-scale, and in 2010, the DDR process was put to a halt again in view of the resumption of tensions around the presidential elections. After the electoral crisis, demilitarization came back high on the agenda. The modalities of the Ivorian DDR process still largely drew on the procedures developed in the 2000s, but a new institution replaced the CCI and the PNRRC, the ADDR (Autorité pour le désarmement, la démobilisation et la reintegration). If the name change was mostly symbolic, two main adjustments were made. First, a noteworthy increase in terms of financial compensation: while the previous safety net had been set at 499,500 francs CFA, in 2012, it was decided to provide more per ex-combatant (800,000 CFA francs), with flexible disbursement conditions. Second, there was a change in definition of who was considered to be a combatant (hence a change in who had access to financial benefits). Before 2012, the Ivorian DDR process integrated a large diversity of profiles in the definition of who was considered "ex-combatant" (from fighting to support tasks), but after 2012, the definition took a more restrictive turn, and individuals who wanted to be part of the official DDR process had to be identified as fighters by their respective commanders and had to pass a weapons-handling test. With respect to the dismantling of pro-governmental militias, ADDR had planned to process 23,000 individual applications out of a total of 74,000 for the entire process. At the end of January 2015, 46,031 ex-combatants, all categories taken together, had benefited from support, according to ADDR statistics. These successes were only relative though, and the ADDR director was not hiding the persistence of many difficulties. Mistrust of some former militia groups allied with the former regime was one of them, as many were fearing reprisals if they officially integrated the process. Direct observations conducted in Duékoué in May 2015, however, showed that some former pro-Gbagbo militias had been taken into account in the process and had received 800,000 CFA francs in cash transfers (with some in fact having benefited twice, in 2006 and in 2013).

At the time of writing (November 2017), the use of the term "militia" finally seems to have disappeared in western Côte d'Ivoire, for the best. ADDR officially announced the end of the DDR process in June 2015, and more recently, in June 2017, the UN peacekeeping mission, which was in charge of controlling part of the DDR process, put a term to thirteen years of mandate. Empirical work is still needed, however, to document the impact of the ADDR program and to see—among other things—if the doubling of amount of the cash transfers led to different uses.

Magali Chelpi-den Hamer is lecturer/researcher at Aix-Marseille Université and at the Institut des Mondes Africains (IMAF). She holds a

Ph.D. in social sciences from the University of Amsterdam and a French doctorate in anthropology from the École des Hautes Études en Sciences Sociales (cum laude). She has extensively published on local processes of militarization and demilitarization, education, and certification of learning in situations of forced displacement, especially in Côte d'Ivoire. Her current interests include transitional justice and the development-humanitarian nexus. She has consulted for various institutions (USAID, World Bank, UNICEF, Norwegian Government), and in the early 2000s, she was involved in humanitarian program coordination.

Notes

1. For detailed information on the process, see Chelpi-den Hamer 2011: 77–84.
2. At the time of doing fieldwork (2006–2007), disarmament in Côte d'Ivoire had not yet started on a massive scale for the main belligerents, and the dismantlement of pro-government militias had only partially occurred.
3. Deutsche Gesselschaft für Technische Zusammenarbeit, International Services (German Organization for Technical Cooperation).
4. 125,000 CFA francs are equivalent to €190 or $235 (US).
5. Initially planned on 29 October 2006, it was delayed a month.
6. Access to land must not be considered a given, even for autochthonous populations (here, Guérés), who formed the base of the majority of the respondents. Out of the people interviewed, some mentioned that they could rely on their father's forest to start their own plantation, but others reported having to buy a piece of land to be able start on their own.
7. *Deux-chambres-salon* is the local term to designate a small house with two bedrooms and a living room.
8. "Quand vous êtes resté quelque part sans salaire pendant des années, tu vis au jour le jour. Cet argent, on ne pouvait rien faire avec."
9. Most respondents could not do anything productive with their money until the third installment.
10. Duékoué is the site where militia recruits were gathered and officially demobilized under PNDDR and ONUCI supervision. The money was given in a protected compound, but as soon as people got out, they were prone to abuse.
11. One respondent could not avoid giving half of his safety net. He was relieved of 70,000 CFA francs from his first installment, 80,000 from the second, and 100,000 from the third.
12. Some added that those willing to give were nonetheless very welcome.
13. APO stands for Accord Politique de Ouagadougou, a comprehensive peace agreement signed on 4 March 2007 by President Gbagbo and the Secretary-General of the Forces Nouvelles Guillaume Soro.

References

Akindès, Francis. 2009. "Côte d'Ivoire since 1993: The Risky Reinvention of a Nation." In *Turning Points in African Democracy*, edited by A. R. Mustapha and L. Whitfield, 31–49. Woodbridge: James Currey.

Ball, N., and L. van de Goor. 2006. *Disarmament, Demobilization and Reintegration: Mapping Issues, Dilemmas and Guiding Principles*. The Hague: Netherlands Institute of International Relations "Cligendael" — Conflict Research Unit.

Bayart, J. F., and P. Geschiere. 2001. "'J'étais là avant' – problématiques politiques de l'autochtonie." *Critique Internationale* 10: 126–128.

Banégas, Richard. 2010. "Génération 'Guerriers'? Violence et subjectivation politique des jeunes miliciens en Côte d'Ivoire." In *L'adieu aux armes? Trajectoires d'anciens combattants*, edited by N. Duclos and D. Garibay, 360–397. Paris: Karthala.

Boshoff, Henri. 2005. "Demobilisation, Disarmament and Reintegration: A Key to Peace in Côte d'Ivoire." *African Security Review* 14 (2): 55–56.

Chauveau, J.-P., and K. S. Bobo. 2003. "La situation de guerre dans l'arène villageoise." *Politique Africaine* 89: 12–32.

Chauveau, J.-P., S. Bobo, N. Kouassi, and K. Moussa. 2012. *Milices et sociétés rurales en Côte d'Ivoire durant le conflit — Reconceptualiser le "dispositif milicien."* In Sociétés en guerres – Ethnographies des mobilisations violentes, edited by R. Bazenguissa-Ganga and S. Makki, 12–43. Paris: Éditions de la Maison.

Chelpi-den Hamer, Magali. 2011. *Militarized Youths in Western Côte d'Ivoire: Local Processes of Mobilization, Demobilization and Related Humanitarian Interventions (2002–07)*. Leiden: African Studies Centre.

Dembele, Ousmane. 2003. "Côte d'Ivoire: la fracture communautaire." *Politique Africaine* 89: 34–48.

Dozon, Jean-Pierre. 1997. "L'étranger et l'allochtone en Côte d'Ivoire." In *Le modèle ivoirien en questions. Crises, ajustements, recompositions*, edited by B. Contamin and H. Memel Fotê, 779–798. Paris: Karthala-Orstom.

Hanlon, J. 2004. "It Is Possible to Just Give Money to the Poor." *Development and Change* 35(2): 375–383.

Humphreys, M., and J. Weinstein. 2007. "Demobilization and Reintegration." *Journal of Conflict Resolution* 51(4): 531–567.

Jozan, R., and O. Ray. 2009. "Introduction thématique: De la fragile à la violence — Les organisations internationales à l'épreuve." *Afrique Contemporaine* 232(4): 23–38.

Knight, M., and A. Ozerdem. 2004. "Guns, Camps and Cash: Disarmament, Demobilization and Reinsertion of Former Combatants in Transition from War to Peace." *Journal of Peace Research* 41(4): 499–516.

Willibald, S. 2006. "Does Money Work? Cash Transfers to Ex-combatants in Disarmament and Reintegration Processes." *Disasters* 30(3): 316–339.

Chapter 12

Cash Transfers in Rural Niger
Social Targeting as a Conflict of Norms

Jean-Pierre Olivier de Sardan and Oumarou Hamani

It solves problems at the household level but creates them at the village level!
—Mayor of Tébaram

The White Man's money belongs to the whole village. So everyone must be allowed to benefit from these handouts.

There's no shortage of abuse, especially when it comes to enjoying the help provided by projects or the state. So bringing everyone together under the palaver tree only makes for more cheating. People have lost their dignity and their sense of honor because of the many forms of support they have grown accustomed to. That's why they are forever scheming to be always among the beneficiaries.

—Y.D., Simiri

Introduction

Discrepancies exist everywhere between policies as defined on paper (or in terms of their logical framework and procedural manuals) and policies as implemented in the field: these discrepancies constitute what is known as the "implementation gap."[1] However, just how big, significant, or apparent these discrepancies are depends on the situation. They are particularly important in the context of cash transfers (CTs) in Niger because, in Niger, CTs are injected into a rural social context where a

---

Notes for this chapter begin on page 321.

"rentier culture" already exists due to aid dependency. Strategies for capturing "development resources" and development "rent" are highly developed at all levels (farmers and chiefs, voters and mayors, investigators and project workers, civil servants, etc.). Moreover, Nigerien villages are deeply divided, fragmented, and characterized by conflicts of varying degrees of latency and by contradictions that lie at varying degrees below the surface. They constitute, therefore, prime "spaces of suspicion," and these suspicions are inevitably fanned when money is involved.

In Niger, CTs are new arrivals in "Aidland" (Mosse 2011). The first experiment involving this system was conducted by the British Red Cross in 2005, and its outcome was considered positive. CTs then went through a period of expansion in Niger from 2010 onward, with multiple schemes and operators and the generation of multiple chains of subcontracting activities: donors (World Bank, ECHO, WFP[2]); NGOs from the northern hemisphere for the management of the operations (ACFASB,[3] Concern, the British, French and Irish Red Cross organizations, etc.); local NGOs providing services in relation to awareness-raising, targeting, and surveys (Karkara, Kaydya, AREN,[4] the Nigerien Red Cross, etc.); local microfinance institutions (for the actual distribution of the cash); and, finally, the local recruitment of investigators, key informants, guides, and committee members.

Moreover, while the vast majority of CT interventions are designed to help the poorest populations cope with an economic food crisis (production shortages, an unusual rise in cereal prices, a particularly difficult lean season) through emergency aid with a fixed time limit (four months), another system of CTs exists in Niger. Rather than providing sporadic aid, this "social safety net" project developed by the World Bank in 2010 is aimed at strengthening the resilience of vulnerable households (Hamani 2013b). It is not included in the forms of CT examined in this chapter.[5]

This chapter concerns the CT programs operated by NGOs. It is based on a large number of interviews (445 formal and numerous informal interviews) conducted in twenty-one villages by a total of eight investigators (researchers and their assistants[6]) from the Laboratoire d'Etudes et de Recherche sur les Dynamiques Sociales et le Développement Local (LASDEL) in Niamey. All of the investigators worked in the local languages, have a proven track record, and are highly trained in the use of qualitative methods. Ten CT operations involving thirteen NGOs were examined in the study.

The issues identified, which are exemplified by the quotations, featured repeatedly in our interviews and in all five locations. In other words, the quotations in our reports are not marginal comments or exceptional cases, but a reflection of the convergent observations of the large numbers of people we interviewed.

Three stages can be distinguished in the CT process: targeting, distribution, and the use made of the sums received. The targeting is the element that causes the most problems by far. Distribution, for its part, happens without impediment. As for the use of CTs, they bear witness both to anticipated effects (in terms of resilience and food security) and unanticipated ones (redistribution and "ill-advised expenditures" — in the view of CT program workers).

In this chapter, we will focus on the social targeting of the most vulnerable households. Indeed, this is the most complex and sensitive process within the CT system in Niger, and the one that attracts the most suspicion, dissatisfaction, and criticism among local populations. We will examine the following points: the social targeting methods used by NGOs, the central paradox of CTs (the imposition of external and incoherent rules), and the revenge of contexts.

Targeting: A Complex Combination of Methods

The targeting of very vulnerable households is a complex and defining phase in the implementation of CT operations. Two levels of targeting can be identified: the *geographical targeting* of districts and villages and the *social targeting* of households within the selected villages.

The Survey Methods

The HEA (Household Economy Approach) is the most widely used method by NGOs for social targeting. It consists of quick (often rushed) surveys of the socioeconomic situation of the participating households, which are conducted by salaried workers who are assisted to varying degrees by village auxiliary workers. A considerable number of managers of humanitarian NGOs acknowledge the summary nature of the HEA surveys. They have also been the subject of numerous criticisms by local public servants and frontline NGO workers for their shoddiness and superficiality. "The HEA method is a good one if the time allocated is long enough to do a good job. But the problem is that we are always given very little time to do the work. Usually, we get two weeks to come up with the lists using HEA, so we can never produce anything worthwhile. . . . The big problem is that our partners want everything to be done quickly: to act quickly and to get fast results as well" (NGO worker, Olléléwa, quoted in Issaley 2013).[7]

Another issue concerns the competence and conscientiousness of the paid investigators recruited by the NGO. According to one report, instead of the planned four days of door-to-door surveys (social safety nets), "the surveys were done within one day and a half under the palaver tree and brought together all the heads of households in Gatawan and its hamlets" (village chief, quoted in Adamou 2013). That implies that each of the two investigators (students) administered five-page questionnaires to fifty family heads within a day (Adamou 2013).

Beyond the surveys, the typical targeting process is underpinned by a particularly complex imported structure, as we will see now.

The General Assemblies of the Local Populations

General assemblies (GA) are organized at the village level to inform the local populations, but also, in the name of a participatory approach, to (1) decide on the criteria for classifying the population into four categories according to their standard of living; (2) to establish and/or approve a list of the most vulnerable households; and, finally, (3) to appoint what could be termed "CT village auxiliaries," who will work alongside NGO workers, either to compile the list that is subsequently validated by the GA or to collaborate on rapid surveys of the vulnerable households so that the final list can be produced. These "village auxiliaries" may have different names depending on the operators involved (similarly, their profiles and their duties can vary slightly): key informants, focus groups, selection committees, targeting committees, monitoring committees, etc.

The list of vulnerable households is not the subject of any real debate in the GAs. Various strategies are adopted—for example, the inclusion of all of the households in the village on the "vulnerable" list or the shouting out of relatives' names, which no one will dare to contradict, as observed by Issaley (2013): "During the GA, no one protests, even when someone's name rich or close to the chief is shouted." Issaley (2013) quotes a beneficiary from Baboulwa: "The young men shout out very loudly the names of their close relatives and other family members. Hypocrisy and Fulani good manners prevent anyone from opposing the designation of beneficiaries at a GA."

Indeed, contrary to the "democratic" expectations of the NGOs, for which a GA should be an arena for public debate and transparency, a village GA is more often than not a space for social control, where taking the floor to contradict a speaker, denounce a cheating neighbor, or, to go even further, publicly criticize the chief—and, on top of that, in front of strangers—is seen as unseemly behavior and widely stigmatized.[8]

Obviously, this contrast between the GAs that the development institutions dream of and the GAs as they take place in real villages predates CTs, and has been in evidence for a long time in all forms of "participatory" development. Be that as it may, it is still a major cause of distortion in the CT targeting process. "When all the heads of households have to be assembled so that they can be interviewed outside their respective households, it's perfectly normal for some of them to hide part of their wealth so as to be classified as vulnerable. And usually we do not denounce one another in front of strangers, especially when it's an elderly person who does such things" (M.I., Gatawan, quoted in Adamou 2013).

In fact, the key issue of the GAs is the selection of village auxiliary workers. Given that their main task consists in helping to draw up the final list, they are a truly important link in the chain when it comes to the selection process.

The Village Auxiliary Workers for CTs

These casual informants and NGO collaborators who carry out the targeting, which results from the general assembly, are sometimes referred to in Hausa as *idon gari*, "the eyes of the village" (see Oumarou 2013). More often than not, the choice is made by the village or neighborhood chief to the advantage of those close to him. Despite increases in the number of checking procedures at various other stages in the CT process (computerized lists, the introduction of personalized cards for beneficiaries, recourse to micro finance institutions (MFIs) on a competitive bidding basis, mechanisms for providing official witnesses, signatures, and reports at the distribution stage), this is the "weak link" in the targeting process. "The key informants in the village are people who are connected with the village or neighborhood chief. They are involved in most NGO activities or with associations engaged in village projects. It's a closed circuit" (I.M.S., quoted in Hamani 2013a).

It is claimed that the village auxiliaries include their friends or relatives quite systematically among the households to be targeted: "There were three of us who'd been taken to one side by the investigators. The approach we took was that if such and such an informant mentioned some households he was close to, we stopped him so that someone else could mention his own. That's how we approached things" (A., Maïgochi Jackou, quoted in Oumarou 2013). In other cases, the list put forward does not exclude anyone at all in order to avoid any risk or accusation and prevent the creation of divisions within the village: "In the village of Dadin Kowa, so that informants were not exposed to criticism, all heads

of households in the village were mentioned and included in the count"
(A., Maïgochi Jackou, quoted in Oumarou 2013).

The Complaints Committee

At the same time as the selection committee is formed, the NGOs ask the
GA to form a "committee of elders," named *comité des sages*, or a "complaints committee," which is supposed to provide a way of appealing and
monitoring the process. In fact, none of these committees ever existed in
any real sense in any of the cases studied. Adamou (2013) noted that, "just
like the committee of elders, the members of monitoring committees do
not know what their roles are. In addition, the beneficiaries are ignorant
of their existence." In some cases, the committees were not even set up.

Hence, the complaints committees, which, from the standpoint of the
promoters of CTs, are supposed to fulfill a fundamental role as the community watchdog ensuring that the selection criteria are respected and
potential abuses are combated, are a total failure. Even when such a committee formally exists, there is strong latent—and sometimes explicit—
pressure on victims to suffer in silence. Leaving aside the fact that
lodging a complaint would have a very high social cost, it would almost
certainly fail to be upheld. A female nonbeneficiary (quoted in Issaley
2013) considered complaining futile: "I didn't ask for explanations or
who I should complain to, because I know that even if I complain, I won't
win my case."

Another constraint on the public expression of frustration and accusations is the fear that it might drive away the NGO, and put to an end the
supply of "manna" from abroad. Thus beneficiaries and nonbeneficiaries
share a common interest in keeping quiet about abuses in the targeting
process, as the latter always hope to be included the next time around. One
woman, a nonbeneficiary (quoted in Adamou 2013), said:"I am happy for
the other women, because at least there have been beneficiaries in the village. That's better than if the village got nothing out of the project. I hope
that it will benefit from the great project again and that I can be targeted."

Finally, the actual composition of the complaints committees was an
obstacle to their utilization. Given that their members were men, it was
difficult for women (beneficiaries) to appear before them and present their
complaints.

Surveying of Households

The census of households, which enables them to be "written" on the final
list, relies officially on door-to-door observation, looking on each farm for

what might be called the "outward signs of high vulnerability": the type of dwelling, the state of the barns, animal tracks, etc. The survey is aimed at eliminating households that are "not sufficiently vulnerable" and therefore has the feel of a police enquiry about it: "The key informants go from door to door to collect information on the households. They do not ask the members of the household any questions. It is just a case of looking around, which enables the household to be codified" (C.Y., member of the subregional committee, quoted in Hamani 2013a). Hence, this method is the object of numerous criticisms (expressed in private) on the part of non-beneficiaries. "The example they refer to most," reports Oumarou (2013), "is the existence of an animal or anything that points to the existence of one (excrement, stakes) on a farm. However, as they see it, many families keep animals on their farms that belong to other people." An NGO official remarked to us ironically that it was a case of differentiating between households with two-legged chickens and those where the chickens had only one leg.

On a more general level, it should be noted here that, as a cognitive operation, classification in four mutually exclusive categories[9] is very much at odds with local conceptions, which tend only to differentiate between two extremes, with blurred boundaries (i.e., the wealthy, *arzakante* in Zarma and *masu hali* in Hausa; and the poor, *alfukaru* in Zarma, *talaka* in Hausa), between which *tsakan-tsaka*, the entire remainder of the population, is located. The "very vulnerable" category, translated by NGO workers as *talaka talak* or *alfukaru bi*, is not really a local category: it is "suggested" by NGO workers and criticized by the local populations. "M., one of the key informants, told investigators that if what they mean by 'very poor' is a person who doesn't even have a chicken, then there aren't more than four in the entire village. And even then, those people who don't even have a chicken were not at the GA, and that's why they were never counted" (I. A. Roumbou, quoted in Oumarou 2013).

Summoning the heads of households and asking them questions about their possessions is certainly much easier for NGOs' agents, described here by A.B., a key informant from Tébaram (in Hamani 2013a): "When the last census was done, we didn't knock on any doors. Everyone just came all together to the neighborhood chief and then went in one at a time." Sometimes, the operation is simplified even more, as described here by the village chief of Dadin Kowa (in Oumarou 2013): "They came back two days later to collect the information on the surveyed households. It was during the busy period of work on the fields and there was practically no one at home. It was I who gave them this information. But they only took information on eight households that were beneficiaries."

Both the village auxiliaries and the NGO workers carrying out the monitoring surveys are regularly suspected of "favors": "In all cases, you always find census takers who are not very honest" (mayor, in Hamani 2013a). They are the target of numerous accusations. Hamani (2013a) describes the mistrust: "A neighborhood chief in Tébaram quoted this proverb with reference to the targeting workers: 'The cock advises the hens to be wary of the cat, even when he's going on a pilgrimage.' Mistrust is required of the hens (the villagers) when they come face to face with the NGO workers (the cat)."

Other factors can also raise questions about the reliability of the surveys—for example, their timing: "The time devoted to the census is very short, the timing of the targeting is sometimes unfortunate. In 2011, it was conducted during the rainy season. At this time of the year, a large proportion of the population have already returned to the farming area." (mayor of Tébaram, in Hamani 2013a). The timing imposed by the NGOs on the field officers constitutes the main constraint on the targeting process, which is carried out in a very simplified way, which obscures certain stages. This problem is observed at all stages in the process: because they receive the funds late from the donors when the difficult preharvest lean period has already begun, the NGOs have little time in the field to complete the targeting process and start distributing the money to the vulnerable households. To enable the timely distribution of the funds, the NGO managers have the list of beneficiaries compiled as quickly as possible.

The Finalized List

The populations know very little about the definitive targeting methods. "The final choice of beneficiaries is still a stage that always leaves the villagers puzzled because they don't know how it works" (Issaley 2013). This lack of transparency obviously fuels suspicion even more. The objections are directed at the number of households selected per village, on the one hand, and at the individuals chosen within the same village, on the other. In fact, it appears that the basis for this final selection is a quota per village. But how these quotas are arrived at remains a complete mystery to us (and to the local populations). "No one knows why a particular number has been decided on for a particular village" (Issaley 2013). The number of households selected in each village is the object of comparisons in conversations, which expose numerous inequalities that no one can explain. "This was the complaint of one village chief: 'Dan Jaoudi was allocated 16 beneficiaries, whereas my village, which has twice the population of Dan Jaoudi, only had eight beneficiaries'" (in Oumarou 2013). Concerning the households selected in each village, they frequently include individuals regarded as well off and/or close to the village chiefs: "The beneficiaries are the chief's clients or those close to him . . . their friends and relatives may often be old but often they are not destitute as they have children who are wealthy traders or high up in the government" (Issaley 2013). Sometimes the blame is placed on technical problems; however, this does not convince everyone: "When the first cash transfer was paid, I clearly heard my name being read out over the radio as one of the people targeted. On the day the photos were taken, I was informed that my name did not appear on the list. They made the excuse that it was the computer in Tahoua that runs off the names, whereas we know for certain that everything happens at Concern in Tébaram. They are always blaming the power supply or the computer which wipes out some names" (M.K., beneficiary, in Issaley 2013).

Women as Recipients in the Name of the Household

The finalized list contains the names of the women. The CTs target the most vulnerable families and, within each family, a woman must be the beneficiary as, in the eyes of the CT professionals, they offer a better guarantee that the sums received will be used for the benefit of the entire family, particularly the children. This is clearly indicative of the "maternalist" ideology behind the CT system (see Olivier de Sardan and Piccoli, introduction; Piccoli and Gillespie, chapter 6; Nagels, chapter 8).

However, given that many households are polygamous, the programs allocate the responsibility for designating the spouse who will receive the cash to the male head of the family.

The Imposition of External and Heterogeneous Rules: The Central Paradox of the CTs

External and Imposed Rules

CTs in Niger are based on a series of "expert" rules (formulated by experts outside the country) and based on the previous experience of institutions that have operated CT schemes in other countries. In a way, these rules function as "conditionalities" which people must fulfill to benefit from the targeted payments. From this point of view, the unconditional CTs are not really unconditional: qualifying conditions apply (poverty criteria defined by the NGOs, distribution to women, etc.). Rules of the game are imposed on the local populations, which not only have difficulty in understanding them in some cases (even if the procedures planned by the experts are implemented scrupulously by the NGO workers—something that is far from always the case—the targeting procedures are highly opaque to them), but also frequently disagree with them and "circumvent" them or adapt them.

These imported and imposed rules are essentially based on the same "devices"; in other words, they have the same ideological roots and the same general "mechanism," which is to distribute in a meaningful way sums of money to very vulnerable families so as to enable them to overcome a food crisis (food crisis CTs) or develop greater resilience (social safety net CTs). Hence, what is involved here is a new form of "social policy" originating from the aid sector, which assumes a place alongside the other forms of aid (such as the distribution of food and sale of goods at reduced prices) and is intended to replace some of them, in part at least, in the name of greater efficiency. Hence, the aim is to eradicate poverty while limiting the social tensions associated with poverty and enabling the most vulnerable households to attain some autonomy and reintegrate into the local economy. The CTs also have other objectives, which are considered complementary: ensuring greater equality (by targeting the most vulnerable), promoting women (by designating them as the sole recipients of the CTs), curbing migration, fighting malnutrition, etc.

These objectives are "translated" by the different donors and operators into a number of major general common de facto rules, which (apart from a few exceptions) can essentially be summed up as follows:

- Without consulting the communities involved or the local authorities, the donor and NGOs decide on the duration, frequency, and amount of the sums paid and the type of targeting used.
- Only certain communes and villages are involved.
- In the selected villages, only a minority of households are beneficiaries of the CTs (in the majority of cases, four categories are proposed to the villagers, to which they must allocate all of the village households, and only those in the category defined as most vulnerable are eligible).
- The women are the beneficiaries of the CTs within the households.[10]
- The NGO workers survey and monitor the beneficiaries with the help of local actors.
- Apart from some exceptional cases, the local actors playing a role in the process (chiefs, village auxiliaries, elected representatives) are not paid for this work as it is considered to reflect a commitment to the community.

- Institutional architecture is required as tools for a participatory approach (community targeting): the holding of general assemblies, classification of the population in four categories, designation of key informants and various committees, surveys, public distribution events, etc.
- Monthly payments are made to the beneficiaries for a limited period.[11]
- Extensive awareness-raising is usually carried out to ensure that the money is used to buy food (in the case of emergency CTs).

Heterogeneous and Contradictory Micro-rules

Based on this core of external and widely shared general rules, the "micro-rules" that govern the specific mechanisms of the CTs vary considerably from one NGO to another, and this undermines their credibility. The targeting and distribution methods often contradict both each other and other development aid mechanisms.

Internal Inconsistencies within the CTs

The CT operators vary considerably with respect to the concrete measures implemented, not only from one village to the next but also within one and the same village: despite various efforts at their coordination, which have not proved very effective, it is common for several operators to work in the same area. Each operator imposes its own norms without taking into account either those of the other operators or the rules governing previous interventions in the same location.

Thus the social safety nets project, which has now been extended to the entire country, is in a way a separate entity. It does not limit the payments to the lean season. They are made throughout the year, and the sums allocated are different (XOF 10,000 as opposed to XOF 30,000–40,000 for the other CTs). The women are encouraged to put the money they receive into a tontine, which will enable them to invest in income-generating activities.

Regarding the "food crisis" CTs, which promote instead the purchase of grain by the recipients, and are all limited in duration, the parameters governing the distribution of money are nonetheless variable: the duration of the schemes (between one and four months), sums involved (XOF 10,000 to 120,000), and the months in which the payments are made (sometimes two payments in one month or a delayed payment, which is made after the harvest, when the granaries are full).

The nature of the target populations also varies: in the vast majority of cases they constitute the most vulnerable households; however, they sometimes also involve disaster victims (floods, fires), persons who have been displaced (for economic, but also political reasons—for example, in Libya, Mali), or statutory categories related to the traditional target categories of the *zakkat* (Muslim tithe)—the disabled, widows, orphans, etc.

The targeting procedures also vary between lists compiled by the paid investigators and the NGOs and the lists compiled by the village auxiliary workers, or the combination of the two. The classification criteria are supposed to be decided on by the villagers; however, in many cases they are suggested by the NGO workers or combined with the NGOs' or donors' own criteria. Finally, it is important to highlight the variations between the sums distributed and the frequency of the distributions, something that is difficult for the populations to understand. The variation in the sums distributed within one and the same CT operation is particularly puzzling, and paves the way for suspicion. Oumarou (2013) gives one example: "The first version of the program planned to allocate XOF 32,500 per month to each targeted vulnerable household. However, even before it was implemented, the WFP decided to allocate XOF 4,640 per household member to be multiplied by the number of persons in the household. The program was supposed to be carried out over a period of four months with one payment per month. However, the first two payments were both made in September. Moreover, the sums, which were supposed to be the same for all operations, were reduced for the third operation."

The Inconsistencies between the CTs and Other Interventions

In addition to highlighting these "internal" inconsistencies between the rules imported through the CT operations, it is important to note that throughout the country the CTs coexist with other types of response to food crises and support for vulnerable families: for example, "cash for work," "food for work," distribution of specific provisions, distribution of general provisions, warrantage, and, finally, the sale of goods at reduced prices. All of these systems obviously follow different sets of rules.

The main contradiction, which is, in effect, the "mother" of all of the others, is that which opposes the principle of general free distribution (and the sale of goods at reduced prices), to which the populations have been accustomed since 1973 (the first postindependence hunger), with the principle of social targeting (the most vulnerable households), which governs the vast majority of CTs since 2006.

Of course, the general free distribution schemes imply geographical targeting (the communes or villages considered to have been severely affected by a crisis), which is often contested by the inhabitants of non-beneficiary areas[12] based on arguments of both civic equality ("we all pay tax") and general discourses on poverty ("the entire rural population of Niger is vulnerable")—the latter being backed up by international statistics that present Niger as a particularly poor country or even the poorest in the world. However, the general free distribution schemes do not make any distinctions within the selected villages.

In contrast, many people perceive local selection (social targeting) within the villages as illegitimate or arbitrary in that the CTs make a radical (i.e., dichotomous) distinction between "the most vulnerable" and the three other categories. In view of the ultimate practical differentiation between only two broad categories (i.e., the beneficiaries who make up the fourth category, and the nonbeneficiaries who make up the other three), the prior formal classification in four categories, which the NGOs import into the village populations in asking them to define criteria for degrees of vulnerability and classify households based on them, is, in fact, purely rhetorical. This dichotomy, which is typical of the CTs in the eyes of the populations, is the only one that really counts: it is deeply contested by the villagers (and not without good reason).

These contradictions and this lack of coherence merely boost the incentives for opportunistic behavior and for "playing with" the rules with a view to circumventing them.

The Revenge of the Context: Local Strategies

The very principle of a selection process introduced to the village by outsiders is the element that constitutes a problem for many villagers. This has two underlying causes: (1) the introduction of a threshold effect; (2) suspicions of bias in the selection process.

The Introduction of a Very Unwelcome Threshold Effect

In villages where the standard of living and consumption patterns are very similar, in spite of economic inequalities, selection introduces a threshold effect which is seen as being completely arbitrary. This is true, first, in terms of selection between villages, which is seen as systematically unfair: What differentiates a "chosen" village from an "excluded" one? It is equally true in the case of selection between households within the same village. Little or nothing differentiates the last household on the "chosen" list from the first household on the "rejected" list. In this finely graded continuum of ranking households from a socioeconomic point of view, differences are very slight, and to require boundaries to be drawn or barriers to be placed between households classified as "very vulnerable" and households classified as "vulnerable" makes little sense, especially when, as often happens, the selection barrier cuts right through one or other of these categories in accordance with "quotas" that are fixed for each village by the NGO without there being any explanation or transparency in the matter.

Selection as an Object of Suspicion and Maneuvers

A local politician from the commune of Ollélewa told us: "I'm not going to put myself forward for another term. Even when food is being distributed, people are very suspicious; the distribution of money makes them worse. They think that we politicians are always on the make and I find that very upsetting." This quotation is evidence of the many suspicions aroused—sometimes unfairly, often with good reason—among the local populations by the targeting procedures, however fine-tuned they may be technically from the NGO's perspective. We have explored this question at greater length above. The role (real or supposed) played by the chiefs trigger ambivalent reactions among their subjects. On the one hand, the former are condemned in sometimes violent terms (accusations of greed, being referred to as hyenas, etc.); on the other, however, they are excused and their behavior legitimized on the basis of the numerous expenses that must be borne by the chiefs in the exercise of their office and of the support they provide to the populations in various ways.

Cunning Strategies

In any case, one rule of thumb applies: the rules imposed by the partners barely satisfy even those who benefit from the CTs; they are recomposed and transformed as much as possible, but quietly. There is no direct opposition or public expression of discontent (which would risk putting an end to the resource and compromising relations with the "projects" that people are trying to attract); however, it is possible to list some local social norms on which there is a sense of latent unanimity in terms of opposition to the imposed rules:

- The men should be recipients as they are responsible for food and are the heads of the families.
- Selective distribution divides the village. The CTs should be aimed at everyone or, if not, benefit all the village households in turn.
- The category of extreme vulnerability (*talaka talak*) and the criteria proposed by the NGOs are too restrictive.

- At the time of CT distribution, households face many pressures; if these pressures are taken into account, the distributed sums are insufficient.
- All those involved in the process and who devote time to it should be remunerated, particularly if they are not beneficiaries.

Nevertheless, the villagers adapt to the donors' requirements with a combination of fatalism and pragmatism so that they can continue to reap the benefits of their "manna." The solutions widely adopted and implemented on the backs of the NGOs are cunning strategies.

Household Reallocation
In the majority of cases, the women give the sums they receive to their husbands and thereby revert to the habitual norm whereby it is the man who must provide the food for the household. D., a village chief, maintained that "putting money in the hands of the women is a waste! And if you play the biting game, you have to go back to the hyena" (in Issaley 2013). The NGO workers are perfectly aware of these hand-overs, as it is general practice.

It is important to remember the local normative context for the management of resources within households (which are manifestly ignored or underestimated by the designers of the CT system in Niger): the women have their own resources, which they manage independently, but it is the responsibility of the husband to buy food and clothes and to cover medical expenses.

Thus the distribution of money intended for food for the entire household to the women (at the expense of the men) can fuel tension between men and women, and even prevent participation, as reported by Issaley (2013): "For the 'cash transfer' from PACRC, the men refused to allow their wives to be registered because, they say, they [the wives] will say that it is for them and not for the husbands."

Community Reallocation: Pooling
"Pooling" schemes were sometimes organized. This was generally done on the initiative of a chief immediately after the departure of the NGO and MFI officials. The money is sometimes retrieved from the beneficiaries, in the majority of cases for equal distribution to all of the village households—either directly in the form of cash or as provisions purchased with the pooled funds. However, it may also be used to cover general expenses (e.g., payment of tax): "In the village of Fonikoira, all of the money was pooled and took two forms. The first involved each of the first three installments (June, July and August); the money was

pooled and used to pay for provisions which were shared among all the households in the village. The fourth installment was used to pay the village tax" (Issa 2013). Pooling can also be partial and take the form of a contribution to an objective approved by the entire community, as Adamou (2013) reports: "In Sabon Gari, the beneficiaries of the cash transfer contributed XOF 100,000 for repairs to the Lollo Yondi integrated health center."

However, pooling obviously triggered a degree of opposition among the official beneficiaries of the CTs, as this example shows: "The committee members decided that on their own. They withdrew XOF 1,000 from the money for each beneficiary during the first payment [to distribute to nonbeneficiaries]. They intended to continue doing this. However, the people said that they did not agree with it. And, faced with the anger this provoked in the district, they became afraid and stopped. So these are the reasons why this did not continue" (Inhabitant of Alfagey, in Issa 2013).

Pooling necessitates sufficient authority on the part of the chief to obtain the—possibly reticent—consent of his beneficiary subjects. It is important to avoid public complaints at all costs as these could dissuade the NGO from continuing to provide CTs. Hence, when resolute opposition is expressed, pooling comes to an end.

Informal "Remuneration" of the Unpaid Actors Involved in the Targeting Process (Chiefs, Village Auxiliaries)

The "Chiefs' Share"

Despite the fact that the NGO workers frequently convey the message that people should not give anything to the chiefs, the practice remains common. In some cases it is done on a voluntary basis; however, in others it is required by the chief himself, as is described here by Oumarou (2013): "Almost all the beneficiaries interviewed acknowledged having given the chiefs of their villages 'something to pay for *cola*.' They do it because sometimes the chief requires them to do it. . . . 'When we didn't give him something quickly from the fourth, he sent a child to us to tell us he hadn't seen us' (T., beneficiary, Roumbou). . . . 'The village chief leads us far away from the town hall before asking for his share' (Female beneficiary).

In contrast, in some places, the beneficiaries give contributions to the chief on an entirely voluntary basis: "We give a little to the village chief. He does not ask but takes what he is given" (Z.A., beneficiary, Maïgochi Jackou, in Oumarou 2013). "In Ollélewa, for the ASB's CT, the beneficiaries decided to each contribute XOF 500 to the cantonal chief during the second phase in gratitude for his hospitality" (Issaley 2013). A gesture of this kind is both a symbolic sign of respect toward the chief and an acknowledgement of the services he provides.

The "Officials' share"
Apart from a few exceptions, in the majority of cases the gestures involved are symbolic. Issaley (2013) gives an example: "For the French Red Cross cash transfers, the beneficiaries say they are grateful to the local volunteers from the Nigerien Red Cross. They think that the latter put forward their names and, by way of acknowledgement, they assign a small contribution to give to them."

Gratitude, Suspicion, and Chance

The advocates of the CTs (like all aid mechanisms) generally expect—implicitly at least—that the scheme will provide relief for the beneficiaries and earn their recognition. The interviews we held on this level generally testify to the fact that the CTs are successful in this regard. These expressions of satisfaction obviously feature prominently in the standard evaluations and reports. However, it is also possible to observe various unexpected developments in relation to gratitude. The aid donors are generally unknown, and the NGOs that lead the CT operations are credited with the generosity in their provision.

The recognition is aimed mainly at the actors rather than the institutions. Beneficiaries do not express gratitude to the actors involved in the implementation of the CT scheme as representatives of the donor organizations but on a personal basis and for the role they have played in their selection as beneficiaries of this manna. It is assumed, therefore, that the targets of the gratitude were involved in the selection processes in a way that benefited the fortunate recipients. The nonbeneficiaries also suspect that all beneficiary lists are the product of favors. This suspicion involves the same actors located on the interface between the populations and the CT system.

Most beneficiaries and nonbeneficiaries share the same assessment, however: irrespective of the underlying motives (compassion, benevolence, family solidarity, village solidarity, clientelism), the final list is the production of various interventions.

The complex mixture of "external criteria" (HEA surveys) and "community criteria" (constitution of the lists), according to which the institutions operating the CTs aim to carry out the selection process in a way that cannot be contested, is greeted in the villages with suspicion and/or maneuvers in response to this mixture. The targeting process is evaluated by the local populations using the local criteria that they usually apply in their evaluation of local governance, political action, and public action (in which "the widespread exchange of favors" is standard; see Olivier de Sardan 2009). In fact, everyone knows that the official norms decreed from above (the state or development institutions)—and the NGO's CT criteria are a typical case of parachuted official norms—are systematically "adapted," "altered," and circumvented as much as possible in the everyday practices of the actors involved in the implementation process. Paradoxically, it is precisely the "community" criteria that the CTs introduced to the process with a view to involving representatives of the populations that arouse the suspicions about it.[13] It will come as no surprise to learn, therefore, that some people express a preference for "external criteria": "The targeting of the social safety nets did not cause as much trouble as that carried out by the NGO Karkara. This is obviously due to the fact that the selection was made in Niamey where nobody knew anybody who could influence the results" (mayor of Simiri, in Adamou 2013).

Even when the selection is not attributed to the intervention of the chiefs or other actors, luck (or bad luck) is referred to as an explanatory factor and not the criteria applied by the NGOs: "If I wasn't chosen, it is just a question of luck and I hope that luck will smile on me during the big project" (nonbeneficiary woman, Gatawan, in Adamou 2013). Some people go as far as speaking of the "drawing of lots" (*kaley-kaley* or *kozop-kozop*) by the NGOs.

Another reaction triggered by the selection principle is that, in the view of many local actors, there should be a kind of rotation system that would enable other households to benefit from the "manna" in turn: "The village chiefs condemn the NGO workers' 'anti-pooling' discourse and feel that it is not desirable to give the aid to the same people across several phases. According to them, it would be best to reduce the sums paid so that everyone could benefit, to target each installment at new beneficiaries or give them the money as they would know how to prevent there being injured parties" (Issaley 2013).

However, in the NGOs' perspective based on the vulnerability criteria, it is clear that the same list of beneficiaries will be used from one month to the next or one year to the next. The aim of pooling, in effect, is to subvert the differentiation (frequently referred to as "division" by the people) introduced by the CT, through the "clandestine" introduction of egalitarian redistribution. However, the argument presented goes further. As stated by this woman from Danbazi, it suggests that, thanks to the pooling of the cash, each person will be able to help a neighbor in need in the future: "It's good to share the money with everyone. It's good because today you benefit and tomorrow perhaps your neighbor will. So if it happens that you have given to him, he too will think of you when it's his turn" (in Issa 2013). Thus pooling acts as a guarantee of local aid for the future (many people believe that the CT operations will not last and the villages involved will ultimately be left to their own devices). Pooling also has the advantage of enabling the avoidance of the numerous accusations and suspicions associated with the selection and targeting processes.

Nevertheless, the objection could also be made that the traditional mechanisms of intravillage solidarity are blunt, that the inequalities in rural areas have deteriorated, and that without the CTs a lot of poor people would be even poorer and caught in the "poverty trap." But some would point out that the CTs themselves aggravate the erosion of intravillage solidarity by driving the rural population to offload this aid function onto the "projects" and various aid initiatives. The debate is never-ending, and also recurrent among Nigerien leaders.

Conclusion: Aid Dependency

Aid dependency (or "assistentialism") is a fundamental problem that predates the CTs; however, the CTs provide further and more convincing corroboration of its existence. In a context of considerable dependency on external aid, with various strategies used to attract this "rent," many people see the CT as an adjuvant to assistentialism: "The CT is not good for fighting poverty. It teaches people that poverty can become a currency, a livelihood" (Y., project worker, in Issaley 2013). "The '*taymako*' [nickname for a CT program] is not a good thing. It is embarrassing but we have no choice. The CT spoils people because the beneficiaries tend not to try and manage on their own" (dignitary, in Hamani 2013a).

Many people see the "cash for work" mechanism, which combines a principle of exchange (and not donation) and open access (and not selection),[14] as a more suitable one: "Two-thirds of the village benefit from the blessings of the cash for work. Women and men are involved without gender or age discrimination. All you need is the strength to work. In contrast, the cash transfer is highly selective" (chief of Kadri district, in Hamani 2013a). However, "cash for work" is sometimes classified under the same "assistentialist" heading: "There is a lack of management of the work carried out as a result of the 'food for work' and 'cash for work' projects as though the population is waiting for the arrival of another project to maintain the developments" (Issaley 2013).

The problem of sustainability associated with aid dependency is also associated with CTs. The question arises as to whether the Nigerien institutions could take over from the World Bank (for the provision of safety nets) or other donors and NGOs (for the humanitarian CTs). This is doubtful. One example shows the extent to which the sums provided by the CTs exceed the possibilities of the local authorities (and contribute, moreover, to undermining the credibility and even marginalizing the latter): the simple comparison of the budgets allocated to the communes and the sums distributed by the CT programs in the same communes. In effect, providing aid to the poor is one of the responsibilities of the communes; however, they are incapable of fulfilling this task. In the rural commune of Tébaram, XOF 185,500,000 was distributed in 2012 by CT programs (to 1,484 households), which is five times the total budget of the commune for the same year. In the commune of Loga, XOF 562,822,000 was distributed in 2012, which is eight times the commune's budget for that year.

In any case, it cannot be denied that, although the CT system involves aid, the considerable sums distributed have had positive effects for the tens of thousands of families involved, irrespective of whether they were actually very vulnerable or not. The fact must be faced that in view of the food crises arising in succession, external aid will clearly be necessary for a long time.

But are CTs the best form of aid for food emergencies and for fostering resilience? Are they destined to last or are they merely a passing trend? Could they be reformed or combined with other forms of aid? How could they be better adapted to local contexts? What should be done about targeting? Even if they are implicit in this chapter's findings, these questions lie outside its framework and we do not have any answers to them.

In our view, the main conclusion to be drawn from our research would appear to lie in the importance of the gaps between the objectives of the CTs, along with the devices/procedures/rules involved, on the one hand, and the practices and representations of the populations in areas in which CTs were carried out, on the other. Cunning strategies can clearly be seen as a form of "appropriation" by the populations (or a part of them at least); however, it is clearly not the kind of appropriation desired by the CT promoters in introducing this model of intervention in Niger.

Postscript

Four years after the completion of our research in multiple sites, numerous attempts at improving the implementation of the CTs have been observed (inspired in part by the considerations raised by our reports, which were the focus of extensive debate in the NGO sector in Niger). These attempts involve the targeting (timing and duration, strengthening of the role of communities, verification techniques, etc.), the diversification of the support offered to vulnerable households (introduction of the "cash grant" by certain NGOs), the conflict-management structures (emergence of complaints committees composed of women, establishment of help lines by certain NGOs), the coordination of interventions, etc. The World Food Programme decided to devote at least one month per site for implementing the HEA for the targeting process from 2015.

These attempts at improving the system make the CT tools more complex, and reflect the consideration of the importance of the contexts to a certain extent. They open up new areas for the research on CT operations in Niger, particularly around the effects of the changes made by them: are they significant or marginal; do they change the perception of the populations?

More fundamentally, does the introduction of these changes represent an initial step toward a strategic will to take local contexts seriously into account or does it simply involve marginal adaptations that conserve the hegemony of an imported model?

Jean-Pierre Olivier de Sardan is a professor of anthropology at the Ecole des Hautes Etudes en Sciences Sociales (France) and emeritus director of research at the Centre National de la Recherche Scientifique (France). He is among the founders of the Laboratory for Study and Research on Social Dynamics and Local Development (LASDEL), in Niamey, Niger (www.lasdel.net), and is associate professor, in charge of the master's program Anthropology of Health, at Abdou Moumouni University, Niamey. He has authored numerous books in French and in English, and is currently working on an empirical anthropology of public actions and modes of governance in West Africa. Honors and awards include Chevalier des Palmes académiques de la République du Niger, 2004; Docteur honoris causa de l'Université de Liège, 2012; Chevalier de l'Ordre national de la Légion d'honneur de la République française, 2012; and Prize Ester Boserup, University of Copenhagen, 2014.

Oumarou Hamani is a researcher at LASDEL, Niger, and teaches anthropology at University Abdou Moumouni, Niamey, Niger. He has a Ph.D. from Ecole des Hautes Etudes en Sciences Sociales (France), with expertise on justice issues.

Notes

This chapter relies on inquiries realized by Oumarou Hamani, Nana Issaley, Younoussi Issa, Issaka Oumarou, and Hannatou Adamou as part of a research program of the LASDEL (Laboratoire d'Etudes et de Recherche sur les Dynamiques Sociales et le Développement Local), funded by French Cooperation and two NGO's (Arbeiter-Samariter-Bund and Concern).

1. See Bierschenk and Olivier de Sardan 2014. The analysis of the "problem of gaps" is at the heart of the anthropology of development and, more generally, of the anthropology of public policy (Olivier de Sardan 2016).
2. European Commission's Civil Protection and Humanitarian Aid Operations (ECHO), World Food Programme (WFP).
3. Action contre la Faim (ACF), Arbeiter-Samariter-Bund (ABC).
4. Association pour la redynamisation de l'élevage au Niger (AREN)·
5. For a broader description and analysis of CTs in Niger, see Olivier de Sardan et al. 2014; Olivier de Sardan 2014.
6. Five municipalities were studied across the country.
7. All the interviews have been conducted in local langages (hausa and songhay-zarma) and translated in French by the reports' authors.
8. We are, of course, describing a general tendency, and exceptions may well exist involving outspoken opponents or unconventional personalities who express their opinions publicly.
9. These four categories are translated into Hausa as *masuhali, masudaa madaama, talakawa*, and *talaka talak*; and into Zarma as *arzakante, daamante, alfukaru*, and *alfukaru bi*. This classification and the use of these terms were popularized by the NGO workers beyond the different local variants that exist in both languages. Such a technique (asking villagers to classify the whole population in four categories) originated from the "toolbox" of the "participatory rural appraisal" (PRA) (Chambers 1994; for a critique of PRA, see Mosse 1994).
10. Some exceptions exist: CTs for the repatriation of migrants in the town, CTs for flood victims.
11. This may be a lump sum per beneficiary household or a sum calculated according to the number of persons belonging to a beneficiary household.
12. On this topic, regarding the food distributions in 2005, see Olivier de Sardan 2011.
13. There is a common idea among the advocates of the CTs that the recourse to community control is the best way to combat unjustified inclusions in the beneficiary lists. Our study shows that the opposite may, in fact, be the case.
14. What is involved, in effect, is self-targeting: the members of the richest families in the village have little or no motivation to do rather hard work for relatively small sums of money.

References

Adamou, H. 2013. "Les transferts monétaires dans la commune rurale de Simiri (département de Ouallam): entre diversités méthodologiques et gestion locale du CT" LASDEL report, Niamey, Niger.
Benadusi, M., C. Brambilla, and B. Riccio, eds. 2001. *Disasters, Development and Humanitarian Aid: New Challenges for Anthropology*. Rimini: Guaraldi.

Bierschenk, T., and J.-P. Olivier de Sardan. 2014. "Ethnographies of Public
    Services in Africa: An Emerging Research Paradigm". In *States at Work: The*
    Dynamics of African Bureaucracies, edited by T. Bierschenk and J.-P. Olivier de
    Sardan, 35–65. Leyden: Brill.
Blundo, G., and P.-Y. Le Meur, eds. 2009. *The Governance of Daily Life in Africa:*
    Ethnographic Explorations of Public and Collective Service. Leiden: Brill.
Chambers, R. 1994. "The Origins and Practice of Participatory Rural Appraisal."
    World Development 22(7): 953–969.
Hamani, O. 2013a. "Le cash transfer à Tébaram (Tahoua): les perceptions
    ambivalentes autour d 'une innovation importee." *Etudes et Travaux du*
    LASDEL 106.
———. 2013b. "Les Pratiques Familiales Essentielles (PFE) au Niger: Socio-
    anthropologie d'une intervention à base communautaire." *Etudes et Travaux*
    du LASDEL 104.
Harvey, P., and S. Bailey. 2011. *Revue des bonnes pratiques: programme de tranfert*
    monétaire dans les situations d'urgence. London: Humanitarian Practice
    Network, ODI.
Issa, Y. 2013. "Les opérations de transferts monétaires dans la commune de
    Loga (région de Dosso): Logiques des opérateurs, logiques locales et diversité
    d'acteurs." *Etudes et Travaux du LASDEL* 110.
Issaley, N. 2013. "Le cash transfer à Olléléwa: de la fabrique des "vulnérables" à
    la gestion locale de l'aide." *Etudes et Travaux du LASDEL* 109.
Mosse, D. 1994. "Authority, Gender, and Knowledge: Theoretical Reflections on
    the Practice of Participatory Rural Appraisal." *Development and Change* 25(3):
    497–525.
Mosse, D., ed. 2011. *Adventures in Aidland: The Anthropology of Professionals in*
    International Development. Oxford: Berghahn Books.
Olivier de Sardan, J.-P. 2009. "State Bureaucracy and Governance in West
    Francophone Africa: Empirical Diagnosis, Historical Perspective." In *The*
    Governance of Daily Life in Africa: Ethnographic Explorations of Public and
    Collective Service, edited by G. Blundo and P.-Y. Le Meur, 39–71. Leiden: Brill.
———. 2011. "Local Actors' Agency, Far from Media Dramatization: The Niger
    'Famine' in 2005." In *Disasters, Development and Humanitarian Aid. New*
    Challenges for Anthropology, edited by M. Benadusi, C. Brambilla, and B. Riccio.
    Rimini, Italy: Guaraldi.
———. 2014. "La manne, les normes et les soupçons: Les contradictions de l'aide
    vue d'en-bas." *Revue Tiers Monde* 219: 197–215.
———. 2016. "For an Anthropology of Gaps, Discrepancies and Contradictions."
    Antropologia 3(1): 111–131.
Olivier de Sardan, J.-P., with O. Hamani, N. Issaley, Y. Issa, H. Adamou, and
    I. Oumarou. 2014. "Les transferts monétaires au Niger: le grand malentendu."
    Revue Tiers Monde 218: 107–130.
Oumarou, I. 2013. "Les transferts monétaires dans la commune de Dakoro."
    Etudes et Travaux du LASDEL 107.

Index

www.ingramcontent.com/pod-product-compliance
Lightning Source LLC
Chambersburg PA
CBHW070906030426
42336CB00014BA/2315